# Dropping out of Socialism

# Dropping out of Socialism

## The Creation of Alternative Spheres in the Soviet Bloc

Edited by
Juliane Fürst and Josie McLellan

LEXINGTON BOOKS
*Lanham • Boulder • New York • London*

Published by Lexington Books
An imprint of The Rowman & Littlefield Publishing Group, Inc.
4501 Forbes Boulevard, Suite 200, Lanham, Maryland 20706
www.rowman.com

Unit A, Whitacre Mews, 26-34 Stannary Street, London SE11 4AB

British Library Cataloguing in Publication Information Available

**Library of Congress Cataloging-in-Publication Data**

Names: Fürst, Juliane, 1973- editor. | McLellan, Josie, editor.
Title: Dropping out of socialism : the creation of alternative spheres in the Soviet
    bloc / edited by Juliane Fürst and Josie McLellan.
Description: Lanham : Lexington Books, [2016] | Includes bibliographical references
    and index.
Identifiers: LCCN 2016037411 (print) | LCCN 2016051561 (ebook) (print) |
    LCCN 2016051561 (ebook) | ISBN 9781498525145 (cloth : alk. paper) |
    ISBN 9781498525152 (Electronic)
Subjects: LCSH: Europe, Eastern—Social conditions. | Communism and
    individualism—Europe, Eastern. | Communism and liberty—Europe,
    Eastern. | Post-communism—Europe, Eastern.
Classification: LCC HN380.7.A8 D76 2016 (print) | LCC HN380.7.A8 (ebook) |
    DDC 306.09437—dc23
LC record available at https://lccn.loc.gov/2016037411

Printed in the United States of America

# Contents

7   Dropping Out of Socialism with the Commodore 64:
    Polish Youth, Home Computers, and Social Identities          157
    *Patryk Wasiak*

**PART III: DROPPING OUT IN STYLE**                              **177**

8   "We All Live in a Yellow Submarine": Dropping Out
    in a Leningrad Commune                                       179
    *Juliane Fürst*

9   Ignoring Dictatorship? Punk Rock, Subculture,
    and Entanglement in the GDR                                  207
    *Jeff Hayton*

10  "Under Any Form of Government, I Am Partisan":
    The Siberian Underground from Anti-Soviet
    to National-Bolshevist Provocation                           233
    *Evgenyi Kazakov [Ewgeniy Kasakow]*

**PART IV: DROPPING OUT ECONOMICS**                              **253**

11  Living in the Material World: Money in the Soviet
    Rock Underground                                             255
    *Anna Kan*

12  Socialism's Empty Promise: Housing Vacancy and Squatting
    in the German Democratic Republic                            277
    *Peter Angus Mitchell*

Conclusion: Dropping Out of Socialism? A Western Perspective     303
*Joachim C. Häberlen*

Bibliography                                                     319

Index                                                            327

About the Contributors                                           341

# Acknowledgments

The editors would like to thank the UK Arts and Humanities Research Board (AHRC) for their generous support of the project "Dropping out of Socialism: The Creation of Alternative Sphere in the Soviet Bloc" (grant number AH/I002502/1) with a generous Early Career Research Grant, which ran at the University of Bristol from 2011 to 2015. The editors would further like to thank the School of Humanities and Faculty of Arts at the University of Bristol, which hosted the project. We are particularly grateful to Sam Barlow of the Bristol Institute for Research in the Humanities and Arts (BIRTHA), who supported the workshop "Dropping out of Socialism," held 6–8 June 2014. Many of our colleagues in Bristol and elsewhere have offered support and advice at various stages of the project and advanced our thinking with their own research. We are also very grateful to our copy editor Kim Friedlander for getting articles written by people with so many different mother tongues into shape, Brian Hill, for his enthusiasm and support for the book and Eric Kuntzman for patience and help in the publishing process.

# Introduction

## *To Drop or Not to Drop?*

### Juliane Fürst

What does it mean to "drop out"? How does one "drop out"? "Dropping out" from what? Google only has two answers to such questions. Either the researcher is referred to Timothy Leary and the many pages dedicated to his famous LSD-hailing mantra of "dropping out, turning on and tuning in." Or paradoxically, the reader is directed to the vast debate concerning school drop-outs and the social and societal problems their existence poses. The irony is, of course, that the latter might very well be adherents of the former. What is utopia to some is a failed existence to others. Clearly, visions of what "dropping out" entails and how to evaluate it differ significantly. Salvation for one is condemnation for the other. Finding oneself can also mean being lost. Cutting ties can be liberating, or the first step to a future without choice.

As different as these and other interpretations of "dropping out" are, they have one major assumption in common. Almost all existing discussions surrounding "dropping out" are conducted with a highly developed capitalist Western world in mind. Dropping out is a luxury that can only take place against a backdrop of societal wealth. It is assumed that only in modern, liberal societies do people have the choice to "drop out" and reject what so many in the developing world are striving for: wealth, career, and success. Both poor people and people living in authoritarian regimes are assumed not to enjoy the freedom to exit. What do you rebel against, if you are busy feeding your family? Who would risk everything to live a life which is not only materially uncomfortable, but highly dangerous in an authoritarian or impoverished context?

While the question of "dropping out" in the developing, global South is the subject of a separate book, this collected volume sheds light on whether, where, and how people "dropped out" from the socialist East. Our contributors put an end to the assumption that it was only possible to "drop out" out of

1

Western capitalism. They confirm a recent historiographical trend, which for the last decade has suggested that socialist Eastern Europe and the Soviet Union were much more in step with Western postwar developments than the political need for differentiation during the Cold War allowed us to see.[1] Many aspects of cultural and social life in the Western postwar years also left their marks in the East: the global counterculture of the 1960s, the turn toward Eastern esotericism, the anticapitalist boom of punk culture, changes in youth culture caused by technological innovation, just to name a few. Of course, communist leaders did not look benevolently upon such global phenomena, which they resolutely interpreted as Western and bourgeois. As such these countercultures were both persecuted and denied. They did not fit into the socialist canon and hence, so far as the official narrative was concerned, they did not exist.

Yet even at the height of the Cold War, Western observers, of and in, Eastern Europe were highly aware of such phenomena and the "drop-out cultures" they spawned. International reporters and the staff of Radio Free Europe were anxious to present them as harbingers of change and communist decline.[2] Ironically, the end of the Cold War also meant the end of Western interest in Eastern European nonconformists. Those who lived willfully outside the mainstream have remained hidden. Most historical and political interest has focused on either big politics or ordinary life, ignoring the marginal sections of society, and in particular, those who made a virtue of being abnormal. For a long time, while communist censorship existed, only Eastern European insiders knew about "drop-outs," because it was impossible to gather information on them except by direct contact or word of mouth. Now their tales are freely available—as oral history, written memoirs, or through state sources. But for many scholars, the drop-outs' exceptionality and non-representativeness makes them unfit subjects of sustained attention.

Maybe it is not surprising that, just as many of the former socialist Eastern European states are leaving the democratic path, interest has (re-)awoken in socialist subjects who did not conform but were not overt dissidents, who lived outside the norm yet possessed their own normative frameworks, and who rejected socialist norms but also perpetuated them by accepting and fostering their social exclusion. In recent years memoirs, newly available documents, and oral histories have started to shed light on this long-neglected topic of willful marginals under socialism.[3] It turns out that many questions posed by the stories of hippies, punks, yogis, hackers, and nonconformists of all shapes are the same as those that have been asked about their Western peers. What does it really mean to "drop out"? Is dropping out an action that one does or one that is done to one? Is it possible to "drop out" completely? Is "dropping out" indeed the best term to describe the relationship of alternative communities to hegemonic political and cultural power?

And yet there are also questions that are very specific to the world of late socialism and its relationship with its recalcitrant citizens. When any kind of nonconformism is punished by social exclusion, what does dropping out mean? How can we make sense of a "dropping out" that means risking one's life and freedom but has few economic consequences? Is dropping out of socialism more or less radical than dropping out of the capitalist world? Where is the border between mainstream and drop-outs in a society that habitually breaks official norms (as was the case in all late socialist societies)? Was the Bolshevik experiment not once itself a radical attempt to "drop out" from the norm?

The characters who feature in this volume could easily have been the protagonists of a book with different headings. Dissidents, hippies, punks, yogis, nonconformist artists, squatters, pacifists, and religious dissenters have also been categorized as protest cultures, subversive elements, counterculture, subcultures, and opposition. This volume does not mean to argue that they were something else entirely or that the term "dropping out" is in any way superior to the other useful, but also flawed, terms in circulation. Rather it wants to highlight one particular communality of these groups—one which we consider crucial to understanding their character and meaning. The drop-outs under discussion here did not primarily set out to be "subversive," "counter," or "subaltern," even if they might not have excluded these conditions as a consequence of their actions. However, all of them consciously wanted distance—spatial, mental, and ideological—from the regime under which they lived. And they wanted to achieve this aim by *not* doing rather than doing something.

It is the refusal to participate rather than loud actions that is at the center of our investigation. It is the evasion of a system whose identity rested on mobilization that strikes us as significant, especially since it was performed to various degrees by such a large number of late socialist citizens.[4] And, as will be demonstrated, even societies with a very narrow normative horizon offer a surprising multitude of possible ways to drop out. Refusal to participate in normality is what connected Leningrad intellectuals with Berlin squatters, Bosnian Muslim madrassa students, and Romanian yogis. And somehow along this communality of "non-participation," late socialist society started to crack.

## "DROPPING OUT": A NEW LOOK AT A FAMILIAR TERM

In a literal sense the term "dropping out" conveys only an outward move: a drop away from societal, parental, and moral constraints into the nowhere: the nirvana of teenage desires, the bottomless possibilities of abstract freedom, and the promise of the undefined. However, "dropping out" has always contained an implicit constructive element as well. This becomes especially clear when considering that although the term reached prominence in the 1960s, the practice has taken place as long as societies existed. The very society from which Leary wanted to drop out—the United States of America—was to no small extent populated and shaped by "drop-outs" from Europe who looked for spatial separation not only from European repressive states but also from the norms of the mainstream. The Mayflower pilgrims and many of their successors defined themselves consciously as outside contemporary "normality." Wild West pioneers, Mennonites, hippies, and New Agists all interpreted the American dream as the possibility of successful removal from the mainstream. Old Europe, too, had its share of historical drop-outs: religious dissenters, ideological zealots, and countercultural youth. In the twentieth and twenty-first centuries globalization has changed the nature of dropping out. Exterior markers and social practices of many "drop-out" cultures, once highly local and specific to certain groups, are now internationally recognizable and tap into a pool of global alternative thought.

Like many terms that circulate widely in the media and colloquially, "dropping out" has mostly escaped academic scrutiny. It has been left to be defined by popular usage, even though scholars have not been shy to use it when convenient. Yet there is much that is problematic about the term, as is pointed out in a variety of chapters in this volume. It implies a totality that is never fulfilled and indeed unfulfillable. It is reductive, simplistic, and hyperbolic. It covers territory that overlaps with other scholarly paradigms. However, its ubiquity and prominence in common usage makes it difficult to ignore. Especially since the wave of youth countercultural movements from the mid-1960s onwards, the term has clearly captured a mood and engaged the imagination. Unsurprisingly, most of the chapters here deal with phenomena that are either part of this wave of youth countercultures or successors to it. Even today the term "dropping out" conjures up whole landscapes of associations. It is still a desirable state for some and a deplorable condition for others. It is high time then that academics interrogate this term and its usefulness in articulating their findings and interpretations of those that intended to escape the mainstream.

"Dropping out" always held the promise of something better around the corner. Yet, more often than not, this "better" was a variation of the very structures the "drop-outs" rejected. At the same time, however, their vision often seeped out from their niche communities, changing the society they wanted to escape. Some drop-out communities had to accept that a watered-down version of their culture had suddenly become mainstream. Others found that over the years they acquired the same problems and characteristics as the society from which they had run away. "Dropping out" was thus always a rump event, which could not stand on its own. Even O'Leary advocated that the dropped-out, bettered self should "drop in" and carry its improvement back into a new society.[5]

The interplay between the "dropping" and the "being dropped," the "turning on" and the "tuning in," the evasive and creative, the rejection and the missionizing, hence requires careful deconstruction and contextualization. Contrary to the belief of most "drop-outs" themselves, "dropping out" did not start with the decision of an individual or collective to do so. "Dropping out" needed boundaries, which were defined by the "mainstream" (society, state, the ruling system) and tacitly accepted by those dropping out. Only the recognition of borders made it possible to cross them. The first act of "dropping out" was thus an acceptance of a normative definition imposed from the "other side."

The construction of these borders and the creation of outsider communities turn out, at a closer glance, to be a chicken and egg question. Without borders, people could not be considered to have "dropped out." But often nonconformist behavior preceded the definition and construction of normative borders. Boundaries were often constructed in opposition to behavior and practices that were felt to be unacceptable or troubling. It is therefore more accurate to see the process of "dropping out" as a collaboration between those who wish to leave the mainstream and the mainstream itself. Indeed, one could even go further and say that the relationship is symbiotic, since the drop-out culture needs the mainstream for definition, while the mainstream re-affirms its hegemony by the designation of "otherness."

Such observations of interdependence mirror what Gramsci has observed for dominant and subordinate cultures. Indeed, many of the characteristics, functions, and meanings of subcultures, as identified by sociologists, also apply to the act of "dropping out."[6] Subculture too needs a dominant entity to define itself against. Just like "dropping out," subcultural practices require a collaboration between a main culture, which defines the norm, and a subculture, which rejects these norms, yet also inevitably draws on them in their creation of a subordinate set of norms. Here too it is not only the case that neither can exist without the other (mainstream culture has to reaffirm its dominance by designating outsiders), but also that in a bizarre twist of intention the subculture affirms the rules of the dominant culture through its desire to be non-mainstream and different from the norm. Gramsci is quite pessimistic about the effectiveness of achieving true "freedom" for such cultures, which believe they are breaking away from the shackles of dominant cultural norms, yet in reality submit to them: "It implies the active consent of the subordinate group in creating and maintaining its subordinate status . . . . In this way, subordinate groups actively choose from the dominant group's agenda, maintaining a semblance of freedom while reinforcing the dominant group's interests."[7]

Yet Gramsci's assumption is a political one. Ultimately the desire for victory over a dominant regime informs his analysis of the place and role of subordinate cultures. Subcultures (and, even more specifically, drop-out cultures), however, put the emphasis on a different place. The continuous process of being "sub" or dropping out is at the heart of their identity. From their point of view it is irrelevant to what extent their opposition is effective as long as their life is different to what they attempt to escape. Subcultures have been found to frame their resistance against a dominant framework of norms and practices in a nonverbal sphere, which Hebdige aptly defined as "style." Subcultural studies have turned to semiotics to decode and analyze societal phenomena which rarely produce any written declarations, yet whose existence is permeated by an unconscious ideology. Subculture is seen as an accumulation of signs: practices become rituals of identification, visual markers turn into narratives of differentiation and adaption. "Dropping out" is also rarely accompanied by a lengthy, verbal explanation. Rather, it too relies on practices, symbols, and style to convey its message of "distance." It too, as is demonstrated by the following chapters, is best approached by reading the act of "dropping out" as a text that tells a complex and multifaceted narrative and covers the whole spectrum between acceptance and rejection, including mutation, subversion, and *bricolage*. If we accept that every act of "dropping out" necessarily creates a new cultural entity, "drop-out" cultures are by definition subcultures.

Yet there is one interesting distinction between the two terms, which shifts the emphasis of definition. The functional interpretation of subculture has always left the question of agency unanswered. Indeed, semiotics took subjective intention out of the interpretation of subcultures. Was it necessary to desire to be a subculture in order achieve its status? Society knows many outsiders and not all of them wish to be "outside." Many—such as prostitutes, vagrants, gypsies—are forced into marginal spaces by poverty, discrimination, and prejudice. Some of these groups, such as the legendary Paris *clochards*, American hobos, etc., operate on a model that is partially voluntary. Yet in reality their lifestyle closes off future choice. Lack of choice over their "style" does not mean that these collectives are not developing their own norms and values. In a semiotic reading they could indeed be considered "subcultural." The term "dropping out" has no such ambiguities. It has an active implication. It requires a will as well as an action. "Dropping out" can be facilitated by the state or system. Yet it cannot be done by them.

Dropping out does require agency and subjective intention. Yet, again unlike subculture, it does not require a collective. "Dropping out" can be done as a group. But, as many of the articles demonstrate, it can also be a very solitary action. It is a subjective act and hence, even when enacted under the banner of a collective, it has a very individual character. Much more than "subculture," "dropping out" thus emphasizes the moment an *individual* leaves the mainstream orbit—at least in his or her own imagination. This action is rarely a moment of great violence or even noise. Most people describe "dropping out" as a rather quiet process, which they discover only at the moment when it is a *fait accompli*. It is also rarely a single act.

The simultaneously conscious and yet unaware nature of the act brings another term to mind that has been used, in particular in German scholarship.

*Eigensinn* has become one of the many terms that defies translation. It denotes a, "willfulness, spontaneous self-will, a kind of self-affirmation, an act of (re)-appropriating alienated social relations."[8] There was certainly a lot of *Eigensinn* in the decision to "drop out." But there also had to be a lot of *Eigensinn* to come to this decision. *Eigensinn*—the will to have one's very own mind—has both the long-term, simmering quality that underpins "dropping out" as well as the momentary burst of energy that is inherent in the term "drop." It is no coincidence that *Eigensinn* has come to prominence in GDR historiography, a society that had little space for nonconformist styles of life, yet deeply believed in a purpose without which life was wasted. This belief, rooted in the Enlightenment and fostered by Bolshevik thought, existed in all socialist societies—in the highest echelons of power as well as among the opposition and nonconformists. *Sinn* in German has another meaning. It is not only a state of mind, but a moral goal: "Sinn machen" is to give purpose. Underneath the meaning of *Eigensinn* as a will of one's own is thus also a more hidden one—to give purpose to and make sense of one's own life. *Eigensinn* is hence also a challenge to a state or system's monopoly on defining the purpose of life.

"Dropping out" is at the very center of this challenge. It is an act that negates the dominant narrative of "making sense" by withdrawing from it. It is a refusal to participate in something that is seen as corrupt and despicable. "Dropping out" is not necessarily oppositional, but it is an act that is not previewed by the norms. A recent German work has thus put the term *Verweigerung*—refusal—at the center of its investigation in order to find a term that transcends the binary notion of acceptance and resistance. Developed with the artistic scene in mind, this term stresses the "dystopian postulate" of disengaging from any kind of mainstream norm. This aim is bound to fail in its totality, yet informs the very spirit of those movements that were "refusing." In its very inception the term hence contains impossibility—an impossibility, however, it embraces rather than denies.[9]

Adherents of *Verweigerung* therefore encounter the same dilemma as the editors of the current volume met when defining the term "drop out." It is apparent from the first glance that any attempt to completely drop out of society is bound to fail. Yet dismissing the term would mean discarding an important subjective element of the identity of those who professed to "drop out." It seems that rather than measuring the effectiveness of "refusal" and/or "dropping out" as an act, it would be more helpful to look at these terms as descriptors of affect and emotion. This means shifting the analytical glance away from the objective practice to the subjective "feel" of "dropping out." Many participants in drop-out cultures emphasize that it was precisely the moment in which they felt they asserted their own will vis-à-vis a dominant state norm that provided satisfaction and identity. All of the chapters in this

volume report that there was rarely much discussion of whether drop-outs'
actions were anti-socialist or oppositional. What was important was that what
they did was felt to be "theirs."

In the Western countercultural milieu of the leftwing, this desire to "do
something" and "be something" that was not corrupted by the norms of the
establishment was labeled "authenticity." Inspired by Marxist concepts and
language of "alienation," Western alternative milieus invoked this term to
separate themselves from the mainstream and fashion their own identity.[10]
"Dropping out" in the West was part of this search for authenticity, while
in turn the state of "authenticity" or "authentic life" included the notion of
"dropping out." One could not be authentic in the mainstream. The general
idea behind this notion of alternative exclusivity resonated strongly with
drop-out cultures in the East. Here, too, "dropping out" was part and parcel of
a search for something uncorrupted, purer, and truer—in short more "authentic." However, this search was complicated by the fact that the ruling system
derived its own identity from a claim of greater authenticity vis-à-vis the capitalist world. Yet the critiques that were leveled against capitalism in the West
had the same ring as the accusations of Eastern disaffected youth against their
own regimes. Here the term in circulation was "truth." In the Soviet case this
did not refer to the truth expressed in *Pravda* and in the Russian term *pravda*,
but the deeper truth of the term *istina* that went beyond the meaning of merely
being factually true.[11] Dropping out, in the socialist East, was a moment of
truth in the sense of personal salvation from lies.

Last but not least, "dropping out" touches on another approach that has
come to prominence recently: the history of emotions. Indeed, the elusiveness
of "dropping out" cultures might rest precisely in the fact that their world
privileged emotional experience over political and social statements. Analysts
who are interested in their potential for resistance and opposition tend to
ignore the fact that for most of these cultures these terms held little meaning.[12]
Drop-out cultures strive less for physical change of their environment than for
a change in how they *feel* subjectively. This change might require a manipulation of their environment and the development of certain outer markers, but at
the heart of any of the groups discussed in this volume, whether intellectuals
or yogis, is always the desire to create a different "emotional style" in contrast to an establishment that dictates an "unauthentic" or "lying" emotional
regime. "Dropping out" is inevitably an emotional process that combines both
rejection of emotional norms as well as construction of new ones.

## "DROPPING OUT": EXPLORATION OF A CREATIVE ACT

As has become apparent, "dropping out" cannot be understood as a stand-
alone or as a single moment. No matter if one associates it with O'Leary or

educational drop-outs, with Gramsci, or Hebdige, with *Eigensinn* or *Verweigerung*, dropping out always means more than the moment of "dropping out" (and, as has become apparent, this moment can be difficult to pinpoint). It inevitably included a complex exit negotiation from an entity perceived as dominant. And it involved creating something to "drop into"—a universe that was constructed by borrowing from the familiar, drawing from the "other," and manipulating both. This process of creation, just like the process of "dropping," was not a singular moment. Rather, it too was an ongoing development, capable of changing and mutating over time as well as differing among individual members of a drop-out community. The processes of "leaving" the mainstream, "refusal to participate," "negating" existing norms, and creating new spheres intertwined and fed into each other. In short, "dropping out" was a process that had to be negotiated by all parties involved.

There was a whole range of ways for drop-outs to construct an alternative sphere, from intellectual inner emigration to establishing spatial separation from the mainstream. All groups described in this volume looked for spaces which both allowed them to be different and signified their difference at the same time. Squatters looked for buildings not occupied by anybody else. Musicians looked for venues not controlled by the official system. The process of creating alternative spaces for alternative cultures could be pursued in two very different ways. One path to spatial separation was to find places that were as far away as possible from the reach of authorities and the vision of the mainstream. Groups that drew on conspiratorial pasts such as Zitzewitz's Leningrad intellectuals and Costache's yogis in Romania, tended to withdraw into apartments and rural locations where authorities lost track of them. However, a variety of groups chose the opposite strategy. They populated and occupied the most prestigious and reputational public spaces, which provided maximum visibility and exposure. It was, as if the very location near the center of official power (e.g., in the center of Tallinn, on the Arbat in Moscow) attracted them, because here subversion was very easy. Their sheer presence was enough to radically alter the narrative underpinning this space. In an unconscious way they were keenly aware that space was always socially produced and depended on the dynamic interaction of what this space represented and how it was lived.

Yet the tension that existed between "creating" as an act of both "dropping out" and as "entanglement with the official" also becomes obvious here. Since socialism was not just a political doctrine, but a lived reality, it was impossible to find a truly "unoccupied" space—just, as, of course the West did not have ideologically "empty" spaces either. Every redefinition of space hence carried underneath itself the original signifier of mainstream interpretation. Escape into remote spaces led not to isolation but to encounters with different parts of socialist society. Indeed, quite often, as a result of travel and seeking physical distance, alternative cultures knew more about the different facets of life in late socialist society than their normative contemporaries. Some groups tried to circumvent the limitations of physical escape through establishing new mental spaces. Intellectuals looked for textual worlds not allowed by official censorship. And hippies tried to make the imaginary else-wheres a lived reality by traveling into a psychedelic world in their heads. Yet here too, entanglement with other structures was never far. The reading lists of the Leningrad circles Zitzewitz describes orientated themselves by the censor's magnetic needle, reading what they were forbidden to read. They remained guided by the norm. And the few Soviet hippies who got hold of LSD, acquired it from the experimental laboratories of the military.

"Style" was another tool in the repertoire of differentiation. "Style" itself is a conglomerate of various homologous inner and outer attributes and can include dress, makeup, music, artistic practices, language, ritual, and much more. Style, with its many facets, serves us well for studying the inter-twined processes of "dropping out" and "creating one's own." Prospective "drop-outs" tended to test out one element of style and then gradually add to the repertoire until one day they realized that they had arrived outside the mainstream (or the mainstream helped them along by pronouncing their exclusion). Hence, for many rebellious youngsters in the Soviet bloc in the 1960s and 1970s, music was the entry ticket to a world that took them along a path of long hair, secret meeting places, exclusive slang, and eventually a wide variety of practices and rituals that made them feel as if they lived in a different world than the one they had feared might be their fate. However, the emphasis is very much on the "as if." Estonian hippies perfected a stylistic confluence of flowery dress, hippie ideas of love and peace, long hair, and a reverence for nature. East German punks employed the same antimaterialist shock tactics as their Western contemporaries. Siberian rock musicians chose names, lyrics, and attributes designed to rile the defenders of Soviet morals. And yet their attempt to escape the norms of those they despised was both successful and laced with limitations. They surprised, they shocked, and they were soon considered subversive by the authorities. Yet their styles also relied on their habitus and the materials it supplied. They changed the mean-ing of these materials by painting flowers on their jeans or cutting up their shirts. They shocked by taking on the name and style of people reviled in their collective historical memory. But more often than not, they needed the mainstream not only as a counterpoint but also as a supplier.

Differences in "style" were codified by differences in language. In conjunction with the creation of style, new terms were coined to give expres-sion to this style and the practices associated with it. Most drop-out culture slang describes the everyday items in circulation within this culture. By creating a different linguistic universe the creation of a different material world is posited. Having named their objects, drop-out communities then created verbs to describe how they related to them, adding an alternative field of action. *Khippi* was joined by *khippovat'* (to be a hippie). *Vint* was both a type of a drug and a term for arrest, and when you were arrested, *tebia vintili*. More often than not the new language was less a complete fantasy than borrowed heavily from either foreign languages (especially English) or from the culture's mother tongue. Foreign words were naturalized by subjecting them to local grammar. Native terms were subverted by giving them different meaning or changing their sound. Language became hence not only a tool of closed, internal communication, but also a means of identity-building by crafting a vocabulary unique to a particular culture. Yet language was often a double-edged sword for "drop-outs." It codified their world and hence created a new norm, when many of them liked to see themselves as beyond "norms." While they usually wholeheartedly embraced the process (and indeed the term "dropping out"), they were much more ambivalent about putting their parallel worlds into words. Toomistu mentions her subjects' reluctance to be labeled "hippie," while many other groups such as Zitzewitz's intelligentsia, Wasiak's hackers, and the members of Leningrad's commune Yellow Submarine simply evaded the question of what they are called. Implicitly, there was always a fear that by being "too" creative, one became a new norm.

## DROPPING OUT OF SOCIALISM

"Dropping out" acquired yet another set of meaning when it was done "out of socialism." Indeed, until relatively recently the idea that "drop-outs" from socialism could exist was rarely entertained in either the popular imagination or in the historical profession. The existence in the socialist bloc of alternative cultures which rejected mainstream norms, created lives that refused to participate in these norms, and set up new normative frameworks known mostly only to those on the inside and the handful of people who dealt with them professionally in their capacity as, for instance, police officers or staff in psychiatric units. The exception was the political dissident community in Eastern Europe and the Soviet Union who, early on, discovered the potential of Western correspondents in their fight against the system. Ironically, it was this community which in many ways was least radical in its desire to drop out of socialism. Many of its tenets of belief were formed with direct reference to socialist values and norms and its demands tended toward reform rather than withdrawal from socialist life. And yet, as the chapter by Zitzewitz shows, when one goes beyond the activities of familiar names who grabbed the headlines of the time, it becomes apparent that through simple acts of differentiation—such as reading a different canon of works from the mainstream—strong alternative identities could be created, paths into a different intellectual world that operated in different physical spaces than the mainstream.

Recent revelations in memoirs, interviews, and a handful of academic studies (including this volume), demonstrate that that "dropping out of socialism" existed to the same extent and within the same limits as "drop-out" cultures in the West. Yet the crucial question remains: was dropping out of socialism different from dropping out from Western capitalism? Or to formulate the question more precisely: how was it possible to drop out from a society that did not only dislike difference but whose very foundations rested on a notion of equality and normativity? Did dropping out from socialism only look like its Western counterpart or was it essentially the same process? What does it mean for late socialism that these drop-out cultures existed?

First and foremost it has to be noted that "dropping out of socialism" was easier than "dropping out of capitalism." This might be a surprising statement. Yet the reason for this rested less with the radicality of homegrown drop-out cultures in the Eastern bloc (even though there was something in this too, as many émigré counterculturals observed when they came to the West),[13] and more in the rigidness of the socialist system. There is no doubt that socialist states were bound by more rigid norms of conformity than the postwar West (without wanting to downplay the repressive arsenal used against troublemakers in capitalist states), often using legal and medical rules to enforce the conformity on which it was believed socialist wellbeing depended. Being different under socialism carried a higher risk than being different in the West, where much opprobrium came from societal condemnation rather than official persecution. This state of affairs, however, also meant that even small differences could lead to relatively complete outsider status. The Leningrad rock musicians in Anna Kan's chapter did not set out to work in the "underground." They set out to make music they believed in (the Western equivalent of authenticity), which, by virtue of the rigidity of the official music business, meant that they found themselves working in boiler rooms while their music was traded on the black market. Unintentionally, they not only revolutionized the Russian music scene but also undermined its economic structures. As is apparent from this example, the outsider and drop-out status of the musicians dragged yet another group of youngsters into an alternative world: young people who loved their music and saw the possibility of making a little income on the side (or indeed quite a big income for the time) by producing and selling usable copies. Similarly, Asavei's artists chose "being mad" over being persecuted for their art. Their refusal to participate in the official norms of the late socialist art world meant not only that their artistic world was pushed into an alternative sphere, but that their physical location was moved into a world that was literally beyond normality. Josephine von Zitzewitz's intelligentsia was desperate to serve as an intellectual elite for Soviet society, but failing this, chose to be an intellectual underground. Almost all our chapters showcase how late socialism was busy shoring itself up against challenges from the inside and out and consequently created a plethora of underground islands.

All of this begs the question of why socialist states insisted on such a normative rigidity, which ultimately left them fighting on a multitude of cultural and intellectual fronts. The assumption that Western capitalism was a freer society only holds limited value. The history of Western counter- and drop-out cultures demonstrates a number of instances when Western societies and states reacted violently and brutally to challenges by social phenomena which questioned traditional norms. Terje Toomistu mentions the 1971 fateful hippie demonstration in Moscow. This very demonstration was indeed conceived of as an act of solidarity with the Yippie demonstrations in Washington, DC earlier in that year, which were brutally crushed by the American police. And yet overall, Western states were undoubtedly less consistently repressive against cultures that refused to acknowledge mainstream norms.

The answer rests less in the notion of liberty in the West than in the particular history of the socialist idea. Socialism itself had once sponsored drop-out cultures all across Europe: committed revolutionaries living in the underground or exile according to their own norms. It had its own language, spaces, and practices. It was also a culture that made a total demand on people. It was not content with the profession of socialist ideals and ideology. Socialism always demanded to be lived. It was all-encompassing. The fact that socialism emerged from the margins to destroy a dominant mainstream, combined with its jealous claim to a monopoly on people's minds and hearts, meant that socialist regimes were primed to react particularly sensitively to phenomena that gathered outside their normative framework and refused to submit to the totality of socialist life. Of course by the 1960s and 1970s, which is the period most of this volume's chapters look at, socialism had long lost the battle to influence all of human existence—private and personal spaces were not the exception but the hallmark of late socialist society—but it was not going to give up on its ideological monopoly.

This monopoly, however, was not limited to demanding belief in the socialist ideas. In the socialist world, as it had been shaped by Bolshevik discourse and practices, both emotional investment and participation were at the heart of socialist idea. It was not possible to be a passive socialist. At the very least, performative rituals had to be enacted by socialist citizens, even though, or precisely because, their content had become increasingly meaningless for their participants. Withdrawal was hence always going to be more than withdrawal. In the eyes of the socialist state withdrawal was resistance.

Dropping out, refusal to take part, and the redirection of emotions away from the socialist project was akin to treason.

As a result, the frontlines between system and drop-outs were particularly edgy under socialism. But they were by no means less blurred than in the West: possibly even more so, creating a complicated web of alliances, guilt, and mutual exploitation. All chapters in the volume confirm that, of course, it was not possible to leave the socialist world completely, just as it was not possible to shut out Western capitalism entirely. Yet some describe some very complicated entanglements, which arose out of the specific situation of regimes using "drop-outs" to enforce surveillance and control over a wayward community, while "drop-outs" used these very same channels to carve out spaces of existence for their way of life. Jeff Hayton delineates this entanglement in its most extreme form, describing how punks carved out a zone of "ignoring socialism" by serving as informal informants for the Stasi. Kan's musicians too were often less than a step away from collaboration with the KGB, which tried to concentrate them in venues such as the KGB-sponsored Leningrad Rock Club, which nonetheless became a mecca for independent music and independent enjoyment of music. Bringing together drop-outs or potential drop-outs was an effective way of keeping them under surveillance, but it was also a strategy that could backfire. Spaces—both physical and virtual—could quickly be repurposed to drop-out ends: Wasiak describes how the Polish state created and sponsored the computer craze that then so easily slipped out of its control.

On a less tangible level, Zitzewitz's dissidents, Toomistu's hippies, and Costache's yogis all constantly worked with, as much as against, the official structures. The truth was that while socialism as an ideology was very inimical to drop-out cultures, socialist reality was a more ambiguous entity. It made life outside the official structures hard, because there was no part of life that was not supposed to be socialist. But at the same time, the ineffectiveness of late socialism and its general unattractiveness to many of its subjects created zones for drop-out cultures to exist. When socialist regimes made up their mind, they had no difficulty in crushing a movement. Yet by the 1970s, socialist infrastructure was under considerable strain. More and more of life was conducted in a sphere that was outside official economics and social norms. At the same time there was no commercial force to take over the spaces "socialism" had forgotten or simply left to its own devices (and that included large chunks of built-up physical space—like, for instance, the rundown housing in Berlin's Prenzlauer Berg of which Mitchell's squatters took advantage). As a result those who wanted to re-invent and redefine themselves might have found more suitable spaces in the East: in the West, the state might be tolerant, but commercial interest drove its own agenda. Further, while only very few people in the Eastern bloc wanted to be punks, hippies, yogis, or mad artists, a much larger number of people were not very keen on being "socialist." In the resulting vacuum alternative milieus sprang up with great rapidity and considerable intensiveness. By the late 1980s Eastern Europe was littered with subcultures and fringe movements—arguably much more so than the West.

It is certainly striking how socialism and socialist structures unwittingly facilitated the rise and existence of some drop-out cultures. But it is even more interesting how these cultures were linked and entangled with ideas and structures that were not dominant under late socialism, but were gathering strength. The madrassa students described by Madigan Fichter are the most obvious example, where dropping out of socialism meant automatically dropping into another powerful, already-existing idea and environment. However, several other chapters also indicate that, of course, socialism was not the only player on the field. Punks, hippies, and pacifists inevitably engaged with their Western counterparts, either by imitating or rejecting them or more often a more complicated mixture between the two. Yet, for instance, Kazakov's punks tap into something more: a Russian nationalism that was not only on the rise in the radical underground of Siberia, but was also rearing its head on a variety of levels, not least in the literary world that defined the dissident circles of Zitzewitz's chapter. Irina Gordeeva's chapter on Soviet pacifists also demonstrates that dropping out of socialism can mean dropping into the *zeitgeist*. Largely unaware of movements such as the antinuclear demonstrations or the powerful peace movement in Western Europe in the 1980s, Soviet pacifists found themselves making very similar demands under the impact, and their impressions, of the same global events. Yet the reception and trajectory of these demands were very different to the Western experience. Rather than evolving into a mass movement, Soviet pacifists found themselves accused of treason by the regime and of faking ideological dissent in order to emigrate by their peers. The movement never flourished and petered out. Kazakov's Russian nationalist punks, however, saw much of their ideas and music go toward the mainstream in the 1990s as angry punk went commercial and nationalism emerged as socialism's main heir.

Was "dropping out of socialism" thus overall different from "dropping out" of Western, capitalist societies? This question is at the center of Joachim Häberlen's conclusion. As a West German specialist, Häberlen brings a fresh perspective to the volume at the very end. His emphasis on outlining the many obvious and not so obvious similarities reminds us that the Iron Curtain was not impenetrable and that indeed many of our protagonists' aspirations such as self-fashioning and self-improvement have their roots not in the Cold War world but in a shared experience of modernity. And yet, is this volume proof that the East was not so different after all? That one could drop out from socialism as well as capitalism? That, give or take a few terms, this

experience was essentially the same, motivated by similar notions and resulting in similar communities and phenomena?

This is indeed one fruitful way of thinking about "drop-out" cultures. Not
only does an emphasis on similarity provide us with a rich vocabulary and
concepts for approaching Eastern European "drop-out" phenomena, it also
shows respect to the subjective views of their participants, who so often did
wish to align their communities with phenomena elsewhere. It breaks down
geographical and conceptual borders, not only stimulating scholarship on
Eastern Europe but forcing Western scholars to rethink some of their assumptions. If there are hippies in a non-capitalist, non-materialist society, what
does this say about the motivations behind the movement? If there are punks
in a world that collected every piece of waste and gave youngsters a well laid
out future, what does this say about the no-future movement?

And yet as helpful as likening the socialist world of alternative spheres
to the West is, ultimately, it is in danger of simply flipping the previous
assumption about the nonexistence of drop-out cultures in the East onto its
head. Often, under a similar veneer, very different processes and subjective
experiences are at work. Hayton picks up on these allusions of similarity in
his chapter on East and West German punks. While the West Germans cried
"No future," in the East the complaint was "too much future." Both cries were
expressions of desire for a more "authentic" life. But the dread they express
is not the same: one is based on norms perceived to conspire against youth in
the name of establishment and the older generation. The other is a state-sponsored inertia under which people's parents labored as much as their children.
Authenticity was also delivered in different forms: West German punks had
to build up a complex world that affirmed at every step that they were different from the establishment. In the East the hostile and repressive reaction of
the state did much to give "authentic" credentials to nonconformists.

While in some sense drop-out cultures in the East had to work less hard
to drop out, this does not mean that it was easier to be a "drop-out." The
plethora of studies on sub- and alternative cultures under socialism at times
might give the impression that their situation in East and West was indeed
the same: subjected to a certain amount of opprobrium and repression from
the establishment but essentially left alone to "do their thing." This volume
too does not tell many stories of persecution—this trope was too exhaustively
treated in 1970s and 1980s, when the West was fixated on stories of the dissidents' plight. But the fact that current scholarship is more interested in
the practices of alternative cultures than in state persecution does not mean
that persecution did not happen and did not massively impact on the subjective experience of "drop-outs" under socialism. Every single chapter in this
volume makes reference to the dangers that living a life "dropped out" from
socialism posed. Asavei's artists could only survive in the restrictive world

of an asylum. Kan's musicians lived in a precarious world of lowly jobs and KGB observation. Mitchell's squatters knew that their actions might draw not only financial punishment but could land them in prison. The lives of the inhabitants of the Leningrad commune Yellow Submarine were shattered for the crime of living and thinking in a nonconformist way. Repression and persecution was a reality on both sides of the Iron Curtain, but it was a much more frequent and a much harder reality in its Eastern side.

Increased persecution, however, also led to a heightened intensity of experience. For those who chose the lifestyle of the drop-out, it came with an outlaw experience, even if actual acts of repression were not an everyday matter. The socialist regimes drew clear lines of battle and their omnipresence in people's lives ensured that these lines could not be ignored. The result was that living outside the norm in the heavily normed socialist societies acquired a very specific flavor. The few who did manage to emigrate from this "compression chamber" of emotions found that life in the West was dull and meaningless compared to the intensive sense of purpose that had permeated the seemingly hopeless world of late socialism.[14] This was true indeed not only for nonconformists but for large swathes of late socialist populations who lived in a timeless space where nothing ever truly changed and "everything was forever," while the permanent absurdity of life was mastered through irony, parody, and withdrawals from the more unpalatable aspects of official late socialism.[15]

This poses an interesting question: was "dropping out of socialism" de facto a much more common occurrence than the equivalent practice in the West? Was a certain "dropping out" of the official structures in fact part and parcel of late socialism and its peculiar "feel"? There is something to be said for such a radical position. Western drop-out cultures by and large protested against a system of bourgeois capitalism, which in its essence had broad support among the population of the West. Soviet bloc drop-outs withdrew from a system of state socialism and socialist norms that had at best partial support. Of course, the socialist regimes were supported by a multitude of people who conformed and enforced the dominant norms for a variety of reasons, ranging from belief to careerism. But both in the Soviet satellite states as well as in the Soviet Union itself, popular sentiment had acquiesced to reality rather than engaging with it. By the 1970s, nationalist, religious, and intellectual dissent chipped support away from socialism in all the Eastern bloc countries not to mention the economic discontent that informed much of how late socialist citizens perceived their reality. In other words, socialist drop-out cultures dropped out of a world whose hegemony was already very much in question.

Socialism was not defeated in street battles. It slipped away when people left the socialist stage. Dropping out was only moderately harmful to capitalism, which quickly understood how to commercialize the

new phenomenon. For socialism and its need for committed participation it
was fatal. Drop-out cultures in the socialist bloc were less numerous than in
the West. Yet arguably their effect was far more cataclysmic, despite the fact,
or precisely because they largely shunned the outright political stage. They
struck at the battleground of the quotidian experience, which itself was at the
heart of a socialist project that did not know apolitical spaces. The everyday,
however, was also socialism's weak spot and became increasingly more so
as late socialism matured into final-day socialism. A multitude of practices
made "dropping out" of certain aspects of socialism a mass phenomena: there
were few people who did not dabble somehow in the second economy, made
their kitchens or dachas bolt-holes of withdrawal or engaged in activities
that were not sanctioned by the socialist state.[16] And the more radical drop-
out cultures, as described in this volume, accelerated this process. For every
drop-out rock musician there were thousands of youngsters who listened to
his music. For every committed yogi there were hundreds who were more
interested in Eastern religion than in Marxism-Leninism. For every reader
of *samizdat*, there were dozens who had heard of it. These were small but
not insignificant practices. As Becky Beal has observed for the American
skateboarding subculture, the everyday can provide a powerful platform from
which to force social change.[17]

Hence it may be not surprising that within a decade the vast majority of
the alternative cultures described in this volume achieved a quasi-mainstream
status. The most obvious is perhaps Kan's rock musicians, who in the 1990s
achieved not only fame and recognition but also considerable economic success. But to a lesser or smaller extent, none of the protagonists of this volume
remained outside society to the extent they had in late socialism. *Perestroika*
and reforms in Eastern Europe removed many of the frontiers that had rel-
egated them to the nonconformist side of the fence, while an explosion of
youth, cultural, and esoteric phenomena meant that their numbers grew well
beyond the small drop-out communities they had once been.

## NOTES

1. Examples for such an argument are numerous. See among others and only
limited to works on the postwar period (the argument has also been forcefully made
for the prewar era), Susan Reid and David Crowley, eds., *Pleasures in Socialism:
Leisure and Luxury in the Eastern Bloc* (Evanston: Northwestern University Press,
2010); Kristin Roth-Ey, *Moscow Prime Time: How the Soviet Union Built the Media
Empire that Lost the Cold War* (Ithaca: Cornell University Press, 2010); Stephen
Bittner, *The Many Lives of Khrushchev's Thaw: Experience and Memory in the Arbat*
(Ithaca: Cornell University Press, 2008); Juliane Fürst, *Stalin's Last Generation:*

*Soviet Post-War Youth and the Emergence of Mature Socialism* (Oxford: Oxford University Press, 2010).

2. It is not a coincidence that a significant amount of what we know about these groups at the margins still comes from Radio Free Europe/Radio Liberty reports that are now located at the Open Society Archive in Budapest. Some of the journalists who had personal contact with dissidents and the bohemian underground wrote their memoirs after their stints in the Soviet Union: Hedrick Smith, *The Russians* (New York: Quadrangle/New York Times Book Company, 1976) and David Satter, *Age of Delirium: Decline and Fall of the Soviet Union* (New York: Knopf, 1996).

3. This is evident in the sources on which this volume draws, which are predominantly memoirs or interviews and, to a smaller extent, declassified archival sources. In terms of secondary literature, there has been a heavy emphasis on the nonconformist artistic milieu. See for example, Matthew Jesse Jackson, *The Experimental Group: Ilya Kabakov, Moscow Conceptualism, Soviet Avant-Gardes* (Chicago: University of Chicago Press, 2010); Christine Gölz and Alfrun Kliems, eds., *Spielplätze der Verweigerung: Gegenkuluren im östlichen Europa* (Cologne: Böhlau, 2014); Alexandra Schwell, *Anarchie ist die Mutter der Ordnung: Alternativkultur und Tradition in Polen* (Münster: Lit, 2005). On a comparative perspective between East and West, see Timothy Brown and Lorena Anton, eds., *Between the Avant-Garde and the Everyday: Subversive Politics in Europe from 1957 to the Present* (New York: Berghahn Books, 2011). For a rare example of looking at the non-intellectual milieu, see John Bushnell, *Moscow Graffiti: Language and Subculture* (Boston: Unwin Hyman, 1990).

4. The most influential book on this topic has undoubtedly been Alexei Yurchak, *Everything was Forever Until It Was No More: The Last Soviet Generation* (Princeton: Princeton University Press, 2006).

5. Timothy O'Leary, *Turn On, Tune In, Drop Out* (Berkeley: Ronin, 1999).

6. See the work in Stuart Hall and Tony Jefferson, eds., *Resistance through Ritual: Youth Subcultures in Post-War Britain* (London: Hutchinson, 1976); Dick Hebdige, *Subculture: The Meaning of Style* (London: Routledge, 1979); David Muggleton, *Inside Subculture: The Postmodern Meaning of Style* (Oxford: Oxford University Press, 2000).

7. Antonio Gramsci, *Selections from the Prison Notebooks of Antonio Gramsci*, ed. Quintin Hoare and trans. Quintin Hoare and Geoffrey Nowell Smith (London: Lawrence and Wishart, 1971), 253.

8. Mark Fenemore, *Sex, Thugs and Rock 'n' Roll: Teenage Rebels in Cold War East Germany* (Oxford: Oxford University Press, 2007), 12. On *Eigensinn* as a concept, see Thomas Lindenberger, "Die Diktatur der Grenzen," in *Herrschaft und Eigen-Sinn in der Diktatur: Studien zur Gesellschaftsgeschichte der DDR*, ed. Thomas Lindenberger (Cologne: Böhlau, 1999), 23–26. See also Andreas Ludwig, ed., *Fortschritt, Norm und Eigensinn: Erkundungen im Alltag der DDR* (Berlin: Links, 2000); Marc-Dietrich Ohse, *Jugend nach dem Mauerbau: Anpassung, Protest und Eigensinn, DDR 1961–1974* (Berlin: Links, 2003); and Frank Eckart, *Eigenart und Eigensinn: Alternative Kulturszenen in der DDR (1980–1990)* (Bremen: Edition Temmen, 1993).

9. Gölz and Kliems, *Spielplätze der Verweigerung*, 13.

10. Sven Reichardt, *Authenzität und Gemeinschaft: Linksalternatives Leben in den siebziger und frühen achtziger Jahren* (Berlin: Suhrkamp, 2014).

11. Alexei Yurchak "Suspending the Political: Late Soviet Artistic Experiments on the Margins of the State," *Poetics Today* 29, no. 4 (2008).

12. On a recent attempt to look at protest cultures from an angle of the politics of emotion, see Joachim Häberlen and Russell Spinney, eds., "Emotions in Protest Movements in Europe since 1917," special issue, *Contemporary European History* 23, no. 4 (2014).

13. See for example, Aleksandr Dvorkin, *Moia Amerika* (Moscow: Khristianskaia biblioteka, 2013), who gives one of the most detailed descriptions of the difficult transition between the unfree, but meaningful East and the free, but intellectually and emotionally poor West. In a very different genre, Eduard Limonov, *Ia Edichka* (New York: Index Publishers, 1979), also expresses his disappointment upon encountering the West.

14. For the Russian case, see Dvorkin, *Moia Amerika*.

15. Yurchak, *Everything Was Forever*.

16. See, for these phenomena among many publications, Stephen Lovell, *A History of the Dacha, 1710–2000* (Ithaca: Cornell University Press, 2003); Vladimir Shlapentokh, *Strakh i druzhba v nashem totalitarnom proshlom* (Sankt Peterburg: Zvezda, 2003); Lewis Siegelbaum, *Borders of Socialism: Private Spheres of Soviet Russia* (Basingstoke: Palgrave, 2006).

17. Becky Beal, "Disqualifying the Official: An Exploration of Social Resistance through the Subculture of Skateboarding," *Sociology of Sport Journal* 12, no. 3 (1995): 252–67.

*Part I*

# DROPPING OUT IN SPIRIT

*Chapter 1*

# The Biography of a Scandal

## *Experimenting with Yoga during Romanian Late Socialism*

### Irina Costache

This chapter investigates the formation of a yoga subculture in Romania before 1989. However, the apex of this hidden history unfolded long after the execution of Romanian dictator Nicolae Ceaușescu and the subsequent fall of "actually existing socialism," making it a case that illustrates continuities after 1989. Moreover, this case illustrates how ideas and practices, people and books, suspicions and uncertainties also traveled across the two sides of the Iron Curtain, marking the ways in which subcultures develop differently in the center and at the periphery.

Let's begin at the end. On the morning of March 18, 2004, over three hundred law enforcement agents, ranging from antiterrorist units to regular police and even prosecutors, stormed sixteen different buildings in a Bucharest neighborhood. The riot police pulled more than ninety people, some scantily clad, out of their beds at gunpoint, threatened them, and videotaped them while also making a thorough search of the premises. By the end of the morning, almost fifty suspects had been taken into custody and evidence had been loaded into more than twenty police trucks.[1] The police brutality was intensified by the intrusion of the media, which reported the entire operation live, depicting it as an investigation into a widespread network for drug trafficking, human trafficking, and potential terrorism.

This was a point of no return for Gregorian Bivolaru, a local yogi, and his organization, MISA (Miscarea de Integrare Spirituala in Absolut or Movement for Spiritual Integration into the Absolute),[2] since he and the members of his organization were the people targeted by the police actions. Picking up from where the Securitate had stopped, the SRI (Serviciul Roman de Informatii), that is, the postcommunist secret police, had been monitoring the group's activities since 1993 and regularly informing the Ministry of Internal Affairs, the Bucharest judiciary, and the Parliamentary Commission for National Security about what the group was doing. The spectacular police intervention of 2004 was only the grand finale of a decade-long strategy of suspicion and harassment of yoga practitioners in a feedback loop in which secret police surveillance was connected with sensationalist media reporting.[3]

The movement gained many new members after the fall of communism. Its activities usually consisted of various forms of yoga exercises, meditation, Ayurvedic medicine, vegetarianism, sexual advice modeled on the principles of Tantric yoga, nudism on a remote stretch of the Black Sea resort of Costinesti, group meditation, and various processions and devotions that included sexualized dancing and even sex acts. The movement opened branches all over the country and at its height there were up to ten thousand participants in regular yoga classes, ashrams, and retreats.[4] While the police later dropped the charges of organized crime for lack of evidence, Bivolaru himself was indicted for statutory rape, allegedly having had sexual intercourse with one of his under-aged followers.[5] While under investigation, the yogi fled the country and took refuge in Sweden where he was granted political asylum, creating a resounding scandal on the eve of Romania's accession to the EU.

At this point, Bivolaru's case underwent a significant shift: it was transformed from a police investigation carried out in the context of the rules and constraints of the nation-state into an international human rights case pertaining to freedom of belief. In the process, Bivolaru not only turned into an international figure and the focus of an international case, but he also fit the bill as a highly controversial, scandalous yoga guru. But how did such a character emerge so quickly in a peripheral, postcommunist country? What strategies did he use in communist times to learn yoga, educate himself on matters of Eastern spirituality, and build a small group of followers? And, more generally, what was the regime's relationship with controversial spiritual practices such as yoga?

This chapter focuses on the guru's life during socialism and draws on findings from his secret police file in order show that spiritual discovery and police surveillance became indistinguishable experiences that were distilled into the guru's yoga philosophy. Bivolaru's yoga was a spiritual practice guided by the rules of secrecy and gradual revelation, imbued with mystery, and containing many references to conspiracy theories and myths. Before delving into Bivolaru's actual biography and philosophy, a brief discussion of the pre-1989 context is in order.

While public display of spiritual manifestations was severely censored and many of the materials detailing interwar esoteric and mystical traditions were purged from public libraries in the first decade of Romanian communism,[6] in the mid-1960s, along with a general liberalization of the regime itself and the distant impact of the global turbulence of 1968, such practices burst into the open again. With a new leader in charge of the Romanian Communist

Party, society increasingly enjoyed the vibes and perks of a phase of liberalization that ended in the mid-1970s. The post-Stalinist decade not only made possible a Romanian Orthodox revival but also permitted New Age practices such as nudism, rock-and-roll hippies' lifestyles, pre-Christian and indigenous pagan traditions, yoga, and many other practices to pop up from the underground into the public sphere.[7]

What is more, some of these practices were in fact actively encouraged, or at least enabled, by the regime, through the publication of books (e.g., a number of yoga books were published at the Sport—Tineret Printing House), the creation of amateur groups of practitioners, and popular classes on yoga, astrology, homeopathic medicine, and acupuncture which were held in university centers or houses of culture; many of these practices were also enabled by being integrated into the arsenal of therapeutic remedies promoted by the regime.[8] The cultural thaw together with the rise of such practices created the conditions for Gregorian Bivolaru to become interested in yoga and develop into an active practitioner.

The social routes through which these practices were revived or emerged in the socialist setting of postwar Romania were diverse, sometimes overlapping, sometimes completely unexpected, marking in specific ways both the nature of the practices and their further development. I suggest that all these groups, placed at different removes from acceptability to the state and official notions of normality, represented in fact a collective attempt at re-enchanting the socialist world, and they were in effect rising up against socialist realism but also pushing back on the realism and pragmatism of socialist industrialization. This return to spiritual quests largely represented a revival of old, antimodern tropes and sentiments. They were rearticulated in a setting in which socialist industrialism was considered a radical version of modernity, and were encouraged by the regime itself and its political and ideological shifts.

## THE TRANSCENDENTAL MEDITATION AFFAIR

But there was also another important aspect of this spiritual revivalism during socialism. Yoga especially, as the following story will illustrate, had always had an ambiguous and liminal status under the socialist regime and was prone to being suppressed or even banned whenever the political situation and the interests of the Communist Party demanded it. The scandal of the Transcendental Meditation Affair, while only loosely involving Bivolaru, also reveals the wider and paradoxical social, intellectual, and institutional contexts in which yoga and other spiritual practices existed under socialism.

In February 1982, an article in the official magazine of the Ministry of Internal Affairs, *Pentru patrie*, decried a new conspiracy affecting the bodies and minds of the most highly educated people. In inflammatory language, the article described Transcendental Meditation (TM) as a dangerous sect that was fooling people and distracting them from their duties through obscure mysticism. Transcendental Meditation was depicted as a Western imperialist disease, brought into Romania by "spies" and people who wanted to harm the country. "Foreign spies, imperialist interests"?[9] This language had not been heard since the 1950s. What had happened?

According to one narrative, in 1979, a couple of low-ranking party officials met in Paris with a Romanian émigré, Nicolae Stoian, who was also a TM teacher and began their training in the technique. Convinced of its benefits, the officials promised to help introduce the technique in Romania. In fact, Transcendental Meditation was nothing exotic for professionals back in Bucharest. Throughout the 1970s, officially sanctioned psychology studies investigated meditation, deep breathing, hypnosis, and other forms of relaxation as methods of improving cognitive capacities and promoting healing. Research into these areas was conducted at the Romanian Academy's Institute for Psychological Research.[10]

During several visits to Romania in 1979 and 1981, Nicolae Stoian and his wife, Murielle Stoian, initiated a number of other party members, usually friends and co-workers, into the art of Transcendental Meditation. Overall, during the entire period, the secret police recorded the names of 371 participants in TM training sessions.[11] The majority were introduced to TM in a private home (131 people), while other participants experimented with meditation at demonstrations held at the Bucharest Institute of Architecture or at various hospitals and medical centers around the capital. It is worth noting that even employees of the Ministry of Internal Affairs as well as members of the army took to the technique.[12]

These friends were part of the technical and humanist intelligentsia, comfortably connected with the party. They also managed to elicit support for introducing their technique formally, either as a recreational activity or as medical technique. But even though the Stoians and their circles were connected to higher echelons of the party, in order to formally accredit Transcendental Meditation as an officially recognized practice, they had to submit an official request. They therefore wrote a letter about the benefits of Transcendental Meditation to the head of the National Research Council of the Romanian Socialist Republic, asking for official accreditation of the technique. After a series of consultations among state officials, accreditation was denied. Transcendental Meditation was considered neither unique nor new compared to the research already being done.[13] It was deemed inappropriate because it lagged behind developments sanctioned by the regime, not because it was violating any of its rules.

Despite this report, months later there was another attempt to obtain the official seal of approval. Consequently, the Institute organized a week-long clinical trial where the Stoians could introduce their technique to an audience of around sixty people. At these experiments most of the participants were intellectuals, artists, or writers[14] but there were also other people who were interested in Oriental studies and yoga practices. The experiments consisted of sessions of initiation and meditation followed by open discussions about the effects and sensations of the mediation session. The week began with a short initiation rite in which each person offered two apples at an altar to Maharishi Mahesh Yogi and in exchange received a mantra to help him/her meditate. Moreover, the subjects of the experiment were asked by the Stoians to sign a confidential agreement stating that they would not share the technique with others. The experiments were concluded in the spring of 1981, but the final report was once again negative.[15]

After these unsuccessful events, everything settled down until the articles with inflammatory language quoted above stirred things up again. In the wake of these articles and the denunciations in them, the regime organized a series of purges, not unlike the mock trials of the 1950s, albeit less bloody. A series of intellectuals, top-echelon party members, managers of enterprises, army personnel, secret police officers, and many other people were demoted, reprimanded, put under investigation, and even put on trial for alleged conspiracy and treason. Because all of the participants in the aforementioned experiments had to sign a document pledging they would keep their mantra secret, the regime's officials interpreted this as a clear sign of an organized conspiracy against the regime. The entire Institute was disbanded, and its members were laid off and faced disciplinary actions.[16]

One outcome of these purges was the subsequent marginalization of all practices connected to yoga, meditation, Eastern mystical exercises, martial arts,[17] and the study of Far Eastern languages and civilizations as well as the disappearance of psychology as the official discipline in which these preoccupations had a legitimate place that was endorsed by the regime. In their stead, more nationalistic and primordialist claims and practices, such as pseudo-historical claims about the millennial origins of the Romanian population, took center stage. In short, by the mid-1980s the above "oriental" practices started to lose out to nationalist frenzy. They appeared as foreign, non- or even anti-Romanian, a threat to the body of the nation, to its ancestral traditions, and its Christian legacy. Although they had been considered useful therapeutic and healthy activities in the 1960s and 1970s, Eastern spiritual practices became a threat. As such, they had to be prosecuted and erased. Transcendental Meditation offered precisely the perfect pretext for that.

This shift in the status of the above practices vis-à-vis the socialist regime's official politics is best encapsulated in the biography of Gregorian Bivolaru, the local yoga and spiritual guru. In fact, his entire biography expresses perfectly the ambiguities, paradoxes, fascination with, and ultimate rejection of these practices in both the socialist and post-socialist contexts.

# THE MAKING OF GURU BIVOLARU

Gregorian Bivolaru was born on the outskirts of Bucharest and was raised by a single mother in an atmosphere ripe with conflicts. Constantly abused by his drunkard stepfather, he took refuge in yoga, parapsychology, telepathy, and ancient therapeutic practices,[18] which were quite uncommon and rather unsuitable activities for a young communist man. From 1971, Bivolaru pursued these interests by carefully studying books written by Mircea Eliade in the Municipal Library of Bucharest. Eliade soon became his idol and the guru claims to have corresponded with him. In addition, Bivolaru was also interested in folkloric traditions and folk medicine. He also attended postural yoga classes that combined theoretical knowledge and practice at the Casa Sindicatelor Medicale (Medical Trade Union House). After graduating from high school, Bivolaru took a different route from his peers. Instead of going to the university, he chose a low-paid job as a postmaster. This offered him a decent source of income that allowed him to pursue his passion—yoga.

For members of socialist underground scenes around the former Eastern bloc, the strategy of working at a menial job and pursuing one's own interests was widespread and was inseparable from the welfare nature of state socialism. In *The Last Soviet Generation*,[19] Alexei Yurchak describes how these kinds of jobs allowed the creative underground the time and resources to pursue their subversive activities. Removed from concerns about productivity and profit that beset the state and ordinary citizens alike, intellectuals and artists were able to focus on their oppositional work and personal self-fulfillment. The figures of the marginal man/woman and the bohemian were thus inseparable from the image of a state catering for all of its citizens, even at the price of their de-politicization.

In addition, this job made it possible for Bivolaru to familiarize himself with the way the postal system functioned, that is to become familiar with one of the few means of communication with the "outside" world in Ceauşescu's Romania. In the following years, Bivolaru learned to use the state's postal service effectively, while under tight scrutiny and subject to censorship, in order to develop a vast correspondence with foreign disciples, friends, yoga organizations, and the foreign press. The secret police intercepted quite a bit of Bivolaru's correspondence, sometimes before it reached its recipients. (Thus, the Securitate archives now hold a substantial amount of the guru's correspondence and a researcher can easily trace the evolution of Bivolaru's group via the personal correspondence that was amassed.) Furthermore, he used the post office to smuggle yoga materials and erotic literature and photos (all of which were illegal at the time) into the country. Sarah Strauss, who has studied the dissemination of yoga in modern India, shows

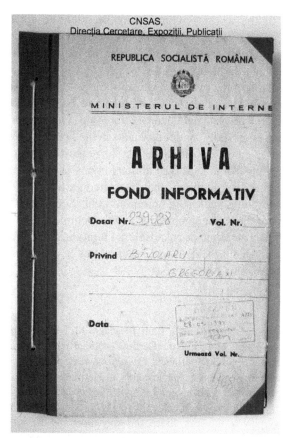

**Figure 1.1** The front cover of Gregorian Bivolaru's (Guru Grig) secret police file.
*Source*: Courtesy of the Consiliul Naţional pentru Studierea Arhivelor Securităţii (National Council for the Study of the Securitate Archives).

how the mail played a similar, significant role in the transmission and creation of a like-minded community of believers around the world.[20]

In light of this atypical trajectory and such unorthodox preoccupations, the opening of a Securitate file on Bivolaru was inevitable (see Figure 1.1). It happened in 1971, in the wake of a ritual murder in his neighborhood.[21] While the original suspicion was dropped, the investigators found out that this young man, who was versed in Eastern philosophy and yoga, had access to numerous sensitive social strata such as young artists, illegal book traders, scholars, and intellectuals with an appetite for Indian philosophy. At the time, even though yoga was a legal pursuit, what worried the investigators were the mystical interpretations of yoga that Bivolaru professed. The investigators saw his view of the world as contrary to the scientific atheism promoted by the socialist state and also as ideas that were opposed to the doctrines of the Romanian Orthodox Church, to which the majority of the population belonged and which the state tolerated.

However, what seemed even stranger to the investigators was the already extensive correspondence that the young man had established both domestically and internationally. At nineteen Bivolaru was writing to magazines, sex education societies, libraries, and individuals in the DDR and West Germany, Sweden, Finland, and the UK. In his letters, he requested either erotic materials or yoga brochures, or at least the publication of short notes announcing his address and his interests, in hopes that interested parties would contact him. In most of his outgoing mail, now preserved in his Securitate file, he decried the prudishness of the Romanian regime and the regime's lack of understanding about the needs of young people. Below I reproduce in full one such letter sent by Bivolaru, which I believe best encapsulates Bivolaru's efforts and the driving force behind his initial quests:

Dear Friends,

I am a young man from Romania, I am 19 years old. I have a great sympathy for the German people and I like the German erotic articles. From unhappiness, Rumanien there are not sexy articles. From your sexy photos I can to see the emancipated comprehension of the sexuality in Germany. It is really extraordinary the uninhibited acceptance and giving of the joyeaus joke of the sexuality in your country. I admire very much your frankness towards the sex. I like very much the sexy photos, the sexy slides, the sexy films and the sexy magazines. I am very interested to buy sexy articles from SPEZIAL YEARS.

I can to pay the sexy articles in DM or USD. Please to write to me what do you prefer DM or USD. I can to send you the payment by registered letter (Do you accept?). Eventually please to send me the catalogue of SPEZIAL VERSAND regarding the sexy photos, sexy films, sexy magazines and the cost price of this articles in DM or USD.

Please very much to answer me! I like very much the sexy articles and it is my intention to get in touch with you. Please to send me your catalogue in a closed envelope with discretion. I finish my letter washing you and your people good health and happiness.

Sincerely yours,
Gregorian
My address Bivolaru Gregorian, Casuta Postala 309, Oficiul Postal Bucuresti 1
Rumaniein[22]

This letter immediately raises a series of questions. What is that irrepressible drive to write such a letter in broken English to some faceless recipients asking for what basically amounts to pornographic images? Who is this person who is making such demands, verging on post-adolescent, exasperated sexual desire, and a hyper-political awareness of the difference between the sexual politics of the DDR and of Romania? Why is he taking the risk of criticizing the sexual politics of state socialism, knowing full well that his letter will be intercepted by the secret police and land him in trouble?

In writing this letter, Bivolaru was in fact writing to the regime itself demanding a freer sexuality. It is easy to dismiss his request as a demand for pornography—something that the secret police was keen to do. Indeed, his demand is for sexually explicit and arousing images of naked women. But instead of uncritically taking a moralizing stance, it is useful to ask whether Bivolaru was not in fact exposing an aspect of the regime itself precisely by formulating his demands as pornographic. Bivolaru is exposing the sadistic character of the regime: the regime was depriving its young people of sexual pleasure and was thoroughly repressing and controlling their sexuality to the point where they felt obliged to take the risk of smuggling pornographic images into the country.

One way to understand Bivolaru's acts is to make a comparison with the Marquis de Sade and his sadistic practices. While of course de Sade was a much more sophisticated character, Bivolaru shared his belief in freedom as an inter-subjective, erotic event. For de Sade, sexuality was an ethical principle elevated to be one of the driving forces of life and death. While Simone de Beauvoir argued for a thorough historicization of the emergence of de Sade's practices as the ultimate sign of a declining aristocracy trying to cling to its former status in the bedchamber,[23] this historical awareness does not fully explain the mysterious character of de Sade's philosophy, his principle of inflicting enjoyment and, more to the point, the principle of *jouissance*. Lacan defined *jouissance* as taking pleasure from an all-consuming activity that runs counter to the pleasure principle. Pleasure emerges in a close relationship with the death drive, from the desire to encounter the threatening Real.

Bivolaru did not engage in sadistic acts but nonetheless he was routinely accused of immoral sexual practices, including seducing young women through his spiritual talk. It is difficult to assess the truthfulness of these reports since most of these accounts come from the records of the Securitate, which wanted to indict him. However, many available accounts do indeed describe him as a dominating figure deriving pleasure from inflicting enjoyment on his followers, who were usually young women, through the act of initiation. As was the case with de Sade, for Bivolaru the bodies of young women represented the site of inscription of his desires and of his *scientia sexualis*.

The guru defended his collection and interest in pornography to the secret police on the basis of his interest in Tantrism. Images, he claimed, allowed him to connect with the women depicted in the photos, while enabling him to develop his non-seminal orgasms: "I use the nude representation of women

to practice Tantra yoga; in this endeavor I am able to look at the pictures
and re-channel my sexual energy toward the achievement of a higher plane
of consciousness. In this way I can connect to the universal consciousness
of humanity that is mostly a never-ending source of love."[24]

His early philosophy was an ingenious, synthetic compilation of religious
and occult ideas drawn from an enormous array of sources. His philosophy
was a kind of postmodern pastiche, a mélange of ideas drawn from the
*Bhagavad-Gita*, Adi Shankara, Vivekanada, St. Augustine, and Mircea
Eliade[25] together with the more prosaic principles of diet and healing belonging to homeopathic and other forms of alternative medicine. One of the key
elements of this philosophical assemblage was the principle of universal love,
an understanding of the body as an entity distinct from physicality. This conceptualization turned the body into a psycho-spiritual constituent, the subtle
body of Tantrism. Bivolaru understood love as ritualized sex, empathy, and
universal communion. In one of his declarations in front of the secret police
dating back to 1972, he explained his interest in yoga: "I drew myself toward
this mysterious science, [because of] the fact that it has as an ultimate goal,
a total annihilation of instincts, preaching the idea of universal love which
opens the path toward the unknown places of the unconscious."[26]

Many forms of Tantric practice do involve explicit forms of ritual transgression. The ritual consumption of meat and wine, and, in some cases,
sexual intercourse in violation of class rules can be employed as a means
of awakening and harnessing the awesome power or *Shakti* (or "Sacti"
as the Securitate spelled it), that flows through all things. Yet at the same
time, Tantra was a conservative tradition that ultimately reasserted the ritual
authority and social status of male Brahmins. Women were seen as tools in
the ritual practices; women have no right to participate in any Vedic ceremonies and have no access to any mantras (sacred words). For the most part,
women were subordinated to males and their ritual role was limited to being
a partner for male adepts.[27]

Tantra was initially a highly esoteric tradition that had little to do with
sensual abandon and sexual liberation and more to do with enlightenment
and transgressing boundaries. Sexuality and magical undertones were added
when European Orientalists discovered these practices in the nineteenth
century and superimposed their own legacies of medieval sexual devotions
on them. This mixture mutated further in the West when Tantra was reduced
to a particular kind of a sexual practice during the nineteenth century and as
such was integrated into the booming market for pornography and sexually
licentious literature that was becoming a notable undercurrent in Victorian
contexts. In interwar reinterpretations articulated in the work of Eliade and
Julius Evola, sexuality was paired with the idea of violence: transgression had

to take the form of destruction to annihilate the forces of modernity in order to return to a pre-modern self.[28]

Bivolaru developed his ideas at the tail end of this convoluted tradition—and in the unlikely context of socialism. While it allowed for various forms of experimentation, transgressive behavior, and alternative states, in Bivolaru's interpretation Tantric sex nonetheless reproduced the subordination of women that belonged to its beginnings. In Bivolaru's practices, women were simply vehicles for his desires and his *jouissance*. While the initiating mechanisms were supposed to liberate the sexuality of both partners, the constant supply of young women from whom the guru benefited points to the hierarchy fundamentally inscribed in these relations.[29] Although the Tantrism performed by Bivolaru had transgressive features in relation to the regime, given the subordination of women in these practices, ultimately it still remained within its patriarchal and heterosexist framework.

Furthermore, Bivolaru conceived of yoga as a "mysterious science." By his own admission, the aura of mystery was what drove him toward this secret science that allows one to know the universe by knowing himself. He was referring here to the reception of Hindu philosophy in the Western tradition as part and parcel of esoteric knowledge. On the other hand, the young guru strived to gather materials on yoga from public libraries around Bucharest, often from books which had been under lock and key in special state archives until the mid-1960s. Most importantly, his spiritual development took place alongside frequent interviews with the Securitate, house searches, and arrests,[30] all of which amplified the aura of secrecy surrounding yoga. Suspicion and a sense of secrecy and conspiracy loom over the guru's philosophy and over MISA materials to this day, inscribing them as powerful objects of desire.

In the letters collected by the Securitate there are numerous examples of Bivolaru claiming to engage in remote communication with his followers. He claimed that a certain form of communication was based on an affective disposition between two partners, usually of opposite sexes, and that this communication could be powered by the channels of sexual energy that existed between the two.[31] To some extent, the possibility of remote communication parallels that of sexual communion. This notion of thought transfer seemed to be particularly useful in giving a sense of community to those like-minded people, who, because of police surveillance, distance, and few means of communication, could not freely engage with each other. Bivolaru envisioned telepathy as an active phenomenon. The sender and the receiver had to prepare for the act of communication through prior training in meditation (which would allow them to access their telepathic powers) and the communication could only take place after they had established an

affective connection. A connection of this type included a history of meditating together which allowed the paths of communication to harmonize in
preparation for telepathy. These rites and rituals ensured and reproduced a
sense of collective identity for the community of yogis, which was always
under surveillance by the state security organs.

After Ceauşescu's regime collapsed, Bivolaru perfected his ideas of telepathic communication. He concluded that collective meditation was the best
practice to clear the channels for thought transfer. To this day, Bivolaru, now
a refugee in Sweden, allegedly uses telepathy to send his messages to his
Romanian followers during two important collective meditation ceremonies.[32]

By 1979, Bivolaru was again under the Securitate's surveillance.
This time he was reported by one of his co-workers for using work time
to translate books about yoga and openly declaring his interest in fleeing
the country. In 1982, he was investigated because he had also taken part
in the TM sessions organized by the Romanian Academy and was thus
caught up in the ensuing scandal. His prior antecedents only confirmed the
suspicious nature of what the Securitate labeled "a religious" group that
gathered around Transcendental Meditation. At this point he was employed
as an unskilled laborer in the Bucharest Metro and was giving yoga classes
in private homes. During the course of the investigation, the secret police
also identified a secret location, a one-bedroom apartment where Bivolaru
and his close followers were depositing an impressive collection of books,
brochures, photocopies, manuscripts of translations, posters, and videos
connected to yoga, occult practices, sexuality, and, of course, pornography.
All these materials were confiscated.[33]

By this time Bivolaru had ceased to be a solitary, marginal figure and
instead had become "Guru Grig," a nickname that acknowledged his status
as the head of a fairly organized underground group of yogis.[34] Its members
dedicated their time to practicing and teaching yoga, translating and discussing materials connected to yoga, reproducing and distributing such items (by
developing a network of supporters with access to photocopiers), selling, or
trading yoga books and erotica to interested individuals and thus developing
even more new networks and new resources in order to continue expanding
the group's assets. After the crackdown on most imports in the last decade of
Ceauşescu's regime, erotica was hard to come by so members begun to produce their own.[35] However, this activity was not solely motivated by austerity
or by a do-it-yourself ethos. It dovetailed with the growth of the group and the
increasing relevance of sexuality for spiritual growth. It is perhaps the only
example of socialist Tantric sex materials in existence today.

In the summer, Guru Grig's followers convened on a remote beach in
Costinesti (generally a popular summer destination for socialist youth) to
spend their holidays practicing nudism and yoga. The choice of a nudist

beach gathering was both spiritual and strategic. Spiritually, it was linked to the direct connection of bodies and the therapeutic effects of the sun; strategically, a remote beach ensured that while the Securitate would keep an eye on them, they would be less likely to infiltrate the group. Harnessing sexual energies was also part and parcel of the summer retreat as documented by a couple of nude photos and long descriptions of alleged experiments involving sex with multiple partners that the secret police archived[36] and which were elaborated on in lavish detail by overtly curious (and fascinated) officers.

While it is easy to understand the role of these collective sexual practices in the spiritual economy of the group, the question that arises here is why did the Securitate allow them to take place? These practices directly contradicted the mores that the regime was trying to cultivate and they were also involved in producing more sexually arousing material. The explanation is that the regime itself was taking pleasure in such interactions. By allowing them, state power was producing its own forms of excitement and *jouissance*, its own dark secret, externalized as a subversive sexual practice. This was the case since Guru Grig's yoga group was a rather closed, underground collectivity with very little potential for spreading its message and practices to a wider audience. Its activities were clouded in mythology and rumor, wrapped in mystery and carried around by whispers. Therefore, its political and subversive potential was quite limited.

But the curious gaze of Securitate officers was also a threatening one. By 1984, Guru Grig had not only been brought in for questioning but he was also charged with exactly the same pursuits that were making him a popular character in Bucharest's bohemian circles. The communist regime charged the guru with crimes such as disseminating mystical literature (article 94 from Law 3/1974), practicing a profession—teaching yoga—without adequate credentials (article 281 of the Penal Code), and disseminating pornography (article 325 of the Penal Code). Under investigation for these charges, the guru managed to or was helped to sneak out of police custody.[37] In his official biography, the event was of course described as a sign of the guru's spiritual powers.[38] In fact, the attempted escape landed him in jail for almost a year. Upon his release, the guru continued to meet with his followers who were also the targets of surveillance and police intimidation.[39]

## THE LEGACY OF GURU GRIG

The fall of communism in 1989 came with a promise of freedom and the feeling that previously imposed inhibitions about sexual activities and spiritual practices could be shed. But instead of the promised opening up, in fact the reality entailed various forms of enclosure.

The rich diversity of spiritual practices during socialism quickly contracted to one dominant form: a powerful revival of Orthodox beliefs, rules, and morals. Under these conditions, sexuality and sexual exploration continued to remain repressed and linked with the devil's work. Public space was imbued with religiosity, which was powerfully connected with the prevailing anticommunism. Since the former regime was considered atheist and antireligious, the revival of Orthodoxy was meant to overcome that legacy. In practice, it led to a new wave of dogmatism and stringent rules.

Economic factors also played a role. There was an initial, brief moment in the early 1990s when people experienced more freedom, especially freedom of the imagination, which reactivated various spiritual quests. This upsurge in spiritual quests led to the formation of an indigenous "hippie" movement that vicariously recuperated global 1968—and then social realities began to creep in. Pragmatism, the quest for a better job, and the pressure to grab every possible opportunity left little space for the idealism and dreams of lofty spiritual quests. Material concerns and interests prevailed and with them a renewed sense of realism and a down-to-earth ideology. As Alexander Kiossev wrote, consumerism, the ability to join the new shopping spree, became the new definition of normality and the embodiment of a post-socialist utopia.[40]

Certainly, some spiritual quests persisted amidst these changes. These included the spiritual journey of Bivolaru and his followers. They founded MISA, which grew into quite a large organization, expanding across social strata and powerfully connecting with international movements related to its mission and spirit. Costinesti remained their summer meeting place, now figuring enticingly in the popular imagination as a place where anything went in terms of sexuality. But MISA too was unable to remain outside broader social pressures, and therefore, while it integrated quite a substantial amount of Orthodox dogma into its mixture of spiritual teachings, it also expanded its soft porn business. Its growing popularity and the alternative sexual practices in which it engaged meant that it continued to attract the gaze of the secret police, which had undergone only minor reforms after 1989.

## CONCLUSION

Sex scandals have shattered the reputations of many Indian and non-Indian gurus among whom Swami Muktananda, the founder of Siddha Yoga, or Bhagwan Shree Rajneesh (Osho) are the best-known examples. Significantly, some strands of yoga have always been surrounded by the suspicion of disordered sexuality. An important reason for this attitude stems from the centuries-long Orientalist interpretation of yoga as a philosophy of the occult and the erotic. As a spiritual practice that makes the liberation of bodily energies a central element of its concerns, yoga is often inseparable from a rethinking of sexuality. To be sure, the popular imaginary simply schematized this complex relationship to the extent that Tantric yoga seems to be a proxy for sexual innuendo, packaged with ideas of wellbeing, physical exercise, and a middle-class lifestyle and consumption practices. More generally then, the sexual imaginary surrounding the practice of yoga and its practitioners, and the recurrent scandals that continue to arise point in fact to a much more complex relationship between the Western world and its various colonial imports. Indeed, while yoga seems to be such a common practice for many Westerners with a certain standard of living, almost to the point where it is on the verge of being incorporated into the West's popular cultural canon, the contradictions and friction this encounter generates have yet to be properly addressed in a scholarly manner.

The sex scandals surrounding Guru Grig also need to be contextualized beyond the framework of the Iron Curtain. Perhaps they should also be examined in terms of the dynamics of the global circulation of spiritual practices in which Eastern spiritualities raised eyebrows—and suspicions—within the former real existing socialisms of Eastern Europe.

Moreover, as I have shown throughout this chapter, Bivolaru's spiritual pantheon developed in conditions of scarcity where intellectual resources were not only difficult to come by but also significant commodities to be traded among other fellow travelers. For this reason, Bivolaru's yoga philosophy reads like the outcome of a methodology for scraping things together, combining whatever resources were available into a more or less coherent message about wellbeing, love, and enhanced consciousness.

Another key feature of yoga groups during Ceaușescu's Romania was the secret police's constant surveillance of their practices. The shadow of the Securitate molded the interactions among the participants as well as the philosophical interpretation of yoga proposed by local writers such as Gregorian Bivolaru.

To bring the story full circle, since 2006 Guru Grig has managed to internationalize his group and his teachings. MISA opened new branches in Denmark, Sweden, and Norway and slowly moved toward the holy lands of India (where it is known as Satya). In 2011, another sex scandal involving former MISA instructors burst onto the Indian media. Allegedly, a Chennai branch of MISA has once again been shut down for productions of dubious erotica.

## NOTES

1. Gabriel Andreescu, *Misa: Radiografia Unei Represiuni* (Iasi: Polirom, 2013).

2. MISA was formally established on January 23, 1990. See the official website, *YogaEsoteric: Ce Este Mișcarea Pentru Integrare Spirituală În Absolut?* http://www.yogaesoteric.net/content.aspx?lang=RO&item=3531.

3. Andreescu, *Misa: Radiografia*, 10.

4. These numbers can be found on the MISA website.

5. In 2013, Gregorian Bivolaru was sentenced to six years in prison for rape but he was cleared of a number of other charges including human trafficking. The final decision from Romania's highest court can be found at http://www.scj.ro/dosare.asp? view=detalii&id=100000000256023&pg=1&cauta.

6. Including books by Mircea Eliade.

7. For a characterization of the countercultural milieu during Ceaușescu's liberalization, see Madigan Fichter, "Rock 'n' Roll Nation: Counterculture and Dissent in Romania, 1965–1975," *Nationalities Papers* 39, no. 4 (2011): 567–85. Youth subcultures were later hijacked by the state and incorporated into the nationalist ideology promoted by Ceaușescu. See Caius Dobrescu, "The Phoenix That Could Not Rise: Politics and Rock Culture in Romania, 1960–1989," *East Central Europe* 38, nos. 2–3 (2011): 255–90.

8. Doina Jela, Catalin Strat, and Mihai Albu, *Afacerea Meditatia Transcendentala* (Bucharest: Humanitas, 2004), 71.

9. Monica Lovinescu, *Posteritatea Contemporană—Unde Scurte III* (Bucharest: Humanitas, 1994).

10. Jela, Strat, and Albu, *Afacerea.*

11. Document published in Marius Oprea, *Banalitatea Raului: O Istorie a Securitatii in Documente 1949–1989* (Iasi: Polirom, 2002), 395. For the original document, see Consiliul Național pentru Studierea Arhivelor Securității (National Council for the Study of the Securitate Archives; hereafter CNSAS), file D3, vol. 4, 239. The documents in this subcollection of file D3 focus on the Transcendental Meditation milieu. They include lists of participants in TM events in Bucharest, formal letters and other paperwork circulated among different institutions in Romania and in France involved in organizing the TM sessions in Bucharest, and statements from participants in those sessions.

12. CNSAS archive, file D3, vol. 4, 239.

13. Jela, Strat, and Albu, *Afacerea*, 48.

14. Some of the most well-known names on the lists of participants were art historian Andrei Pleșu, sculptor Ovidiu Maitec, and poet Marin Sorescu.

15. Jela, Strat, and Albu, *Afacerea*, 168.

16. Jela, Strat, and Albu, *Afacerea*, 227.

17. CNSAS, file D3, vol. 2, 48.

18. CNSAS, file I1688, 45. File I1688 is Bivolaru's Securitate file.

19. Alexei Yurchak, *Everything Was Forever, Until It Was No More: The Last Soviet Generation* (Princeton: Princeton University Press, 2006).

20. Sarah Strauss, *Positioning Yoga: Balancing Acts across Cultures* (Oxford: Berg, 2005).

21. CNSAS, file I1688, 10.

22. CNSAS, file I1688, 223.

23. Simone De Beauvoir, *Must We Burn De Sade?* trans. Annette Michelson (London: Peter Nevill, 1953).

24. CNSAS file I1688, 230.

25. See a list of books found at Bivolaru's premises during a police search: CNSAS, file I1688, 312.

26. CNSAS, file I1688, 126.

27. Hugh B. Urban, *Tantra: Sex, Secrecy, Politics, and Power in the Study of Religion* (Berkeley: University of California Press, 2003), 45.

28. Urban, *Tantra*, 89.

29. A secret police informer mentioned that "while at work [Bivolaru] often speaks on the phone with different young women giving them different pieces of advice; such phone calls are even prolonged for up to 2 hours; sometimes young women come and pick him up from work and Mr. Bivolaru holds them in his arms right in front of the school and on the street," CNSAS, file I1688, 220.

30. Between 1971 and 1989, Gregorian Bivolaru was interviewed by the Securitate on nine different occasions and he was detained on at least three occasions. In 1984, he served a jail sentence of sixteen months after trying to escape from Securitate headquarters. In 1989, he was judicially interned in a mental institution for an undetermined period but served only three months (from October to December 1989).

31. Bivolaru claimed that he once meditated his way out of jail. CNSAS, file I1688, 330.

32. *YogaEsoteric*, "Telepatia," http://www.yogaesoteric.net/content.aspx?lang=RO&item=6135.

33. CNSAS, file I1688, 330.

34. By 1984, the secret police had identified twenty people who were close to Bivolaru. They also laid out a further course of action to prevent them from engaging with the guru or practicing yoga. Such measures included excluding Bivolaru's fellow adepts from university studies, disciplinary work sanctions, being forced to change one's residence, secret police surveillance, and positive influences on the part of undercover agents who had infiltrated the group. CNSAS, file I1688, vol. II, 20. For personal narratives of other group members, see Gabriel Andreescu, *Reprimarea miscarii: Yoga in anii 80* (Iasi: Polirom, 2008) and, *MISA: Radiografia*.

35. CNSAS, file I1688, vol. 2, 39.

36. CNSAS, file I1688, vol. 2, 88.

37. Gabriel Andreescu interprets Bivolaru's 1984 escape as a plot orchestrated by the secret police in order to bring new charges against the guru for attempted escape from police custody. See Andreescu, *Misa Radiografia*, 320.

38. *YogaEsoteric*, "Biografie," http://www.yogaesoteric.net/content.aspx?lang=RO&item=196.

39. Human rights activist and political scientist Gabriel Andreescu documented the repression directed against the followers of Gregorian Bivolaru through oral history interviews. See Gabriel Andreescu, *Reprimarea miscarii*.

40. Alexander Kiossev, "Introduction," in *Post-Theory, Games and Discursive Resistance: The Bulgarian Case*, ed. Alexander Kiossev (Albany: State University of New York Press, 1995), xii–xx.

*Chapter 2*

# The Imaginary Elsewhere of the Hippies in Soviet Estonia

## Terje Toomistu

In the fall of 1970 there was a rumor about a major hippie gathering on the Town Hall Square in Tallinn. Although this never became a reality, it did enough to awaken some sense of community for those who longed to be part of the legendary Summer of Love or the Woodstock festival in the United States in the late 1960s.

Aare, then a seventeen-year-old kid in the eleventh grade, craved rock 'n' roll and freedom, which he identified with a world beyond the Iron Curtain. It was challenging for him to obtain things he rejoiced in such as Led Zeppelin and Janis Joplin albums and books on Eastern philosophy and yoga. But, he could sit in the cafeteria and smoke a joint of marijuana since nobody knew what this strange-smelling "tobacco" really was.

Around the time when the rumor about the hippie gathering was circulating, he noticed some men following him to school every day. Soon afterward Aare was asked to go to the teachers' lounge, where he was questioned about the gathering and warned about his future and the wellbeing of his family. Sufficiently intimidated by this, Aare decided to not go to the meeting and instead to delve into the mesmerizing sound of rock music. This gave Aare the first taste of the vast potential of internal dreamscapes.

Standing by a road, Aare raised his thumb to go on a journey to seek out people who shared his views and interests. To his surprise, he discovered a whole network of "free spirits" across the urban underground Soviet Union. Not only did they call themselves *sistema* (the system),[1] but it appeared that these people had indeed formed their own system within the system. The Soviet system had not only created a "Soviet man" and a "Soviet woman," but also its own hippies.

41

## INTRODUCTION TO THE FLOW

The hippie movement, which culminated in the US with highlights from San Francisco and its legendary Summer of Love in 1967, and the Woodstock Festival on the East Coast (in upstate New York) in 1969, had its own trajectory in the Soviet Union. Affected by perceived Western freedoms and inspired by various spiritual traditions, a counterculture of flower children developed in the Soviet Union.[2] Disengaged from the official Soviet ideology of atheism, authoritarianism, and Soviet morals, the Soviet hippie movement[3] found its expression through rock music, the cult of love, pacifism, actual and "cosmic" travel, and self-fashioning of a type that was generally considered unacceptable for Soviet citizens.

This chapter[4] engages with the formation of the youth counterculture in 1970s Soviet Estonia, which is seen as a coinciding effect of global cultural flows and a local sociopolitical context. While the hippie movement in Soviet Estonia manifested a global cultural flow of transnational origin, the sociocultural appropriations embedded in the context of their appearance generated distinctive enactments. These enactments produced a common ground for communicating with kindred spirits across the urban Soviet Union, which quickly expanded into a subcultural network often referred to as the *sistema*. On the one hand, the hippie movement in the Soviet Union illustrates global cultural flows in which media has enabled rhizomatic[5] communities with "no sense of place." However, the engagement with rock music and occasional representations in the official and non-official Soviet media depicting the youth counterculture movements in the West led to a collective envisioning that went beyond merely admitting that their contemporaries in the "free world" were rocking in the spirit of "Make love not war." The particular context of the late Soviet period, the available materials, scattered information, even the sense that state socialism was eternal,[6] provoked certain imaginaries that were in direct contrast with the outside world and formed a constitutive part of Soviet Estonian nonconformist youth subjectivities. Before elaborating on the conceptual framework of my inquiry, it is necessary to mention the historical development of the hippie movement in Soviet Estonia.

Within the Soviet Union, Estonia (often dubbed the Soviet West)[7] was known for its relatively more relaxed atmosphere and greater exposure to Western influences, especially through its contacts with Finland. The breath of fresh air brought by Khrushchev's Thaw (1956–1964) resulted in the emergence of a substantial number of Beat bands in Estonia.[8] Nonetheless, the stagnation that accompanied Brezhnev's rule (1964–1982), which was further marked by the events of 1968 in Prague, seemed to dissolve young people's hopes that their active participation in Soviet culture and politics could in any way satisfy them. That led to the burgeoning of a youth culture that deliberately distanced itself from Soviet ideology, prevailing societal norms, and the officially approved practices of youth culture. With what little was known about the counterculture movements in the West, these youth started to associate themselves with proximate and distant others, whose bodies and practices seemed to materialize what "we" could allude to as "the hippie culture."[9]

The first individuals to associate themselves with the hippie movement in Soviet Estonia appeared in the late 1960s, while the movement itself lasted throughout the late Soviet period involving various generations. Supported by the growing network of alternative youth across the urban Soviet Union, the movement took a form of a subculture[10] by the mid- to late 1970s with characteristics such as communal activities, shared codes of communication, and a distinctive slang language and social spaces. In larger cities certain places emerged where hippies could find others who shared their views, and whose appearance and manners made them recognizable as fellow hippies. In Moscow some hippies already started referring to themselves as *sistema* (the system) in the late 1960s, but often other words were used such as *tusovka, sistemnyi* (which is derived from *sistema*), *volosatye*, and *pipel*.[11] Between *sistemnyi* hippies, information about gathering places and music festivals was shared, as well as the addresses and phone numbers of other people who belonged to the "system." As a result, it became possible to travel to a strange city and immediately find new friends, because, as one of my collaborators put it, "the system existed there." From 1972 on, it became a tradition to gather in Tallinn on May 1, which marked the start of the hitch-hiking season. One of the first hippie summer camps in 1977 was also held in Estonia, in Viitna. Among the circuits of nonconformist Soviet youth, Estonia was known for its distinctive rock music scene, which drew visitors from hippie circles near and far.

The community of hippies in Soviet Estonia was highly heterogeneous and amorphous, but not to an extent that would exclude the following attempt to conceptualize the movement in its relations to the notions of power, agency, and "dropping out." I conclude with a suggestion that the hippies in Soviet Estonia could be considered a community of shared affect that was based on their engagements with the imaginary elsewhere and which drew them into mimetic communication with their imagined counterparts in the West as well as among themselves.

## A COMMUNITY OF SHARED AFFECT

In his oft-cited essay "Disjuncture and Difference in the Global Cultural Economy,"[12] anthropologist Arjun Appadurai distinguishes five dimensions of global cultural flows: ethnoscapes, technoscapes, mediascapes, ideoscapes, and financescapes. These constructs are influenced by the historical, linguistic, and political positions of different actors, from nation-states to more intimate social groupings. As global flows of ideologies, chains of ideas, terms, and images that in their movement connect agents from geographically distant regions,[13] ideoscape could be a useful concept for thinking about various contra-ideologies, such as ones that drove the hippie movement. Hippies, both in the West and in the Soviet bloc, positioned themselves against the established order. In the US the established power structures were intertwined with rigid ideas about race, gender, class hierarchies, a normative model of the family, morals, colonial power, and institutionalized order; while in the Soviet Union, they were more likely to be associated with authoritative discourse, morals, militarism, censorship, cultural repressions, and proclaimed atheism. These were the dominant power structures that hippies were keen on resisting:

> At the age of twelve or thirteen I already started doubting the school propaganda and the superiority of Soviet reality and power. That was the starting point for me. Being a little bit different. The rock music: Woodstock sessions, rock 'n' roll, the Beatles, the Rolling Stones, etc. The hippie movement started. I knew about it from early on. First from the radio, then there were publications in the Soviet media. They criticized hippies a lot, described them as completely crazy—strange clothes and protest against capitalist society. Basically it was a protest against the well-established system. That was also the case in the Soviet Union. We couldn't protest against capitalism, because we didn't have it here. But we had the same bureaucrats, rednecks, and just very box-headed people.[14]

This extract from an interview demonstrates the extent of influence of what was known about the counterculture movements in the West. It also underlines the core of their struggle, seeing their activities as protests against the established system and simultaneously differing from their Western counterparts inasmuch as there was difference between their respective dominant ideologies. But, how might we understand this "protest" as a practice with respect to the notion of "dropping out"? Did they resist by fighting back or were they trying to avoid contact with the dominant power structures, instead creating a world of their own? Could we conceptualize the hippies in Soviet Estonia as a group bounded by political protest or by something else? And in direct reference to the core question of this volume, was it really possible to "drop out" from the dominant power structures? To answer these questions, first it is necessary to address the complex relationship of Soviet Estonian youth to the "politics" of the time and the workings of cultural memory.

In the Baltics, young people usually condemned the Soviet state in more or less explicit ways. But, as the regime was perceived to be so unalterable, young people did not envision any possibilities for conversion and change, with or without their political engagement. Moreover, since the community was not large, it was not seen as capable of introducing political change. Additionally, young people usually identified politics narrowly with Soviet political structures such as the Komsomol (Young Communist League) and the Estonian Communist Party, and communist ideology. Because politics had such a rigid meaning for Soviet youth, the hippies wanted to see their activities as apolitical. "Politics" was usually the last thing they wanted to deal with.

One of the vestiges of Stalin's regime was also the long-implanted fear of being constantly invigilated: "the all-seeing eye is everywhere!" Thus, instead of active participation in or protest against the Soviet regime, the hippies tried to remain invisible—so that, "they wouldn't touch us, and we wouldn't touch them." Nevertheless, my collaborators have also framed the movement as "a passive protest" or "passive resistance."[15] As with all recollections, this particular form of reflection might be activated by the context of its appearance, which is related to the complex processes of cultural memory.[16] Memory is what combines identity with history and vice versa.[17] Thus, the past is never a given nor is it unchangeable but rather, it is continuously reconstituted and represented, both individually and collectively. This means that personal recollections of the past are also in constant flux in relation to their current sociopolitical context, ideologies, discourses, and a personal sense of self at a particular moment in one's life course. What might have been a subjectively truthful way of being in the world, with the right "feel" to it[18] and with affective engagements with the imagined world on the other side of the Iron Curtain, is only now, after the dissolution of the Soviet Union, seen as a protest, as resistance.

Having said that, I still believe the movement nevertheless took a strong political stance. The hippies opposed Soviet norms through various means of self-expression such as music, other arts, travel, self-fashioning, and spiritual quests. It was indeed more of an emotional practice[19] than a political movement. Nonetheless, this emotional practice was the site of their agency in resistance to societal norms. In the traditional moral philosophy linked to Immanuel Kant, agency as an individual's capacity to act could be equated with an autonomous will. This conception has been disrupted in parallel with profound changes in philosophical understandings of the workings of power. Especially since Michel Foucault's contributions to the notion of power, we can argue that there is no autonomous will outside of power. One of Foucault's central notions, and consequently one central to Judith Butler's[20] work has been the paradox of subjectivation, which is based on the idea that there is no subject "I" that stands outside of power. Being subjected to power is the very condition that brings the subject into existence. In other words, the subject is itself an effect of power.

Following the Foucauldian notion of power as productive, the norms that shape the dominant views and practices in society also shape non-normative subject positions. In Soviet Estonia the power of the norm was manifested every time distressed parents sent their sons to insane asylums, and whenever young men had to walk around for months with their hair combed back "decently" with sugar water, or had to endure being arrested by the *militsiia*, or visits from KGB informers who were looking for excuses to punish "deviants." When power is seen as productive, as something which inevitably encompasses us, it would seem to be impossible to really "drop out" from socialism since this is the context upon which the subject's very existence relies. A Soviet hippie is not a Soviet hippie without the Soviet context. Their identity depended to a significant extent on their difference from mainstream Soviet society but it was the Soviet world, with its economy, public institutions, infrastructure, geography, etc., that shaped their practices.

When there is neither subject nor action outside of power, what did the Soviet hippie's agency encompass? In performativity theory, which derives largely from the work of Judith Butler,[21] the subject emerges through endless reiteration of certain norms. Performativity should not be read as a single "act" or "performance," but it is rather a discursive practice, which forms the subject and by which identities are thus constructed. Agency here would be resistance to dominant social norms. Dick Hebdige[22] has stated about subcultures that opposition to hegemonic norms is often not expressed directly, but through meaningful practices of style. For Soviet hippies, their practices of music, the arts, travel, fashion, or spirituality were precisely their site of agency, their resistance to social norms. Even if the hippies did not get involved with politics directly, their symbolic expressions bore their performative agency,[23] their opposition to Soviet society, its bleak promise, and prevailing norms.

In poststructuralist feminist thinking, agency is not understood only as arising in the negative paradigm of subjectivation, but rather, norms can be performed and experienced in various ways. As Saba Mahmood put it, agency cannot not be conceptualized "simply as a synonym for resistance to relations of domination, but as a capacity for action that specific relations of '*subordination*' create and enable" (emphasis in the original).[24] While Soviet hippies escaped normative assumptions about *Homo Sovieticus*, they were simultaneously inscribed in different sets of norms, for example, what they imagined a hippie to be like in the West or what had become normative within their own community. Thus, specific forms of agency are always already embedded in the context of their appearance.

In its essence, Soviet hippie identity was linked to the struggle for agency in the Soviet context. In that sense the hippie identity bore a political stance, even if it is difficult to see hippies as a group bounded by political protest.

The hippies in Soviet Estonia did not share a clear oppositional ideology. They were rather different in their involvement in artistic activities, spiritual practices, and critical thinking about politics. Thus, I find it useful to see Soviet hippies as a community of shared affect rather than as a defined oppositional ideology. By stressing a distinctive emotional style as the core element of Soviet hippies, Juliane Fürst[25] has noted that they "wanted to feel differently by looking different from the 'grey masses.'"[26] I take her stance by arguing that what drove the hippie ideoscape in Soviet Estonia was a shared affect.

Since the mid-1990s the humanities and social sciences have witnessed a turn to affect. Extending discussions on the body, culture, and subjectivity that were influenced by poststructuralism and deconstruction, affect theory foregrounds emotion and dynamism in bodily matter.[27] Affect marks the intensities or stickiness[28] in relationships between bodies, discourses, or even historical-cultural formations. As Gregory Seigworth and Melissa Gregg[29] have put it, "[a]ffect arises in the midst of in-between-ness: in the capacities to act and be acted upon." Emerging between two bodies, or between bodies and the world, affect is also crucial in the production of collective identities and affinities.

To explore what drove Soviet hippie subjectivity, I elaborate on the notion of the imaginary elsewhere based on affect theory. While I have also drawn from performativity theory, which provides the framework for understanding *how* the material culture of the Soviet hippies emerged and *how* it affected the bodies involved, the notion of the imaginary elsewhere helps to understand *why*. I argue that Soviet hippie subjectivity was deeply ingrained with a craving for the imaginary elsewhere. The imaginary elsewhere is a much broader concept than the imaginary West,[30] since it encompasses not only associations with *zagranitsa*, but also altered states of consciousness, dreams, fantasies, and spiritual quests—all of which formed a substantial part of the Soviet hippie lifestyle. The imaginary elsewhere holds the transcendent experiences that hippies pursued through spiritual practices, using psychedelics, or the sensory experiences generated by fuzzy and distorted sounds of rock music.

This phenomenologically grounded and affect-theory driven stance also provides another angle to deal with the notion of "dropping out" from socialism. Namely, the imaginary elsewhere provided the means to drop out from Soviet daily reality. It allows the subject to emerge in a perpetual space of becoming, in which subjects both define and are defined by imaginaries of an "elsewhere." Affect plays a central part in the lived experience of the imaginary elsewhere. In the framework of affect theory, a body is webbed in its relations, pulled beyond its surface-boundedness through affective encounters, which eventually compose a body.[31] In a Spinozan-Deleuzian sense, the human can be perceived as an "envelope of possibilities" rather than a fixed individual organism.[32] Soviet hippies who strived for their imaginary

elsewhere wanted to lift their bodies away from their daily environment.
They wanted to open their bodies to perpetual becoming, to be in constant
movement toward the promises of the imaginary elsewhere. In affect theory
what drives affect is precisely its promise, its "not yet."[33] Since here the elsewhere to strive for is imaginary, it is always more of a promise than the actual
and material here-and-now. Yet I believe this promise was precisely the key
element that captivated hippie youth in Soviet Estonia.

The imaginary elsewhere also formed the constitutive outside of Soviet
daily reality. In Judith Butler's terms, the constitutive outside refers to the
unspeakable, the unviable, the non-narrativizable[34] that signify the limits of
intelligibility. By its forces of exclusion and abjection, through its negative
relation to the Other, the subject as well as what stands as "reality" are simultaneously constructed. Butler writes: "Fantasy is not the opposite of reality;
it is what reality forecloses, and, as a result, it defines the limits of reality,
constituting it as its constitutive outside."[35] To that extent, the imaginary
elsewhere is understood by indicating the limits of intelligibility of the general Soviet public and the proclaimed sense of "reality." Thus the imaginary
elsewhere functioned as the productive space on the axes of the potential and
the everyday reality. I will subsequently elaborate my argument based on
the practices, which were often intertwined, that catered to the drive for the
imaginary elsewhere for hippie youth. These are music, the connection to the
imaginary West, the use of psychedelics, and spiritual practices.

## TURN ON, TUNE IN . . . THE RADIO, AND THEN, DROP OUT

While former Harvard professor Timothy Leary was preaching about "Turn
on, tune in, drop out" in the late 1960s in the United States, which was
meant to encourage people to counter existing social conventions by using
psychedelic drugs, young people in Soviet Estonia practiced another kind of
"tuning in." Radio Luxembourg and various other foreign radio broadcasts
kept people updated not only about events, but also about new trends in
music elsewhere in the world. For Estonia especially, the access to Finnish
television was a key source of divergence. Young minds were captivated by
the iconic hippie-era albums from the UK and the US, which were illicitly
distributed, copied on reel tapes, and exchanged within networks of friends
and music lovers.

One of the very first psychedelic rock bands in the Soviet Union, Keldriline
Heli (Basement Sound), was established in 1970 in the basement of the
Tallinn Polytechnic Institute (today's Tallinn University of Technology).
As noted by music critic Margus Kiis,[36] the band modeled itself on the clas-
sic hippie band from San Francisco, Jefferson Airplane. Their songs relied on

psychedelic structures and metaphorical lyrics while emphasizing the use of effect pedals and visuals for shows. Keldriline Heli played several shows until one of them was perhaps too radical. The stage was covered with candles and the hall filled with balloons at the show on March 26, 1971,[37] after which the group was banned from performing in public, but for a while they continued under a different name, Väntorel.[38] One of my interlocutors described the fatal concert in highly emotional terms, as if, "the whole crowd was breathing together that night." Recalled with such specificity over forty years later, it demonstrates that the band succeeded in delivering the affective promise of something "more," which impacted the audience in meaningful ways.

Estonia soon became known among the networks of hippies and music lovers across the Soviet Union for its innovative rock music scene.[39] As was the case in various other spheres in the Soviet state, there was no total ideological control of the music scene, but it depended extensively on the particular personal preferences or methods of those in power.[40] All bands (then officially called vocal-instrumental ensembles) had to register and obtain a permit each time they wanted to perform. But most of the time the playlists were handled creatively. For example, the band Con Amore used to write John Lennon down as Johannes Lennuk, Paul McCartney as Paul Maakaart or

**Figure 2.1  Making music with some handy instruments to induce a trance state.**
*Source*: Courtesy of Tõnu Sampu, 1980.

Deep Purple's song "Into the Fire" as "Igavene tuli" (which can be translated as "Eternal fire" which could well be interpreted as something archetypically "Soviet").[41] The freedom to play live cover songs by Western bands depended on how open a venue's manager was to rock music or his or her willingness to take a risk. Many influential bands, most prominently Ruja, had a fluctuating relationship with the authorities: sometimes they were banned from performing, at other times their albums were released by the official Soviet record label Melodiia.[42] While music certainly functioned as an important social scaffold, the new sound of psychedelic rock, with its distorted guitar sound and extended solos, triggered the imagination of the youth in remarkable ways:

> We played music on tape or record player, settled in a comfortable position and just let go. Only some basic indispensable phrases interrupted it. The rest was just music. You could close your eyes. Some just stared at one point. You could, but it was certainly not compulsory to use something in order to get in the right mindset. The music alone was enough.[43]

Thus, the sound of rock music, whether experienced at a concert or at any of often ritualized, private listening or jamming sessions as shown on Figure 2.1, prompted the mind to travel to unknown dimensions. This affectively engaged experience held the promise of an imaginary elsewhere, not only because of the radically new sound of psychedelic rock music, but also because this was the music usually produced in the West.

## IN A VACUUM, EVEN A FART IS AIR

The global youth movement of the late 1960s and 1970s also transformed the imaginaries of Soviet youth. First, various signs and symbols, scattered information, and images of celebrities from political spheres and popular culture were available and open for reuse and reinterpretation by Soviet youth, for example, slogans such as "Make love not war," the oft-cited notions of love, peace, and freedom, or sex, drugs, and rock 'n' roll, the peace symbol, etc. In addition, public figures and rock idols such as Jimi Hendrix, Janis Joplin, Mahatma Gandhi, or Srila Prabhupada were sources of inspiration. Images—of people and ideas—were available mainly through non-official, but to some extent also through the official media. While dispersed yet definite in their visibility, these symbols functioned as floating signifiers,[44] open to various re-workings and interpretations. "In a vacuum, even a fart is air," commented the Estonian cult poet Johnny B. Isotamm (1939–2014) on witnessing a group of young people in early 1970s in Tartu trying hard to read the community newspaper *The New York Free Press*, the so-called hippie journal that someone in a prominent profession had brought back from a trip to the United States.[45]

The availability of potent images and scattered information for reworking and a sense of community with global youth informed the sense of an imaginary elsewhere. The notion of the imaginary elsewhere is closely connected to the notion of the imaginary West introduced by Alexei Yurchak in *Everything Was Forever Until It Was No More*.[46] In the Soviet Union, the West was perceived as the "free world" beyond the zone, so the imaginary elsewhere was amplified by the fact that it was generally unattainable. Yurchak explains[47] that *zagranitsa* was not necessarily about any real place, but it was its archetypical manifestation, which existed only when the real West could not be encountered. As foreign cultural forms were simultaneously promoted and critiqued within the state's cultural policy, the imaginary West was a constitutive element of late Soviet culture.[48] For Soviet youth in late 1960s, the imaginary West held the powerful promise of the global youth counterculture movements.

The images of youth movements in the West that traveled to Soviet Estonia evoked certain styles of self-fashioning, predominantly long hair and bellbottom trousers, preferably jeans. These symbols were used to manifest the wearer's subject position, to resist societal norms through symbolic expression, and also to converge emotionally with young people in the West. They also provided a way to recognize those who felt and thought the same way. Anna Gibbs[49] has written about mimetic communication as contagious processes between bodies in which affect plays an integral role. Mimetic communication in her view[50] is the corporeally based forms of imitation, which can take place both voluntarily and involuntarily across heterogeneous networks of media, images, bodies, and things. The aim of this communication is emotional convergence. Especially during the early years of the Soviet hippie movement, Soviet hippies practiced mimetic communication based on what they had learned about hippies and rock music culture in the West. They aimed to converge emotionally with the global youth counterculture. Even if some of these people did not identify themselves as hippies, they recall feeling a strong connection to members of their generation in other parts of the world: "I wasn't a hippie, but I was young and personally influenced by this movement as this was something that made us feel free even behind the Iron Curtain. To feel being part of world youth and their spirit of protest."[51]

Another framed it even more explicitly as a particular generational phenomenon that distinguishes them from generations born earlier or later:

The generation born in the late '40s and early '50s flourished at the peak of the hippie culture. That movement, in whichever corner of the world it occurred, resonated in many areas. That generation had a unique feeling of liberty and

open-mindedness, more so than generations born at any other time. The interest
in who we are and where we are is greater, deeper, and more genuine when it
comes to them.[52]

Later mimetic communication grew exponentially within the community of
Soviet hippies. Based on appearances that often diverged substantially from
the rest of Soviet society, they recognized and had an effect on each other.
As one of my collaborators said, hair was their flag of freedom. Embroidered
jeans, decorated jackets, colorful *ksivnik*'s (a small, pocket-shaped bag hanging around neck, where documents were usually kept), and bracelets were
important markers of the "hippie look." This mimetic communication with
the imagined global youth was turned into the source of their performative
agency in order to manifest their opposition, their difference from, or indifference, to the Soviet norm, and their striving for elsewhere.

## THE PSYCHEDELIC REVOLUTION

Images acquired from a variety of media and the rock music scene stimulated
the imagination of hippie youth, but a different kind of "toxicity" also had
its effect on the imagination. While the Western youth counterculture of the
1960s is often referred to as "the psychedelic generation," LSD and other
psychedelic substances that were widely used in the West were generally not
available in the Soviet Union. Instead, the flower people of the late 1960s and
early 1970s in Soviet Estonia were fairly sober.
    Around the time when Timothy Leary came out with his League for Spiri-
tual Discovery (LSD) and the Merry Pranksters organized a series of Acid
Tests in California, several articles appeared in Estonian media reporting on
the popularity of LSD among the Western youth and the drug's dangers, for
example, "Kaheksa tundi illusoorset maailma" ("Eight hours of an illusionary
world") in the newspaper *Edasi* (1966); "LSD ja Ameerika noored" ("LSD
and the American youth") in *Noorte Hääl* (1967); "LSD—uks hullumeelsusse või paradiisi?" ("LSD—the door to madness or paradise?") in *Edasi*
(1968). The point of these articles was to warn against the drug and ridicule
its users, pointing to the haunting dangers of persistently returning to a world
of hallucinations[53] or the devastating effects on the user's bloodline.[54] Drug
use was also framed as evidence that capitalist, bourgeois society had failed.[55]
    This coverage aroused young Soviet people's imagination, and this excite-
ment was subsequently channeled into emerging forms of rock music (e.g., bands
such as Keldriline Heli and Suuk), multimedia art (e.g., the works of Kaarel
Kurismaa), animation (e.g., Rein Raamat, Avo Paistik, and Ando Keskküla),

graphic art (e.g., Aili Vint and Vello Vinn), or into experiments with available substances: "We didn't have many material needs. I still don't. My needs are downright ascetic. Hedonism of the mind is most important."[56]

Sometimes even more welcome than the use of alcohol, marijuana was the most widely available mind-altering substance after wine. Weed was not grown locally, but brought in from the southern Soviet regions (from Ukraine, the Caucasus, and Central Asia) by fellow hippies, or from Moscow where the drug scene was bigger. Usually it was not exchanged for money. The most common form of marijuana consumption was to roll a joint inside the tubes of Belomorkanal cigarettes. Of the prescription drugs available, seduxen, dimetrol, and cyclodol were experimented with. A psychoactive tea was also made from Astmatol cigarettes, which were intended for asthmatics. Some reckless experimenters inhaled Sopals, a cleaning agent produced in Latvia, the main active ingredient of which was ether. Later in 1970s opium poppy tea became popular among some circles.[57]

Affect is a predominant element of altered states of consciousness. Bodily sensations are intense and imbued with an initial sense of ecstasy that can later give way to the torments and constraints of addiction, which happened to many people who experimented with the poppy tea. Although the widely used slang term *kaif* can refer to various things that just feel good, such as sex or music, the notion of ecstasy or *kaif* became important to some circles of friends, especially as a result of their drug-infused practices. The affective quality of *kaif* is galvanized by curiosity and a desire for unforeseen spiritual adventures and bodily sensations on the plains of altered states of mind:

> You see all kinds of hallucinations, kind of like dreams. But these dreams have a special quality. You feel as if they're real. Much more real than this reality. Often newcomers got really crazy. Because you realize for a few seconds that now you are completely awake and this is the moment you're born into reality. Everything which came before, all the years of your life, was a complete illusion. Nothing, just illusion. Garbage, nothing else. You see that everything was fake. Everything becomes nothing. And at that exact moment you become completely enlightened. You understand everything, the whole truth about the world. But you can't express it. If you try, nobody understands.[58]

This description highlights yet another aspect of the affective promise of experiences induced by mind-altering drugs. The altered states seem to hold the promise of not only a better, but often a more "truthful" reality. This further set hippies apart from Soviet daily reality. Hence, drugs produced detachment, but the opposite was also true—disengagement from and indifference to Soviet life paved the way for experimentation with drugs. Psychoactive drugs generated the sense of being elsewhere that those who took them sought. The experience of elsewhere was precisely the drugs' affective promise; thus, it arose as a significant praxis of the Soviet hippie imaginary elsewhere. In hippies' searching for further mental detachment from Soviet daily life, psychoactive drugs offered a way to "drop out" from socialism.

## FREE AS GOD

For some people, the drive for an imaginary elsewhere was externalized though experiments with mind-altering substances, but it was pursued more widely through various spiritual practices. The buzz around American rock opera *Hair* (which premiered in 1967), which claimed that the new Age of Aquarius had begun, also stimulated a New Age discourse in Soviet Estonia. This led to growing interest in Eastern religions, mysticism, meditation, and yoga. Some young people turned to Russian Orthodoxy, or, in Estonia, more likely locally grounded Protestantism. While in the West hippies searched for spiritual paths that transcended the limitations of institutionalized religion, in the officially atheistic Soviet Union, any spirituality was an alternative, which provided a way to break away from gray daily reality.

Hippies combined pieces of information and spiritual guidance from partially available Western media, *samizdat* literature, Buddhist studies which emerged in the University of Tartu in Linnart Mäll's classes and research, and encounters with a few local gurus such as Gunnar Aarma, Uku Masing, and Mihkel Ram Tamm. Tallinn was also one of the early centers of the Hare Krishna movement in the Soviet Union.[59] In 1978 the first public mantra singing took place on Town Hall Square in Tallinn and a few radio broadcasts with Anatoli Pinyayev were produced[60]:

> My husband and I were searching for spirituality, this materialistic life wasn't suitable for us. We visited different churches, we were seekers. Everything was interesting, but nothing was perfect. Until we met Hare Krishna followers from Moscow who had come to visit Rein Metsniin [widely known as Rein Mitšurin—T. T.]. When they talked about their philosophy, we immediately knew that this is what we need[ed].[61]

Whether it was the Hare Krishna or the Jesus movement, yoga or black magic, all of these allowed people to bypass the Soviet discourse of atheism. One of my collaborators said, "[S]pirituality was a hidden form of intellectual protest." Their "intellectual protest" led them to redefine their relationship to reality. It opened up different realms with affective promises other than those that the dominant Soviet discourses offered: "Esotericism can be used as a means of dealing with such a depressing totalitarian system, where it seems as if society is always acting stupid. When everything is wrong. Esotericism takes your feet off the ground."[62]

The forbidden status of any esoteric or religious knowledge further exoticized these realms. See, for example, Riina's comment on her "sacred notebook":

> This old notebook—I don't even know who wrote the manuscript. I got it from [my classmate] for just one day, and she was really nervous, saying, "This is a secret text" and "make sure you bring it back to me tomorrow!" I stayed awake all night, copying the whole book in handwriting. Later on I read it many times and didn't find it had any "secret knowledge" anymore—regular yoga, breathing techniques, diet recommendations. Back at the time it was so exciting, because when you were trusted to read such manuscripts, you were as if the "chosen one."[63]

In the late twentieth century a tendency to center alternative beliefs around a guru developed in the West. For example, Srila Prabhupada, Maharishi Mahesh Yogi, Timothy Leary, and Terrence McKenna were important figures in Western youth counterculture movements. Did Soviet hippies also have their gurus? Arguably yes, at least in Soviet Estonia. One of the figures who stood out was philosopher Mihkel Tamm, known as Michael Ram Tamm (see Figure 2.2).[64] He became popular among hippies in Estonia and attracted visitors from elsewhere: "Going to Ram became sort of a fashion. If you hadn't been to Rama, you weren't 'with it.' Many people got a great experience, which they might not have gotten elsewhere."[65]

According to classic social anthropologist James George Frazer, the two main elements of a religion are the belief in higher forces and practices that try to please them.[66] The first could be seen as the theoretical side of a religion, the second as the practical, which includes activities, prayers, etc. The hippies in Soviet Estonia certainly engaged with the first one—there was a belief in and openness to something higher than everyday ordinariness. However, it is more difficult to draw conclusions about their religious practices. Not only was there limited access to organized religions, but more significantly, their principal opposition to any system often restrained them from piously following any institutionalized religion: "It was about the feeling of personal freedom, being free as God."[67]

Thus, the hippies were influenced by various religions and spiritual trends such as the Hare Krishna movement, Buddhism, Christianity, Russian Orthodoxy, and even shamanism, but they rarely limited themselves to one of them. Hippies wanted to engage in spiritual practices to step aside, physically, intellectually, and intuitively, from the norms of Soviet society. Considering the bodily sensations that come with practices of piety, meditation, or yoga,

**Figure 2.2   Aare and Julia visiting Rama in the mid-1970s.** An Estonian philosopher and an expert on Sanskrit, yoga, and meditation, Mihkel Ram Tamm became a guru for many hippies in Soviet Estonia and from elsewhere. *Source*: Courtesy of Vladimir Wiedemann.

and a belief in higher forces, the spiritual relationship to the world is an affective one. Through their affective engagements with the "otherworldly," hippies opened up new imaginary spaces of elsewhere.

To return to a collaborator who was introduced at the beginning of this chapter, on his travels inside the borders of the Soviet Union, Aare has probably covered a distance equivalent to going around the globe twice. At present he has spent about two years of his life fasting. During one of my most recent conversations with him, he pithily summarized a point that I have highlighted in this chapter. In his view hippies were just looking for what historically people in many cultures have sought—a deeper understanding of the world: "It is not about whether you are in favor of or against something [like the Soviet state], but it's rather about stepping aside from it all. You allow someone [or something] to observe the world through yourself."[68]

Just as the imaginary West existed only because the West was unattainable in practical terms, the imaginary elsewhere in spiritual terms encompasses the indefinite becoming of an inward-looking journey, the unattainability of the transcendent, the impossibility of grasping this "someone" that Aare referred to in his words.

## TOWARD INFINITY

By viewing Soviet hippies as a community of shared affect, I have argued that the craving for an imaginary elsewhere was deeply ingrained in Soviet hippie subjectivity. The imaginary elsewhere encompasses not only the perceived West as the locus of "freedom," but also the transcendent experiential realms that hippies pursued through spiritual practices, by using mind-altering drugs or through sensory experiences generated by the distorted sounds of rock music. I have also shown how this imaginary elsewhere, in some ways, provided the means to "drop out" from the Soviet daily reality. The hippies in Soviet Estonia wanted to open their bodies to perpetual becoming, to be in constant movement toward the affective promises of the imaginary elsewhere. By deriving its force from its practical unattainability, in the process of self-formation the imaginary elsewhere was the motor of indefinite becoming.

The public discourse addressing Soviet hippies often centered around their looks and their lack of participative action. Remmel[69] and Ohmann[70] have noted, based on the few available official reports from 1970, that around that time hippies were not seen so much as an ideological problem as an esthetic or moral problem. The emphasis on appearances is directly connected to practices of regulating bodies. In the context of Cold War propaganda, the authorities framed longhaired young people who engaged with rock music as people who had become infected by Western influences. This use of infectiousness as a powerful metaphor represents certain population groups or certain kinds of affect as infectious agents and thus, as something dangerous for societal wellbeing. Here, the metaphor of infectiousness projected onto some groups (such as hippies) or certain "toxic" affects (such as an interest in rock music) functions as a differentiating instrument.[71] That led to the authorities' further politicization of the community and resulted in several measures designed to rein in young people such as strategic surveillance by the KGB, constraints on cultural activities, expulsions from schools, universities, and other educational institutions, forced treatment in psychiatric hospitals, and arrests on the basis of public performances or appearances.

While hippies were often punished or subject to surveillance because they failed, or rather refused, to create the exterior appearance necessary to remain within the norm, they also used their bodies as the sites of affect to attract others to their community, their ideas, and ideals; "Following us, many people turned into hippies. Artist and writers—they all became hairy later on. It caught on . . . ."[72]

This highlights what is characteristic of affect—it is contagious. It holds the power to captivate bodies in mimetic communication. And when the affect behind this mimetic communication stood for something "higher," something much more promising than the dominant Soviet discourses, dark with their authoritarian rhetoric and atheism, the light of freedom shimmered in the distance.

## NOTES

1. The origin of the word *sistema* is often associated with a charismatic person from the early Moscow hippie scene who was known as "Solntse" (Sun). Supposedly he called his *tusovka* (crowd) the *solnechnaia sistema* (solar system). Vassilii Long, interview with the author, Moscow, July 29, 2014.

2. For example, Juliane Fürst, "Love, Peace and Rock 'n' Roll on Gorky Street: The 'Emotional Style' of the Soviet Hippie Community," *Contemporary European History* 23, no. 4 (2014): 565–87; William Jay Risch, "Soviet 'Flower Children': Hippies and the Youth Counter-Culture in 1970s L'viv," *Journal of Contemporary History* 40, no. 3 (2005), 565–84; Sergei Zhuk, "Religion, 'Westernization,' and Youth in the 'Closed City' of Soviet Ukraine, 1964–84," *Russian Review* 67, no. 4 (2008), 661–79; Živilė Mikailienė, "The Hippie Movement in Soviet Lithuania: The Tension Between Official and Unofficial Youth Culture and State Violence" (paper presented at the conference "Culture: Popular and Mass Culture in Late Soviet Society," St. Gallen, January 24–25, 2013); Madigan Fichter, "Rock 'n' Roll Nation: Counterculture and Dissent in Romania, 1965–1975," *Nationalities Papers* 39, no. 4 (2011); Vladimir Videman [Vladimir Wiedemann], "Khippi v Estonii. Kak eto nachinalos," (2013), http://www.liveinternet.ru/users/644802/post297896425/.

3. Throughout this chapter, my use of the words "hippie" or "the hippie movement" is conditional. Not all the people whom I take as the subjects of this analysis identified themselves as hippies. Nevertheless, they were all influenced by the movement in the West or in the Soviet Union to a greater or lesser extent. Those influenced by the movement in the West or the Soviet Union included a variety of people: the so-called real hippies, the radical "drop-outs" who tried to lead their lives independently of the Soviet system, and those who wore hippie attire and enjoyed the rock scene without any enduring contact or identification with Soviet hippie communities (the so-called "*hipitsejad*" in Estonian). See Meelis Tasur, "Eesti hipid olid rohkem hipitsejad [Interview with Hannes Varblane]," *Maaleht*, May 19, 2013, http://maaleht.delfi.ee/news/uudised/kultuur/varblane-eesti-hipid-olid-rohkem-hipitsejad.d?id=66129516.

4. This chapter relies on an independent anthropological research project with which I have been involved since 2011. As part of a wider transmedia documentary project, I have conducted video-recorded interviews with thirty-four people: seventeen individuals from the hippie generation in Estonia and seventeen individuals from that generation in Russia, Latvia, and Ukraine. However, this chapter draws mostly on the material collected in Estonia. In addition, I have done archival work, and have had many shorter conversations and online communications with people associated with Soviet Estonian hippie culture. The work has resulted in a multimedia exhibition, "Soviet Hippies: The Psychedelic Underground of the 1970s Estonia" that Kiwa and I co-curated. It was exhibited at the Estonian National Museum in 2013, at the Moderna

Museet in Malmö, Sweden in 2014, at the Uppsala Konstmuseum in Sweden in 2014, at the Presentation House Gallery in Vancouver, British Columbia, Canada in 2014, and at the Red Gallery in London, UK in 2016. At the time of writing, a feature-length documentary film is in production with an expected release date in 2017.

5. Gilles Deleuze and Felix Guattari, *A Thousand Plateaus: Capitalism and Schizophrenia*, trans. Brian Massumi (Minneapolis: University of Minnesota Press, 1987).

6. Alexei Yurchak, *Everything Was Forever, Until It Was No More: The Last Soviet Generation* (Princeton: Princeton University Press, 2005).

7. William Risch, "A Soviet West: Nationhood, Regionalism, and Empire in the Annexed Western Borderlands," *Nationalities Papers* 43, no. 1 (2015).

8. Vello Salumets, *Rockrapsoodia* (Tallinn: Eesti Entsüklopeediakirjastus, 1998).

9. While writing this chapter I struggled with the tension between the disciplinary uses of the notion of culture in anthropology and cultural studies. "Hippie culture" as a certain set of practices, beliefs, appearances, materialities, etc. enacted by subjects across various nations or localities reflects the approach commonly used in the field of cultural studies. However, in the field of anthropology, my "home discipline," culture is usually seen as a more inclusive locus, an indeterminable context within which certain claims are explored. In this analysis I am simultaneously drawing on both of these disciplinary approaches, using whatever proves most fruitful for the material under discussion.

10. In the sense of, for example, Stuart Hall and Tony Jefferson, eds., *Resistance through Rituals: Youth Subcultures in Post-War Britain* (London: Routledge, 1990) and Dick Hebdige, *Subculture: The Meaning of Style* (London: Routledge, 1979).

11. Liva Zolnerovica, "Hippies in Latvia SSR" (unpublished paper, quoted with permission of the author).

12. Arjun Appadurai, *Modernity At Large: Cultural Dimensions of Globalization* (Minneapolis: University of Minnesota Press, 1996), 27–47.

13. Ibid., 36–37.

14. Vladimir (b. 1955), interview with the author, Tallinn, September 4, 2012. I identify my collaborators by their first names. All the video-recorded interviews took place in 2012–2013, various informal communication followed until 2015.

15. The complex relationship between the apolitical intentions of the hippies and external politicization is also discussed in a paper about the hippies in Soviet Lithuania, Živil Mikailien, "Soviet Lithuania," and in Fichter, "Rock 'n' Roll Nation."

16. See, for example, Maurice Halbwachs, *On Collective Memory*, ed. and trans. Lewis A. Coser (Chicago: University of Chicago Press, 1992); Astrid Erll, "Cultural Memory Studies: An Introduction," in *Cultural Memory Studies: An International and Interdisciplinary Handbook*, ed. Astrid Erll, Ansgar Nünning, and Sara B. Young (Berlin: Walter de Gruyter, 2008), 1–18; Jan Assmann, "Communicative and Cultural Memory," in Erll, Nünning, and Young, *Cultural Memory Studies*, 109–18.

17. Ene Kõresaar, "Mälu, aeg, kogemus ja eluloouurija pilk," in *Mälu kui kultuuritegur: etnoloogilisi perspektiive*, ed. Ene Kõresaar and Terje Anepaio (Tartu: Tartu Ülikooli Kirjastus, 2003), 8.

18. Fürst, "Love, Peace and Rock 'n' Roll."

19. Ibid.

20. Judith Butler, *Bodies That Matter: On the Discursive Limits of Sex* (New York: Routledge, 1993), 15.

21. Ibid., Judith Butler, *Undoing Gender* (New York: Routledge, 2004).

22. Hebdige, *Subculture,* 18.

23. Butler, *Bodies That Matter.*

24. Saba Mahmood, *Politics of Piety: The Islamic Revival and the Feminist Subject* (Princeton: Princeton University Press, 2011), 18.

25. Fürst, "Love, Peace and Rock 'n' Roll."

26. Ibid., 585.

27. Patricia T. Clough, "The Affective Turn: Political Economy, Biomedia, and Bodies," in *The Affect Theory Reader*, ed. Gregory J. Seigworth and Melissa Gregg (Durham: Duke University Press, 2010).

28. Sara Ahmed, "Happy Objects," in Seigworth and Gregg, *The Affect Theory Reader.*

29. Gregory J. Seigworth and Melissa Gregg, "An Inventory of Shimmers," in Seigworth and Gregg, *The Affect Theory Reader*, 1.

30. Yurchak, *Everything Was Forever.*

31. Ibid., 3.

32 Anna Gibbs, "After Affect: Sympathy, Synchrony, and Mimetic Communication," in Seigworth and Gregg, *The Affect Theory Reader*, 187.

33. Seigworth and Gregg, "An Inventory of Shimmers," in Seigworth and Gregg, *The Affect Theory Reader*, 3.

34. Butler, *Bodies*, 140.

35. Butler, *Undoing Gender,* 29.

36. Margus Kiis, "Estonian Psychedelic and Dissident Rock" (paper presented at the exhibition "Soviet Hippies: The Psychedelic Underground of the 1970s Estonia," curated by Kiwa and Terje Toomistu, Estonian National Museum, Tartu, Estonia, March 15–August 25, 2013).

37. Martin Jõela, "Intervjuu: Andres Valkonen," *Müürileht,* April 9, 2014, http://www.muurileht.ee/intervjuu-andres-valkonen/; Salumets, *Rockrapsoodia.*

38. Changing the band's name was a common strategy for musicians who were banned from performing in public.

39. Other emerging, influential collectives which used experimental, psychedelic and prog rock elements in their repertoire were Kooma (with charismatic singer Joel Steinfeldt), Meie (an experimental band with vocalist Tajo Kadajas and guitarist Kalle Vikat), Psycho (an improvisational collective with Paap Kõlar on drums and Andres Põldroo on guitar), Mess (often claimed to be the Soviet Union's first progressive rock band formed by then-seventeen-year-old Sven Grünberg) and Suuk (a psychedelic rock band from Tartu which stood out for its collaboration with Aleksander Müller). In 1969, Kooma recorded a hard-rock-style song called "I Wash My Teeth with Blood," which, in Kiwa's analysis, "signaled the change, from the dreams of the last decade, into a cynical phase." Kiwa, "The Sound Culture in Soviet Estonia," in *Out of Sync. Looking Back at the History of Sound Art*, ed. Ragne Kukk and Kati Ilves (Tallinn: The Art Museum of Estonia—Kumu Art Museum, 2013).

40. Atko-Sulhan Remmel, "Veel kord hipidest ja komsomolist ning mõningatest katsetest piirata roiskuva Lääne mõju Nõukogude noorsoo seas," *Tuna* 2 (2014).

41. Herbert (b. 1954), interview with the author, Tallinn, January 30, 2013.

42. Adam Garrie, "When Tallinn First Rocked the World," *Estonian World,* June 17, 2013, http://estonianworld.com/culture/when-tallinn-first-rocked-the-world/.

43. Aare (b. 1953), interview with the author, Tallinn, January 4, 2013.

44. Claude Lévi-Strauss, *Introduction to the Work of Marcel Mauss*, trans. Felicity Baker (New York: Routledge and Kegan Paul, 1987).

45. Well-known blues artist Aleksander Müller (1947–2013) described this. His house in Tartu used to be a popular place for artists and bohemians to hang out. See Margus Kiis, "Aleksander Müller end maha ei kanna [Interview with Aleksander Müller]," *Muusika* 10 (2004).

46. Yurchak, *Everything Was Forever*, 158–206.

47. Ibid., 159.

48. Ibid., 165.

49. Gibbs, "After Affect."

50. Ibid., 186.

51. Maire, e-mail communication with the author, February 18, 2013.

52. Aare.

53. G. Borovik, "Kaheksa tundi illusoorset maailma," *Edasi,* November 1, 1966.

54. I. Pappel, "LSD—uks hullumeelsusse või paradiisi?" *Edasi,* June 6, 1968.

55. J. Aldrige, "Intellektuaalne enesetapp," *Rahva Hääl*, December 24, 1966.

56. Jaakko (b. 1948), interview with the author, Tallinn, June 26, 2012.

57. Opium use was a topic on which my collaborators were often reluctant to comment. The variation in the amount of opiates in the seeds made it difficult to dose properly, hence many lost their friends from overdoses of this substance.

58. Vladimir.

59. Ringo Ringvee, "Hare Krišna ja Eesti," *Mäetagused*, no. 49 (2011): 173.

60. Anatoli Pinyayev (renamed Ananta-Shanti Das) started spreading Krishna consciousness in the Soviet Union after meeting with Bhaktivedanta Swami Srila Prabhupada, the founder of the Hare Krishna Movement, in Moscow in 1971. See Ringvee, "Hare Krišna," 172–73.

61. Lilamrita, telephone interview with the author, April 28, 2013.

62. Enn (b. 1946), interview with the author, Tartu, August 9, 2012.

63. Riina (b. 1949), written communication with the author, February 15, 2013.

64. Mihkel Ram Tamm was born near Tartu, Estonia, in 1911. He emigrated in 1939 and went to study at the Berlin Technical University. During World War II he lived in Sweden. In the early 1950s he decided to move to India to live in an ashram, but before leaving Europe, he wanted to visit his relatives in Estonia. On entering the territory of the Soviet Union, he was immediately arrested. As a person without citizenship, he remained under close surveillance by the KGB for decades. During that time, he developed his most widely recognized theory, his theory of null-energy. See Mihkel Ram Tamm, *Theory-Hypothesis-Null* (Asrama Rama-Tam-Om, 1988).

65. Aare.

66. James George Frazer, *The Golden Bough: A Study in Religion and Magic* (Mineola, NY: Dover Publications, 2002), 50.

67. Vladimir (b. 1955), personal communication with the author, May 10, 2013.

68. Aare.

69. Remmel, "Veel kord hipidest."

70. Valdur Ohmann, "Eesti hipiliikumine komsomoli fookuses," *Tuna* 3 (2013).

71. Mel Chen, *Animacies: Biopolitics, Racial Mattering, and Queer Affect* (Durham: Duke University Press, 2012), 192.

72. Päärn (b. 1943), interview with the author, August 10, 2012.

*Chapter 3*

# Art and "Madness"

## *Weapons of the Marginal during Socialism in Eastern Europe*

### Maria-Alina Asavei

In this chapter, I analyze subtle forms of artistic/everyday resistance during the late socialist period in Eastern Europe, focusing on the artistic practice of several artists who were considered "mad." I survey several individual forms of artistic self-estrangement, arguing that political resistance can take place in different force fields: not only in mainstream institutions and in the public sphere, but also in the remote zones of the "inner self" where one's inherent "reality" and its subversive performance become the expression of an existential rebellion. The concept of resistance assumes "the unassimilated nature of something in a new distressed context."[1] In addition to explicit forms of artistic opposition like "defying authority" or "beating the system," which overtly and publicly questioned the legitimacy of the regime, there were also subtle forms of resistance such as feigning madness or obsessively documenting the "average everydayness" of socialist everyday life. The association between critical art and madness is not accidental. Many artists throughout the Eastern bloc spent years in mental institutions (or were confined to their home and placed under a physician's supervision) although many of them did not actually have a mental disorder. In this case, psychiatry was used as a means of social and political control and sham psychiatric diagnoses were imposed on perfectly sane people. However, one could analyze the other side of the same coin, namely situations in which mental hospitals or/and the invocation of "madness" were used to protect people from worse fates at the hands of the regime. Artists frequently used "insanity" to disguise their political protest through art. By focusing on "madness" as an existential and cultural symbol of "dropping out" rather than as a medical problem, this chapter scrutinizes various ways in which artists departed from communist-imposed "reality" via internal escape routes. This self-inflicted marginality and self-estrangement was a way and, in some cases, a strategy, to transcend cultural and political conformity and the values embedded in such conformity.

The argument of this chapter is that some artists from the former Eastern bloc managed to "drop out" of socialist reality through artistic madness. This madness, which was usually feigned, functioned as a cultural practice and as strategy of re-individualization and dis-identification from collective identification with the communist regime. The purpose of this chapter is to extend the list of "drop-outs" from socialism by examining artistic madness from the perspective of unassimilated resistance. I argue that the retreat from "reality as it was supposed to be" by means of "artistic madness" is a political response to a politicized society's surveillance of the individual. Withdrawal from "communist reality" took the form of both physical self-exile to the margins of society and (artistic?) retreat to the inner margins of a disen-chanted self. Both forms of retreat can be regarded as strategies for dropping out of socialist reality. While someone in external, physical self-exile on the margins of society was still subjected to the omnipresent surveillance of the state (because the artist could still be seen and punished), the retreat into mad-ness instantiated a peculiar form of artistic-political resistance that those in power could not necessarily decipher.

## A "MORE REAL" REALITY AS CULTURAL POLICY

The stereotypical image of the socialist Central and Eastern European "pan-optic regime of modernity" divides art and cultural production into strict binary oppositions of "official" and "unofficial." In turn, this is translated into an imposed antagonism between Socialist Realism—as a unique style of artistic and cultural production—and modernist/neo-avant-garde art practice. Socialist Realism was not only the official style (canon) of art in the Soviet Union and its satellites from the late 1940s, but it was also a system for the production and consumption of culture.[2] Although imposition of this unique style was relaxed in many Eastern European countries after Stalin's death, it remained more or less in "limited force" as the official canon of art and cultural production until as late as 1989. However, it must also be said that the particular historical and political changes in Eastern European, state-sanctioned cultures complicated the line between "official" (Socialist Real-ism) and "unofficial" art. For example, in the former socialist Yugoslavia after the Stalin-Tito split (1948), Socialist Realism was known as "National Realism." Stalinist cultural orthodoxy was officially rejected and replaced with self-managed socialism of a national (Yugoslavian) type. In Romania, Socialist Realism remained the official canon of all art, and it even gained momentum after Ceaușescu's notorious 1971 "July Theses" and the 1983

"Mangalia Theses," when the communist leader rebranded it as "socialist humanism." In Hungary, Socialist Realism reigned as the compulsory style until the early 1960s but after the Hungarian revolution of 1956 the new cultural policy of the "Three Ts" (Tiltás, Türés, Támogatás or "Prohibition," "Tolerance," "Support") started to gain authority. As Péter György posits, "The party expected no one to believe in the ideas of Socialist Realism; it only expected the artists to abide by the rules of the game."[3] This does not mean that the artist was completely independent and free to produce whatever she/ he wanted. Artistic success depended on the ability to find the right balance among the "Three Ts." This trading on the "Prohibition-Tolerance-Support" card can also be detected in other Eastern European countries. These "grey zones" (and shades of gray) still need to be illuminated and disentangled if we want to overcome the widespread take on the socialist era as a period that was structured by strict binary oppositions.

However, it is still a common assumption both in the region and in the West that Socialist Realism was a robust monolith programmed by ideologues to reject individualist art (the "demiurgic" role of the individual artist-genius) for the sake of collectivism. In the socialist context, collectivism is defined in contrast to individualism, connoting a "selfless community" and capitulation to the *status quo*.[4] This vision of collectivity also appears in the formal obligation to produce an art which reflects a singleness of purpose and the "collective voice" as opposed to individualistic and deeply personal ruminations and anxieties. The "zhdanovization" of all cultural life[5] narrowed the scope of art, leading to "an obvious loss without any apparent compensation."[6] Individualist, "subjective" artistic expression was often attacked as capitalist wickedness devoid of human and social content. This lack of "human and social content" was understood as a "devil-may-care attitude" and ideological indifference. The purpose of art was not to express deep private feelings or emotions, but to transform human consciousness for the benefit of the proletarian masses. The artist's mission was not to express reality in a subjective, personalized mode, but to reflect the official politics of the moment and its "reality." Thus, "political art" was the only accepted and acceptable kind of art (at least until Stalin's death).[7] Officialdom understood art as "political art," which disseminated communist values. The artist was not allowed to produce "non-political" works: "artists think that politics is the business of the government and the Central Committee. (. . .) We demand that our comrades both as leaders in literary affairs and writers, be guided by the vital force of the Soviet order—its politics."[8] In other words, Socialist Realist art was the only possible kind of "political" art. In the former Soviet Union, party officials censured, for example, the poetess Anna Akhmatova, who was charged with writing "empty and *non-political* poetry" (emphasis mine).[9]

The official discourse also stressed the artist's duty to reflect "reality in its revolutionary development."[10] The argument that Socialist Realist ideologues used was that art had to be "realistic" and artists had to use a "realist" method. But what kind of "reality" was art supposed to reflect? The "average" reality (reality as it is) or "reality" as it was supposed to be? Obviously, Socialist Realism fostered its own realism, one where people and events were not represented as they really were, but as they were supposed to be. Socialist Realism did not depict average miners, *kolkhoz* women, industrial workers, and factories but rather, "heroes," "super humans," and "new men." The official canon rejected any attempt at depicting average reality or "average everydayness" on the grounds that such depictions were forms of "degener- ate" rather than "political" art. Therefore, the censorship machine attempted to prevent any artistic production which had to do with something that was "unclear and tenebrous," "depressing or ugly," "painful and distressing," "mystical," "anti-human," "abject," "ill," "imperfect," and so on. In this ideo- logical framework, not all art mediums were equally important and relevant. For instance, painting was deeply cherished and it was considered radically different from photography. Photography was subject to overt disapproval because the artist could not transform reality and, reality, as brutal as it was, was not an appropriate subject of art.

As Romanian conceptual artist Ion Grigorescu says:

> In painting the artist has a role, has a mission, because he transforms reality. Reality is not the "regular" one because art has the great mission of intervening in reality. In [an artist's] interpretation, reality becomes more "real." In paint- ing, the artist strives to find his own territory. In the case of photography, the photographer disintegrates or, in other words, the photography explodes the author. In a communist reading, photography which is mixed with painting is "ideologically dangerous" because a document (the photograph) is distorted by the intervention of the artist's hand.[11]

According to the rhetoric of official art, every "ugly," "uneasy," or "distress- ing" detail of existence had to be beautified, improved aesthetically because art's mission was not only to educate and to transform human consciousness, but also to "powerfully attract." To give just one example, the most favored official artist of the Ceaușescu era, the mural painter Sabin Bălașa,[12] used to "beautify" all the subject matter he painted. The most "attractive" element in Bălașa's official paintings was the use of a special shade of blue with which the painter wanted to "powerfully attract" the viewer. His paintings are not depictions of reality as such, but deliberate attempts to beautify reality. In Bălașa's *Homage to the Miners* (1978), miners—one of the most favored social groups in socialist Romania—are painted as shiny characters, bearing miraculous blue minerals in their hands. Blue is also the predominant color of the whole composition and its function is to "heroicize" the figure of the miner. After 1989, some Romanian art critics[13] emphasized that the ways Sabin Bălaşa produced attractiveness are cacophonic and his blue is not a plastic color, but "a cheap medical color, which can be bought from an average shop for a bit of money."[14]

Although art had to be attractive and visually appealing, all artistic production was expected to be appreciated in accordance with some distinctive aesthetic rules. The aesthetic experience was not understood in terms of unmediated pleasure and cognitively uninfected perception (what is known via Kant as "free aesthetic judgment"), but in terms of usefulness and "political" functionality. The politics of both art production and reception that was imposed on artists and the public occasioned conflicting art histories and conceptions of the cultural public sphere which differed from those in the West. The official cultural sphere was subjected to state-controlled conceptions of art and art institutions that are ubiquitous in the West (such as private galleries, art societies, or private art collectors) did not exist in the same form in the former Eastern bloc.

Yet, this does not mean that the artists and other cultural producers of those times did not develop alternative or countercultural spheres. This did happen, especially after the Thaw. Individual artists, each pursuing her/his own identity, came together many times to establish a collective identity or an alternative culture. By refusing to "buy into" the *status quo*, these artists withdrew voluntarily from social life and confined themselves to the margins of society. In what follows, I will examine artistic madness as a means of re-individualization and dis-identification from collective identification with the communist regime.

## DISSENT FROM "REALITY" AS IT WAS SUPPOSED TO BE

Artists of many stripes started to contest socialist reality and its stylistic "realism," which was imposed from above. Withdrawing from social life and living the life of an outsider were just some aspects of this multifarious contestation. Artistic dissent employed many vocabularies which escaped the constraints of the *status quo*, representing not only overt criticism of the system, but also "a mixture of resignation, suppression of dissatisfaction, random cunning, melancholy and humor combined with carefully calculated submission, self-limited criticism, tactical control of the marginal profile and intelligent use of opportunities."[15] By the 1980s, self-censorship had become a state of mind, especially in Romania and Bulgaria. Many artists conformed to this state of affairs precisely because carefully calculated submission allowed them to be visible and exhibit and, from time to time, to escape the constraints of the wooden language of propaganda. This tactical self-censorship did not necessarily mean the artist was resigned in the face of a "reality" that she perceived as eternal, but rather, it was a psychology of doubling—a protective strategy of adjustment which does not necessarily accept authority and the futility of resistance. For some visual artists and writers, living and producing art behind this "doubleness" was unavoidable. Despite the fact that "you can hardly play piano with the same hand that you cut wood with," as Bulgarian dissident and novelist Blaga Dimitrova brilliantly put it, "some artists did manage to master this art of doubleness."[16]

There are many narratives of artistic dissent from communist "reality," but this chapter focuses on "madness" as an act or a strategy of self-estrangement and self-exclusion. The association between resistant art and madness is not accidental. Artists frequently used insanity as a disguise for their political protest through art. The invocation of "artistic madness" was possible because it coincided historically with the modern conception of "productive madness" according to which the artist was a reclusive and *alienated* "genius" and "madman" whose insanity was not clinical but essential, intellectual, and artistic. Even if socialist officialdom initially rejected any trace of aesthetic Modernism in official art, ideas about the artist as someone who is reclusive, disturbed, and misunderstood were fairly well known and sometimes tolerated although not overtly acknowledged. Sometimes artists engaged in various forms of constructive escapism and even tried to find peace of mind in a psychiatric asylum or create their own asylum. Slovakian photographer Milota Havrankova confesses that "if we had wanted to do a social documentary, it would have been impossible. People doing that were imprisoned. I tried to create an asylum where, with students and through our own fantasies, we created our own world."[17] Creating "your own world" as a voluntary internal or external exile or as a means of self-exclusion from "reality" as it was supposed to be was understood as the only way out of communist reality. Many of these "outsider artists" considered philosophical ideas about madness—especially the alleged connection between genius and insanity—fundamental to the cultural history of European insanity.[18] The theory of divine insanity, which, according to Plato, was characteristic of prophets, poets, and lovers, was constantly fueled by stories about "poetic melancholy" and rumors about insane artist-geniuses.[19] By the same token, some artists took Hans Prinzhorn's work on psychiatry and artistry as a guide, seeking inspiration in the art of outsiders (children, the folk, and the mentally ill). Sometimes this cultural and philosophical background allowed them to escape the norms of their society.

On the other hand, it is useful to recall that officialdom did label many artists and political dissidents as "mad" and declared them "insane." As a result, they were confined to their homes, and placed under a physician's supervision. In these cases, a spurious medical or psychiatric diagnosis was imposed on perfectly sane people. Psychiatry was used as a means of social and political control and dissent was often "medicalized." Statements made by communist leaders justified this practice: for example, in 1964, after Khrushchev visited the Manezh Gallery in Moscow, which included "a display of abstract paintings," he declared these artworks to be "private psycho-pathological distortions of the public conscience."[20] In a similar vein, at the Third National Conference of the Union of Plastic Artists in Bucharest in 1968, Nicolae Ceauşescu ordered artists to depict "specific national features," attacking individualist artistic expression as "a capitalist evil devoid of human and social content."[21] A few months later he declaimed that "only *madmen* could question the vitality of socialism in Romania" (emphasis mine).[22] "Philosophical intoxication" and "sluggish schizophrenia" were also terms widely used to refer to mental disorders in cases where artists and intellectuals disregarded officialdom and the rules of the game. These kinds of statements became "the official rationalization that allowed for the routine use of psychiatry against non-official artists and intellectuals."[23]

While a great deal of attention has been paid to documenting and analyzing the political abuses of psychiatry in the Soviet Union and its satellites, much less attention has been devoted to the other side of the same coin, that is, the use of mental hospitals as a safeguard against worse fates at the hands of the regime.[24] Sometimes artists used mental hospitals as a subterfuge to avoid socialization into communist society. Although this topic deserves further elaboration, the purpose of this chapter is limited to examining artistic madness as an existential and cultural symbol of "dropping out" of socialism rather than as a medical question. However, further studies on mental institutions as places of protection from communist persecution would greatly contribute to a better understanding of the ways in which artists and intellectuals (and others) managed to drop out of the system. As an example of this, it is worth mentioning that several pavilions of the Gătaia Psychiatric Hospital (in Timiş, Romania) hosted painters, writers, musicians, philosophers, and poets who were hospitalized as patients but had been diagnosed as having relatively minor mental problems (like amnesia).[25] As Gabriela Haţegan, the director of the Gătaia hospital and some psychiatrists, including Dr. Mircea Lăzărescu, recount, the artists/patients found a tranquil refuge in the psychiatric hospital, a place where they could create their art freely. In fact, many people called the psychiatric asylum the "Gătaia Art Academy" because several artists produced their works there. This does not mean that these artists and other intellectuals were necessarily dissidents. Their aim was not to confront the regime. All they wanted was to avoid communist "madness." As one of the former patients puts it, "madness was outside and not inside the psychiatric hospital." On the other hand, from the time when it was established in 1966, the Gătaia Psychiatric Hospital was well known for its staff's use of art therapy and psychodrama as two of their main therapies. The use of these therapeutic practices, which are based on artistic production, could also account for the large number of patients from artistic backgrounds who received treatment in the hospital.

Terrified of politics, or just bored with parroting an aesthetic vocabulary imposed by the propaganda machine, some artists attempted to escape by withdrawing from social life. This withdrawal from "reality" was regarded as a coping strategy or as a voluntary exile (either internal or external). Those who decided to withdraw had to choose between an external, self-imposed exile to the physical margins (the asylum, the remote village, the basement, the forest, the outskirts) and the internal way out of communist "reality": withdrawing from adult life and living in a state of mind of perpetual immaturity in which they rejected the adult *status quo*;[26] dreamlike states of mind; and self-induced, euphoric states of mind. External self-exile took place not only in spaces of freedom such as the forest or the mountains, but also in architectural spaces of enclosure within the urban spaces where disciplinary control distributed bodies in space (such as those described by Michael Foucault—the asylum, the home, or even the prison).

In some cases, "mad" artists attempted to combine physical (external) and mental (internal) escape routes. These retreats to the internal or external margins ought to be understood not only as a voluntary alienation from an appalling reality ("based on a subjective feeling that the social world is simply not worth participating in"),[27] but also as a distinctive form of political resistance. These "outsider" artists did not necessarily consider their self-estrangement "rebellious" or "political." On the contrary, they deliberately chose to stay away from politics. As Polish writer and poet Jolanta Stefko posits in her novel *Possible Dreams*, using the character Bolek as her proxy: "I am for nobody, just for myself . . . . Besides, I do not like to talk about politics, I do not like politics, I do not like politicians, because they usurp the right to decide how other people have to live, why they have to live, and if they should live at all."[28]

Yet, as I will argue, the aesthetic interjection of marginal and self-excluded artists and other cultural producers counted as political through and through. By rejecting politics they actually chose a clear political position. They turned their voicelessness into a kind of a political voice precisely because they were confined, *chose* to be confined, to a certain space of exclusion. This "silence," denial of involvement with politics, and remoteness are not apolitical acts because "the political" is defined not only by explicit and direct political action, but also by what Konrád calls "anti-politics"[29] or "the power of the powerless."[30] Political resistance then can take place in different force fields:

not only in mainstream institutions and the official public sphere, but also in the remote zones of our spirituality or in our induced states of mind. Through its unassimilated nature, this resistance is not necessarily purposeful or a matter of clear consciousness. This internal exile from an imposed "reality" functioned both as a form of politics and as prophetic activism. Sometimes, the artist acted like a prophet (or a holy fool) outside the traditional sacred structures mediated by religion. This mental and/or physical retreat from "reality as it was supposed to be" had a psychospiritual dimension. As Tom Block posits, "the true challenge of being human takes place inside in each person's head, not in overcoming the latest prediction of doom. What is called for in each epoch is a positive response to the interior confusion of being human, in a time of calamity. And those that can best offer this affirming impetus to help heal the fragile human soul are the seers and shamans—the prophets."[31] The self-estrangement from communist reality took several distinctive forms in the visual arts. In the following sections, I will briefly examine several instances of this withdrawal from communist reality, focusing on artists from different Eastern European countries who worked in various media. What these artists have in common is the fact that their fellow citizens thought that they were insane. At the same time, their artistic practice may be regarded as what Alexei Yurchak calls a distinctive "politics of indistinction."

## THE OBSESSIVE FORBIDDEN GAZE: MIROSLAV TICHÝ

Miroslav Tichý's photographs are an example of internal self-confinement artistically manifested at the level of personal obsessions. Miroslav Tichý was a Moravian "Art Brute photographer" whose lifelong performance of self-confinement consisted of obsessively taking photographs of the women of Kyjov, his hometown. He returned again and again to the same subject matter: dreamlike women in their everyday surroundings. This artistic obsession was labeled by some art critics as "compulsive behavior" or "borderline psychosis."[32]

For more than fifty years he lived in Kyjov as a complete recluse, at the periphery of the art world, exhibiting his self-constructed madness through the lenses of his camera as an obsession with an eroticized reality. For decades it seems, Tichý's neighbors avoided him because he completely ignored the rules of personal hygiene, stopped shaving and cutting his hair, and preferred to sit on the roof of his mother's house all day simply enjoying the sun while others were hard at work, building "the new world of socialism." When he was not contemplating the sun, he would take thousands of photographs of women, who were usually unaware that they were being photographed. From the 1960s until 1985, Tichý took black-and-white photographs of women on a daily basis (about ninety pictures a day): women in bathing suits, women in negligees, women playing cards, young women, old women, skinny women, sensual women, fleshy women, women waiting on a bench for someone, women behind shop counters, women aware and unaware of being gazed at from a distance.

Tichý emerged out of oblivion late in the 1990s, only after his neighbor, the Czech art collector and Zurich-based psychiatrist Roman Buxbaum (who currently enjoys worldwide acclaim for presenting Tichý to the art world), "discovered" his thousands of blurry photographs of local women. Until his death in 2011, Tichý continued to live in Kyjov in deep seclusion without even attending art exhibitions. Meanwhile, the international art world grew fascinated with his "charming oddity" and his photographs were on display in art museums from Switzerland to the United States. A 2009 report in the art magazine *Vice* described his confined existence: "These days, Tichý continues to live in Kyjov but is essentially unreachable. He suffers from dementia and has to be taken care of by his neighbor. He has most likely destroyed the majority of the work he produced over the course of his life in what can romantically be described as fits of artistic madness."[33]

Curator Michael Hoppen describes him in the following terms:

A student at the Academy of Arts in Prague, Tichý left following the communist overthrow of 1948. Unwilling to subordinate to the political system he spent some eight years in prison and psychiatric wards for no reason, other than he was 'different' and considered subversive. Upon his release he became an outsider, occupying his time by obsessively taking photographs of the women of his home town, using homemade cameras constructed from tin cans, children's spectacle lenses, rubber bands, scotch tape and other junk found on the streets.[34]

Because art students in communist Czechoslovakia were required to work within the Socialist Realist canon, Tichý left the Academy of Arts, where he had initially been studying painting. Women and nudes were no longer the subject matter of painting; miners, workers, and "the new man" took their place. Tichý refused the canon and the "new reality" altogether. His refusal to produce an art which respected the ideology of the Communist Party could be interpreted more as a form of critical exit than as a type of straightforward activism. His resistance and criticism reside in his willingness to live and create an art free of any ideological constraints. Women in bathing suits or in negligees are not what Tichý's art is all about. His art is motivated by his visceral and painful struggle to live and to "see," freely and without distortion, two irreconcilable worlds: the one imposed by the communist regime and the one he saw naturally, through the lens of his improvised camera. It is clear that he did not overtly criticize the communist regime. What he did was slightly different: he obsessively documented the other reality in an attempt to re-eroticize the feminine body through art under the pressure of a political regime that controlled childbirth, the length of women's skirts, cookbooks, and the amount of makeup and jewelry a woman was allowed to wear. His photographs did not display women as mothers whose reproduction was strictly regulated by the regime or as "revolutionary comrades" but as motifs, fairies, and appealing beings. The incessant interest in womanhood untrammeled by the state was meant to replace the communist obsession with motherhood. That is why Tichý's women are rarely mothers too.

Yet to some extent, his photographs can be interpreted as instances of a blurry and vague erotic art which engages the viewer's imagination but does not leave space for any traditional aesthetic conventions. The artist's obsession ought not be understood as one man's obsession with the act of eroticism but rather as an obsession with the idea of eroticism in a context in which "erotica was just a dream." Contemporary art historians posit that Tichý himself once said that he was not interested in chasing women or in getting along with them because for him woman was a motif and nothing else interested him anymore: "Even when I see a woman I like—and perhaps I could have tried to make contact—I realize that I'm not actually interested. Instead, I pick up a pencil and draw her. The erotic is just a dream, anyway. The world is only an illusion, our illusion . . . . Enjoyment is a concept that I absolutely disallow."[35]

His intimate close-ups of women should not be interpreted as a merely voyeuristic practice but rather, as an escape route taken on the outer margins of the art world. Tichý's photographic obsession has nothing to do with chasing women or visualized sexual encounters; it is instead about chasing a politically constructed "reality" that left no place for an idiosyncratic lifestyle or a tender affection for femininity. His art is about the forbidden gaze, an obsessive self-internment in one's mind, self-exile, and melancholy. The photographs are not easy to read or to take pleasure in, and, as one art critic puts it:

> [W]ithin Tichý's gaze, there is no pleasure principle at work. Here again, voyeurism and desire become another mere excuse to define the bars of the cage that has always irremediably separated Tichý from reality, while taking on the dimension of a much more generic argument specific to his era: the fundamental alienation among the human being and its historical present.[36]

Unlike other distinctive subversive visual art pieces produced under communism in which the female body epitomizes political resistance, Tichý's photographs do not criticize socialist reality at the expense of the women represented in his art by sexually objectifying them because pleasure does not seem to be the locus of resistance for him.[37] The female bodies in his photographs and drawings look esoteric, mysterious, and outwardly beautiful without necessarily serving specifically masculine desires "for political liberation in pleasurable ways."[38] The beauty of these dreamy photographs is not an eye-catching, disinterested, and pleasure-seeking type of beauty, but a difficult and traumatic one. Through the eye of his improvised, low-tech camera Tichý displays a certain poetics of femininity without necessarily making claims of political rebellion via female erotica or "the erotic as power." In other words, the artist refuses the pleasurable gaze and "enjoyment *despite*"[39] as artistic-political strategies, apparently opting for the obsessive forbidden gaze as both self-therapy and political critique. His artistic retreat from "reality as it was supposed to be" is a political response to the Soviet panopticon's surveillance of the individual. At the same time, we can understand Tichý's low-tech, homemade cameras and obsessive "voyeurism" as an alternate, perhaps a rival, system of surveillance.

## LIVING A SUNFLOWER'S LIFE: ŞTEFAN BERTALAN'S ART OF COMBINED PARADOX AND NEUROSIS

Ştefan Bertalan became a "case" in Romanian contemporary art when art theorists and art historians decided that his work was difficult to recuperate for art history because it combined a certain form of neurosis and paradoxical impersonations. Bertalan was born in 1930 in Hunedoara, Romania. He worked as a teacher at the Art High School in Timişoara and he was a founding member of the artistic collectives Sigma and Group 111. His artistic production is still difficult to assess. In art theorist Călin Dan's interpretation, Bertalan was not "a political dissident, but a dissident from reality, as we all experience it as social conformists, and his distancing from this conformity increased through the years until complete silence."[40] In 1960, Bertalan began to question state-sponsored art by abandoning all figurative representation. He researched Western art and then produced a Romanian formalism that was eventually transfigured into a highly spiritual approach to abstraction. Bertalan's artistic production can be read as a document of his own personal tragedy. By the same token, Romanian curator and art critic Coriolan Babeţi interpreted Bertalan's tragedy in terms of "creative *neurosis*" (emphasis mine).[41]

Bertalan merged visual interpretations of natural phenomena with his own lifestyle. His art displayed and portrayed the subtle mechanisms of individual alienation. In a ritual practice, he observed and documented the destiny of a plant from its creation to its disappearance. His "Prolix Diary" became the keeper of all the details of daily routine. Every detail of everyday everydayness is photographed or sketched in the diary, including the plant's evolution and all its changes in growth. Then, the sunflower turned into the artist's beloved interlocutor. Allegedly, he used to speak with a specific sunflower from his garden, and, as a result of these conversations, Bertalan performed the artistic action entitled *I have Been Living with a Sunflower for 130 Days* (at the Architecture Institute in Bucharest in 1979). The work consisted of an installation focusing on a dead sunflower with pages from the diary, drawings, and studies documenting the plant's growth and development hanging from the dead plant. In the same year, Bertalan displayed several other artistic actions (happenings, installations, and performances) in different but "peripheral" locations: *Neuer Weg, Swimming Through the Working Pocket* (1979, in his own studio in Timişoara); *Eternity—the Juice of Raspberry for the Last Night of the Year* (Gârda de Sus, in the Apuseni Mountains); *I am Dispassionate and I am Proud of the Epoch in Which I Live . . . . So I Have to Rest, Do Not Be Agitated Because Tomorrow Again We Have No Possibility* (Banat, Semenic Mountains) and *In His Dream a War-like Telegram Lost Its Left Leg* (Timişoara). His self-marginalized artistic actions were not conceived for presentation to a larger public: the artist performed a task for himself rather than performing in a show for others. His performances have a teleological dimension rather than a spectacular aspect. In a similar fashion, in a 2006 interview, visual artist Geta Brătescu told me, "[W]ell, art is a matter of interiority . . . I never enjoyed big manifestations because of the masses . . . I don't know why I don't like the masses and I don't want to be involved in this type of events. Art is a privilege, an individual privilege, a way of understanding which differs from person to person."[42]

Bertalan's way of understanding and performing art coincides with his understanding of alienation as a severe form of the inability to adapt. His art pieces are chronicles about himself. A diary full of drawings, dated 1977, was entitled "Self-Therapy." On one of its pages, Bertalan wrote: "Every morning I have to finish a drawing in order to cure myself. They want to transform our spirit into slaves. They watch me all day long."[43]

Although apparently there is no proof that the Secret Police (Securitate) really spied on Bertalan, in his mind and work this danger was real and ubiquitous. Many times he confessed to his friends: "[L]ook at these holes (pointing to the wood fence that separated his yard from unknown and hostile neighbors), I'm being watched at every step."[44] As Babeţi puts it, he thought that the Securitate disguised themselves as forest workers or tractor drivers and they were responsible for preventing him from taking refuge in the mountains. Another of Bertalan's obsessions was that an airplane was always following him in the Apuseni Mountains. In response to these worries, the artist used abstract drawings to record "the everyday routes the patients of the wards moved along in the hospital aisles."[45]

Bertalan's art displayed the mechanisms of refusal, alienation, and trauma. As Babeți put it, "Bertalan did not search for the limitations of art and forms and he never seemed to me to pay attention to how much novelty he created. There was as much originality in his work as the amount of drama he had to communicate."[46] His artistically neurotic description of everyday life is a lucid diary about existence as such: "Bertalan makes his work the trace left by this flabbergasted perplexity when faced with history. He is just the sensor of his fellow men and of history dramatically experienced in the first person."[47] By experiencing history in the first person the artist refused both the official narrative and the effort of dealing with it. He found refuge and peace of mind in a vegetal Eden, "where he can be away from the authoritarian pressure of a violent power that threatens his existence all the time, as he, in turn, refuses to recognize its authority, and confronts it by opposing it with the paradise of the plants, a space where protest, delight, understanding and happiness, find a meeting point."[48] Bertalan not only loved plants and followed their growth but he also lived in symbiosis with them. Like his beloved plants, he exploited disaster to meet his special needs: he shared with them the tendency to prioritize private life and the struggle for survival. Both the artist and the vegetal employ medium-specific "hair-raising strategies" to engineer apocalypses and catastrophes.

## THE NECROREALISTS' MADNESS AS "POLITICAL INDISTINCTION"

The Necrorealists emerged in Leningrad's unofficial art scene in the 1980s during *perestroika*. The art collective was not formed by professional artists. The founding members included Vladimir Kustov, Evgenii Iufit, and Sergei Serp. Because the group accepted basically everyone (factory workers, students, nurses, librarians, and others), it is hard to detect any homogeneous set of aesthetic concerns. However, their predilection for cinematic underground, radical aesthetics, and dark humor triggered the development of a distinctive artistic method—the "necro-method." The very first pieces produced by Necrorealists were staged photographs displaying the group's members wearing zombie makeup. Not long after this stage, their artistic production started to diversify, including spontaneous performances that simulated fights, extreme violence, and failed suicides. Other impromptu performances displayed naked men running aimlessly; a full-size mannequin (stolen from the Institute of Criminological Medicine) beaten with wooden sticks in the streets; various impersonations of cruelty and "un-deadness"; and clownish hooliganism. Later on, the group started to circulate short *samizdat* films in which the public could experience absurd and grotesque representations of death and pain. All these visual productions were not intended as "art production" but rather as public provocations. These series of provocations performed as "experiments" spread rapidly among young people (and other artistic circles in Leningrad), and, as Alexei Yurchak points out, they "became known in slang as *klinika* (psychiatric clinic)."[49] The public's reception of these provocations emphasized the "madness" and the "absurdity" of these performances. The curators of a 1993 exhibit of the Necrorealists' work in the US compiled responses to the Necrorealists' performances, voiced in 1989 by viewers of the popular Leningrad TV show *Piatoe koleso* (*The Fifth Wheel*). As these responses (which appear in the exhibition catalog, *Russian Necrocrealism: Shock Therapy for a New Culture*) stress: "From the artistic standpoint it is ordinary junk: Insanity! Total absurdity! These people who made this, are they mentally all right? Horrifying! No meaning in it whatsoever. This is a dreadful pathology . . . ."[50]

Yet, the Necrorealists were not concerned at all (at least at the beginning) with "the artistic standpoint." Evgenii Iufit and his colleagues were not sure whether they should think of themselves as artists or not. By the same token, they had doubts about whether their pieces had any political connotations at all. Yurchak claims that the Necrorealists' performances and "provocations" are not political in the usual sense because these actions are neither oppositional nor dissident.[51] He supports this claim with declarations from the Necrorealists, who considered politics "uninteresting" and "irrelevant," arguing that their search for truth was organic rather than ideological. Yurchak attempts to theoretically frame his argument about the Necrorealists' radical aesthetics by relying on Niels Bohr's seminal distinction between "clear truth" (the opposite of which is a lie) and "deep truth" ("opposed by another equally deep truth"). According to this interpretation, the Necrorealists were preoccupied with their search for *istina* (the Russian concept of truth, which parallels Bohr's "deep truth"). In other words, they were not interested in politics because they did not feel they were Soviet citizens and they were not interested in unmasking Soviet lies about reality and restoring *pravda* (Bohr's "clear truth"). Their organic difference consisted of their complete separation (both spatial and temporal) from what a Soviet citizen was supposed to epitomize and what being a Soviet citizen was supposed to entail. At first glance the Necrorealists' absurd actions and "experiments" look apolitical since these people were neither supporters of nor dissenters from the Soviet system.

However, in a later study, Yurchak reconsiders the political dimension of these actions and ways of living by introducing the concept of "political indistinction," which is inspired by Giorgio Agamben's "zones of indistinction."[52] This kind of politics goes beyond dissident opposition and it was indecipherable to the Soviet authorities. It is exactly this illegibility that renders the Necrorealists' actions political. Although the Necrorealists expressed their total disinterest in politics, for Yurchak, like Agamben and Foucault, there is no "outside" of politics. The Necrorealist's actions should not be understood as "negations of politics"—nor as an escape from the political—but as forms of subversion. Their *insane* actions did not attempt to contest the system's representations of reality but instantiated selves, practices, and lifestyles that the Soviet system could not represent at all. In other words, their artistic practice does not operate within the political boundaries of "for" or "against" (the Soviet state) because it circumvents this dichotomy by occasioning an unassimilated form of resistance. For the Soviet state this form of resistance was not only difficult to grasp but also hard to assess. Yet, as Yurchak argues, the group's name (*necro* = death and realism) came to mean two things simultaneously: a distinctive interest in death (and its materializations and representations) and an ironic attempt to locate this art movement within a genealogy and history of existing art styles (such as Realism, Socialist Realism, Neorealism, Neo-Documentary-Realism, and so on).[53] The very name "Necrorealism" is paradoxical because death is combined with realism (which alludes to life or living). However, the bare fact that the artistic collective's name also signifies an ironic attempt to localize the movement in the larger picture of Real-*isms* (Socialist Realism included) implies a certain degree of politicality because, as theorists of irony posit, "all irony is political."[54] At the same time, the Necrorealists' attempt to impose a style (a necro style) on the "real" makes it another "ism." The irony is indeed very bitter: since Socialist Realism attempted to impose a certain "style" (socialist) on reality, Necrorealism emphasizes the condition of the human being on the verge of death, in the words of one expert, "indicating some pathology." As many art curators and theorists suggest, Necrorealism—"full of absurdity and black humor and based on forensic medicine textbooks"—was born as a form of social-political protest: "this genre overturned the established Soviet concept of death as the only possible heroic 'death in the name of Motherland.'"[55] Necrorealists staged the boldness of death as such, disembodying it from ideological heroism.

At the same time, death and extreme violence also targeted the New Man promised by the communist *status quo*. The New Man's image is replaced with the image of "absolute death" (not alive and not dead). Insane behavior and excesses such as decomposing cadavers in the Necrorealists' films might be understood as an uprising against the Soviet regimes of discipline and representation. Yet, at the same time, as Yurchak argues, they undermined the meanings the system gave to the political without directly confronting these meanings. Although Yurchak envisions the politics of the Necrorealists as overcoming the binary of oppression/resistance and locates their politics in a "zone of indistinction," we can still envision resistance as an unassimilated moment (neither separated from nor fully integrated). The fact that "resistance" is not envisioned as a matter of clear consciousness does not annihilate its subversive power.

## CONCLUSION

As I have shown, "artistic madness" in the Eastern bloc sometimes assumed the form of an internal retreat from the imposed "reality." In the panoptic regime of socialism, some artists disturbed the omnipresent surveillance by choosing internal escape routes of "madness." External, physical self-exile on the margins of society was still subjected to the omnipresent surveillance as the artist could still be seen, and being seen meant being exposed and vulnerable. However, although the guards in the tower could watch all the prisoners without being watched in turn (which is the main premise on which a panoptic regime functions), the guards did not have access to what was going on in the prisoners' minds, unless the prisoner, as Foucault pointed out, "inscribed in himself the power relation in which he simultaneously plays both roles, becoming the principle of his own subjection."[56]

However, as this chapter argues, there is no clear-cut dialectic between hegemony and the powerless because the "mad" is not rendered disempowered. The artistic retreat to the inner margins can be regarded as a strategy of "dropping out" of communist reality by instantiating new forms of politics. These tiny acts of resistance operate in a different *durée*, embodying an inherent reality and its subversive performance, which becomes the expression of an existential rebellion. The crux of the matter is that even "voicelessness," the retreat to one's inner self, the lack of awareness of being involved in an anti-politics, the denial of political involvement and reclusiveness are all political acts because they instantiate a form of dissensus (what Ranciére calls "the real politics" as opposed to *"façade* politics").[57] Although, these forms of creative internal exile did not openly and loudly confront the official politics, they cannot be rendered as ineffective or powerless because resistance takes place in different force fields, and sometimes in the most unexpected places and spaces. Such places can be Tichý's homemade cameras and his obsessive "voyeurism" as an alternate, perhaps rival system of surveillance or Bertalan's meticulous diaries of visual surveillance, which counter the "reality" of the public sphere. The self-inflicted marginality of "mad artists" overcame their physical marginality by rendering the "mad man" powerful.

## NOTES

1. Peter Fritzsche, "On the Subjects of Resistance," *Kritika: Explorations in Russian and Eurasian History* 1, no. 1 (2000): 147–52.

2. Socialist Realism was the Soviet Union's official cultural policy, which Stalin institutionalized in 1934. As a consequence, the arts and cultural production turned into a form of government propaganda. Art was reduced to being merely a source of ideological information and artists were reduced to "singleness of aspirations, singleness

of idea and singleness of aim" as Bernice Glatzer Rosenthal puts it in *New Myth, New World: From Nietzsche to Stalinism* (University Park, PA: Pennsylvania State University Press, 2004), 323. Any other artistic efforts had to be suppressed. However, there is still an ongoing debate on the paternity of the doctrine of Socialist Realism. On the one hand, some cultural historians, such as Sheila Fitzpatrick, argue that this cultural policy was the product of Joseph Stalin's totalitarian state. According to Fitzpatrick, before Stalin, the state's attitude toward the arts and artists was "soft," more relaxed. In this context, Socialist Realism was the result of Stalin's ambition to solidify his power. In other words, for Fitzpatrick, the artistic oppression instituted by Socialist Realism is envisioned as the product of a single leader's will. See Sheila Fitzpatrick, *The Cultural Front: Power and Culture in Revolutionary Russia* (Ithaca: Cornell University Press, 1992), 105. For other cultural historians, Socialist Realism was not fundamentally a Stalinist doctrine. Although Stalin officially implemented the doctrine, Socialist Realism was "the logical continuation of the actions and values of the early Bolshevik state . . . the concept of controlling artists and using them to serve the Soviet people was a part of Bolshevik mindset and practice from the very beginning of the regime." Maya Krishnan, "Transformation of the Human Consciousness: The Origins of Socialism Realism in the Soviet Union," *The Concord Review* 21, no. 1 (2010).

3. Péter György, "Hungarian Marginal Art in the Period of Late Socialism," in *Postmodernism and the Postsocialist Condition: Politicized Art under Late Socialism*, ed. Aleš Erjavec (Berkeley: University of California Press, 2003), 179.

4. It should be mentioned that "collectivism" does not always connote submission to authority and "selfless" communities as it did in socialist and communist contexts. For instance, the term "collectivism" in Bakunin's sense connotes a group of cooperating producers and consumers. It has nothing in common with later usage in which the term comes to mean "state socialism's ownership."

5. A close associate of Stalin, Andrei Zhdanov was in charge of the Soviet Union's cultural policy, 1946–1948. Some sources indicate that toward the end of his life, Zhdanov lost favor with Stalin and died in a sanatorium as a result of an intentional misdiagnosis. See Jonathan Haslam, *Russia's Cold War* (New Haven: Yale University Press, 2011), 104.

6. Victor Terras, "Phenomenological Observations on the Aesthetic of Socialist Realism," *Slavic and East European Journal* 23, no. 4 (1979): 448.

7. For more on the meanings of "political art" under socialism, see Maria-Alina Asavei, "A Theoretical Excursus on the Concept of Political Art in Communism and its Aftermath," *Studia Politica* 11, no. 4 (2011): 647–61.

8. *Literaturnaia gazeta*, September 21, 1946, 83. My translation is from the Russian.

9. Ann Demaitre, "The Great Debate on Socialist Realism," *The Modern Language Journal* 50, no. 5 (1966): 265.

10. Andrei Zhdanov's "Speech at the First All-Union Congress of Soviet Writers 1934," in *Modernism: An Anthology of Sources and Documents*, ed. Vassiliki Kolocotroni, Jane Goldman, and Olga Taxidou (Chicago: University of Chicago Press, 1998), 525.

11. Ion Grigorescu, interview with the author, Bucharest, April 14, 2007.

12. Sabin Bălaşa ranked highest among Ceauşescu's preferred painters. At present, his paintings are still appreciated by those who are nostalgic about communism, and they sell for very large sums. Contemporary art critics consider Bălaşa's paintings very kitschy. Yet despite this, the artist saw his work as art "beyond time."

13. Such as Pavel Susara, Radu Ionescu, and Vladimir Bulat.

14. Vladimir Bulat, "Sabin Bălaşa o Fosila Prosperă şi Sfidătoare," http://www. nettime.org/Lists-Archives/nettime-ro-0502/msg00018.html.

15. Mihai Botez, *Intelectualii în Europa de Est* (Bucharest: Fundaţia Culturală Română, 1993), 52–53.

16. Interview with Blaga Dimitrova quoted in Boyko Vassilev, Lucie Kavanova, Anita Komuves, Wojciech Kosc, Sinziana Demian, and Pavol Szalai, "The Arts: An End to "Doubleness," *Transitions Online*, October 9, 2009, 63.

17. Interview with Milota Havrankova quoted in Boyko Vassilev et al., "The Arts," 70.

18. Here the term "outsider artists" refers to the artists' status and not to formal (stylistic) criteria of the pieces. Work coming out of peasants' homes or mental institutions was not called "art" until French artist Jean Dubuffet gave it his seal of approval. Influenced by Hans Prinzhorn's work on psychiatry and artistry, Dubuffet coined the term "Art Brut" in 1945.

19. For more on philosophical conceptions of insanity, see Angela Brintlinger and Ilya Vinitsky, *Madness and the Mad in Russian Culture* (Toronto: University of Toronto Press, 2007), 169–72.

20. Andrei Erofeev, "Nonofficial Art: Soviet Artists of the 1960s," in *Primary Documents: A Sourcebook for Eastern and Central European Art since the 1950s*, ed. Laura J. Hoptman and Tomáš Pospiszyl (New York: Museum of Modern Art, 2002), 42. Erofeev is cited in Claire Bishop, "Zones of Indistinguishability: Collective Actions Group and Participatory Art," *E-flux* 29 (2011), http://www.e-flux.com/journal/zones-of-indistinguishability-collective-actions-group-and-participatory-art/.

21. Nicolae Ceauşescu, quoted in Kenneth McBride, "A Fiery Lens Aims at Surface," ch. 2 in "Eastern European Time-Based Art and the Communist Project of Emergence and Post-Communist Disintegration" (PhD diss., Plymouth University, 2009), agora8-art documents, agora8.org/kennethmcbride_thesis/kennethmcbride_thesis_8/.

22. Nicolae Ceauşescu, quoted in Vladimir Tismăneanu, "Behind the Façade of the Ceauşescu Regime," Radio Free Europe Radio Liberty, June 28, 2008, http://www.rferl.org/content/Behind_Facade_Ceausescu_Regime/1145867.html.

23. McBride, "A Fiery Lens."

24. There is a great deal of scholarship on the political abuse of psychiatry. Significant work includes Sidney Bloch and Peter Reddaway, *Soviet Psychiatric Abuse: The Shadow over World Psychiatry* (Boulder, CO: Westview Press, 1985); Ben Bursten, *Psychiatry on Trial: Fact and Fantasy in the Courtroom* (Jefferson, NC: McFarland, 2001); Paul Calloway, *Russian/Soviet and Western Psychiatry: A Contemporary Comparative Study* (New York: Wiley, 1993); Zhores A. Medvedev and Roy A. Medvedev, *A Question of Madness: Repression by Psychiatry in the Soviet Union* (New York: Macmillan, 1971).

25. For more information on the Gătaia Psychiatric Hospital before 1989, I consulted Anton Borbely's article "Ospiciul din Gătaia-Refugiu pentru Intelectuali in Perioada Totalitara," *RL/România Liberă*, October 30, 2006, http://www.romanialibera.ro/actualitate/locale/ospiciul-din-gataia-refugiu-pentru-intelectuali-in-perioada-totalitara-78469; Ioan C. Cucu and Toma I. Cucu, *Psihiatria sub Dictatura* (Piatra Neamț: f.e., 2005); Ioan C. Cucu, Dragoș Marcu, and Andrian Miclea, *Represiunea Psihiatrică in Romania Comunista* (Bucharest: Editura Foaia Nationala, 2011), http://www.memoria.ro/marturii/perioade_istorice/perioada_comunista/represiunea_psihiatrica_in_romania_comunista/2107/.

26. Svetlana Vassileva-Karagyozova, "Voluntary Social Marginalization as a Survival Strategy in Polish Postcommunist Accounts of Childhood," *Sarmatian Review* 29, no. 1 (2009): 1436.

27. Nick Couldry, "Culture and Citizenship: The Missing Link?" *European Journal of Cultural Studies* 9, no. 3 (2006): 326.

28. Vassileva-Karagyozova, "Voluntary Social Marginalization," 1436.

29. See György Konrád, *Antipolitics: An Essay*, trans. Richard E. Allen (San Diego: Harcourt Brace Jovanovich, 1984).

30. Vaclav Havel et al., *The Power of the Powerless: Citizens Against the State in Central-Eastern Europe* (London: Routledge, 1985).

31. Tom Block, "Prophetic Activist Art: Activism Beyond Oppositionality," *International Journal of the Arts in Society* 3, no. 2 (2008): 23.

32. See for example, Susie Garden's "Tichy's Madcap Voyeurism," *No New Enemies Network*, May 7, 2012, http://nonewenemies.net/2012/05/07/tichys-madcap-voyeurism/.

33. "Miroslav Tichy," *Vice Magazine*, July 2, 2009, http://www.vice.com/read/miroslav-tichy-933-v16n7.

34. "Unique Photographs, Previously Unseen in the UK, at Michael Hoppen Gallery," *artdaily.org*, http://www.artdaily.com/index.asp?int_sec=11&int_new=37704&int_modo=1.

35. Interview with Tichý conducted by Roman Buxbaum in *Miroslav Tichý*, ed. Quentin Bajac (Paris: Centre Pompidou Editions, 2008), 16.

36. Natasha Christia, "Miroslav Tichý-Forbbiden Gaze," *Eyemazing* (Summer 2009), http://www.mutualart.com/OpenArticle/Miroslav-Tichy---Forbidden-Gaze/4D1E0833A892523C.

37. Especially the satiric films from pre-1989 Eastern Europe, which use the female body to convey a political critique at the expense of women's sexual objectification under the gaze of the male characters and directors (e.g., Péter Timár's *Egészséges Erotika/Sound Eroticism* [1985] and Jiri Menzel's *Closely Watched Trains* [1966]). My claim is that Tichý does not want to convey a political critique at the expense of women's sexuality.

38. Lilla Töke, "Not through My Skin: Political Resistance and the Female Body in Péter Timár's Egészséges Erotika/Sound Eroticism (1985)," *Studies in East European Cinema* 4, no. 2 (2013): 129–42.

39. The term "enjoyment *despite*" connotes "a transgressive pleasure that defies the communist state's hegemonic position." Töke, "Not Through My Skin": 140.

40. Călin Dan, "East Art Map Romania," on Stroom Den Haag's website, http://www.stroom.nl/media/dan.pdf.

41. See Coriolan Babeți's article "The Bertalan Case: The Artistic Experiment as an Exercise of Neurotic Sublimination," in *Primary Documents, A Sourcebook for Eastern and Central European Art since the 1950s*, ed. Laura J. Hoptman and Tomáš Pospiszyl (New York: MOMA, 1999), 53–56.

42. Geta Brătescu, interview with the author, Bucharest, May 2006.

43. Ştefan Bertalan, "Prolix Diary," (May 22, 1977, unpublished diary/artistic object). I consulted the "Prolix Diary" when it was in Bertalan's possession. Since his death, its whereabouts are unknown.

44. Babeți, "The Bertalan Case," 54.

45. Art critic Coriolan Babeți identified the place as the mental institution in Gătaia. Babeți received all the information about the period the artist spent at this institution from Bertalan himself.

46. See Coriolan Babeți's article "The Bertalan Case" published in the catalogue *Experiment in Romanian Art since 1960*, edited by Soros Center for Contemporary Art (Bucharest, 1997), 198.

47. Ibid.

48. Erwin Kessler, *The Self-punishing One: The Art and Romania in the 80s and 90s* (Bucharest: Romanian Cultural Institute, 2010).

49. Alexei Yurchak, "Necro-Utopia: The Politics of Indistinction and the Aesthetics of the Non-Soviet," *Current Anthropology* 49, no. 2 (2008): 202.

50. This retrospective exhibition of Necrorealist art was organized at the Dorothy Uber Bryan Gallery in Columbus, Ohio (USA) in 1993. The exhibition was curated by Ellen Berry, Jacqueline S. Nathan, and Anesa Miller Pogacar. See Ellen Berry, Jacqueline S. Nathan, and Anesa Miller Pogacar, eds., *Russian Necrorealism: Shock Therapy for a New Culture* (Columbus, OH: Bowling Green State University, 1993).

51. Yurchak, "Necro-Utopia," 199.

52. Yurchak, "Necro-Utopia," 199–215.

53. Alexei Yurchak, "Suspending the Political: Late Soviet Artistic Experiments on the Margins of the State," *Poetics Today* 29, no. 4 (2008): 713–33.

54. Linda Hutcheon, *Irony's Edge: The Theory and Politics of Irony* (London and New York: Routledge, 1993), 6.

55. "Necrorealism Alive and Well in Moscow," *ArtKabinett*, September 20, 2011, http://www.artkabinett.com/ak-file/necrorealism-alive-and-well-moscow.

56. Michael Foucault, *Discipline and Punish: The Birth of the Prison* (London: Allen Lane, 1977), 202–3.

57. Jacques Ranciére, *Dissensus: On Politics and Aesthetics* (New York: Continuum, 2010).

*Chapter 4*

# Student Activists and Yugoslavia's Islamic Revival

## *Sarajevo, 1970–1975*

### Madigan Andrea Fichter

In early January 1972, the students at one of Sarajevo's oldest educational institutions refused to attend classes. Like many of the era's other rebellious youth, these young people used public confrontation with authority as a means of asserting their demands. Distinguishing them from other members of their cohort, however, the strikers were students at Yugoslavia's premier madrassa, or Islamic religious school, and many were also advocates for a new and updated form of Islam that would be relevant in the modern world and global in scope. The young people at the Gazi Husrev-bey madrassa were, therefore, simultaneously part of Yugoslavia's wider, and for the most part secular, student movements, as well as early participants in what scholars have referred to as Bosnia's "Islamic revival."[1] The intersection of student activism and Islamic revival helps us to re-evaluate two distinct areas of scholarship that have not previously been considered together, while also allowing us to consider the issue of dropping out of socialism.

The students at Gazi Husrev-bey, and particularly the opinions they advanced through their journal, *Zemzem*, show that Yugoslav student activism extended well beyond the more commonly studied student Left. In their willingness to openly confront the authorities with complaints and demands, and in the specific content of their goals and interests, the madrassa students were clearly part of the complex and multifaceted student movements of Yugoslavia. Even if the madrassa students' ultimate aims did not completely align with those of the secular student leaders in Belgrade or Zagreb, these young Muslims shared with their counterparts the desire for a more participatory education, better employment opportunities, a responsive state apparatus, an interest in anticolonial politics, a sense of connection to a wider, global movement, and an assertion of the vanguard role of youth in addressing these perceived wrongs. Investigating the madrassa students' activities therefore deepens our understanding of Yugoslavia's student opposition movements.[2] Rather than only taking a narrow view of student politics as inherently of the Left, this more expansive analysis shows us the richness and complexity of Yugoslav student rebellion, which encompassed far more political and cultural identities than acknowledged by the scholarly literature.

While the scholarship on Yugoslavia's student movements has entirely omitted Islamic activism, making this connection allows us to better see the complexities of Yugoslav political Islam. The Islamic revival was not just the product of radical influences from abroad, but also the continuation of the country's tradition of student rebellion, which was itself embedded in the local-global framework of the 1960s and 1970s. As Bosnian Muslim activists began to emerge as prominent members of the dissident community in the 1980s, among them former pupils of the Gazi Husrev-bey madrassa, critics accused them of plotting to overthrow the Yugoslav state and impose *shari'a* law.[3] In response, sympathetic observers argued that Bosnia's religious Muslim community was, on the contrary, remarkably understated in its activities and goals.[4] Zachary Irwin, Mitja Velikonja, Xavier Bougarel,[5] Ivo Banac, Anto Knežević,[6] and Sabrina Ramet have all focused on the late 1970s as the moment in which political Islam developed. These scholars particularly highlight the growing conflict between the socialist state and Islamic dissidents that culminated in the 1983 trial of Alija Izetbegović and thirteen others on charges of "counterrevolutionary" activity, and conspiracy.[7]

However, this chronology entirely omits the activities of the earlier contributions of the madrassa students, and leaves unnoted the fact that the students of Gazi Husrev-bey had long been discussing many of the same issues for which the dissidents were later prosecuted, suggesting an even longer trajectory for the movement's development. Furthermore, the major aims of Gazi Husrev-bey's Islamic activists were neither as passive as some supporters might have argued, nor as extreme as their opponents charged. In the period under examination here, *Zemzem*'s contributors sought to promote a variant of Islam that encouraged greater religiosity and observance of Islamic principles, was active in defense of Muslims and in opposition to colonial repression, but still comfortable in the modern world, and tolerant of other beliefs and systems of thought.

The students' commitment to Islam also provides an interesting analytical frame through which to further consider the notion of "dropping out of socialism," and specifically, what that could have meant for religious Yugoslavs and their relationship to the state. The daily rituals and practices of Islam compelled one to temporarily step away from socialism, and carved out a space in which one was encouraged to think about values, relationships, and traditions other than those fostered by the socialist state. Furthermore, through their engagement with global Islamic trends, the students of Gazi Husrev-bey were dropping *in* to a network of fellow Muslims and activists in pursuit of an Islamic revival.[8] But, at the same time, the madrassa students were not seeking to permanently or fully withdraw themselves from either the Yugoslav state, or from the society in which they lived. Members of the Islamic revival appear, in these early stages, relatively convinced that they could prod the state into change, and therefore sought to compel officials into better respecting their needs as religious Muslims, and the Islamic hierarchy into better accommodating their needs as students and young people.

I therefore propose that dropping out of socialism was not necessarily a permanent or an absolute condition. Rather, these Islamic activists show us that attending prayers, refusing to attend classes, identifying as a member of an observant religious community, or imagining oneself as a member of a wider, global Islamic world did not necessarily mean that one had to sever all ties to mainstream Yugoslav life. People had complicated, multifaceted connections to the world in which they lived, and they were capable of dropping out of some aspects, remaining engaged in others, and positioning themselves within frameworks beyond the boundaries of socialist Yugoslavia. The concept of moving in, out, and between socialism and other cultural and political networks reveals a greater flexibility on the part of the socialist state and society than is often assumed, while also accounting for the nuanced relationship that many people had toward the major structures in their lives.

This study primarily draws on *Zemzem,* the newspaper published by and for the madrassa's students, focusing on the years between 1970 and 1975. As the major source of information readily available about these students, *Zemzem* allows us to explore the activities of Bosnia's religiously inclined young people as reported by them. Still, the wider Islamic revival most likely included individuals not associated with the paper or the madrassa or even the *Islamska vjerska zajednica* (Islamic Religious Community), the administrative body charged with organizing and overseeing Muslim religious affairs within socialist Yugoslavia. This chapter is therefore not a comprehensive view of an entire movement, but rather a particular, youthful piece of it.

## THE EVOLUTION OF A MOVEMENT

The Gazi Husrev-bey madrassa was established in Sarajevo in 1537 as part of a larger endowment from the eponymous sixteenth-century Ottoman governor. Although local Muslims eventually established a number of other Islamic educational institutions, by the socialist era Gazi Husrev-bey was the only remaining madrassa in Bosnia and Herzegovina and one of two in the entire country of Yugoslavia.[9] By the early 1970s, the madrassa taught five grades of boys, aged roughly thirteen to eighteen in both secular and religious subjects, preparing them for careers as imams, muezzins, or other religious workers. The vast majority of students came from Bosnia, although some hailed from Herzegovina, or the Sandžak region of Serbia. Enrollment at the institution grew steadily over the socialist period, quadrupling between 1950 and 1975.

This growing interest in a religious education and activism resulted from the confluence of several local and global factors. Internationally, the 1970s saw a heightened interest in a more observant and globally minded version of Islam.[10] Domestically, socialist Yugoslavia's particular approach to handling national diversity and negotiating the balance of power between the federal center in Belgrade and the constituent republics also played an important role in encouraging the development of a more politicized Islam. In the 1960s, elite debates over the centralization vs. decentralization of the country's structure ultimately tilted toward the continued devolution of power to the republics.[11] Concomitantly, Communist League officials increasingly encouraged individuals to claim membership in a particular national group, rather than the supranational Yugoslavism of the early postwar period. Here, the newly empowered republican-level communist leaderships leaned on national identification as a way of circumventing calls for democratization.[12]

The rise of nationally based politics was particularly complex for Bosnian Muslims, for whom, by the late socialist period, a "Muslim" identity was neither firmly religious nor national.[13] Sunni Islam had arrived in the Balkans with the expansion of the Ottoman Empire, which solidified its grip over the territories of Bosnia and Herzegovina over the course of the fifteenth and sixteenth centuries.[14] Although Bosnian Muslims were Slavs who shared the South Slavic language of their neighbors, Islam did not take on a strong national connotation as did Orthodoxy for Serbs and Catholicism for Croats over the course of the nineteenth century.[15] While religion set Muslims apart from Bosnia's other ethno-national groups, their lack of fixed national identification made them an appealing target for Serb and Croat nationalists, who occasionally claimed Muslims as a lost part of their own national group.[16] In the socialist period, due to the state repression of religious institutions and expression, and because of a general process of secularization, Islam came to represent "only one of the many facets" of Bosnian Muslim communal identity.[17] Many Muslims abandoned religious observance, or used the non-national identification of "Yugoslav."[18]

Thus, when communist officials recognized Muslims as a "constitutive nation" in 1968, it was in hopes of drawing interest away from identification with the now officially abandoned notion of Yugoslav ethnicity.[19] Furthermore, scholars have argued that another motivation for the official recognition of this new national category was to demonstrate Yugoslavia's care for Muslim needs to the Islamic countries of the Non-Aligned Movement.[20] This new national category was, however, envisioned as secular, omitting Islam from the concept of "Muslim."[21] The emergence of a movement promoting a religious identity was, according to scholar and former *Zemzem* contributor Fikret Karčić, partially a reaction against official efforts to de-emphasize the Islamic aspect of Muslim heritage. At the same time, Karčić notes that the first generation of Bosnians who had gone abroad to pursue graduate degrees in Islamic theology in the Middle East were now returning, bringing with them ideas about reinvigorating Islam. Furthermore, Yugoslavs who had gone to work in Western Europe were now prosperous enough to send home the remittances that financed a major project of constructing and renovating mosques across the country.[22]

It should be recalled that the youthful Islamic activism at the Gazi Husrev-bey madrassa also occurred within the context of Yugoslavia's remarkably vocal student movements. Since roughly 1965, university students in most of the country's major cities had begun to organize campaigns in opposition to the Vietnam War, militarism, and racism, while openly criticizing the shortcomings of Titoist Yugoslavia, and expressing frustration with the conditions in which they, as students, lived and studied. Most famously, in June 1968, students across Yugoslavia, including Sarajevo, launched a week-long series of strikes and demonstrations to demand a fairer and more participatory socialist system.[23]

The students at Gazi Husrev-bey were also not the first examples of Yugoslav high-schoolers participating in the world of student oppositional politics. For example, teenagers took part in a riot that erupted during a 1966 anti-Vietnam War demonstration in Zagreb, leading to the destruction of the US consulate's façade.[24] In the fall of 1967, students at Belgrade's Nikola Tesla high school revolted, "almost [. . .] to the point of riots," against being required to wear blue uniform blouses, which they insisted contradicted Yugoslavia's system of self-management.[25]

By the early 1970s nationalist and religiously inflected student activism was appearing across Yugoslavia. This development emerged out of disillusionment with Tito's failure to implement promised reforms, out of the larger turn toward national politics initiated at the elite level, as described above, and partially due to longstanding complaints regarding national rights. Zagreb became the center of a vigorous and increasingly uncontrollable student nationalist movement, many of whose leaders openly embraced Catholicism.[26] The Croat student movement crested with a massive student strike in November–December of 1971, which authorities suppressed only with great difficulty.[27] In Serbia too, religion, and particularly religious mysticism began to appeal to some groups of nonconformist youth. For example, in 1972, police investigated a hippie commune in the town of Subotica, Serbia, where members had reportedly been engaging in séances, a "nudist show," political discussions, Bible readings, prayer meetings, and "musical-literary acts."[28] Thus, when

Sarajevo's madrassa students went on strike in January 1972, it was in the context of a longer trajectory of student rebellion, and a growing engagement with national and religious-based activism. To put the madrassa strikes into perspective, just weeks earlier, police had stormed the dormitories at Zagreb University, and they were still actively rounding up student nationalist leaders across the city.[29] The activities at the Gazi Husrev-bey madrassa therefore clearly fit into the broad spectrum of the era's rebellious youth politics, which, despite their incredible diversity, were united by a desire for more autonomy, less authoritarianism, and the belief that young people had the right, and even the duty to make their demands known.

## THE NEW ISLAMIC PATH

While the proponents of the Islamic revival had a broad vision for modernizing the religion, a necessary first step was the task of familiarizing potential adherents with the basic principles and practices of Islam. To this end, the contributors to *Zemzem* described to their readership the significance of various holidays, and explained the importance of keeping the Ramadan fast.[30] They sought to explain why events such as Muhammad's flight from Mecca to Medina, known as the Hijra, were relevant in the contemporary world, and it instructed readers on the religion's most significant features, such as monotheism and "obedience and total devotion to God."[31]

Another important aspect of building a modern Islam lay in encouraging a positive view of the historical contributions of Muslims. *Zemzem* thus regularly featured short biographies of historical figures, and featured an ongoing graphic cartoon series that depicted Islamic history through the adventures of "Hasan and Omer."[32] Although the general history of Islam and early Muslims was an important aspect of *Zemzem*'s content, contributors were particularly determined to promote the historical achievements of Bosnian Muslims, whom they felt had even been unfairly labeled as members of the Ottoman Empire's "dark vilayet."[33] Writers promoted Bosnia's rich cultural tradition, and the lengthy history of education and scholarship which, an author noted proudly, predated that of Croatia by 130 years.[34]

This focus on their ancestors' historical achievements strongly resembled a tactic employed by other student movements across the Balkans in this period—particularly the student movements with nationalist inclinations. For example, Romanian youth often drew on their country's cultural history and peasant traditions as a means of subtly opposing, or at least distinguishing themselves from the socialist present.[35] Nationalist student activists in Croatia used the anniversaries of major historical events to galvanize their fellow students and remind them of both the glories and repression of past and current epochs.[36] With *Zemzem*, though, the deployment of historical achievements was in the cause of a strengthened religious identity, rather than the promotion of a national one.

The students were rather conflicted about their focus on the historical achievements of Islam, however. On the one hand, a number of contributors to *Zemzem* were profoundly troubled by what the comparison between the past and present revealed. One article noted that in contrast to the intellectual and scientific prowess of the past, today, seventy million of the one hundred million Arabs were illiterate, while another asserted that it was Muslims' passive relationship to the Qur'an that had allowed the European colonial powers to occupy their territories with essentially no resistance.[37] One contributor, despairing of the possibility that Islam would be able to "propagate itself without repeatedly citing examples of the greatness of our ancestors," crossed into potentially dangerous political territory in a socialist state. Arguing that Muhammad "succeeded where no other revolution, ideology, or man has," the author added that, "the spiritual and moral renewal of our man is only possible through the Qur'an and strict adherence to its wise regulations," thus offering little hope for the development of Islam in the contemporary world.[38] Another writer anxiously wondered if Islam could survive this crisis.[39] On the other hand, some viewed the Islamic past with pride and as a source of inspiration, noting how much early Muslims were able to accomplish even without going to school or acquiring a university education.[40] Those following this more optimistic strand of thought urged readers to abandon their habit of negatively comparing the contemporary era to the past, and to instead use history as an inspiration for a new and vigorous approach to Islam.[41]

The exact shape that this new and more relevant form of Islam should take was a major topic of discussion within the pages of *Zemzem*, and beyond. Sarajevo's observant, young Muslims were self-conscious about the perception that their religion made them "backwards and conservative," and were eager to prove themselves as part of the wider, "progressive and contemporary" world.[42] A student, writing to *Preporod* (*Rebirth*), one of Sarajevo's other major Islamic periodicals, complained that he believed in science and progress, but that he did not understand how Islam fit into his conception of *savremenost* (contemporaneity, or modernity).[43]

*Preporod*'s response was essentially identical to the ideas circulating within *Zemzem*, and revealed the careful balancing act that activists were attempting in calling for a modernized Islam that still rejected the aspects of the contemporary world they considered incompatible with their religion. Articles in both papers condemned pornography, smoking, alcohol, the "weird, extravagant" behavior of the hippie movement, and the allure of "a beautiful girl in a miniskirt," to which it was "very difficult to remain indifferent."[44] One contributor lamented that "whenever we hear about something originating in the European West, we hurry recklessly to accept it."⁴⁵ Suggesting that temptations did not only come from the West but also from the secular socialist world, two Bosnian youths who were studying abroad cautiously reported back to *Zemzem* that the erotic Yugoslav magazines *Čik* and *Eva i Adam* were available in Kuwait.⁴⁶ According to Sarajevo's Islamic activists, the alternative to the dangers of secular "contemporaneity" lay in understanding the term as being defined by "moving forward, overcoming, surviving life circumstances, [and] working toward achievement," which matched their understanding of Islam.⁴⁷

The contributors mostly agreed that rapid advances in science and technology had alienated many from the modern world, encouraging some to turn back toward religion and spirituality. However, rather than rejecting these trappings of modernity, the writers of *Zemzem* argued that religion and science could and should be reconciled. The journal noted that the Qur'an repeatedly calls for Muslims to embrace research and learning,⁴⁸ and that the findings of faith and science were actually compatible with one another.⁴⁹ The writers called for openness to technological advances, citing the resistance that the leader of Saudi Arabia faced when he attempted to introduce the telephone as an example of the sort of regressive, ossified Islam that was holding back the Muslim world.⁵⁰ One article reported that Arabs, and one presumes all Muslims, were eager to close the technological gap between themselves and the West.⁵¹

Activists were also eager to convey that this more updated version of Islam lacked extremism and could coexist peaceably with other religions. Contributors emphasized the passages of the Qur'an that called on Muslims to live in harmony with non-Muslims, and argued that it was perfectly acceptable to socialize with those of other faiths.⁵² However, while *Zemzem*'s writers understood Islam as a peaceful religion, they were also determined to prove that Muslims would no longer be passive when attacked, since the Qur'an allowed for defensive warfare.⁵³ In one creative short story, a student described the search for his inner *mudžahid* (mujahid, pl. mujahideen), although here too, the writer emphasized the defensive nature of Islamic warfare: the story's fictional *mudžahid* was a "warrior" and a "victor," as much as a "fugitive" and a "victim."⁵⁴

## A GLOBAL ISLAM

Another of the activists' major preoccupations was the connection between the madrassa's students and the wider, Islamic world. *Zemzem*'s consistent coverage of events abroad kept students updated on the construction of a mosque in London, a Qur'an reciting competition in Malaysia, and the

Muslim community in Australia.[55] The editors took particular pains to build student awareness of how other young Muslims experienced life and religion. For example, in one article, two Bosnian students who had moved to Kuwait described their classes and social interactions abroad.[56] After a class trip to Bulgaria and Turkey, students published several articles describing their excitement at meeting other madrassa students in Istanbul, with whom they communicated in Arabic, and their dismay at the difficult circumstances endured by Bulgarian Muslims.[57] Columns frequently noted that Sarajevo's Islamic community was part of a "group of around 700 million Muslims on all continents," while others self-consciously reminded students that "the eyes of . . . colleagues in . . . Egypt, Libya, Iraq, Kuwait, and Morocco, are fixed upon us."[58]

This determination to be part of a larger movement closely matched that of Yugoslavia's secular students, although Islamic youth were claiming membership in a worldwide religious network, while their secular counterparts asserted their connection to the era's global student activism. Furthermore, secular and Islamic students shared a focus on a number of specific topics. Like their colleagues, Gazi Husrev-bey's students saw the Israeli-Palestinian conflict, anticolonial revolutionary movements, and global racism as crucial issues about which it was their duty to comment and raise awareness. For the most part, *Zemzem*'s coverage of Palestine differed little in content from what one would find in secular student newspapers, such as Belgrade's *Student*, Zagreb's *Studentski list*, or Sarajevo's *Naši dani*. Articles emphasized the human rights abuses suffered by Palestinian refugees, by, for example, publishing a photograph of a dead or severely injured child with a caption reading, "Have I not the right to live peacefully?" or with short stories that dramatized the violence suffered by civilians during the 1967 Six-Day War.[59]

In another tactic virtually identical to that of the other student movements, *Zemzem*'s writers also focused on the revolutionary politics of the Palestinian activists, as well as other anticolonial struggles, such Algeria and Libya.[60] However, *Zemzem*'s interpretation diverged from the era's relatively standard student support for anticolonial, revolutionary politics in pointing to Islam as a major source of inspiration, albeit in conjunction with socialism, for resistance to colonial repression. Students also presented Islam as both an argument against, and an antidote to racism. Noting that Muhammad refused to distinguish between the skin tones of his supporters, student writers insisted that Islam had presented its followers with the slogan of "Liberty! Brotherhood! Equality!" long before the French Revolution.[61] Another way in which the Islamic student movement differed from that of Belgrade or Zagreb University was in their lack of attention to issues such as the war in Vietnam. This however, may have had less to do with their interest in Islam, and more to do with the fact that the war was beginning to wind down.

## LOCAL COMMUNITY

Importantly, the Islamic world abroad was not the only community with which
the students at the Gazi Husrev-bey madrassa hoped to build connections. As
part of their goal of a rejuvenated and confident Islamic movement, students
also placed themselves at the center of an effort to strengthen the sense of
community between Muslims across Bosnia and Herzegovina, as well as the
other Yugoslav republics. Students declared Bosnia to be an "oasis of Islam
in Europe," and insisted that they would not allow the "light [of Islam] to go
out in the Balkans."[62] The editors of *Zemzem* saw the paper's publication as
itself being a major step toward this goal. While, they explained, they had initially intended the paper to only serve the immediate students at the madrassa,
they were delighted to find that the paper now circulated across Yugoslavia,
and even as far as the United States, Australia, New Zealand, and Germany.[63]
Letters to the editor requesting a subscription to the paper, such as one from
Muharem Bašić in St. Louis, suggest that émigrés from Yugoslavia formed
*Zemzem*'s main audience abroad.[64]

One way of building community awareness within Yugoslavia was
simply reporting on the activities of Muslims in other republics. For
example, one article discussed the small but active Muslim community of
Ljubljana.[65] Another lamented the lack of academic cooperation between the
Gazi Husrev-bey madrassa in Sarajevo, and the only other one located in
Yugoslavia, Pristina's Alauddin madrassa.[66]

*Zemzem* also regularly covered a student activity that both served to
strengthen Islamic practice within Yugoslavia, and was an essential part of
the students' religious training. Throughout the year, and particularly around
major holidays such as Ramadan, Sarajevo's madrassa sent students to lead
prayers in Muslim communities across Yugoslavia.[67] This provided crucial
experience to young people, and *Zemzem*'s publication of feedback on the
students' performance became an annual ritual.[68] Beyond this educational-
professional aspect, however, this practice also served to deepen interest in
Islam, or at least provide some sort of contact with a population that was often
weakly self-identified as religiously Muslim. Indeed, students cited such
encounters with the madrassa's students in their local mosque as having been
crucial to their decision to enroll at Gazi Husrev-bey.[69] One future student
described such a meeting as itself being a nearly transcendent experience:
"What elegance, what harmony, I thought to myself [. . .] I was rapt with
ecstasy as I stared at these youth [the madrassa students]." After the service,
he sat on the riverbank of the Drina, "and thought about these youth [. . .] and
as if speaking to me, the Drina told me 'Go to the madrassa, go, go . . . .'"[70]

Although *Zemzem*'s contributors saw themselves as working to build
a strong community of Yugoslav Muslims, one important question from

which the publication essentially removed itself was the debate as to whether Bosnia's Muslims should be defined as a separate national group. In fact, *Zemzem* barely registered the existence of the conversation, other than asserting that Yugoslavia's Muslim population should be allowed to declare membership in any national group they desired, including "Muslim."[71] Was this reluctance to tread too firmly into a potentially delicate topic the result of the self-censorship and generally repressive political atmosphere within Bosnia?[72] Or, were Islamic activists simply more interested in promoting a religious identity rather than engaging with the question of a national one?

## AN ISLAMIC STUDENT MOVEMENT

While *Zemzem* was in one sense the vehicle for students and sometimes their teachers to think through and advocate a new and updated form of Islam, it was also a product of the student body, and therefore reflected a number of the less spiritual concerns of those at the madrassa. The journal often worked to provide a sense of community within the school, by, for example, providing space for students to publish poems and short stories, or featuring short articles in which students would describe why they chose to attend the madrassa. Students described school trips, and discussed the challenges they faced when they traveled to remote villages to lead holiday services.[73]

Beyond acting as a forum for recording the more mundane occurrences of student life, *Zemzem* also revealed growing friction between students and administrators, and between students and the other official organs with which they came into contact. While the sources unfortunately do not explicitly detail the nature of the disagreements within the madrassa, we can still detect a few of the sources of tension. The first point of anger appears to have centered on the lack of student control over *Zemzem*. That the student body was unhappy with the perceived disempowerment surrounding their publication became evident around 1970, when an editorial in the year's first edition expressed hope that *Zemzem* could improve itself and better satisfy readers.[74] An article from the same edition announced that more responsibilities were being handed over to the "young people of *Zemzem*," strongly suggesting that there had been internal disagreements as to the level of autonomy that the paper should enjoy.[75] Importantly, it appears that young people had won this round of disputes with the school administration.

The next source of student dissatisfaction surfaced in 1971, when a rather defensively worded article went into great detail as to the numerous extracurricular opportunities enjoyed by the madrassa students, including the right to watch television on Saturdays.[76] This article clearly spoke to what must have been an ongoing, but otherwise undocumented, debate surrounding the students' perception that their educators were overly authoritarian in their policies and inattentive to student needs. Additionally, a number of these complaints surrounding the right to watch television and participate in extra-curricular activities would surface later in the madrassa strike of 1972, suggesting that the current policy was ultimately deemed unacceptable.

Evidence of a final source of frustration emerged in the very next edition, where students complained that the lack of a university-level Islamic Faculty in Yugoslavia meant that they would have to go abroad if they wanted to continue their religious studies after graduating from the madrassa.[77] Unlike the previous two, this complaint was less related to the failings of authorities at the madrassa, and more to the state's failure to accommodate their needs as Muslims. Although too late to be immediately useful to the students graduating from high school in 1971, Sarajevo's Faculty of Islamic Studies did finally open in 1977.

As we can see, neither the complaint about students lacking control over their own publication nor the one about the educational system's authoritarianism was particularly related to Islam. In fact, some variant of these grievances could be found at universities and schools across Yugoslavia, and indeed much of Europe. Students across the country had been calling for a less authoritarian educational system since the mid-1960s, and by the late 1960s and early 1970s nearly every major student-run newspaper and periodical in Yugoslavia had battled educational and state authorities over the autonomy of their publications.[78] While the issue of needing to travel abroad to complete an Islamic education was somewhat specific to the students' status as Muslims, here too we can see a close parallel to the secular students, who frequently complained that the failures of the Yugoslav system compelled many of their generation to leave the country for employment.[79]

Gazi Husrev-bey's students also fit into the wider spectrum of Yugoslav student activism in regards to timing. Nineteen seventy-one marked the highest level of student activism across Yugoslavia since 1968. When the madrassa students went on strike in January 1972, a massive nationalist student strike had paralyzed Zagreb and a number of Croatia's other university centers just a few weeks earlier, and authorities were still actively engaged in subduing the remnants of the movement. While *Zemzem* never referenced the activities of students unassociated with the madrassa, information about Yugoslavia's other student movements was readily available through other sources such as Sarajevo University's student newspaper, *Naši dani*. These movements were also widely covered in the mainstream Yugoslav press. It is doubtful that Gazi Husrev-bey's students had contact with any of the other student movements active at the time, but we can safely assume that the madrassa's students were well aware of them.

Frustrations with the madrassa's authoritarianism and the lack of concern for student needs came to a head in early January 1972, when the students at the madrassa went on strike.[80] According to a contemporary Reuter's report, 320 students refused to attend classes at the madrassa until the headmaster, whom they accused of having an "authoritarian attitude" was replaced, and until subjects such as logic, mathematics, English, and philosophy were added to the curriculum. The students also called for more free time, better recreational facilities, and more television-viewing privileges.[81] The crisis dragged on for two months, during which time Islamic authorities closed the madrassa altogether until they felt able to "normalize" the situation.[82]

When they finally announced the school's reopening, the authorities sternly warned that in the future, students were "absolutely forbidden" from using strikes as a method of making their demands heard. They further complained that through the distribution of leaflets and comments to the "public media," students had engaged in actions that they knew would be "morally and materially damaging to the Islamic community."[83] This comment in particular points to what Sabrina Ramet noted was a strategy adopted by Yugoslavia's Islamic leadership, to avoid attracting official attention as much as possible—in contrast to the leaderships of the Catholic and Orthodox communities, which were growing increasingly confident and outspoken.[84] It seems, though, that many of the younger generation did not share this aversion to public confrontation, and like their counterparts at secular educational institutions, saw it as their right to openly make demands when they deemed it necessary. Ultimately, the Islamic leadership did recognize that some steps needed to be taken to address the students' complaints. The announcement included discussion of eventual "changes to the educational plans," and as well as the possible relocation of boarding-school facilities, which would presumably address other aspects of student discontent. Finally, while it is unclear whether this was related to the strikers' demands, by the following year, 1973, the school's director had been replaced.[85]

While this appears to have been the last example of activity as rebellious as a strike, students, occasionally joined by sympathetic teachers, became much more vocal in expressing dissatisfaction both with their treatment as students, and their treatment as Muslims. An article covering the yearly meeting of the madrassa's student assembly reported complaints that the previous year's leadership had been "inadequate."[86] Students complained that "indolence" on the part of their elders occasionally hindered the publication of *Zemzem*, while an article in *Preporod* asserted that school officials had not made sufficient effort to locate opportunities for their students to lead prayers in local mosques, thus hindering their professional advancement.[87]

Other recurring grievances were directed toward the financial burden of education at the madrassa. In a complaint nearly identical to that of secular university students, bitterness over the rising fees for room and board aroused criticism that the madrassa favored students from privileged families. An angry article demanded to know when it would be realized that most of the students were the children of workers and peasants.[88] When, in 1974, school officials neglected to follow through on a promise of an expanded school canteen that would feed all of the students, a writer acidly noted that "this wasn't the first time that a promise for something that would improve our lives was unfulfilled."[89]

Beyond dissatisfaction with living standards and institutional responsiveness, increasingly, student anger was directed both at Islamic officials and the socialist state, for failing to take the steps necessary to protect their rights as Muslims, and to advance the cause of Islam. Despite the existence of a law stating that all students were to enjoy the same rights, students at the madrassa did not have adequate access to health insurance, were unable to apply for support from the children's supplementary fund, and were unable to delay their mandatory army service.[90] In an example of socialist authorities' lack of concern for their needs that students found particularly galling, given their lack of healthcare, one article complained that as a reward for participation in a blood drive, two students had been invited to a seaside state resort, only to find the food had been cooked with pork fat.[91] Even the Islamic hierarchy appeared to be unable or unwilling to take the necessary steps to promote Islam. A sympathetic teacher noted that by not allowing young people a greater role, and with its "non-Islamic" division between the older and younger generations, the administrative body encouraged dogmatism and prevented the "rejuvenation" of the religion. In an article that connected the overall fate of Islam to young peoples' struggles and frustrations, one writer noted that "we can see how many victims there are on the path to Islam."[92]

## DROPPING OUT OF SOCIALISM?

The concept of dropping out, or removing oneself from the socialist system and its structures of power, recasts the socialist period as having been more complex than the older portrayal of an all-powerful totalitarian state. As the various punks, hippies, and other rebels who populate the pages of this volume reveal, those living under socialism deployed a multitude of strategies by which they evaded, mitigated, and rejected the power and logic of their states. And, indeed, many of the religious activities of the madrassa's students inherently required a certain level of dropping out of socialism. In performing daily prayers, attending services at a mosque, and observing religious holidays, Muslims were inscribing themselves in a system of belief and behavior that existed beyond the grasp of the socialist state. Furthermore, one could not be a member of the Yugoslav League of Communists and be a member of any religious congregation, Islamic or otherwise, therefore necessitating a certain distance between state and the religiously observant.[93]

Still, other aspects of the madrassa students' activities remind us that dropping out of socialism could itself be a complex and multifaceted concept. Firstly, these activists were not simply withdrawing into a separate, parallel world. They were actively drawing on the strategic repertoire of student rebellion developed by activists from Berkeley to Paris to Belgrade, and they imagined themselves to be participating in a movement of young Muslims from Jakarta to Dakar. Secondly, in a number of important aspects, the madrassa students did not *want* to fully drop out of socialism or secular society. In fact, as their demands from the 1972 strike reveal, they sometimes wanted more access to the secular pleasures of television viewing, for example. In other instances, they demanded that the state adjust itself to their needs, thus allowing them to more fully participate in socialist society on their own terms.

Taken as a whole, the madrassa students' actions fail to position them clearly in either the realm of dropping out or staying within socialism. We can see, therefore, that both the socialist state, and the practices involved in resisting, challenging, retreating from, or thinking beyond it were not necessarily permanent, absolute, or unchanging. As the madrassa students reveal, the citizens of socialist countries sometimes negotiated between global and local frames of reference, and between the rejection of and participation in various aspects of life in the socialist state.

## CONCLUSION

The student activists at Gazi Husrev-bey madrassa present a fascinating look at how Yugoslavia's many political and cultural movements intersected and overlapped in the 1960s and 1970s. In blending standard concerns about student rights and Third World revolutionary politics with a more unique interest in strengthening religious observance and rejuvenating Islam, the madrassa's students compel a reevaluation of Yugoslavia's student and Islamic movements. We see that the era's student movements were not confined to the Left, but incorporated a wide range of identities and political orientations that are often omitted from studies of student politics. Furthermore, we see that the early years of Bosnia's Islamic revival were characterized by advocacy for a vigorous, though not inherently violent or intolerant form of Islam.

The ways in which student and Islamic politics intertwined and reinforced one another are particularly important to keep in mind in understanding the later trajectory of Islam in Bosnia. As the late Yugoslav regime grew increasingly sensitive to criticism and dissent in the late 1970s and 1980s, Islamic activists, as well as leftists and nationalists, became targets of repression. In one of the more publicized examples of late Yugoslav anti-dissident measures, in 1983, Bosnian authorities targeted Alija Izetbegović, later president of wartime Bosnia, and a group of younger Islamic activists, including former contributors to *Zemzem*, for writing the *Islamic Declaration*.[94] Although the defendants were accused of plotting to overthrow the socialist state on the way to the establishment of global, *shari'a*-based government, the *Declaration* had actually been written in the early 1970s, and advocated for a version of Islam closely related to that promoted in the pages of *Zemzem*.

In returning to the theme of dropping out of socialism, I maintain that the madrassa's students show us the numerous ways in which one could pass back and forth across the line of withdrawing from some aspects of the state and society, while demanding a fuller inclusion in others. In attending prayers, in not eating pork, in imagining oneself as part of a global community of Muslims, students were temporarily dropping out of socialism, or at least marking themselves as clearly distinct from it. At the same time, writing critical articles and making public demands were not acts of dropping out, although they were clearly acts of opposition and defiance. Therefore, I suggest that we might see dropping out as one of a number of tactics by which student activists, dissidents, and rebels could critique, make claims upon, avoid, or challenge the state and society in which they lived.

In more recent years, the discussion of Islam's position in Bosnia, and the Balkans more broadly, has generally been dominated less by the question of its relationship to socialism and more by anxieties that the region provides a foothold in Europe for dangerous Islamic extremism.[95] And, it is true, several of the 9/11 hijackers fought or were trained in Bosnia during the 1992–1995 war.[96] But, rather than further encouraging paranoia about the dangers to European civilization that may be lurking in the Balkans, the students of the 1970s show us that political Islam is not necessarily a new and startling development. Rather, there is a rich history of activists who advocated for a vigorous and observant form of Islam, who participated in and dropped out of the socialist state, and who were enmeshed in many of the same, global trends as their secular counterparts.

## NOTES

1. Fikret Karčić, "Islamic Revival in the Balkans 1970–1992," *Islamic Studies* 36, no. 2–3 (1997): 565–81.
2. For a particularly useful summary of Yugoslavia's leftist student movements, see Hrvoje Klasić, *Jugoslavija i svijet: 1968* (Zagreb: Naklada Ljevak, 2012).
3. Neven Andjelic, *Bosnia-Herzegovina: The End of a Legacy* (Portland: Frank Cass, 2003), 46.

4. S. P. Ramet, "Islam in Yugoslavia Today," *Religion in Communist Lands* 18, no. 3 (1990): 226–35.

5. Xavier Bougarel, "Bosnian Muslims and the Yugoslav Idea," in *Yugoslavism: Histories of a Failed Idea, 1918–1992*, ed. Dejan Djokić (London: Hurst & Company, 2003).

6. Anto Knežević, "Alija Izetbegović's 'Islamic Declaration': Its Substance and its Western Reception," *Islamic Studies* 36, no. 2–3 (1997): 483–521.

7. Ibid., 498; Andjelic, *Bosnia-Herzegovina*, 46.

8. My thanks to Juliane Fürst for suggesting this notion.

9. Karčić, "Islamic Revival," 571.

10. Zachary T. Irwin, "The Islamic Revival and the Muslims of Bosnia-Hercegovina," *East European Quarterly* 17, no. 4 (1984): 437.

11. Ana Dević, "The Forging of Socialist Nationalism and Its Alternatives: Social and Political Context and Intellectual Criticism in Yugoslavia between the Mid-1960s and 1992" (PhD diss., University of California, San Diego, 2000), 30.

12. Ibid., 45, 315.

13. Ivo Banac, "Bosnian Muslims: From Religious Community to Socialist Nationhood and Postcommunist Statehood, 1918–1992," in *The Muslims of Bosnia-Herzegovina: Their Historic Development from the Middle Ages to the Dissolution of Yugoslavia*, ed. Mark Pinson (Cambridge, MA: Harvard University Press, 1994), 146. The figures under discussion in the present study would probably now be identified as "Bosniak," a term that now has a specifically national connotation. However, this chapter uses the term "Muslim," since none of the sources under discussion here utilized "Bosniak."

14. Mitja Velikonja, *Religious Separation and Political Intolerance in Bosnia-Herzegovina*, trans. Rang'ichi Ng'inja (College Station, TX: Texas A & M University Press, 2003), 55.

15. Ibid., 68.

16. Ibid., 132.

17. Ibid., 222–23.

18. Tone Bringa, *Being Muslim the Bosnian Way: Identity and Community in a Central Bosnian Village* (Princeton: Princeton University Press, 1995), 28–29.

19. Velikonja, *Religious Separation*, 223–24.

20. Aydın Babuna, "Bosnian Muslims during the Cold War: Their Identity between Domestic and Foreign Policies," in *Religion and the Cold War: A Global Perspective*, ed. Philip Muehlenbeck (Nashville: Vanderbilt University Press, 2012), 194.

21. Karčić, "Islamic Revival," 567.

22. Ibid., 568.

23. Klasić, *Jugoslavija i svijet*.

24. "Demonstracije širom Jugoslavije protiv rata u Vijetnamu," in "Marx i revolucija. Jun-lipanj 1968: Dokumenti," special issue, *Praxis* no. 1–2 (1969): 10.

25. Milan M. Misić, "Pobuna protiv plavih bluza ili u stš, 'Nikola Tesla' samoupravljanje ide na 'popravni,'" *Student* 23 (1967): 11.

26. Pero Kvesić, "Ponovno izbori na filozofskom fakultetu," *Studentski list* no. 1–3 (1971): 2.

27. For a description of the Croatian student nationalist movement, see Tihomir Ponoš, *Na rubu revolucije—Studenti '71* (Zagreb: Profil International, 2007).

28. Open Society Archives at Central European University, Budapest, Hungary (HU OSA), 300-10-2/27, Arrests, 1971–1975 ("Jedan 'hipi' u zatvoru," February 23, 1972).

29. Hrvatski državni arhiv (HDA), Policijska uprava Zagreb (PUZ), Studentska događanja (SD)/2, Kronologija studentskih zbivanja 1972. god. (KSZ), (Untitled chronology of student events).

30. Šaban Imamović, "Ramazanski post i njegov značaj," *Zemzem* 7–8 (1970): 1–2.

31. Šaban Imamović, "Hidžret i njegov značaj," *Zemzem* 3–4 (1970): 1–3; Šaban Imamović, "Uz ovogodišnji mevlud," *Zemzem* 5–6 (1970): 1–3; Muhamed Behej, "Islam je vjera, a ne filozofija," *Zemzem* 3–4 (1971): 3–4.

32. See for example, Nesib Talić, "Hasan i Omer," *Zemzem* 5–6 (1971): 32.

33. Rešad Kadić, "Gazi Husrevbegova medresa u Sarajevu (Kuršumlija) prva je visoka škola na Balkanu," *Zemzem* 5–6 (1970): 14–15. A *vilayet* was an Ottoman administrative region.

34. Kadić, "Gazi Husrevbegova medresa," 14–15.

35. Madigan Fichter, "Rock 'n' Roll Nation: Counterculture and Dissent in Romania, 1965–1975," *Nationalities Papers* 39, no. 4 (2011): 567–85.

36. HDA, PUZ, SD/2, (Spisak: prijavljenih osoba i lišenih slobode zbog krivičnih djela protiv naroda i Države).

37. Ibrahim Kovačević, "Islam i muslimani, nekad i danas," *Zemzem* 7–8 (1972): 2–3; Fikret Karčić, "Značenje religije danas," *Zemzem* 1–3 (1974): 4–6.

38. Islam Kadić, "Vratimo se Islamu," *Zemzem* 5–6 (1970): 10–11.

39. Kovačević, "Islam i muslimani," 2–3.

40. Jusuf Zahiragić, "Naša stvarnost," *Zemzem* 1–2 (1972): 6.

41. "Riječ urednika," *Zemzem* 9–12 (1972): 1.

42. Zahiragić, "Naša stvarnost," 6.

43. "Mladi u pitanju—mladi u odgovoru," *Preporod* 32 (1972): 4. My thanks to Professor Jane Burbank for pointing out the importance of distinguishing between "modernity" and "contemporaneity."

44. "Cvatući biznis i pornografija," from *Večernje novine*, March 21, 1970. Republished in *Zemzem* 3–4 (1970): 19; "Svaka deseta smrt—zbog pušenja," from *Oslobođenje*, March 1, 1970. Republished in *Zemzem* 3–4 (1970): 11; Hasan Hilić, "Pojedinci piju zajednica plaća," *Zemzem* 9–12 (1970): 15–16; "Mladi u pitanju," 4; Husein Smajlović, "Prostitucija," *Zemzem* 3–4 (1972): 8–9.

45. Ishak Alečević, "Pornografija i njen štetan uticaj," *Zemzem* 1–2 (1970): 10–11.

46. "Utisci iz Kuvajta," *Zemzem* 3–4 (1970): 20–21.

47. "Mladi u pitanju," 4.

48. Osman Nuri Hadžić, "Muhamed a.s. i Kur'an o nauci i prosvjeti. Rad islamskih naučnika u prvim stoljećima po Hidžeretu," *Zemzem* 3–4 (1970): 5.

49. Mustafa Spahić, "Razmišljanja o vjeri, svijetu i životu," *Zemzem* 9–12 (1975): 1–2.

50. Fikret Karčić, "Značenje religije danas," 4–6.

51. Ćamil Eminagić, trans., "Muhamed a.s. u očima njemačkih orjentalista," *Zemzem* 7–9 (1973): 1–3.

52. Fadil Mekić, "Tolerancija u Islamu," *Zemzem* 7–8 (1972): 16–17.

53. Fikret Karčić, "Rat i muslimani," *Zemzem* 9–12 (1972): 7–9.

54. Fikret Karčić, "Susret ili priča o strancima," *Zemzem* 4–6 (1973): 38.

55. "O Islamu sa svih kontinenata," *Zemzem* 4–6 (1973): 26–27; Muhammed Rida, "Intervju sa najpoznatijim mukriom (učačem) Kur'ana na svijetu," *Zemzem* 3–4 (1970): 18; "Iz štampe," *Zemzem* 7–8 (1972): 21.

56. "Utisci iz Kuvajta," 20–21.

57. Fikret Karčić, "U gradu na Bosforu," *Zemzem* 9–12 (1972): 18–20.

58. Imamović, "Hidžret," 1–3; "Riječ urednika," 1.

59. Karčić, "Rat i muslimani," 7–9; Ismet Dautović, "Priča oaze Sevsen," *Zemzem* 1–2 (1972): 7.

60. Fikret Karčić, "Prikaz: Sunce nadžicom: Pjesma palestinske revolucije," *Zemzem* 3–4 (1972): 16–17; Karčić, "Značenje religije danas," 4–6; F. K., trans., "Islam je vječno kretanje," *Zemzem* 4–6 (1974): 18.

61. Salih Čolaković, "Došla je istina," *Zemzem* 1–2 (1971): 1; Mirsad Ćeman, "Islam i humanizam," *Zemzem* 3–4 (1975): 6–7.

62. Imamović, "Uz ovogodišnji mevlud," 1–3; Alija Čoso, "Borba na Božijem putu," *Zemzem* 3–4 (1972): 2–3.

63. Redakcija, "Oproštaj sa starom redakcijom," *Zemzem* 3–4 (1971): 1–2.

64. Muharem Bašić, "Draga redakcijo," *Zemzem* 1–2 (1972): 19.

65. "Bajram-namaz u Ljubljani," *Zemzem* 1–2 (1971): 9.

66. Nijaz M. Sukrić, "U susret fakultetu islamskih studija u Sarajevu," *Zemzem* 4–6 (1974): 4–9.

67. See for example, "Bajram-namaz u Nikšiću," *Zemzen* 3–4 (1971): 22.

68. See for example, "Odbori Islamske zajednice o našim učenicima," *Zemzem* 9–12 (1971): 8.

69. "Zašto ste se odlučili da pohađate Medresu?" *Zemem* 1–2 (1972): 10.

70. Ibid.

71. "Nacionalnost sandžačkih i crnogorskih muslimana," *Zemzem* 1–2 (1971): 18.

72. Banac, "Bosnian Muslims: From Religious Community," 145.

73. Meho Zahirović, "Nažalost, i to se događa," *Zemzem* 7–12 (1974): 17; Muhamed Efendić, "Vjera ili egoizam," *Zemzem* 5–6 (1975): 37.

74. Šaban Imamović, "Poziv na saradnju svim odborima islamske zajednice Glavni i odgovorni urednik," *Zemzem* 1–2 (1970): 25.

75. Šaban Imamović, "Na pragu trećeg godišta," *Zemzem* 1–2 (1970): 1.

76. Rešid Bilalić, "Rad đačkog udruženja 'Gazi Husrevbeg' u prošloj godini," *Zemzem* 3–4 (1971): 20–21.

77. "Kuda poslije mature?" *Zemzem* 5–6 (1971): 11.

78. Ralph Pervan, *Tito and the Students: The University and the University Student in Self-Managing Yugoslavia* (Nedlands: University of Western Australia Press, 1978), 134; HU OSA, 300-10-2/493, Youth 1970–1971(Zdenko Antic, "Yugoslav Youths' Rebellious Press," May 29, 1970).

79. Akcioni komitet demonstranata i zbor studenata u Studentskom gradu, "Rezolucija studentskih demonstracija," June 3, 1968, in "Dokumenti," special issue, *Praxis* 1–2: 62–63.

80. HU OSA, 300-10-2/425, Students, 1972 (1 of 2) ("Sarajevo Students Reported Boycotting Classes," Reuters, January 17, 1972).

81. Ibid.

82. "Obustava nastave u Gazihusrevbegovoj Medresi," *Preporod* 34 (1970): 5.

83. "Gazi Husrevbegova medresa uskoro počinje sa radom," *Preporod* 36 (1972): 3.

84. Ramet, "Islam in Yugoslavia Today," 230.

85. O. Asim, "Reorganiacija života u domu," *Zemzem* 7–9 (1973): 15.

86. "Godišnja skupština Udruženja," *Zemzem* 3–4 (1972): 12.

87. Bajro P., "Bismillahir-rahmanir-rahim," *Zemzem* 5–6, 7–8 (1975): page unnumbered; "Odbori iz o učenicima medrese," *Preporod* 8 (1973): 10.

88. "Iz života medrese," *Zemzem* 7–12 (1974): 16.

89. Ibid.

90. Ferhat Šeta, "Da li je Medresa zaboravljena," *Zemzem* 3–4 (1975): 1.

91. "Zašto se učenici medrese nisu odazvali pozivu zavoda za transfuziju krvi?" *Zemzem* 9–12 (1972): 22.

92. Šeta, "Da li je Medresa zaboravljena," 1.

93. Bringa, *Being Muslim the Bosnian Way*, 204.

94. Knežević, "Alija Izetbegović's 'Islamic Declaration,'" 483–521.

95. Brian Whitmore, "Saudi 'Charity' Troubling to Bosnian Muslims," *The Boston Globe*, January 28, 2002.

96. "9/11Commission Staff Statement No. 16," (2004), http://www.nbcnews.com/id/5224099/ns/us_news-security/t/commission-staff-statement-no/#.VTF6hyFViko.\.

*Part II*

# DROPPING OUT INTELLECTUALLY

*Chapter 5*

# Reader Questionnaires in *Samizdat* Journals

## *Who Owns Aleksandr Blok?*

### Josephine von Zitzewitz

*Samizdat*, the production and circulation of texts outside the official channels, was one of the most distinctive phenomena of the late Soviet Union. *Samizdat* was a writing culture: the unofficial intellectuals were prolific writers, and one of the central functions of the journals was to substitute, at least to some degree, for the lack of publication opportunities for people not wishing to conform to the rigid official aesthetic. However, *samizdat* was above all a reading culture. Periodicals in particular provided an entire alternative repertoire of reading materials: new literary texts and essays, written by the unofficial intellectuals themselves, were offered alongside contemporary texts that were censored or banned, as well as rare pre-revolutionary texts and Western writings in translation. Friendships and informal literary groupings were often based on shared reading experiences.

This chapter lists some of the insights arising from the project "Reading Habits and Dissent during the Period of Stagnation in the Soviet Union, 1960s–1980s," a study that seeks to problematize the relationship between "official" and "unofficial" culture during the Brezhnev era.[1] In this chapter, I will examine one particular instance of this relationship: unofficial writers' reaction to an event in official culture, namely the centenary of Aleksandr Blok in 1980.

My research concerns alternative culture in Leningrad and, more narrowly, the typewritten periodicals that began to replace individual publications (manuscripts or almanacs) as the most popular form for circulating *samizdat* from the mid-1970s onwards. The journals and the communities that formed around them offered a platform for young intellectuals who eschewed the official Soviet cultural process to meet for discussions, as well as showcase their own work. Titles such as *"37,"* *Chasy*, *Severnaia pochta*, and *Obvodnyi kanal* became the underground poets' primary vehicle for distributing their own literary texts and critical writings. The unofficial sphere in Leningrad was small and self-referential, and the same people tended to be involved with various journals. A look at the editorial boards of the journals named above confirms this: Viktor Krivulin was co-founder and literary editor of *"37"* and editor-in-chief of *Severnaia pochta.* Sergei Stratanovskii co-founded and/or co-edited *Chasy,* in many respects a sister journal of *"37"* and the longest-running *samizdat* periodical, publishing eighty issues between 1976 and 1990, *Dialog* (three issues, 1979–1981), and *Obvodnyi kanal.* Boris Ivanov, an influential cultural critic who published copiously in *"37,"* was the founding editor of *Chasy.*

Official ideology afforded great power to the written word, which is evident in the rigid censorship, rote learning of literary classics in schools, encouragement to readers to acquire their own libraries, etc. Virtually all the poets and writers who went "underground" in the 1970s began writing as adolescents in the 1960s, attending the after-school poetry circles and LITOs set up by official institutions, including the Writers' Union, with the explicit aim of encouraging new literary talent.[2] Had it not been for the conservative turn in official ideology in the late 1960s, it is likely that at least some of them would have joined the intellectual and literary elite. Thus, the unofficial intellectuals' cult of the written word—the claim for the exceptionality of literature and the benefits of reading—can be regarded as a natural result of Soviet education; in this respect they were model citizens. On the other hand, the unofficial writers undermined the parameters of Soviet culture by reading (and writing) the wrong texts, often going to extraordinary lengths in order to gain access to texts that were not available, hidden in libraries' special reposi-tory (*spetskhranilishche*), or smuggled in from abroad. The truth claim with which the written word was invested in the Soviet Union turned their love for literature into a highly charged venture.

*Samizdat* was much more than just the circulation of texts—old or new, rare, banned or never published—in typewritten form in order to counteract a scar-city of information and still intellectual hunger. *Samizdat* in its mature form, during the 1970s–1980s, was a subculture that constituted a special form of "inner emigration." In the words of veteran dissident Liudmila Alekseeva, the circles of friends which, among other things, produced periodicals and orga-nized unofficial seminar, "often replaced non-existent, inaccessible or for various reasons unacceptable institutions—publishing houses, lecture halls, exhibitions, notice boards, confessionals, concert halls, libraries, museums, legal consultations, knitting circles . . . and also seminars on literature, his-tory, philosophy, and linguistics."[3] For many poets of the Leningrad "under-ground," *samizdat* poetry was not just a practice, but a lifestyle that required them to forego all the usual material comforts of Soviet everyday life, includ-ing professional success and better housing:

The non-recognition was expressed in a lifestyle that sharply differed from the Soviet lifestyle. Going to work every three days and books—that is how one could casually describe the non-Soviet lifestyle. Books were the greatest joy and keenly sought after. Refined and profound knowledge of Russian, but especially of foreign literature and history were considered the trademark of the aristocrat, a highly artistic person who had nothing in common with the working masses.[4]

These self-styled intellectual aristocrats were social marginals, and they accepted their precarious status as a consequence of staying true to their poetic vocation. Many worked as lift attendants, boiler room stokers, caretakers, and at similarly menial jobs.[5]

*Samizdat* was a form of inner emigration without a complete break with the "primary" culture. All the names used to describe *samizdat* culture—unofficial culture, second culture, underground, alternative culture, counterculture—point to the close relationship between this phenomenon and the official sphere from which the *samizdat* writers sought to distance themselves. In the case of literary *samizdat*, this relationship was especially complex. In the 1950s and 1960s, official and unofficial literature (in the sense of groups that did not seek contact with institutions) developed side by side, and it was not too difficult to cross from one sphere to the other. However, the course taken by official culture in the late 1960s deprived an entire generation whose aesthetics were deemed too experimental of publication opportunities and a wider readership and forced them to create opportunities themselves. It is important to remember that unlike the *samizdat* texts produced by the human rights movement, unofficial literature as a form of opposition had no direct political goals and certainly did not seek confrontation. Olga Sedakova, a Moscow poet and critic who published in Leningrad *samizdat* journals and wrote perceptively about her peers' poetry, confirms this: "For us, culture in its broadest historical aspect was that very freedom and height of the spirit denied to us by the Soviet system. . . . . We all emerged from some kind of protest movement, which was not so much political as aesthetic or spiritual resistance."[6] Even more importantly, as we shall see, those who had gone underground never entirely renounced their aspirations to be published writers.

## UNOFFICIAL INSTITUTIONS AND THE TURN TOWARD LITERARY CRITICISM

When asked retrospectively to assess the achievements of their own movement, many unofficial intellectuals exhibit an ambivalent stance, in particular when the relationship between unofficial and official culture is concerned.

The extremes of this position are exemplified in these two statements: "I would call this a shattered generation, because it did not create anything. It was an alternative generation. Alternative generation means it was negative. There was no change of configuration. It was the same stuff, only black instead of white."[7]

These pessimistic words belong to Arkadii Dragomoshchenko, a Leningrad poet and member of the editorial board of *Chasy*, who became well-known after the collapse of the Soviet Union. For a vigorously positive evaluation, we can turn to Anna Katsman, an ex-wife of Viktor Krivulin, who states: "The cultural chasm after the poetic pleiad of early twentieth-century Petersburg had to be filled—by us. And this impression was correct, as time has shown."[8]

What is beyond doubt is that the similarities between individual features of the cultural underground and official culture were extensive. The alternative structures were much more than channels to share new writing. With access to printing presses strictly regulated by the state, *samizdat* journals were typewritten and subsequently corrected by hand; often the carbon copy was barely legible. However, the conception of most journals was highly professional. With their sections for poetry, prose, criticism, and book reviews, unofficial periodicals seemed closely modeled on Soviet literary "thick" journals, such as *Novyi mir*, *Zvezda,* or *Moskva*. Many journals regularly published booklets, showcasing a particular writer in the manner of the "literary supplement" operated by some large journals.[9] Like official journals, they had dedicated section editors and submission procedures. *Chasy* even operated a subscription scheme[10]—subscribing to one or several journals was a common practice in the Soviet Union. They also featured sections for interactions with readers, such as "letters to the editor"[11] and questionnaires, a genre I shall explore below. For now, I suggest that all these features are evidence of the editors' ambition for their journals to be much more than poetry pamphlets.

*Samizdat* journals were in practice publishing ventures that effectively promoted their "house authors." Moreover, the unofficial sphere produced a handful of first-rate literary critics. Viktor Krivulin and Sergei Stratanovskii in particular were prolific scholars and critics who discussed historic works as well as contemporary writing.[12] Other figures instrumental for the conceptualization of unofficial culture are the now well-known art critic Boris Groys[13] and the thinker and critic Boris Ivanov.[14]

All over the world, the institutions of publishing houses and literary criticism have a vital influence on making the literary canon, and Soviet unofficial culture was no exception: the literary institutions of the underground created a distinctive canon, quite separate from the Soviet canon of the time. However, it seems that the rationale behind unofficial literature was not the creation of a self-contained cultural space. The relationship between official and unofficial literature was much more ambivalent. A number of factors indicate that the unofficial poets conceived of themselves as the real heirs to the Russian poetic tradition. Their literary output exhibits an intense intertextual engagement with the classical tradition in Russian poetry; their aesthetics was oriented toward the Silver Age. And indeed, the Leningrad underground made a sustained attempt at restoring the cultural and spiritual continuity with Modernism that was interrupted by the 1917 revolution, and in doing so it effectively bypassed fifty years of Soviet literature. Viktor Krivulin confidently maps out the place unofficial poetry occupies within twentieth-century literary history in his article "Dvadtsat' let noveishei russkoi poezii."[15] There, he exposes continuities between Modernism and 1970s poetry and describes the renewal of poetic language after 1960. History has proven him right: it is figures such as Viktor Krivulin himself and Elena Shvarts who are now remembered as "poets of the 1970s."[16]

The underground's turn toward literary criticism at the turn of the 1980s coincided with a wave of persecution directed against individual members and groups in the unofficial sphere, such as the emigration in July 1980, as a result of KGB harassment, of Tat'iana Goricheva, one of the founding editors of *"37."*[17] The journal was discontinued a year later, once again under pressure from the KGB.[18] At the same time, a number of new *samizdat* journals were founded, some of them short-lived, that are evidence of a shift in concern. The needs of *samizdat* authors and readers—overlapping but not synonymous groups—had evidently changed. The priority was no longer the publication of rare texts (a result of better availability, at least in *samizdat*, one would assume). The journals had likewise moved away from the objective voiced in the first issue of *"37,"* namely "to lead the conversation culture beyond its pre-written stage."[19] Rather than catering for an eclectic mixture of interests ranging from patristic theology to avant-garde poetry under a single cover, the new journals focused more strictly on the original literary work of unofficial writers, as well as on literary criticism. The preoccupation with criticism is reflected in the very titles of the second-generation *samizdat* journals. *Obvodnyi kanal* (19 issues, 1981–1993), for example, bore the subheading "Literaturno-kriticheskii zhurnal"; its short-lived predecessor, *Dialog* (three issues, 1979–1981), was called "Zhurnal kritiki i polemiki." *Severnaia pochta,* founded in 1979 as "Zhurnal stikhov i kritiki" was discontinued after the eighth issue in 1981 after the KGB applied pressure. Subsequently, one of the editors, Sergei Dediulin, was forced to emigrate.[20]

On the one hand, the emergence of secondary structures, such as a school of literary criticism, a journal dedicated solely to cataloging and reviewing material published in other journals,[21] and conferences,[22] simply indicated that over the three decades of its existence *samizdat* had managed to mature into a fully fledged literary process. It is rare for a countercultural movement to survive long enough to reach the stage of sophisticated self-reflection. However, I propose that in the case of late Soviet *samizdat*, the proliferation of literary institutions was also a sign of the symbiotic relationship between official and unofficial culture. While *samizdat* culture represented a form of inner emigration—detachment from the Soviet lifestyle and values, including literary ones—the unofficial poets never totally renounced their aspiration to become published writers, that is, to gain access to a readership not limited to their own circle. The ultimate goal of the unofficial writers remained being accepted into official literary institutions, albeit without having to conform to the aesthetic and, to a lesser degree, political standards required by these institutions, and it was precisely the condition of remaining uncensored that rendered the goal unattainable.

Evidence of this was plentiful in the decade preceding *perestroika*. In 1974, a group of five poets (Iuliia Voznesenskaia, Boris Ivanov, Viktor Krivulin, Konstantin Kuzminskii, and Evgenii Pazukhin) submitted a poetry anthology, entitled *Lepta* (*The Contribution*) and featuring work by thirty-two unofficial poets, to the *Sovetskii pisatel'* publishing house. The anthology, which would have legalized the unofficial poets' contribution to the literary process, underwent the review process but was ultimately turned down.[23] According to Boris Ivanov, the collapse of the *Lepta* project was instrumental in the foundation of the *samizdat* journals *"37"* and *Chasy* in 1976; materials earmarked for publication there found entry into the first issues of both journals.[24] In 1978, Oleg Okhapkin submitted a collection for publication to *Lenizdat*, but refused to comply with the request of his reviewers to remove terminology referring to the life of the soul. Only after his hope for a substantial official publication had been dashed did he agree to serve as literary editor for the religious *samizdat* journal *Obshchina*, which was suppressed by the KGB after the first issue (no. 2).[25] A seminal event in 1981, which at first seems a turnaround, in fact confirms the thesis of the symbiotic relationship between unofficial and official culture. Following an unsuccessful attempt at establishing a legal literary association at the library of the House of Teachers, Boris Ivanov and other editors of the journal *Chasy* reached an agreement with the KGB and the Writers' Union. The outcome was the first-ever official organization of unofficial writers, called *Klub-81* (Leningradskoe professional'noe ob"edinenie literatorov, 1981–1988). A large number of prominent unofficial writers, including Viktor Krivulin and Sergei Stratanovskii (who became a board member) joined this organization, which held regular evenings and readings.[26] The KGB's reason for effectively legalizing and protecting the activities of nonconformist writers was the desire to limit the amount of texts these writers sent abroad for publication; in this respect the collaboration had only limited success, as texts from Leningrad's second culture continued to appear in émigré publications.[27] In 1985, Sovetskii pisatel' published

Klub-81's first and only almanac, a rather slim miscellany called *Krug* (Circle).[28] Eight of the fourteen authors featured in *Krug* had contributed to the unsuccessful *Lepta* venture eleven years previously. It is thus evident that the desire to access the institutions of official literary culture remained strong among unofficial writers, overridden only by the even stronger desire to remain true to their own aesthetic standards.

## WHO OWNS ALEKSANDR BLOK?

Literary criticism was high on the agenda of the official institutions in the 1970s, which wanted to harness criticism for the purpose of shaping the mass readership's literary preferences. In January 1972, the Central Committee of the Communist Party passed the resolution "On Literary Criticism," emphasizing the necessity for criticism to remain accessible to the general reader. The journal *Literaturnoe obozrenie* (*The Literary Review*) was founded in 1973 as a direct response to the Party resolution; it focused on criticism but was addressed to a non-specialist audience.[29] Official journals not infrequently invited well-known writers to comment on cultural topics and/or their own artistic philosophy; *Literaturnoe obozrenie* in particular used this format several times in the 1970s and early 1980s.[30] Unofficial journals began using this format, too. The questionnaires we find in some of them represent a further step in the development of unofficial literary criticism. They also take the interdependence of the official and unofficial literary process to a different level.

It is worth nothing that responses by specifically chosen figures to questionnaires on particular authors (see below) or cultural phenomena[31] were only one type of the "reader feedback" *samizdat* journals published. There were also replies to questionnaires of a more "administrative" character, including some that invited readers to comment on the journal in question and propose improvements.[32] Engaging with readers in this way is, of course, editorial policy in journals all over the world. However, I believe it is fair to presume that in choosing their particular format for reader feedback, *samizdat* editors were looking toward Soviet official journals. Sometimes, the respondents employ Soviet jargon in way that can be read as ironic.[33] A further step in this direction was Boris Ivanov's satirical *samizdat* journal *Krasnyi shchedrinets* (1986–1990), a phenomenon of the *perestroika* years. Alongside satirical writings it published persiflages of the feedback sections in Soviet newspapers and journals, such as "Workers' Letters."[34]

For our investigation into the relationship between the official and unofficial literary process, questionnaires that focus on particular authors are the most rewarding field of study. If the *samizdat* journals and their criticism constitute an attempt at reclaiming the literary process, then these questionnaires, created on the occasion of the centenaries of the Symbolist poet Aleksandr Blok (1880–1921) and the Futurist Velimir Khlebnikov (1885–1922) respectively, were explicit attempts at reclaiming pre-revolutionary writers whom the unofficial poets regarded as part of their own heritage. Apparently, the Blok Questionnaire (Anketa o Bloke) was modeled on a similar one, published by Kornei Chukovskii on the centenary of the nineteenth-century poet Nikolai Nekrasov in 1921. In claiming that the need to publish an anniversary questionnaire arises "when the real feelings of the public clearly don't correspond to the arrangement of the anniversary that is celebrated, and when the person whose anniversary is celebrated evokes contradictory feelings in us" Konstantin Butyrin, who compiled the questions, appeals to a tradition of writers resisting the appropriation of poets by Soviet official culture—Nekrasov, a civic poet, was a favorite of the Bolsheviks and his writing was held up as exemplary.[35]

The Blok Questionnaire and seventeen responses to it by well-known unofficial poets and intellectuals—we can call them the alternative, self-proclaimed Leningrad canon of the time—were published in issue no. 3 (1980–1981) of the *samizdat* journal *Dialog*;[36] nine of the original responses were subsequently republished in *Severnaia pochta* no. 8.[37] The Khlebnikov Questionnaire and nineteen responses, five of which came from people who had also responded to the Blok Questionnaire, were published in *Obvodnyi kanal* no. 9.[38]

These questionnaires, examples of the work of unofficial culture's secondary institutions, generated a further level of secondary text. They attracted criticism from another, mostly younger, group of Leningrad *samizdat* writers for the choice of respondents and the opinions expressed. The poet Ry Nikonova (pseudonym of Anna Tarshis), one of the editors of the avant-garde journal *Transponans*, accused the respondents to both questionnaires of elitism and, more significantly, of aping official culture. After ridiculing some of the pronouncements made on Blok, Nikonova proceeds:

> The official barometer jerked and pointed at Khlebnikov. Editions, festivities and articles were churned out. Our Leningrad elite "responded to the call," too. The elite drew up a questionnaire . . . . Suddenly more orthodox than officious culture, these individuals synthesized a thought worthy of a genius: Well, since Khlebnikov is a genius (everybody calls him a genius now!) that means he's not an avant-garde poet.[39]

Nikonova herself was among the respondents to the Khlebnikov Questionnaire, alongside Sergei Sigei, her fellow editor at *Transponans,* Dmitrii Volchek, Vladimir Erl', and the Moscow conceptualist poet Dmitrii Prigov;

in the case of Khlebnikov, Stratanovskii, and Butyrin, the authors of
the questionnaires on both Blok and Khlebnikov, had thus taken care to
include respondents who upheld avant-garde poetics. Nikonova's criticism—
unfounded, perhaps, and/or infused with not a small dose of irony—is most
probably levied primarily at those influential editors (Stratanovskii, Butyrin,
Krivulin, and others) who were setting the tone in the majority of unofficial
publications but were rather conservatively minded (i.e., not "avant-garde").
Evidence of factional strife of this kind is to be expected in a developed literary scene, but Nikonova's spite highlights a specific feature of the late Soviet
underground, namely the constant presence of official culture as a realm situated outside *samizdat* that nevertheless had the power to define the value of
most things said or written by *samizdat* authors.

The rest of the discussion will focus on the Blok Questionnaire. While
Khlebnikov, who gained popularity among unofficial writers in the 1970s,
remained virtually unpublished after 1941 and was "rediscovered" by official culture only shortly before his centenary in 1984,[40] Blok constituted an
exception among the Silver Age poets in that his work was well promoted
during the Soviet years. Blok's favorable position was a result of his apparent
welcoming of the 1917 revolution and in particular his poem "The Twelve"
("Dvenadtsat'"), written in 1918. His centenary in 1980 was the occasion for
many events, including a formal evening in the Bolshoi Theatre attended by
several high-ranking members of the Communist Party (Grishin, Kirilenko,
Suslov)[41] and several conferences.[42] In Leningrad, a museum (*muzei-kvartira
A. A. Bloka*) opened in the house in which the poet had spent his last years
and died (ul. Dekabristov 57). A new TV film, called "I vechnyi boi . . . Iz
zhizni Aleksandra Bloka" and based on episodes from his life, was shot and
aired, the state publishing house Khudozhestvennaia literatura published a
collected works in six volumes,[43] and the series *Literaturnoe nasledstvo* produced four volumes of materials on Blok.[44] Issue number 11 for 1980 of the
reputable and widely read literary monthly *Novyi mir* dedicated a large section to the memory of Blok. In her reply to the Blok Questionnaire in *Dialog*,
Elena Ignatova mentions a Blok questionnaire for visitors in the Dvorets
kul'tury in Leningrad.[45]

Official Blok scholarship worked hard in order to present Blok primarily as
a civic poet, and the materials published on the occasion of the anniversary
were typical in this respect: "Blok's exhortation to the intelligentsia to 'listen
to the music of the revolution,' and his immortal poem 'The Twelve,' permeated as it is by the sensation of the majestic steps of the revolution, remain
for us a clear example of the civic spirit in art and of the artist's faithfulness
to his obligation before history and his people."[46]

"Civic poet" is not the first term that comes to mind when reading Blok, if
it comes to mind at all. Blok was primarily a representative of the mystical

current of Russian Symbolism. His early poetry is heavily indebted to the teachings of the religious thinker Vladimir Solov'ev, and his writings, not least "The Twelve" itself, remained permeated by religious imagery. This aspect of Blok's work, which sits uneasily with the emphasis on his revolutionary credentials, was of particular importance to the unofficial poets. For the Leningrad poets high culture—epitomized in the culture of the Silver Age—held spiritual significance; they studied religious philosophy and Silver Age literature, and many of them wrote poems replete with elaborate religious and/or Christian imagery.[47] Significantly, those who responded to the Blok Questionnaire, gave importance to the religious/mystical element in Blok's work, with only one exception (Elena Ignatova). It is worth noting that both editors of *Dialog*, Kirill Butyrin and Sergei Stratanovskii, had attended a special seminar on Blok at Leningrad State University in the 1960s, as had several of the other respondents, for example, Viktor Krivulin.[48]

The difference between the Blok Questionnaire and an official journal questionnaire lies not in the format, or in the language of the questions, but in the replies, which interpret Blok in a way that is very different from that given by official Blok scholarship.[49] We can assume that Butyrin and Stratanovskii counted on their respondents for this effect; Stratanovskii even published his own responses. Let us now look at some of the responses in greater detail. Question 4 asks: "What does the religio-mystical aspect of Blok's poetry mean to you? What do you think of his poetry's attitude toward the relationship between poetry and religion (first and foremost Christianity) and toward mysticism in the broad sense?"[50]

The emphasis on religion notwithstanding, the question itself is not necessarily subversive, provided the respondents can be expected to downplay or condemn this aspect of Blok's work. But the unofficial poets relished the opportunity to highlight it instead. Tat'iana Vol'tskaia writes: "The religio-mystical aspect of Blok's poetry is very important for me. As has been said before, I look at his poetry through the prism of Christianity."[51] Elena Pudovkina adds, "It seems to me that poetry is always linked to religion."[52] Iurii Kublanovskii, on the other hand, calls Blok's approach to religion "outdated," because it is beset by "decadence and the traditional complexes of the intelligentsia."

Question 5 reads, "In your opinion, is the poem 'The Twelve' an aide or an obstacle to understanding Blok's work as a whole, especially before 1917?"[53] This question's potential for provocation is even higher than Question 4, placing as it does under scrutiny the very cornerstone of Blok's reputation in Soviet official culture. Some of the answers warrant quotation in full. Tamara Bukovskaia's answer is tongue-in-cheek and expresses open contempt for the famous poem:

What the writer has written cannot be an 'obstacle' if you want to see what is rather than what you would like to see. What helps—as a comment—are the memoirs of G. Ivanov, who writes that before his death Blok destroyed all copies of "The Twelve" he had to hand and called [to his wife] "Lyuba, that bastard Briusov still has a few copies, go to him, collect them and burn them!"[54]

In a much more sober tone, Elena Ignatova refutes the default standpoint of official criticism: "'The Twelve' neither helps nor hinders 'perception of [Blok's] work' since it is a creation in its own right rather than a key to the poet's work as a whole."[55] Viktor Krivulin's assessment is perhaps the most enlightening: "'The Twelve' . . . is the Trojan Horse of Symbolism and the religio-mystical quest in the acropolis of Soviet literature. Had Blok not written 'The Twelve' we who started school after the Second World War would not only be unaware of the name of Aleksandr Blok, but would also have no way into the culture of the early twentieth century—no approach at all."[56]

Rather than downplay the importance of the poem, Krivulin interprets its popularity in the interests of unofficial culture. Blok thus turns into a kindred spirit, the source of precisely that poetic key in which the unofficial poets are writing. It follows that they are his rightful heirs and, since Blok is a renowned classic, heirs to the classical tradition.

Two further questions, 2 and 7, give the respondents ample opportunity to declare the Soviet official approach to Blok invalid or at least skewed. Moreover, both questions insinuate that official culture is ignorant of other Silver Age writers who might be more deserving. In their responses to Question 7, several unofficial writers decry the lack of erudition and/or discernment of the typical Soviet reader, thereby implicitly placing themselves outside or above this group: "How do you explain Blok's popularity with the mass readership and Soviet literary scholarship, especially in comparison to his peers? Is this situation just?"[57]

Tamara Bukovskaia asserts that Blok would not be popular if his work was not so widely available and considered "safe" for readers and researchers alike: "With the fact that [his work] is permitted and available. The Russian reader is lazy and lacks curiosity. The literary scholar is obsessed with the pathos of remunerated enlightenment—he writes when his writings can be published. Let's not forget that Blok died of natural causes, and that he died in Russia; this is very important for literary scholarship."[58]

In a similar vein, Tat'iana Vol'tskaia reckons that Blok's popularity can be ascribed to ideological considerations rather than literary merit. "I think that in as far as Soviet official literary scholarship is concerned, Blok's poem 'The Twelve' and his so-called 'acceptance of the revolution' had a significant impact on his popularity."[59] Moreover, by labeling Blok's acceptance of the revolution "so-called" Vol'tskaia contends that the ideological justification for his popularity may be incorrect. Question 2, on the other hand, enables the respondents to showcase their own erudition: "Do you consider Blok the first poet of the 'beginning of the century,' or perhaps even the best Russian poet of the 20th century? If not, who do you prefer to Blok?"[60]

In order to appreciate the invitation to provocation in this question, we must bear in mind that official culture habitually hailed Blok as the greatest poet of the Silver Age: "From the middle of the last century onwards and up to our days Blok is in the very center of poetic attraction . . . . From our historical distance, the magnificent 'Silver Age' of Russian poetry already presents itself as the Blok pleiad . . . ."[61] The issue at stake here is not so much the centrality of Blok in official criticism but rather, the fact that official culture had been skeptical of the majority of Silver Age writers for most of the Soviet period. Modernism had been repressed during Stalinism (this included the physical annihilation of many outstanding writers) and was rehabilitated slowly from the 1960s onwards. The aesthetics of Leningrad unofficial poetry, on the other hand, was heavily indebted to Modernism; moreover, many unofficial poets were experts on one or several Silver Age writers.[62] In other words, the unofficial writers' claim to cultural superiority over official culture was objectively justified when the Silver Age is concerned. Viktor Krivulin's answer was a display of erudition and evidence to a taste that is resolutely opposed to the official dictate: "I don't consider Blok to be the first poet of the early twentieth century. I prefer Khlebnikov, Mandel'shtam, even Khodasevich. I think Mandel'shtam was right when he labeled Blok a provincial poet (in the article 'The Badger's Hole')."[63]

All the names listed by Krivulin had been contentious only a few years ago. Khlebnikov, famous for his transrational (*zaum*) poetry, was little known in the Soviet Union until the 1970s.[64] The first substantial Soviet collection of the work of Mandel'shtam, who had died in the Gulag in 1938, was published in 1973.[65] Khodasevich was an émigré and as such suspicious.[66] By citing his favorite Mandel'shtam's denigrating view of Blok, Krivulin insinuates that official criticism has not risen above the very provinciality Mandel'shtam decries.

To sum up, this is how the unofficial poets perceive Blok: he is not the most important representative of the Silver Age aesthetic, "The Twelve" is neither his most important poem nor a key to this work as a whole, while religion and mysticism are inalienable constituents of his creativity. This conclusion opposes the main tenets of the official stance on Blok. To borrow Krivulin's expression, the quasi-official format of the Questionnaire has the function of a Trojan horse—an instrument popularized by the official literary process is used to express an attitude toward Blok that is anything but Soviet and to reclaim a contested writer for the unofficial sphere. The unofficial poets' contribution to Blok scholarship was formally recognized in 2011 when the Questionnaire was republished in a collected volume of new research on Blok that forms part of a regular series.[67] The Blok Questionnaire has effectively come full circle.


## EVALUATION

How does the Questionnaire—its very existence, its format, and its content— help us clarify the relationship between the official and unofficial literary process? One might be tempted to see in the Questionnaire an example of what Sergei Oushakine, in his study of the language of political *samizdat*, calls "mimicry."[68] Oushakine elaborates on how dissidents used the official language of a given political system ("the authoritative discourse") in order to criticize that very system, for example, when they wrote letters exhorting the authorities to abide by the Soviet constitution. Drawing on Michel Foucault's concept of "mimetic resistance" and the work of scholars including Bakhtin, Gadamer, and Homi Bhaba, Oushakine concludes: "This mixture of inten- tions caused by being constituted by the authoritative discourse as well as by being constituted at a location different from that of the authorities finally produces a 'replication' of the dominant discourse that 'terrorizes authority with the *ruse* of recognition, its mimicry, its mockery.'"[69]

There certainly exist parallels between political dissidents and unofficial writers. To start with, literary and other "cultural" *samizdat* texts were politi- cal in that they existed outside Soviet official culture, which tolerated no out- siders. This "politicization by default" already justifies calling the members of this subculture if not "dissidents," then certainly "dissenters." Indeed, some definitions of "dissident" can be applied to Leningrad's unofficial writ- ers and thinkers with only minor adjustments, for example: "Dissent implies taking a critical stance with *no* intention of replacing the government or political order."[70] This definition is accurate if we substitute "cultural order" for "political order" and are prepared to regard the officially unacceptable aesthetics of the Leningrad underground as a "critical stance." Moreover, the activists of unofficial culture shared the fate of many political dissidents, including social marginalization and quasi-forced emigration.

Looked upon in isolation, then, it makes perfect sense to conceptualize a device such as the Questionnaire as "mimetic resistance." However, in the overall context of unofficial culture the concept of "mimicry" is of limited utility as a definition of the linguistic devices employed by the unofficial poets in their quest to make Blok their own. Ultimately the agenda of the unofficial poets in relation to the official literary process was very different from that of the political dissidents in relation to the authorities: the objective was not to correct the course of the literary process but rather to claim a space within that very process.

The unofficial writers were masters of *stiob* (pronounced "styob")—the undermining or ridiculing of literary or cultural discourses by first copying and then transplanting their symbols into an alien context. The explanatory note accompanying the republished Questionnaire in *Severnaia pochta* is a perfect example of this technique: "The Questionnaire was offered to a number of men and women of letters through the Leningrad journal *Dialog* on the occasion of the one hundredth anniversary of the birth of A. A. Blok. We thank the editors for the possibility to republish the poets' answers on the pages of *Severnaia pochta*."[71] The words do not disclose that the "Leningrad journal" in question is an illegal stapled typescript that circulated in no more than twenty-four copies.[72] More importantly, the respondents are identified here as "men and women of letters" and "poets," implying that they enjoy a certain standing in society. Nothing hints at the fact that the works of these authors cannot be acquired in a bookshop or found in a library. The stock phrase "We thank the editors for the opportunity to republish . . ." conceals the fact that the editors of both journals were close friends.

In short, the high-flying words constitute a sharp contrast to the poor carbon copy in which they appear. The Questionnaire's format belongs to an official journal with several hundreds of thousands of readers. Its use in a self-made publication that could hope for maybe a hundred readers, mostly drawn from among the friends of the authors, throws into sharp relief the vast distance between the two cultural spheres, highlighting unofficial culture's shabbiness and its courage while exposing the contingency of official culture's symbols and methods. There is a "rhetoric of absolute non-belonging, radical alienation" from the official literary process in those replies that seem deliberately to contradict the official doctrine on Blok. Simultaneously, these replies are by definition references to official culture and as such demonstrate "an unconscious and obtrusive dependence on the object from which one is distancing oneself"; thus the Questionnaire exhibits the defining characteristics of *steb* according to Boris Dubin.[73] However, as this chapter has once again shown, unofficial culture's alienation from the official literary process can hardly be called "total"—the third characteristic of *steb*.[74]

The unofficial poets maintained a stance of unabashed superiority to the official literary process, as is evident in their complex poetry with its multilayered references to Silver Age authors, Russian and Western classics, and Scripture that was intended for a reader of similar tastes and erudition. At the same time, they entertained a symbiotic relationship with the official process that was ultimately driven by the desire to participate, albeit without compromising their own aesthetics. The Blok Questionnaire as a whole neatly reflects these tensions. Its very existence may be an instance of *steb*, the ironic misappropriation of an authoritative discourse. But the individual replies, many of which are thoughtful and scholarly (e.g., those by Krivulin,

Okhapkin, and Stratanovskii) testify to a more complex, multilayered relationship between the official and unofficial literary process, which coexisted uneasily but increasingly closely until *perestroika* and the fall of the Soviet Union rendered this division of Russian literature obsolete.

## NOTES

1. Information on the project can be found on http://www.mod-langs.ox.ac.uk/russian/reading-dissent/.

2. For very detailed information on this phenomenon, see the first part of Emily Lygo's *Leningrad Poetry 1953–1975: The Thaw Generation* (New York: Peter Lang, 2010). Consulting the biographical entries for figures such as Krivulin, Stratanovskii, Elena Shvarts et al., in D. Severiukhin, V. Dolinin, B. Ivanov, and B. Ostanin, eds., *Samizdat Leningrada: 1950e—1980e gody: Literaturnaia entsiklopediia* (Moscow: Novoe Liternoe Obozrenie, 2003) shows that, for example, a large number of unofficial poets attended the LITOs led by Gleb Semenov in the 1960s. See also Elena Pudovkina's memoir on literary youth clubs and their teachers "Klub 'Derzanie,'" *Pchela* nos. 26–27 (2000), http://www.pchela.ru/podshiv/26_27/club.htm.

3. "chasto zamenia[li] liudiam nesushchestvuiushchie, nedostupnye ili po raznym prichinam nepriemlemye uchrezhdeniia—izdatel'stva, lektorii, vystavki, doski ob"iavlenii, ispovedal'ni, kontsertnye zaly, biblioteki, muzei, iuridicheskie konsul'tatsii, kruzhki viazaniia . . . a takzhe seminary po literature, istorii, filosofii, lingvistike." Liudmila Alekseeva and Paul Goldberg, *Pokolenie ottepeli* (Moscow: Zakharov, 2006), 91.

4. "Nepriznanie vyrazhalos' v rezko otlichnom ot sovetskogo obraza zhizni. Rabota sutki cherez troe i knigi—vot kak mozhno lakonichno opisat' nesovetskii obraz zhizni. Knigi byli samoi bol'shoi radost'iu i tsel'iu okhoty. Utonchennye i glubokie znaniia otechestvennoi i osobenno zarubezhnoi literatury i istorii schitalis' priznakami aristokrata, cheloveka vysokoi tvorcheskoi organizatsii, u kotorogo nichego obshchego net s rabochim liudom." Natalia Chernykh, "Kontsert dlia geniia pervonachal'noi nishchety," http://nattch.narod.ru/nbmironov.html.

5. Boris Grebenshchikov, frontman of the legendary rock group Akvarium, dedicated a song to his contemporaries, aptly entitled "Pokolenie dvorniikov i storozhei" ("The generation of caretakers and nightwatchmen"). Viacheslav Dolinin, a Leningrad *samizdat* activist and himself a boiler room stoker, remembers his place of work in the title of his memoirs: *Ne stol' otdalennaia kochegarka: Rasskazy, vospominaniia* (St. Petersburg: Izdatel'stvo Novikovoi, 2005). Boris Ostanin, editor of *Chasy*, works in a boiler room to the present day. There was even a serial almanac that only published texts by authors who worked in boiler rooms, supposedly addressing a cultural cliché with irony, *Topka* (1988–1992); the title means "furnace" or "stoking," but also transcribes the acronym Tvorcheskoe Ob"edinenie Preslovutykh Kotel'nykh Avtorov (Creative Association of the Notorious Boiler Room Authors).

6. Olga Sedakova and Slava I. Yastremski, "A Dialogue on Poetry," in Olga Sedakova, *Poems and Elegies*, ed. by Slava I. Yastremski (Lewisburg, PA: Bucknell University Press, 2003), 11–20, here, 15.

7. "Ia nazval by (eto pololenie) pokoleniem, razbitym vdrebezgi, ibo ono ne sozdalo nichego. . . . ono bylo al'ternativnym pokoleniem. A al'ternativnoe pokolenie—eto negativ. Eto ne izmenenie konfiguratsii. Eto to zhe samoe, tol'ko obratnogo tsveta." Arkadii Dragomoshchenko and Nikolai Beliak, "My govorim ne o meste, a o sud'be pokoleniia. Beseda s Tat'ianoi Koval'kovoi," in *Sumerki Saigona*, ed. Iu. Valieva (St. Petersburg: Samizdat, 2009), 146–48, here, 147.

8. "Kul'turnyi proval posle poeticheskoi pleiady Peterburga nachala veka dolzhen byl byt' zapolnen—nami. I eto oshchushchenie, kak pokazalo vremia, bylo pravil'nym." Anna Katsman (Krivulina), "Kofe s limonom—vkus vremeni," in Valieva, *Sumerki Saigona*, 261–64, here, 261.

9. To give a single example, *Chasy* published works by the following authors in the form of "literaturnoe prilozhenie": Arkadii Dragomoshchenko, Viktor Krivulin, Elena Shvarts, Elena Ignatova, Alain Robbe-Grille, Grigorii Pomerants, Sergei Stratanovskii et al. For a full list see: http://arch.susla.ru/index.php/%D0%A1%D0%BE%D0%B4%D0%B5%D1%80%D0%B6%D0%B0%D0%BD%D0%B8%D0%B5_%D0%B6%D1%83%D1%80%D0%BD%D0%B0%D0%BB%D0%B0_%C2%AB%D0%A7%D0%B0%D1%81%D1%8B%C2%BB._%D0%9F%D0%A0%D0%98%D0%9B%D0%9E%D0%96%D0%95%D0%9D%D0%98%D0%AF.

10. Described, for example, by Boris Ostanin, "'Bez redaktsii starykh bol'shevikov andergraunda' ili shto takoe *Chasy*," *Cogita!ru*, October 8, 2011, http://www.cogita.ru/news/sobytiya-i-anonsy-2009-2011/abbez-redakcii-staryh-bolshevikov-andegraundabb-ili-chto-takoe-abchasybb.

11. For example, in *"37"* no. 11.

12. A list of their critical writings can be found under their biographical entries in *Samizdat Leningrada*. Both published most of their criticism under pseudonyms, Krivulin as A. Kalomirov and Stratanovskii as N. Golubev.

13. One of the first theoretical discussions of conceptualism, Boris Groys's now iconic "Moskovskii romanticheskii kontseptualizm" was first published in *"37"* no. 15 (1978).

14. Alongside his publications in *samizdat* periodicals it is also worth looking at Boris Ivanov, "Po tu storonu ofitsial'nosti," in *Samizdat: Po materialam konferentsii '30 let nezavisimoi pechati. 1950–80 gody'* (St. Petersburg: NITs "Memorial," 1993), 82–93; "V bytnost' Peterburga Leningradom: O leningradskom samizdate," *NLO* 14 (1995): 188–99; "Evoliutsiia literaturnykh dvizhenii v piatidesiatye-vos'midesiatye gody," in *Istoriia leningradskoi nepodtsenzurnoi literatury*, ed. B. Ivanov and B. Roginskii (St. Petersburg: DEAN, 2000), 17–28.

15. A. Kalomirov [Viktor Krivulin], "Dvadtsat' let noveishei russkoi poezii," *Severnaia pochta* no. 1–2 (1979).

16. Shvarts is widely published in foreign languages, including English. The renowned Bloodaxe publishing house has produced two full collections, *Paradise* (1993) and *Birdsong on the Seabed* (2008). In addition, she is represented in anthologies, such as Evgenii Bunimovich and J. Kates, eds., *Contemporary Russian Poetry: An Anthology* (Champaign, IL: Dalkey Archive Press, 2008) and J. Kates and Mikhail Aizenberg, eds., *In the Grip of Strange Thoughts: Russian Poetry in A New Era* (London: Bloodaxe, 1998). The latter also includes work by Krivulin

and Stratanovskii. In my article "Self-Canonisation as a Way into the Canon: The Case of the Leningrad Underground," *Australian and East European Studies* 31, forthcoming in 2017, I discuss the techniques by which the underground poets wrote themselves into the canon.

17. *Samizdat Leningrada*, 153. *"37"* no. 20 was dedicated to Goricheva and contained a short text and photographs taken on the eve of her departure.

18. *Samizdat Leningrada*, 458.

19. "vyvesti kul'turu obshcheniia iz dopis'mennogo sostoianiia." This purpose was proclaimed, in capital letters, in the editor's foreword to the first issue (1976). The first issues in particular devoted a large amount of space to publicizing some of the papers given and discussions held at the sessions of the Religious-Philosophical Seminar and related events.

20. *Samizdat Leningrada,* 450. In his memoir, *Istoriia Kluba-81*, on p. 37. Boris Ivanov states that the discontinuation of *Severnaia pochta* was the KGB's precondition for allowing the foundation of Klub-81 (see below and note 26).

21. Between 1979 and 1982, Sergei Maslov and a number of others published eight issues of *Summa: Referativnyi seminar samizdata. Summa* was republished in book form: *"Summa" za zvobodnuiu mysl'* (St. Petersburg: Zvezda, 2002).

22. In 1979, Boris Ivanov and Boris Ostanin, the editors of *Chasy*, organized two conferences on the significance of the unofficial cultural movement. The materials of these conferences, including some of the papers given, were published in *"37"* no. 19 (1979) and *Chasy* nos. 21, 22 (1979), 23, 24 (1980). See also V. Nechaev, "Nravstvennoe znachenie neofitsial'noi kul'tury v Rossii: Materialy konferentsii v musee sovremennoi zhivopisi," *Poiski* 1 (1979), 303–14.

23. For information on the *Lepta* affair, see *Samizdat Leningrada*, 419. The documentation relating to the *Lepta* case, including the table of contents, the protocols of the editorial committee meetings, and the correspondence with Sovetskii pisatel' are published in *The Blue Lagoon Anthology*, vol. 5B.

24. Boris Ivanov, "V bytnost' Peterburga Leningradom," 192.

25. Okhapkin's comments on the events of 1978 can be read in "Khristianskii Seminar," *Vol'noe slovo* 39 (1981): 92. The editor's suggestions for cuts he described as a suggestion to "maim my poems" ("mne predlagaiut iskalechit' svoi stikhi").

26. Klub-81 is described in *Samizdat Leningrada*, 410–13. A list of members and foundation documents are held in the archive of the Research and Information Centre "Memorial," St. Petersburg. Shortly before his death in 2015, Boris Ivanov published the entire history of Klub-81, including foundation documents and correspondence with official bodies: *Istoriia Kluba-81* (SPB: Izdatel'stvo Ivana Limbakha, 2015).

27. Eduard Shneiderman, himself a member of Klub-81, describes this process and provides a list of new *tamizdat* publications in "Klub-81 i KGB," *Zvezda* no. 8 (2004): 209–17.

28. B. Ivanov and Iu. Novikov, eds., *Krug: Literaturno-khudozhestvennyi sbornik* (Leningrad: Sovetskii pisatel', 1985).

29. Discussed in Stephen Lovell, *The Russian Reading Revolution: Print Culture in the Soviet and Post-Soviet Eras* (Basingstoke: Macmillan, 2000), in particular, 50 ff.

30. *Literaturnoe obozrenie* ran a rubric called "Literatura i chitatel.'" In nos. 7 and 8 (1977) nine writers published their thoughts on the relationship between the writer and his/her audience (four questions) under the heading "Naedine so vsemi." *Literaturnoe obozrenie* no. 8 (1981) explicitly invited comments from readers.

31. The editors of *"37"* were keen to publicize fellow unofficial intellectuals' opinions on the relationship between religion and culture. In no. 14 (1978), they published the artist Vadim Filimonov's responses to a questionnaire on the topic of "Christianity and Art"; in no. 16 (1978) we find the responses of the poet Iuliia Voznesenskaia to the questionnaire "Christianity and Culture." *Obvodnyi kanal* no. 6 (1984) published a questionnaire asking unofficial Leningrad writers to comment on the art exhibition in the Young Pioneer's Palace. The four respondents include Viktor Krivulin and Arkadii Dragomoshchenko.

32. For example, in *"37"* no. 17 (1979); the questionnaire invites the reader to comment on how much time they spent reading the journal and which section they preferred. The questionnaire plus responses are in the copy of no. 17 that survived, in the Keston Archive (Baylor University, Texas, USA); they do not appear to have made it into every copy of the issue. A draft that looks similar to this questionnaire is preserved in the personal archive of Viktor Krivulin (fond 71) in the archive of the Centre for the Study of Eastern Europe (Forschungsstelle Osteuropa), University of Bremen, Germany.

33. "I think that the editors ought to struggle relentlessly for the interests of the reader. Materials that are written for oneself or a very narrow circle of readers need to be curtailed." ("Mne kazhetsia, chto redaktsiia dolzhna bezzhalostno borot'sia za interesy chitatelia, te materialy, kotorye pishutsia dlia sebia ili dlia kraine uzkogo kruga, nado otsekat.'") *"37"* no. 17 (1979). The expression "ought to struggle relentlessly" is a set phrase in Soviet officialese.

34. *Samizdat Leningrada*, 414. Issues of *Krasnyi shchedrinets* can be found in the archive of the Research and Information Center "Memorial" in St. Petersburg.

35. "provodit' [iubileinye ankety] imeet smysl, kogda real'nye chuvsta obshchestvennosti zametno ne sovpadiut s iubileinoi ustanovkoi i kogda sam 'iubiliar' vyzyvaet u nas protivorechivye chuvstva." In "Anketa ob A. A. Bloke v zhurnale 'Dialog.' Predislovie," in *Aleksandr Blok: Issledovaniia i materialy*, ed. E. I. Goncharova, N. Iu. Gradkova, and A. V. Lavrov (St. Petersburg: Pushkinskii dom, 2011), 543–46, here, 546. The centenary questionnaire on Nekrasov was published in *Letopis' Doma literatorov*, no. 3 (1921) in Prague. Butyrin remembers compiling the questions for the Blok Questionnaire, but the idea itself seems to have been a joint project that involved him and Sergei Stratanovskii, his co-editor.

36. See: V. E. Dolinin, B. I. Ivanov, B. V. Ostanin, D. Ia. Severiukhin, eds., *Samizdat Leningrada 1950e–1980e: Literaturnaia entsiklopediia* (Moscow: Novoe Literaturnoe Obozrenie, 2003), 402–3. Copies held in private archives.

37. The original respondents were Viktor Antonov, Andrei Ar'ev, Tamara Bukovskaia, Konstantin Butyrin, Tat'iana Vol'tskaia, Iurii Dinaburg, Boris Ivanov, Viktor Krivulin, Iurii Kublanovskii, Georgii Levinton, Ivan Martynov, Aleksandr Mironov, Oleg Okhapkin, Elena Pudovkina, Sergei Stratanovskii, Fedor Chirskov, and Vladimir Shenkman. The responses of Bukovskaia, Vol'tskaia, Ignatova, Krivulin, Kublanovskii, Okhapkin, Pudovkina, Stratanovskii, and Shenkman were republished in *Severnaia pochta*.

38. The respondents were Konstantin Azadovskii, A. Aleksandrov, Andrei Ar'ev, Grigorii Benevich, Dmitrii Volchek, Elena Ignatova, I. K-V., Viktor Krivulin, Vladimir Lapenkov, Tat'iana Nikol'skaia, Ry Nikonova, Evgenii Pazukhin, Dmitrii Prigov, Sergei Sigei, Sergei Stratanovskii, Vladimir Ufliand, Fedor Chirskov, Eduard Shneiderman, and Vladimir Erl'.

39. "Ofitsial'nyi barometer vzdrognul i pokazal na Khlebnikova. Pokatilis' izda-niia, iubileii stat'i. 'Otkliknulas" i Leningradskaia elita. Elita soorudila ankety . . . . Vdrug okazavshis' pravee ofitsioza, eti osoby sintezirovali v sebe genial'nuiu mysl'" da, raz Khlebnikov genii (a skazano teper' vsiudu: genii) znachit, on—ne avangard-ist." "Anketnaia ikra Obvodnogo kanala" *Transponans* no. 34 (1986).

40. The only exception is a 400-page volume of his poetry that appeared in the *Biblioteka poeta* series during the Thaw: V. Khlebnikov, *Stikhotvoreniia i poemy* (Leningrad: Sovetskii pisatel', 1960).

41. Reported in *Literaturnaia gazeta*, December 3, 1980 and *Pravda*, November 27, 1980, 3.

42. Conferences took place on November 24–26, 1980 at the Moscow Literary Institute (Pushkinskii Dom Akademii Nauk SSSR); on November 19–20, 1980 at the Philology Faculty of Moscow State University; on November 21, 1980 in Kiev; there was also a Blok Anniversary Conference in Tartu.

43. *Sobranie sochinenii v shesti tomakh* (Leningrad: Khudozhestvennaia literatura, 1980).

44. M. B. Khrapchenko and V. R. Shcherbina, eds. *Aleksandr Blok: Novye mate-rialy i issledovaniia*, vol. 92: 1–4, *Literaturnoe nasledstvo* (Moscow: Izdatel'stvo "Nauka," 1980–1987).

45. I have been unable to find further reports on this questionnaire or the question-naire itself.

46. "Prizyvy Bloka k intelligentsii "slushat' muzyku revoliutsii," ego bessmertnaia poema "Dvenadtsat,'" naskvoz' proniknutaia oshchushcheniem derzhavnoi postupi revoliutsii, ostaiutsia dlia nas iarkim primerom grazhdanstvennosti v iskusstve, vernosti khudozhnika svoemu dolgu pered narodom i istoriei." Introduction to the materials published on the occasion of the one hundredth anniversary of the birth of A. Blok, in *Novyi mir* 11 (1980): 224.

47. Sergei Stratanovskii has studied this link in four articles on his contemporaries, "Religioznye motivy v sovremennoi russkoi poezii," published in the journal *Volga*, nos. 4, 5, 6, and 8 (1993). I have commented extensively on the use of religious imag-ery in *samizdat* poetry in *Poetry and the Religious-Philosophical Seminar (Leningrad 1974–1980): Music for a Deaf Age* (Oxford: Legenda, 2015).

48. See *Samizdat Leningrada*, 229, 402.

49. Konstantin Butyrin defines the main reason for publishing the questionnaire as "to give a voice to those poets and critics whose opinion could not possibly be heard in the official press, at least not in an appropriate way, but was valued . . . in sufficiently large circles within unofficial culture" ("Dat' vozmozhnost' vyskazat'sia tem poetam i kritikam, ch'e mnenie zavedomo ne moglo prozvuchat' v ofitsial'noi pechati, po kraine mere v adekvatnom vide, no tem ne menee tsenilos' . . . v dostato-chno shirokikh krugakh neofitsial'noi kul'tury"), in "Anketa ob A. A. Bloke v zhur-nale 'Dialog.' Predislovie," 544.

50. "Kakoe otnoshenie imeet dlia Vas religiozno-misticheskii aspekt poezii Bloka? Chto Vy dumaete ob otnoshenii ego poezii k religii (prezhde vsego, khristianskoi), k mistike v shirokom smysle slova?"

51. "Religiozno-misticheskii aspekt poezii Bloka dlia menia ochen' vazhen. Kak uzhe skazano vyshe, poeziia ego viditsia mne skvoz' khristianskuiu prizmu."

52. "Mne kazhetsia, poeziia vsegda sviazana s religei."

53. "Meshaet ili pomogaet Vam poema 'Dvenadtsat'' vosprinimat' tvorchestvo Bloka v tselom, osobenno tvorchestvo do 1917 goda?"

54. "Napisannoe poetom 'meshat'' ne mozhet, esli khochesh' uvidet' to, chto est', a ne to, chto khochetsia. A pomogaiut—v kachestve komentariia—vospominaniia G. Ivanova, kotoryi pishet, chto Blok pered smert'iu unichtozhil ostavshiesia u nego ekzempliary 'Dvenadtsati' i krichal 'Liuba, u svolochi Briusova eshche ostalos' neskol'ko shtuk, poezzhai, zaberi i sozhgi!'"

55. "'Dvenadtsat'' ne meshaet i ne pomogaet 'vosprinimat' tvorchestvo,' ibo eto samotsennoe tvorenie, a ne shifr ko vsem tvorchestvu."

56. "'Dvenadtsat'' . . . troianskii kon' simvolizma i religiozno-misticheskikh iskanii v akropole sovetskoi slovesnosti. Ne napishi Blok 'Dvenadtsat',' nam, poshedshim v shkolu posle voiny, ne tol'ko imia Aleksandra Bloka ne bylo by izvestno, no i nikakikh putei ne vidno k kul'ture nachala veka—nikakikh podstupov."

57. "Chem vy ob"iasniaete bol'shuiu populiarnost' Bloka v chitatel'skoi masse, ofitsial'nom sovetskom literaturovedenii—osobenno v sravnenii s ego sovremenni-kami? Spravedlivo li takoe polozhenie veshchei?"

58. "Razreshennost'iu i dostupnost'iu. Russkii chitatel' leniv i neliubopyten. Lit-eraturoved oderzhim pafosom oplachennogo prosveshcheniia—pishet, kogda mozhno opublikovat'. Ne zabudem, chto Blok umer svoei smert'iu i na Rodine, dlia literaturo-vedeniia eto kraine vazhno."

59. "Dumaiu, chto v ofitsial'nom sovetskom literaturovedenii na populiarnost' Bloka sil'no povliiali ego 'Dvenadtsat'' i tak nazyvamoe 'priniatie revoliutsii.'"

60. "Iavliaetsia li dlia Vas Blok pervym poeteom 'nachala veka,' mozhet byt' voob-shche luchim russkim poetom XX veka? Esli net, to komu Vy otdaete predpochtenie pered Blokom?"

61. "S serediny proshlogo veka po nashi dni Blok stoit kak by v tsentre poet-icheskogo pritiazheniia . . . Velikolepnyi 'serebrianyi vek' russkoi poezii iz nyneshnei istoricheskoi dali uzhe risuetsia nam kak blokovskaia pleiada . . . ." I. Rodnianskaia, "'Muza Aleksandra Bloka,' from the materials published on the occasion of the 100th anniversary of the birth of A. Blok," in *Novyi mir* no. 11 (1980): 230.

62. Krivulin wrote his master's thesis on Innokentii Annenskii. Oleg Okhapkin was the first host of the unofficial seminar on Nikolai Gumilev, "Gumilevskie chteniia," in 1976. Gumilev, who was shot in 1921 as a counterrevolutionary, was still taboo in 1976, as Evgenii Pasukhin remembers in his memoir *Zerkalo slavy* (Samizdat, 1988), 14. OBERIU, the last Modernist group, was "rediscovered" only in 1967, through A. Aleksandrov's and Mikhail Meilakh's paper at the Tartu student conference in 1967. See *Materialy XXII Nauchnoi studencheskoi konferentsii* (Tartu: Tartuskii gosu-darstvennyi universitet, 1967), 101–4, 105–15.

63. "Ia ne schitaiu Bloka pervym russkim poetom nachala XX veka. Predpochitaiu emu Khlebnikova, Mandel'shtama, dazhe Khodasevicha. Dumaiu, chto prav Mandel'shtam, otsenivaia Bloka kak provintsial'nogo poeta (v stat'e 'Barsuch'ia nora')."

64. See note 40.

65. In the series "Biblioteka poeta." His final cycle, "Voronezhskie tetradi" (1934–1937), was published in 1966.

66. The re-emergence of Silver Age names in the 1970s is described in V. V. Ivanov, "Metasemioticheskie rassuzhdenie o periodike 1968–1985 gg.," in *Semidesiatye kak predmet istorii russkoi kul'tury* in *Rossiia/Russia,* 1 (9), ed. K. Iu. Rogov (Moscow: OGI, 1998).

67. E. I. Goncharova, N. Iu. Gradkova, A. V. Lavrov, eds., *Aleksandr Blok: Issledovaniia i materialy* (St. Petersburg: Pushkinskii dom, 2011), 543–98. The previous volumes of this series appeared in 1987, 1991, and 1998.

68. In his article "The Terrifying Mimicry of Samizdat," *Public Culture* 13, no. 2 (2001): 191–214.

69. Homi Bhabha, *The Location of Culture* (New York: Routledge, 1994), 115 (Bhabha's emphasis). Quoted in Oushakine, "The Terrifying Mimicry of Samizdat," 203.

70. Jouni Järvinen, *Normalization and Charter 77—Violence, Commitment and Resistance in Czechoslovakia* (Helsinki: Kikimora Publications, 2009), 46. I owe this reference to Barbara Falk.

71. "Anketa byla predlozhena riadu literatorov leningradskim zhurnalom 'Dialog' v sviazi so stoletnim iubileem A. A. Bloka. Blagodarim redaktorov za vozmozhnost' perepechatat' na stranitsakh 'Severnoi pochty' otvety, dannye poetami."

72. *Samizdat Leningrada,* 449–50. *Dialog* only came out in eight copies (ibid., 402–3).

73. B. V. Dubin, "Kruzhkovyi steb i massovye kommunikatsii: K sotsiologii kul'ternogo perekhoda," in B. V. Dubin, *Slovo—pis'mo—literatura: Ocherki po sotsiologii sovremennoi kul'tury* (Moscow: Novoe Literaturnoe Obozrenie, 2001), 163–74, 164.

74. Ibid.

*Chapter 6*

# The Spirit of Pacifism

## *Social and Cultural Origins of the Grassroots Peace Movement in the Late Soviet Period*

Irina Gordeeva

Translated by Margarit Ordukhanyan

Pacifism is an ideology of the fundamental rejection of violence in international, social, and interpersonal relations. In the nineteenth century the ideas and values of pacifism, which were originally rooted in religion, expanded beyond the boundaries of the small number of peacemaking sects, were secularized, and grew into social movements. After World War I, pacifism grew into a formidable political force in Europe and America.

The Russian pacifist movement emerged at the end of the nineteenth century as an outgrowth of the Tolstoyans' sociopolitical self-determination. The pacifism of the Tolstoyans was radical in nature, which is to say that it was aimed at social action and directed toward totally reshaping every aspect of society through a peaceful, nonviolent transformation of the individual, his ideals, and values. It also sought to change daily life in all its aspects and to rework all interactions between people. The Tolstoyans' ultimate goal was to establish the universal brotherhood of all of humanity through a peaceful, spiritual revolution.

After Tolstoyan pacifism was repressed in the 1930s, ideas about nonviolence receded into oblivion for decades in the Union of Soviet Socialist Republics (USSR). The only form of a peace movement that was possible was one belonging to the official social organizations. Among these, the main one, from when it was founded in 1949, was the Soviet Committee for the Defense of Peace (SCDP). In the historical memory of former Soviet people, the official peace movement remains only as "dreary and hypocrisy-laced tedium."[1] Only a few people remembered that Russia had its own pacifist tradition; these were mainly the very few surviving Tolstoyans and some members of the intelligentsia and the youth subcultures.

The dissenters and dissidents of the 1960s and 1970s were quite indifferent to issues of peace and nonviolence.[2] Among them, only Iurii Galanskov (1939–1972)[3] called himself a pacifist and put forth the idea of creating a *local* peace movement. Until the 1980s there were only a few, unofficial peacemaking initiatives. These were Andrei Sakharov's antinuclear and antiwar speeches; Aleksandr Solzhenitsyn's conceptual work "Peace and War" (1973); a handful of protests against sending Soviet troops to Afghanistan; the open letter of the people of the Baltic republics demanding that the Baltic Sea, along with Estonia, Latvia, and Lithuania, be included in the Northern European non-nuclear zone (1981); and the Soviet hippies' pacifist protests, which they attempted to carry out sporadically from 1971 on. However, these were all separate acts, none of which was aimed at the creation of a social movement.[4]

By the end of the 1970s the period of détente had passed, and the international situation grew increasingly tense. Fear of nuclear war, fanned by official propaganda, was added to the fear of war that had remained with the Soviet people since 1945. These emotions became an inextricable part of everyday Soviet existence. At times they manifested themselves in rather odd ways: "fighters for peace" who wanted to prevent nuclear war popped up, even in psychiatric hospitals. In 1979 the general fear of war was compounded by dread of war with Afghanistan, although the majority of the Soviet people chose to remain silent on the subject.

Peace advocates' grassroots self-organization only began in the USSR in 1982 with the emergence of two organizations, the Group for Establishing Trust between the USSR and the USA (the Trust Group, which was later called Between East and West) and Free Initiative. The simultaneous emergence of two local peace organizations was both completely unexpected and made sense in the broader context.

If *Vesti iz SSSR* (*News from the USSR*) is to be believed, the now obscure Group for Establishing Trust between the USSR and the USA (hereafter, Trust Group) turned out to be both the group most doggedly persecuted by the Soviet authorities and the one best known overseas. According to Iuliia Vishnevskaia, a correspondent for Radio Liberty, in the mid-1980s, the dissident movement in the USSR went through an "extremely difficult time." Under the conditions of the new waves of mass arrests, when "almost all existing independent social associations were either forced to cease open activity completely or were clearly breathing their last breath of resistance," the "energy and perseverance" of the Soviet independent peace movement "impressed its friends and foes alike."[5]

The formation of the Trust Group was announced on June 4, 1982 at a press conference for members of the foreign press which took place in the Moscow apartment of nonconformist artist Sergei Batovrin (b. 1957). Batovrin read a declaration entitled "An Appeal to the Governments and People of the USSR and the USA," copies of which were sent to Brezhnev and Reagan, as well as TASS, the newspaper *Pravda*, and the Soviet Committee for the Defense of Peace.

In this "Appeal," which became the group's program-setting document, its founding members wrote:

> The USSR and the USA have the means to kill in proportions such that the history of mankind would end.
>
> A balance of terror cannot be a reliable guarantee of safety in the world. Only trust between peoples can create firm assurance of a future.
>
> Today, when elementary trust between the two nations has been completely lost, the problem of trust has ceased to be simply a question of bilateral relations. This is the question: Will mankind be wiped out by its own destructive capabilities or will it survive?
>
> This problem demands immediate action today. It is, however, very obvious that political leaders of both sides are incapable of coming to any sort of agreement about significant arms limitations in the near future . . . to say nothing of genuine disarmament.
>
> Due to their political interests and circumstances, politicians find it difficult to be objective on disarmament issues . . . .
>
> We are convinced that the time has come for the public not only to confront decision-makers with the issue of disarmament, but to participate in the decision-making process with the politicians.
>
> We are in favor of four-way dialogue—for dialogue in which average Soviet and American citizens are included on an equal footing with political figures.[6]

The document's authors called for proposals from average Soviet and American citizens on ways to establish trust between the USSR and the USA as well as the creation of international social and research groups to analyze such proposals.

The "Appeal" was written by eleven people: artist Sergei Batovrin, engineers Maria and Vladimir Fleishgakker, psychiatrist Igor Sobkov, mathematics teacher Sergei Rozenoer, physicists Gennadii Krochik, Viktor Blok, and Iurii Khronopulo, dental technician Mikhail Ostrovskii and his wife Liudmila, and mathematician Boris Kaliuzhnyi. Within the very first days of the creation of the "Appeal," many people, including, among others, Vladimir Brodskii, geographers Iurii and Olga Medvedkov, philologist Oleg Radzinskii, economist Lev Dudkin, and physicist Valerii Godiak and his wife, added their signatures to the document. By July 6 of the same year, the "Address" had collected 170 signatures.[7]

The initiators of the creation of an independent peace movement were all members of the intelligentsia living in Moscow and Dolgoprudnyi. Later, similar groups (albeit very few and not very stable ones) appeared in Novosibirsk, Rybinsk, Odessa, Leningrad, Kuibyshev, Vilnius, Gorkii, Riga, Lvov, Kiev, and Baku.

The Trust Group's statement on defending peace was unique in the late Soviet period in at least two ways. Firstly, the primary goal set by the group was not negative but rather, positive: to fight not *against war*, but rather *for peace*, the guarantor of which was trust. According to the members of the group, it was precisely the absence of trust between the USSR and the USA, between East and West that was responsible for the nuclear threat to humanity. In their opinion, "antinuclear protests must be accompanied by large mass positive actions aimed at humanizing relations [between the two countries]," and at establishing broad civilian connections, collaboration, and free exchange of information and people, and discussions and dialogue.[8] This was the idea of large-scale "public diplomacy," which was intended as a safeguard against World War III.

Secondly, the Group's organizers strove to create a mass local movement. They voiced their dissatisfaction with the results of the implementation of the Helsinki Final Act, which had stipulated measures for strengthening the friendly ties and trust between countries, including the development of collaboration and exchanges in the areas of culture and education, but had bypassed average citizens by tasking governments with addressing all the issues that they had outlined.[9] The Trust Group's organizers believed that the fight for peace must cease to be the monopoly of politicians and instead must become the "daily task of thousands and thousands of people." Thus, the first slogans of the movement became "Peace: trust plus disarmament" and "Fighting for peace is everyone's job."[10]

Once its members announced the group's creation, proposals from the public on ways of establishing trust poured in. These were analyzed and included in letters addressed to the governments and the general public of the USSR and the USA. Among the suggestions received and approved by the group were children's exchange programs between Soviet and American host families, the development of international tourism, regular presentation of joint Soviet-American television discussions, propagation of peace in school textbooks, facilitation of postal exchange, the creation of a Soviet-American marriage bureau, and the development of a program of joint space exploration.[11]

The group began actively sending appeals to the governments and the general public of the USSR, the USA, and other countries, calling for an immediate end to nuclear testing and proposing measures for establishing trust. The Trust Group did not receive a single official written response from the Soviet organs (or from members of the US government, for that matter). The initiatives of unofficial Soviet fighters for peace garnered tremendous interest from foreign correspondents and representatives of Western pacifist organizations, who expressed their approval and support, and later took an active part in protecting Soviet "peaceniks" from persecution.

From the moment the Trust Group was created, the locations of its members' meetings attracted intense scrutiny by the Soviet *militsiia* and KGB alike. Employees of the "organs" repeatedly tried to break into the apartments of the group's members, who were routinely stopped in the streets for the purposes of "verification of identity." Group members regularly received summons and telephone calls asking them to present themselves at *militsiia* (police) precincts, the offices of the executive committee and the procurator, or the KGB. They were detained and taken in for questioning, received telephone threats, or had their telephone service disconnected altogether. At work they were subjected to pressure and blackmail, and were even blocked from entering each other's apartments. Since the KGB could not directly accuse the group members of participating in a peace movement, charges of hooliganism or anti-Soviet agitation and propaganda were fabricated against them.[12]

Despite the repressions and the emigration of its activists, the Trust Group regularly held its sessions and research seminars, collected proposals on establishing trust, wrote letters and appeals to the public and members of the government, disseminated petitions, prepared peaceful actions, and tried to organize art exhibits. The Trust Group established contacts with representatives of the Western peace movements. Abroad, support groups for Soviet peace fighters were created; they organized acts of solidarity and, through various foreign media outlets, made public information about the persecution of Trust Group members.

Gradually and unavoidably, the Trust Group's activities began to incorporate the issue of the protection of rights; in addition to antinuclear issues, from 1984–1985 the scope of the Trust Group's work grew to include both environmental concerns and properly pacifist ones. The group's transition to a strictly pacifist agenda occurred in the spring of 1984 when two active members of the youth counterculture joined its ranks. These were Aleksandr Rubchenko (b. 1960) and Nikolai Khramov (b. 1963). Rubchenko was a hippie and an artist, a Tolstoyan and a vegetarian for a brief period in 1979, and later an active participant in the formation of Andrei Chukaev's underground Revolutionary Social-Democratic movement.[13] Nikolai Khramov, a journalism student at Moscow State University, fell in with the hippies toward the end of 1982 and considered himself a pacifist.[14]

Rubchenko and Khramov soon became some of the most active members of the Trust Group. For this they were mercilessly persecuted: they were detained and arrested on numerous occasions, threatened and beaten. Rubchenko was forcibly committed to a psychiatric hospital; Khramov was expelled from the university and drafted into the army, and even pressured to leave the country.[15] Rubchenko and Khramov attracted a substantial number of radical youths from various countercultural organizations to the Trust Group. Toward the end of the 1980s, when the majority of the group's initial members either emigrated or distanced themselves from the movement for various reasons, the counterculture came to be the primary reference group for the Trust Group.

Such was the history of the group. In a short time it grew into a real pacifist organization, mastered contemporary political jargon, and became experienced in open struggle, engaging with the authorities as well as resisting them, conducting various forms of initiatives, collaborating with foreign organizations, and becoming capable of mounting the legal defense of its adherents. During *perestroika* group members actively engaged with the processes of democratization, and in the first post-Soviet years they managed to complete the historical mission of Russian pacifism when, with their vigorous participation, a law on alternative military service was enacted. The Trust Group may also be viewed as one of the first proto-party formations whose experience, reputation, and connections were used by some social-political organizations of the *perestroika* period for their own political ends.

In December 1982, almost at the same time as the Trust Group, a second independent peace group called Free Initiative was created in Moscow. Its membership consisted exclusively of hippies, and its leaders were Iurii Popov (aka "Diversant," 1954–1999) and Sergei Troianskii (1954–2004?).

The group's first appeal, likely composed in mid-December 1983,[16] was entitled "Appeal to Young America," and, like the "Appeal" of the Trust Group, it was built on the idea that it was necessary to establish trust between Soviet and American young people.[17] The text, disseminated through *samizdat*, was accompanied by eighty-nine signatures of people, mostly hippies who belonged to the "system."[18]

Free Initiative's distinctive character resided in the fact that in many ways it resembled a game, a mystification, or simply Popov's and Troianskii's dream of creating a system-based movement in the spirit of 1968 in the USSR, a dream that for a number of reasons they were unable to realize fully. This explains why many of the people whose signatures appeared under the "Appeal" were not even aware of the text's existence. It appears that in the majority of cases Popov and Troianskii took the license of putting their friends' and acquaintances' names on documents, convinced that the latter would not refuse to sign their names to documents voicing such great ideas.

Popov and Troianskii considered John Lennon their "ideological guide and leader." "Our ideological base was the amalgamation of Tolstoy's and Gandhi's ideas with a touch of the flower culture," Popov later said, "We represented the face of the hippie system that existed in Moscow. We managed to get organized, to find a common direction, and to go a bit further than the youth who simply hung out at social gatherings. We truly wanted our voices to be heard by our Western peers."[19]

Troianskii, who considered himself an anarchist, wrote a radical appeal to his fellow hippies. Entitled "To June 1, 1981," it openly brought up the subject of protest against the war in Afghanistan.[20] At that time the Trust Group did not dare raise the problem in similar terms. Even in the dissident milieu, to say nothing of the milieu of regular Soviet people, any expression of open opposition to this war was highly unusual. However, concern with the war in Afghanistan continued to be important for Free Initiative.[21]

From 1980 on, wanting to organize a movement, Popov and Troianskii tried to make the annual gathering of hippies in Tsaritsyno on June 1 (International Children's Day) a tradition. (Such gatherings had taken place sporadically throughout the 1970s).[22] Furthermore, the pair tried to imbue the gatherings with a distinctly ideological character, going so far as to prepare leaflets with reminders of the system's pacifist traditions for the occasion.

From 1981 on, annual rallies commemorating John Lennon, in which Free Initiative participated, took place on the observation platform in the Lenin Hills. The rallies were usually broken up by the police. On the eve of the event, Free Initiative regularly distributed flyers referring to the day of commemorating John Lennon as the "day of antiwar action." One of these flyers, currently in our possession, contains a quote from Tolstoy: "Everything that unifies people constitutes kindness and beauty; everything that divides them—evil and ugliness."[23]

Before long, the group's social engagement caught the attention of the authorities. All the participants of the June 1, 1983 rally in Tsaritsyno were detained and brought in by the *militsiia*. *Vesti iz SSSR* and other sources reported that:

[T]he next day the park was completely cordoned off by the police. The raid continued until June 2, 1982, and two hundred people were detained as a result.[24] On June 1, 1982, flyers calling for the abolition of the death penalty and, by some accounts, for an end to the war in Afghanistan, were discovered. The detainees were interrogated in connection with the flyers. In the course of the interrogations, the police collected evidence that the flyers had allegedly been prepared by Iurii Popov.[25]

Popov was arrested and charged with article 224, part 3 of the RSFSR Penal Code (possession of narcotics with no intent to sell). After spending time in the Butyrskaia prison and the Serbskii Institute for Social and Forensic Psychiatry, he stood trial in the summer of 1984 and was subsequently committed to Sychevka, a special psychiatric hospital in Smolensk *Oblast'*, before being relocated, two years later, to a regular psychiatric hospital located at the Stolbovoi station of Moscow *Oblast'*'s Chekhovskii region.[26] Troianskii was arrested and committed to Sychevka on the same charges in

October 1986, because Free Initiative pacifist *samizdat* was discovered in his possession and confiscated during a search. Popov's, Troianskii's and other hippies' lifestyles made it easier to persecute them.[27]

In 1987 a hippie manifesto entitled "There is No Turning Back" was disseminated on behalf of Free Initiative.[28] The manifesto was published in the unofficial Soviet press as well as abroad in the journal *Strana i mir* (*Country and World*).[29] The manifesto declared the need for the hippie movement to transition from nihilism and a negative conceptualization of freedom to a positive program founded on ideas of love and nonviolence. From 1988 to 1991, on behalf of the "independent, anarchist-pacifist group" Free Initiative, Iurii Popov published a typewritten magazine entitled *Svoboda* (*Freedom*) that he disseminated among his friends.

In the 1990s Popov and Troianskii ceased to be involved with Free Initiative's activities. According to notebook entries made by a group member, at this point "Diversant" considered the group's program mostly completed.[30] Iurii Popov died in 1999; he perished in the street under unclear circumstances. Sergei Troianskii, who had completely retreated from society by that time, disappeared in 2004. Almost none of the people who were directly involved in the history of Free Initiative are still alive.

The members of the Trust Group cite their "preoccupation" with the "nuclear issue" as the primary reason for the emergence of the local peace movement in the USSR.[31] However, outside observers repeatedly questioned the sincerity of their commitment to peacemaking. The mistrust was largely driven by the group's social makeup as well as the fact that the dominant majority of the Trust Group's founders soon emigrated.

The social makeup of the local peace movement was surprisingly variegated. Its key participants belonged to the following social, cultural, and professional groups: scientists (physicists, mathematicians, and others), a group that included a large number of refuseniks;[32] refuseniks, among them many scientists and Jews, who were eventually joined by religious dissidents, mainly Pentecostals;[33] and hippies, artists, and other representatives of the cultural underground (which also included quite a few refuseniks or people simply wishing to emigrate). Also involved in the local peace movement were various groups marginalized by Soviet society, such as activists fighting for the rights of disabled people, individual dissidents, including religious ones, people who were interested in parapsychology, and representatives of the nascent New Age movement in the USSR. In a socio-psychological sense, what unified all of them was their shared status of being unwilling or voluntary apostates within Soviet society.

Attempts to "expose" the movement's true goals were initiated by its contemporaries and even various members of the movement itself. For example, Oleg Radzinskii, who was among the first people to join the Trust Group and who was arrested in October 1982 and was charged under art. 70-1 of the RSFSR Criminal Code in 1984, wrote an open letter from prison to the members of the group's Moscow chapter, in which he claimed that most of the group's members were interested in emigrating and not in fighting for peace. He insisted that the group's original intention was truly peacemaking, but that with time it had been hijacked by people who had no interest in fighting for peace.[34]

Yet another attempt to publicly expose the Trust Group's true motives was made by Nikolai Khramov's father, Evgenii L. Khramov (1932–2001), who was a member of the Writers Union, a journalist, and a translator. On April 17, 1986, the Russian office of the *Novosti* press agency published the "Open Letter by Evgenii Khramov," in which he insisted that his son had fallen under the influence of the refuseniks in the Trust Group, people who called themselves fighters for peace but in reality were exploiting the idea of peacemaking to obtain exit visas. The writer added that the Trust Group used his son Nikolai, an ethnic Russian and a student enrolled at a prestigious university "to bring new color into the otherwise monotonous portrait of a bunch of loafers."[35]

Another revelatory testimony about the allegedly true motives behind Trust Group's work was given by Aleksandr Shatravka, a man with a fantastical life story that he himself described in his autobiography *Pobeg iz raia* (*Escape from Paradise*). Shatravka, the only blue-collar worker in the Trust Group, attempted, together with his brother and two friends, to cross the Soviet-Finnish border in 1974 and had consequently ended up in a psychiatric hospital.[36] Shatravka maintained that the sole true purpose for creating the Trust Group was to facilitate members' emigration from the USSR. On an Internet site containing Batovrin's nostalgic reminiscences, Shatravka wrote: "Sergei, why be so tragic? We got into the whole Trust Group business to get out of the USSR painlessly (avoiding imprisonment)."[37] It should be added that in a personal message to the author of this chapter, Shatravka did not deny the fact that upon his release from prison he was surprised to discover that the Trust Group truly fought for peace.

The group's stated aims confused some of the Soviet dissidents as well. Pinhas Podrabinek, who once attended one of the group's meetings, recalls being astonished by how divorced from life the questions they discussed were ("a dozen and a half Manilovs discussing . . . hopeless projects").[38] According to Podrabinek, everything started to make sense once he found out that Medvedkov was a refusenik.

Irina Krivova's story about visiting Andrei Sakharov upon his return from exile is similarly illustrative:

> Our group's visit to Andrei Sakharov was brutally disappointing. One of our speaking points was a call to reject the development of nuclear energy in the

way it was conducted in the USSR. We wanted to hear the opinion of Sakharov, who had just returned to Moscow. We were greeted in the hallway by Elena Bonner who said that 75 percent of our group were refusenik Jews and that we had to go our separate ways. She said they had no intention of emigrating anywhere. Sakharov showed himself for literally a minute and said that he was in favor of the development of nuclear energy and that he didn't support us.[39]

In his 1986 article in *Strana i mir*, Mark Reitman lists some of the accusations most frequently leveled against the Trust Group and attempts to address them.[40] Reitman examines in detail the most common accusation: that the majority of the Trust Group consisted of refusenik Jews whose primary goal was to secure permission to leave the USSR and who had no intention of continuing their peacemaking endeavors once they had gone abroad.

Indeed, Reitman confirms that "there were five Jews among the eleven people who signed the first appeal to the governments of the USSR and the USA in June 1982." He acknowledges that there were quite a few Jews among those people who joined the group later as well, and that many of them had either already filed for exit permits or were intending to do so. "Did it truly have any impact on the movement's gravitas?" asks Reitman:

No question it did. We would have done better with born-and-bred Russians, whom the movement also had in abundance (Shatravka, Kiselev, Medvedkov, Lusnikov, and many others). But we believed that we had no right to limit the parameters of the movement based on ethnic membership. The refuseniks had suffered enough discrimination at the hands of Soviet state institutions. The last thing they needed was for independent social organizations to join the persecution campaign as well![41]

When explaining this social effect, Reitman writes that once the idea of the Trust Group had already emerged and its initiators began searching for contacts, the easiest ones to find were always the refusenik groups in various cities. This might have to do with the fact that:

The refuseniks had already crossed the psychological barrier which stopped the rest of the Soviet citizens on the doorstep of any form of social activity not sanctioned from above. The refuseniks were less fearful of losing their jobs (many had already lost them) or their freedom (most were convinced that they were going to lose it sooner or later). This explained why the refuseniks, unlike others, were interested in improving the international situation and in peace-building.[42]

At the same time Reitman, a refusenik himself, juxtaposed his own position with that of the "pure refuseniks:" "After all, we always opposed any form of isolationism. Once bombs begin to fall, they are devoid of any prefer-ences."[43] He insisted that when they joined the Trust Group, most refuseniks had already bid farewell to any hope of an impending departure. However, an easily explicable metamorphosis took place: "if initially the 'exit' was priority number one for many and 'world peace' was the second priority, eventually 'world peace' became the main concern," because "such was the ethical platform constructed over the course of ten months of difficult and dangerous social work."[44]

Interestingly, works detailing the history of the Jewish emigration move-ment contain practically no mention of the Trust Group. Paradoxically, while many contemporaries of the emigration movement considered its history a mere episode in the history of the refuseniks' plight as people trying to leave the USSR, the Trust Group is completely absent from the historical annals of the refusenik movement. It appears that the group's organizers were outsiders not only in Soviet society but also within the refusenik movement. It is useful to attempt to analyze the reasons for this paradox.

There were only ten refuseniks among the original members of the Trust Group. By applying for exit visas, the refuseniks automatically abdicated their Soviet citizenship. The motives for abdicating one's citizenship could vary, but people who joined the Trust Group most frequently cited their moral-ethical objections to Soviet citizenship, specifically their "total rejec-tion of the Soviet lifestyle, excessive demagoguery and hypocrisy, and sup-pression of the individual."[45] For example, Dr. Vladimir Brodskii told OVIR that he did not wish to live in a totalitarian state.[46] In her 1981 appeal to the Presidium of the Supreme Soviet with a request for permission to give up her Soviet citizenship, artist Nina Kovalenko declared that her motive was the "absolute and completely conscious rejection of the social and political structure of the USSR."[47]

Marina Morozova, a scholar of the refusenik movement, noted that one of the characteristic traits of life in "refusal" was that people could not know when or whether they would be granted permission to leave and hence could not make long-term plans. This made people feel that "life is passing by, and there are very few changes and events in it." Therefore, in order to create a semblance of normalized life, the refuseniks strove to keep themselves busy with something, "to fill life with some content, to do something positive on a daily basis." To this end, they organized scientific and cultural seminars that were characterized by free discussions on various social or intellectual problems.[48] The creation of the Trust Group was connected with just such an unofficial seminar.[49]

The members of the Soviet Committee for Defending Peace referred to the Trust Group as a "band of hooligans with academic degrees."[50] It is easy to explain why scientists, mostly physicists and mathematicians, became involved in the group. At some point, that particular professional group began

to occupy a privileged position in the USSR and had a level of social awareness that was unprecedented in the Soviet era. "Academic" physicists were
guaranteed relative freedom by the authorities "in exchange for their work on
creating weapons for that very government," and this freedom "could in turn
become a resource for forming a critical outlook on the state policies overall."[51] As early as the beginning of the 1960s, socio-cultural initiatives were
rapidly developing in the various associations of physicists and mathematicians; these initiatives were later to lay the groundwork for the phenomenon
of Soviet academic dissidence.

In the academic milieu the general moral atmosphere prevailing in scientific circles fostered the emergence of the idea of trust, which became the
fundamental premise of the local peace movement. However, scientists' relative ease of access (certainly in comparison to ordinary people) to Western
sources of information, including sociopolitical ones, a general awareness of
Western scientists' engagement in the peace movement, and the dissemination of Sakharov's antinuclear articles also helped the idea of trust to emerge.
Scientists, who were part of transnational production processes and dissemination of knowledge by virtue of their profession, were among the first people
in the USSR to detect and understand the currents of globalization, which
resulted in their consciousness becoming cosmopolitan and the emergence
of the feeling of "cosmopolitan responsibility" for the future of the entire
world. It was precisely in the context of this emerging cosmopolitanism that
the fundamental ideas of the Trust Group were born.

Gennadii Krochik recalls how in 1977 his academic adviser Iurii Khronopulo
set up a laboratory for research on lasers in the town of Dolgoprudnyi, near
Moscow. In the course of the many "kitchen-table seminars" held there,
Krochik and his friends Vladimir Blok and Iurii Khronopulo did not simply
conduct scientific research but also discussed "everything: from UFOs and
Indian yogis to Soviet totalitarianism and freedom to leave the country."[52]
They were also interested in parapsychology, yoga, and spiritualism, and they
frequented the bioelectronics laboratory in Furman Lane.[53] By the spring of
1980, the kitchen-table chats in the house in Dolgoprudnyi had expanded into
an unofficial, scientific research seminar in Moscow which soon began to
convene at regular intervals. The seminar discussed issues of social relevance,
and focused, in particular, on the problem of scientific modeling of social
processes, that is, making models of collective behavior, so mass psychology
and parapsychology were examined alongside issues of war and peace.[54]

This seminar broke up into several independent ones. Among these there
was one dedicated to reporting on issues of war and peace, discussions of
"nuclear winter," and mathematical modeling of the "nuclear nightmare"
scenario. The seminar's participants discovered for themselves the ideas of
the British Quaker Lewis Fry Richardson, a polymath and pacifist who was

the founder of the science of peace as well as a physicist and mathematician. As Reitman put it, "we voraciously devoured works by him and his numerous followers and then began attempting to create similar things."[55]

In an announcement "Concerning the Trust Group" that the Moscow-based scientists created on or shortly after October 5, 1982, the reasons for creating the group were described thus:

> In most developed nations, the year 1980 marked the beginning of the latest economic downturn. In some countries, problems of energy, raw materials, and the ecology became worse. Other countries had problems with food supplies, technology, and management. This downturn was severe and lengthy, unlike, for instance, the economic difficulties of 1974–1975. Realizing that various efforts to revive their economies were ineffective—and in order to draw their peoples' attention away from their day-to-day economic problems—governments had to resort to an old and effective remedy in capital investment into long-term military programs. This step, easily justified in the eyes of the populace in the name of external military threats, has another attractive characteristic—it facilitates the consolidation of the nation under the banner of patriotism. Unavoidable consequences of this are the inculcation of a martial spirit, increasingly closed societies, a reduction in democratic freedoms and human rights. All this will strengthen and bring to power military-industrial complexes and the merging of political positions with those of the military.[56]

The scientists worked out a method for computing an "index of hostility" that was based on data from newspaper articles and speeches by political leaders. Their index of hostility allowed them to "identify instances of intentionally created hostilities by the opposing sides toward one another, especially on the eve of scheduled significant political events."[57]

Using mathematical modeling and drawing on historical examples from tsarist Russia and a few other countries, the scientists concluded that increasing human exchange (by means of tourism, emigration, and work trips) could bring the arms race under control.[58] They decided that they could no longer remain silent. Aware of the existence of a pacifist movement in the West and dissatisfied with the effectiveness of the SCDP, the scientists decided to "act on their own" and create a grassroots social movement that sought to establish trust between the USSR and the USA and bring about a rapprochement between the cultures of the two blocks that would be based on shared values.[59] The "Appeal" of the Trust Group reflected the ideas developed by the participants of the research seminar.

The founders of the Group declared that they did not consider themselves citizens of a particular country but rather, *citizens of the world*—people unencumbered by any political borders.[60] The cosmopolitan motif is observable in some form or another throughout the group's reports.

In the life history of Iurii Vladimirovich Medvedkov (b. 1928), doctor of geographical sciences and a member of the Trust Group, one sees a similar story about how a global, "cosmopolitan" consciousness was adopted as a life choice by a scientist in the late Soviet period. Medvedkov's research interests and high professional qualifications made him an active and visible member of the transnational association of geographers. When the Soviet authorities curtailed his professional growth and mobility, he made an attempt to emigrate and subsequently, after his request was denied, became actively involved in the Trust Group.[61]

In January 1983 the scientific sector of the Trust Group separated into a group called Friendship and Dialogue, which established a seminar under the heading of "Peace and Social Research." In 1986 the seminar grew into an independent group known as Social Research and Research on Issues of Peace.[62] The Trust Group and Friendship and Dialogue conducted collaborative seminars that foreign scientists and pacifists frequently attended. During *perestroika*, the researchers from the Trust Group were actively involved in establishing the "Democracy and Humanism" seminar.

The agenda of the Trust Group, the subjects discussed at the research group's peace seminars, the main direction of their educational work, and later, the focal point of the independent peace movement's newsletters (*Den' za dnem* or *Day after Day* and *Doverie* or *Trust*) were all distinctly cosmopolitan. They included discussions of current problems in international relations, religious and cultural history, customs of different countries and peoples, convergence between religion and science, the militarization of the economy, the causes and the biomedical consequences of industrial disasters and pollution, the history of science and the fine arts, and many other topics.

Sociologist Ulrich Beck describes the contemporary type of cosmopolitan consciousness as the cultural consequence of globalization—one of the primary processes of the "second modernity" whereby the human condition itself has become cosmopolitan.[63] Globalization signifies an empirically experienced removal of national borders in the spheres of the economy, information, the environment, technology, transcultural conflicts, and social interactions. This sensation of the disappearance of borders transforms people's daily lives and compels them to use new, transnational ways of thinking and living which, in Anthony Giddens's definition of globalization, create "activity and (co)existence that do not recognize distance (externally remote worlds, national states, religions, regions and continents)."[64]

The flip side of this "second modernity" is the emergence of global threats and the subsequent realization of the "*fragility* of civilization, which, politically speaking, is capable of forging a common destiny." The realization of interdependence and the concomitant "civilizational community of fate," induced by global risks and crises, foregrounds the issues of peace and of environmental protection.[65] Simultaneously, according to Beck, what is destroyed is the "default of social decisions being made behind closed doors. What once was discussed and decided upon by executives and scientists, unbeknownst to the general public, must now receive its substantiation in heated public debates." Collective concerns about universally relevant problems lead to the formation of "transnational commonality" in order to solve shared problems. The public begins to master new, transnational spheres of political activity, which leads to the emergence of transnational movements.[66] These movements can be defined as "networks of actors organized at the local, national, and international levels in order to mobilize people beyond national borders for the purpose of accomplishing a common goal."[67]

Therefore scientists, for whom generating and disseminating knowledge were key professional activities, were among the first people in the USSR to react to the dismantling of the foundational premise of the "first modernity," that is, people's conviction that they lived in "closed, delimited spaces and nation-states and therefore in national societies."[68] In the scientific milieu of the late Soviet period, this perception of oneself and one's activities in the context of a global society, along with the realization that there were global risks, an awareness of the global nature of the threats facing the humanity, and the desire to respond to present-day global problems made extensive external contacts with the wider world necessary. This, in turn, resulted in a new form of social identification and activity with a transnational outlook (the "grassroots" peace movement). For such people, the desire to emigrate, like their engagement with global problems, frequently stemmed less from wishing to live in more evolved societies or from seeking financial stability abroad than from this cosmopolitan outlook. This was the outlook that drew scientists, refuseniks, hippies, and other nonconformists into a single organization.

The other socio-cultural group that proved receptive to the contexts of the "second modernity" in the late Soviet period was the cultural underground— hippies and other nonconformists such as nonconformist artists, religious seekers, alienated intellectuals, rock musicians, and other outsiders.

The Trust Group counted a few nonconformist artists and hippies among its active participants, and the number of representatives of the cultural underground in the local peace movement only grew with time. The founder of the Trust Group, Sergei Batovrin, was both an artist and a hippie. Iurii Kiselev, whose signature appears on many of the Trust Group's documents, was an artist. He was disabled and eventually left the Trust Group to helm the Initiative group, which was fighting for the rights of disabled people. Later, artists A. Rubchenko, N. Kovalenko, M. V. Zotov of Togliatti and M. Zvonova and A. Zilber from Gorkii joined the Trust Group as well. Emigration was the goal for Kovalenko, Zotov, Zvonova, and Zilber. The cultural underground's support for the Trust Group became especially prominent during *perestroika*.

Socially, the nonconformist artists and hippies can be considered the equivalent of a Soviet bohemia. Sociologist Elena Zdravomyslova identified their primary characteristics as "self-exclusion in terms of basic social structures, a relative lack of professional success, the absence of broad social acceptance, irregular and insignificant income, a barely perceptible psychological state of melancholy, a largely idle lifestyle, free sexual norms, an indeterminate future, a propensity for self-destructive practices; . . . spleen as a psychological condition, . . . deep aversion to the meaninglessness of events."[69] This population's absolute revolt against Soviet reality was manifested through negative freedom, escapism, and self-exclusion from society. All of this came at a high cost: early deaths, broken families, and self-destructive behavior such as drug addiction, alcoholism, suicidal tendencies, and links with the criminal underworld.[70]

One of Soviet hippies' key concepts was the notion of "belonging/non-belonging," which encompassed a "general escape from reality," and "final, principle-based non-citizenship."[71] The acknowledgment of one's "non-citizenship" in the USSR served as the departure point for the development of a cosmopolitan outlook and opposition to national borders. Hippie culture aimed to construct aesthetic, religious, and ideological alternatives to Soviet reality.

At some point, for many representatives of the Soviet underground, the burden of "negative freedom" and their marginalization, denial, rejection, escapism, and destructive practices were all replaced by the need for a system of ideas that offered a more positive vision of the world. The Soviet cultural underground, and Soviet hippies in particular, were clearly explorative in nature; the mission of all its members was to search for their proper place in society, their religion, and their ideology. Within the space of the underground, the period of juvenile nihilism was turning into a period for acquiring new values.

In the 1970s many members of the cultural underground experienced this kind of a need for positive ideals. Among these were Sandr Riga (b. 1939), Aleksandr Ogorodnikov (b. 1950), Vladimir Poresh (b. 1949), Andrei Madison (1952–2009), Sergei Batovrin, Mikhail Bombin (1951–2011), Sergei Moskalev (b. 1958), Alik Olisevich (b. 1958), Aleksandr Lobachev (1953–2011), Georgii Meitin (b. 1958), and many others.

Ogorodnikov, a hippie and the organizer of underground religious seminars in the mid-1970s, wrote in 1978 that one of the most important markers of the epoch was the creation in the USSR of a "second cultural reality," which allowed for the realization of young people's need to "soar beyond the limits of the Soviet horizon, to tear down the boundaries of Soviet thinking and [the Soviet] lifestyle." He claimed that:

This culture touches practically every sphere of human activity (literature, philosophy, history, art, and so on); we are observing the creation of island communities that carry a radically new spirituality and are capable of molding people with a non-Soviet consciousness and mode of action. The new spirituality, breaking free from the kingdom of need and social coercion, looks to the future and seeketh the celestial. The topographic universe of this new spirituality is structured around two coordinates—love and freedom, and art is its lifeblood.[72]

"We wouldn't so much as sit down to dinner without first ascertaining God's existence,"[73] as Mariia Remizova remembers the spirit of the hippie movement of the 1980s. She goes on to say:

I have never again met people who were so all-around knowledgeable and interested in random topics . . . . The system [*sistema*—Soviet hippies] knew everything—what books to read (what's more, it actually owned those books, in the original and even in its members' own translations, in both rare editions and Xerox copies stamped "rare books collection"), what music to listen to, what films to watch. The moment someone unearthed something worthwhile, he or she became an indefatigable advocate and disseminator of the knowledge acquired. The social gatherings were places of uninterrupted exchange of "cultural artifacts" and "information," as well as [exchanges] of opinions about what each person had seen, heard, read, and experienced.[74]

Andrei Madison, a member of the older generation of hippies, describes his reading experience during this period of searching:

The substance for this new identification consisted of an unlimited number of components: *melting pot*. In the course of the 1970s and 1980s, I sampled, in no particular order: Tolstoy, Laozi, Confucius, Mozi, Zen Buddhism, Krishnamurti, Vivekananda, Wilfredo Pareto, Adorno, Berdyaev with Sergei Bulgakov and the like as well as Rozanov, Konstantin Leontiev, Sufism, Bakunin, Nechaev, Fanon, Paris of 1968, Abby Hoffman, Jerry Rubin, Novalis, Jean Paul, Shalamov, Solzhenitsyn, Ciliga, Nietzsche, Spengler, Avtorkhanov, Chakhotin, Ellul, Henry Thoreau, Ken Kesey and—enough.[75]

This searching led to aesthetic and, more frequently, religious[76] epiphanies, but some of these were ideological as well. One of the ideological (in some cases religious-ideological or ethical) choices for the cultural outsiders of the late Soviet period was pacifism, or the idea of nonviolence in its various interpretations and manifestations.

Nikolai Khramov believed that the hippies' involvement in the pacifist movement meant they had chosen a "more conscious and purposeful protest."[77] He explained his "political" choice by the fact that the hippie movement in the West had lost its revolutionary spirit and had become a fashion. It was compromised by pseudo-hippies, who liked the external attributes of the movements but rejected political struggle, abandoned society, and retreated "into themselves, into the drug-infused hallucinogenic world." According to Khramov, for Soviet hippies this created the need for a positive ideal, that is, to create a movement built on equality and brotherhood, "where there are no distinctions between nations, where love will be the primary factor bringing people together."[78]

The authors of the Free Initiative manifesto also declared their need for a positive ideal, for positive solidarity, to overcome the negative consequences of the "Great Refusal." They stated:

> The hippie is an apostate. This is the only way he can learn about the common disease . . . . But there is a limit to how useful loneliness can be. In order for the spiritual disease to be cured, loneliness must be followed by interaction. The poison of apostasy is useful only in limited doses; otherwise, it kills . . . . At first, the interaction is passive. Hippies are bonded together by their nihilism, by their shared rejection of the old order and of the restrictions placed by society and the state on the apostates. However, interaction cannot develop on the basis of the shared negative emotions alone. With the complete erasure of the old values emerges a spiritual void that must be filled with positive ideals. Each individual must develop his or her own ideals, and it fills you with joy to realize that you are not alone . . . . At the next step, individual ideals are synthesized into common ones . . . . This synthesis is our ultimate positive goal. It can be achieved only through collaborative practical actions, collaborative work, collaborative life.[79]

Efforts to find a positive ideal to overcome hippies' escapism can be clearly traced in the life of Sergei Batovrin, one of the founders of the Trust Group. Sergei's father was a Soviet diplomat, and his family lived in New York from 1965 to 1970. Sergei was familiar with American culture and fluent in English. According to American journalist David Satter, who interviewed Sergei later in Moscow, "the younger Batovrin grew up in New York believing that his distant Soviet homeland was the freest country in the world." Satter found Batovrin to be astonishingly American-like and even remarked on the latter's "non-Soviet" traits: "[I]n a country where suspicion is all pervasive, he was notable for his openness and lack of suspicion." He noted "his endless capacity for optimism," decency, sincerity, and directness, and thought he was just the kind of a person who "might easily have grown up in New York or Washington to become a leader of the US peace movement."[80]

Upon his return to the Fatherland, Sergei came face to face with the "falsehood of the Soviet system." In 1968 he was expelled from school for discussing the events in Czechoslovakia, and this prompted him to become a hippie. However, the ideals of Soviet hippies did not entirely appeal to him, because the latter did not intend to reform Soviet society but rather, simply strove to avoid it.[81] During this time Batovrin became an artist and began searching for a positive alternative to both Soviet society and the nihilism of the hippies. His father arranged for him to be admitted to the Institute of World Economy and International Relations (known by its Russian acronym of IMEMO)— a prestigious university for the children of the Soviet elite. Batovrin was stunned to discover his peers' complete lack of interest in politics not to mention communism: they were only interested in commerce. (Almost all of the students were children of government officials who worked abroad and sent home packages with items for resale on the black market.)[82]

Sergei dropped out of the institute and joined the artistic hippie group Hair, becoming part of the inner circle of the notorious Ofeliia (Svetlana Barabash, 1950–1991). The members of this group expressed themselves mostly through their lifestyles, their aesthetic preferences, and a form of actionism—the group organized a few exhibitions of nonconformist art, which were shut down by the authorities.[83]

Batovrin's family made the decision to leave the USSR in 1976. Sergei and his mother already had been weighing the idea of emigration for some time, but Batovrin's involuntary commitment to a psychiatric hospital became the last straw.[84] A battle for an exit permit ensued, but, working through Batovrin's father, who by this time already had another family, the authorities raised formal obstacles, making emigration impossible. Therefore, for Batovrin, the idea of creating the Trust Group became the logical next step in politicizing his countercultural ideas, and he successfully channeled them into the local peace movement.

Nonetheless, it would be misleading to suggest that the idea of creating a social movement on the basis of pacifism found broad support in hippie circles. The members of the system (*sistema*) did not trust the Trust Group then, and they do not trust it now. The cause of this mistrust was "Soviet" hippies' sharply negative reaction to "politics," because "politics" implied any form of participation in social life (such as dissident activism) or even a public expression of ideas and values. "Political" engagement was in stark contrast to the hippies' position of pure escapism—complete non-inclusion in Soviet reality.[85]

The traditional symbol of Western hippies is the peace sign. The peace sign was very popular among "Soviet" hippies as well. However, for most of them it served as a symbol of nonconformism, of excluding themselves from the space of state-sanctioned violence, and of belonging to the hippie brotherhood, rather than the symbol of conscious adherence to the ideals of peace and nonviolence. People who wore the peace sign in the late Soviet period could not be considered fighters for peace for a variety of reasons. Soviet hippies were not drawn to the traditional spheres of the Western counterculture's social activism. Their pacifism more frequently manifested itself as a vague, conceptually unstructured mood which came out of a protest against the "lies" of the Soviet system and their own parents, against systems of coercion which they encountered in their homes, at school, in the Pioneer and Komsomol organizations, the army, the mass media, and cultural institutions. It was an anti-disciplinary protest, a negative pacifism, or pacifism expressed as nonconformism.

The ambiguous semantics of the notion of "pacifism" as well as its complicated history in the context of the late Soviet period led to an inevitable distortion of hippies' collective memory about the role of pacifism in the life of the *sistema*. These contradictions are especially poignant in contemporaries' recollections about the June 1, 1971 rally. (It is not even clear how many of them actually took part in the event). At the time, *The Chronicle of Current Events* reported:

> On June 1, International Children's Day, young men who refer to themselves as "hippies" and "long-hairs" gathered in the courtyard of the former historical faculty of Moscow State University in order to march with anti-war slogans to the US embassy in protest. No sooner had their "leader" unfurled a poster with the English-language inscription "Make Love, Not War!" (the traditional hippie slogan) and they entered the arc leading to Gertsen street than he and the rest (about 150 people) were surrounded by special response units and *militsiia* members who had been positioned there for some time . . . . Allegedly, a few days before the rally, a person nicknamed "Solntse"[86] (an authority among the Moscow hippies) had told them that the demonstration had been permitted by the All-Union Central Council of Trade Unions . . . .[87]

The version of the events most commonly circulated among hippies is based on Maksim Kapitanovskii's (1948–2012) account, which is found in his memoirs, *The Beatles Are To Blame*,[88] and later popularized by the eponymous film. According to this version of the story, the rally was planned as an antiwar and anti-American protest instigated by the KGB. However, his account fails to explain why some of the hippies still recall that particular rally so fondly.[89] The events of June 1, 1971 must be subjected to a careful historical scrutiny; sadly, the official archival documents on the subject remain inaccessible to the present day.

Pacifism as a symbol of nonconformism and as fashion (expressed through wearing and drawing the peace sign) was part of the milieu of the cultural underground. Pacifism was also present as a personal ethic, that is, as a personal moral and ethical human choice.

The values of nonviolence, pacifism, the methods of civil disobedience, and the idea of the "new leftists" in the 1970s and the first half of the 1980s can be glimpsed from the rock music of the era and the media associated with it, from fiction and cinema, and from Western philosophical texts that made their difficult way to the Soviet reader, as well as the essays and reports about the Western protest movement that appeared in the official Soviet press. For example, Sasha "Pessimist" (b. 1962) discovered the notion of pacifism through J. D. Salinger's work.[90] Leningrad teenager Roman Iashunskii (b. 1966) encountered his first peace "demonstration" in the early 1980s at his school. He recalls:

> I was pushed into pacifism by the death of John Lennon. I must have been in the eighth or ninth grade, and I remember that our class was on duty that day . . . . Suddenly, in the hallway, right where I had my post, a group of older kids materialized with an improvised poster affixed to the handles of two mops; the poster depicted the peace sign, a portrait of John Lennon in a black frame and an inscription that read "John Lennon Forever." The group staged something akin to a protest by singing something by Lennon, and I was supposed to stop them but I shirked my duty and was just about to join the group myself when the crazy chemistry teacher ran to disperse them, shaking her fists.[91]

There are few, albeit hardly surprising, cases of people discovering pacifism through the teachings of Leo Tolstoy. As a matter of fact, the late Soviet era saw the emergence of a number of hippie-Tolstoyans, most notably Aleksandr Lobachev (1953–2011)[92] from Lviv and Georgii Meitin (b. 1958)[93] from Riga. In 1988–1991 Meitin published *Iasnaia Poliana*, a religious-social journal with a pacifist bent.

"Anti-border" feelings were prominent among the members of the cultural underground of the late Soviet period and were probably the ideological common ground of pacifism that almost all of its representatives shared at that time. These feelings prompted the development of the Soviet grassroots peace movement. They were shared by most of the participants of the Hair group, with which Batovrin and "Diversant" were associated. The group's leader was Ofeliia, a hippie artist who had been expelled from Moscow State University in 1971 for her role in the June 1 rally. Neither the group's aesthetics nor the philosophical outlook and lifestyle of its members fit into Soviet reality.

The Hair group took part in exhibitions of nonconformist art, including the one organized in September 1975 at VDNKh (Vystavka Dostizhenii Narodonogo Khoziaistva or Exhibition of the Achievements of the National Economy) House of Culture. Especially memorable among its exhibits was the huge appliqué-and-embroidery flag Ofeliia had made, with large multicolored slogans that said "Make hair everywhere" and "Peace without borders."[94] As Oskar Rabin recalls:

The flag was displayed the first day, but the next day it was gone. We couldn't get it back, so the guys made another one just like the first overnight. They hung it up in the morning, but it was removed again, despite the fact that we went head-to-head with the exhibition organizers over it. There was a huge scandal. The assistant minister of culture with an appropriate last name (the devil marks a scoundrel)—Shkodin, who curated our exhibit, yelled, "This is anti-Soviet stuff, there can be no such thing as peace without borders!" We objected: "What do you mean? You're a communist! How can there be any borders when communists plan to take over the world?" (As they always declared they would.) Shkodin retorted: "No, even during communism there will be borders . . . ."[95]

According to Beck, not everyone is receptive to the contexts of globalization; some people continue to perceive themselves within the confines of nation-states, while others function within the framework of the global community.[96] This effect could explain the paradoxical perception of the local peace movement in the USSR by those who accused the Trust Group of exploiting the idea of fighting for peace for personal gain. The misconceptions about the motivations of activists in the local peace movement and the lack of trust in their sincerity can be explained by the fact that the people who commented on the history of the movement represented a different type of perception and thinking than those involved in the movement, and included members of the state apparatus, the average philistine, and even some nonconformists and dissidents.

It is commonly accepted that one of the characteristic traits of Soviet man was his "isolation." Much has been written on this by post-Soviet sociologists, who believe that in the USSR the isolation that had always been typical of Russia was taken to the extreme, human contacts were almost completely severed, and "constant efforts, reinforced by frenzied 'patriotic' campaigns on part of the propaganda apparatus were required to maintain the isolation of the Soviet universe."[97] The person who was formed as a result of this propaganda was "internally (in his make-up and habits) isolated from the external world, unready to perceive and understand it, unprepared for dialogue and everything else."[98]

However, the barriers gradually dissolved, and the number of people with an "open" consciousness in Soviet society grew. For a number of reasons, this process first began in the realm of outsiders who had been driven out of Soviet society or had quit it of their own free will. It was among these outsiders that cosmopolitan, anti-border, and pacifist tendencies first arose, leading to the creation of the independent peace movement in the USSR. The local peace initiatives were first and foremost "initiatives of citizens of the world." The ideas of nonviolence and pacifism were cultivated in the unofficial associations of the outcasts, who proved receptive to the globalization trends of the society of the "second modernity."[99]

Therefore, in the 1970s and 1980s, the USSR, just like the rest of Europe, saw the processes of the opposition's transnationalization as processes based on cosmopolitan values. However, the "cosmopolitan" thinking of the members of the grassroots peace movement was foreign and incomprehensible for the dominant majority of their contemporaries before the arrival of *perestroika*, when, for a brief period of time, ideas of openness and nonviolence became popular among broad layers of society.

## NOTES

1. M. I. Reitman, "Mir i ne ot mira sego: Zametki o gruppe 'Doverie,'" *Strana i mir* no. 4 (1986): 43.

2. Vladimir Bukovskii's *Patsifisty protiv mira* (Paris: Le Presse Libra, 1982) helps explain the situation.

3. Iurii T. Galanskov, *Iurii Galanskov* (Frankfurt am Main: Posev, 1980), 76–98.

4. For a brief overview of the history of independent peacemaking during this period, see Sesil' Vess'e [Cécile Vaissié], *Za vashu i nashu svobodu: Dissidentskoe dvizhenie v Rossii* (Moscow: Novoe Literaturnoe Obozrenie, 2015), 275–82.

5. Open Society Archives at Central European University, Budapest, Hungary (hereafter HU OSA), 300-85-12/271, (also available at HU OSA, Radio Liberty research department, 146/85) (Iuliia Vishnevskaia, "The Trust Group on the eve of Vladimir Brodskii's trial," August 14, 1985). All references to sources from the Open Society Archives are to materials from Radio Liberty and materials from the Samizdat Archive. All of the Samizdat Archive records held at HU OSA were published in the periodical *Samizdat Materials*. Some notes cite material from this periodical. For citations of this type, the issue number, date, and, in some cases, a brief description of the contents are given.

6. *Samizdat Materials* no. 1 (1983) ("An Appeal to the Governments and People of the USSR and the USA," June 4, 1983).

7. HU OSA, 300-85-12/271 (Information on persecution of members of the Trust Group in June–August 1982), 1982.

8. HU OSA, 300-80-7/217 (RL 116/83) (Iuliia Vishnevskaia, "The trial of Olga Medvedkova," March 27, 1984); *Samizdat Materials* no. 9 (1983).

9. *Samizdat Materials* no. 18 (1987) (Andrei Krivov and Irina Krivova, "The movement for establishing trust between East and West as a development of the Helsinki Process," April 19, 1987).

10. HU OSA 300-80-7/217 (RL 116/83) (Iuliia Vishnevskaia, "The trial of Olga Medvedkova," March 27, 1984).

11. HU OSA 300-80-7/217 (RL 116/83) (Iuliia Vishnevskaia, "The trial of Olga Medvedkova," March 27, 1984). See also *Samizdat Materials* no. 6 (1983) ("Statement of the Moscow Trust Group," June 29, 1982) and *Samizdat Materials* no. 9 (1984) (Elena Sannikova, "Proposals to the Moscow Trust Group from Elena Sannikova," 1982).

12. HU OSA, 300-80-7/21 (Sergei Batovrin, "Statement on the persecution of Trust Group members between June and November 1982," 1982), 7; HU OSA, 300-80-7/269 (The day of Oleg Radzinskii's trial in Moscow, October 1983).

13. For biographical information on Rubchenko, see HU OSA, 300-85-12/89 (The biography of Aleksandr Rubchenko, member of the Trust Group, pacifist, and vegetarian, July 1984).

14. For biographical information on Khramov, see HU OSA, 300-85-12/89 (Nikolai Khramov, "Autobiography of Nikolai Khramov, written while awaiting arrest and trial for pacifist activity," July 14, 1984).

15. *Samizdat Materials* no. 23 (1985) (Nikolai Khramov, "An open letter of the Trust Group member to M. S. Gorbachev, General Secretary of the CPSU Central Committee in defense of political prisoner A. Shatravka," March 31, 1985).

16. HU OSA, 300-85-12/89 (The biography of Aleksandr Rubchenko, member of the Trust Group, pacifist, and vegetarian, July 1984).

17. HU OSA, 300-80-7/335 (The Independent Initiative Group, "An Appeal to Young America," 1983).

18. "System" (*sistema*) was the term Soviet hippies used to describe themselves. Sometimes it was used more broadly to refer to other relevant organizations of the late Soviet cultural underground (nonconformist artists, musicians, etc.).

19. "Interv'iu uchreditelia gruppy 'Svobodnaia Initsiativa' Iu. Popova," *Express-Khronika*, 26, no. 5 (1988): 6.

20. HU OSA, 300-80-7/7335 (Sergei Troianskii, "Toward June 1, 1981—an appeal from the Moscow pacifist," 1981).

21. "Otechestvo v opasnosti: Manifest 'Svobodnoi Initsiativy,'" *Den' za dnem*, no. 8 (1987): 15–22.

22. "1 iunia—mezhdunarodnyi den' zashchity detei," *Svoboda*, no. 2 (1988): 2.

23. "Prizyv k rovesnikam," the personal archive of O. Romanenko (b. 1959, aka "Pudel'"). See also "Prizyv k rovesnikam," *Svoboda*, no. 4 (1988): 3.

24. Other sources put the number at one hundred.

25. *Vesti iz SSSR* 2, no. 5 (1983): 205; *Vesti iz SSSR* 2, no. 11 (1984): 415; HU OSA, 300-80-7/7335 (Sergei Troianskii, "Toward June 1, 1981—an appeal from the Moscow pacifist," 1981); HU OSA, 300-80-7/335 (Statement on the arrests in Moscow of members of the youth pacifist group "Independent Initiative," 1986).

26. *Den' za dnem*, no. 8 (1987): 3–4.

27. Information about these arrests made it to the West, where Popov and Troianskii were regarded as "prisoners of peace" and victims of punitive psychiatry. See *Vesti iz SSSR* 6, no. 22 (1984); HU OSA, 300-80-7/335 (Statement on the arrests in Moscow of members of the youth pacifist group "Independent Initiative," 1986); *Return Address: Moscow: International News Bulletin on Independent Peace Activity in the USSR*, no. 2 (1984): 18.

28. A. Rubchenko told us he was involved in creating this text. The specifics of the timeframe and circumstances of the text's creation require further research.

29. "Svobodnaia initsiativa: Nazad puti net," *Strana i mir* 42, no. 6 (1987): 142–43. See also "Svobodnaia initsiativa: Nazad puti net," *Den' za dnem*, no. 9 (1987): 23–27; *Samizdat Materials* no. 48 (1987).

30. Gray notebook, entry for December 13, 1989. The author wishes to thank Olga Ponomareva (aka Olia Troll) for providing the materials. The gray notebook was Iurii ("Diversant") Popov's personal notebook. The notebook was part of Olga Ponomareva's private archive but is currently in possession of Iurii Popov's daughter.

31. *Samizdat Materials* no. 21 (1983) (Sergei Batovrin, "Why we refuse our bowls of soup: Hunger strike statement," March 16, 1983).

32. This word is used to describe "people whose requests for permission to emigrate were denied." M. A. Morozova, *Anatomiia otkaza* (Moscow: Rossiiskii gosudarstvennyi gumanitarnyi universitet, 2011), 9.

33. Cécile Vaissié claims that initially there were six refuseniks among the Group's members. Later, they were joined by another six, bringing the total number to twelve. Vess'e [Vaissié], *Za vashu i nashu svobodu*, 502.

34. Memorial Society Archive, fond 103 (collection of Kronid Lubarskii), file 5, d. 8 (Oleg Radzinskii, "An appeal to the members of the Moscow Trust Group," April 5, 1984).

35. HU OSA, 300-85-12/271 (Evgenii Khramov denies the statement of the members of the Trust Group, April 17, 1984).

36. Aleksandr Shatravka, *Pobeg iz raia* (New York: Liberty Publishing House, 2010).

37. "Sergei Batovrin: Bespechnoe puteshestvie s gruppoi 'Volosy,'" *dipart*, September 17, 2012, http://dipart.livejournal.com/51904.html.

38. Pinhas Podrabinek, Politicheskii dnevnik (unpublished manuscript), 1987, 28, Ekspress-Chronika archives, box 92, International Institute of Social History, Amsterdam.

39. Sergei Goncharov, "O chem toskuet 'Russkaia mysl'"? (Beseda s Irinoi Krivovoi)," *Sovershenno sekretno*, August 2001, http://www.sovsekretNo.ru//article/681.

40. Reitman, "Mir i ne ot mira sego," 43–44.

41. Ibid., 47.

42. *Samizdat Materials* no. 20 (1983) (Interview with Mark Reitman, member of the Trust Group on the group's activity, 1983).

43. Reitman, "Mir i ne ot mira sego," 47.

44. *Samizdat Materials* no. 20 (1983) (Interview with Mark Reitman, member of the Trust Group on the group's activity, 1983).

45. Morozova, *Anatomiia*, 9, 35.

46. Ibid., 58.

47. *Samizdat Materials* no. 35 (1986) (Nina Kovalenko, "The artist and Trust Group member's reasons for renouncing Soviet citizenship," July 27, 1986).

48. Morozova, *Anatomiia*, 182–83.

49. Gennadii Krochik, "Iz arkhiva Viktora Bloka," *Chaika*, May 16, 2001, http;//www.chayka.org/node/4071.

50. HU OSA, 300-85-12/89 (Mark Reitman, "Open letter to the chair of the American Peace Council Dr. Mark Solomon," June 1984).

51. Oleg Zhuravlev, "Studenty, nauchnaia innovatsiia i politicheskaia funktsiia komsomola: Fizfak MGU v 1950–1960-e gody," in *Raznomyslie v SSSR/Rossii*

*(1945–2008): Sbornik materialov nauchnoi konferentsii, 15–16 maia 2009 goda*, ed. B. M. Firsov (Saint Petersburg: Evropeiskii Universitet v Sankt-Peterburge, 2010), 128.

52. Krochik, "Iz arkhiva."

53. David Satter, *Vek bezumiia: Raspad i padenie Sovetskogo Soiuza* (Moscow: OGI, 2005), 219.

54. HU OSA, 300-85-12/271 (Information on the Trust Group, 1982).

55. *Samizdat Materials* no. 44 (1983) (Mark Reitman, "Letter to an unidentified addressee about the attitude of the author, a Trust Group member, to problems of emigration, defense of peace, the group's legal status, etc.," 1983).

56. HU OSA, 300-85-12/271 (Information on the Trust Group, 1982).

57. Ibid., *Samizdat Materials* no. 21 (1983) (Content analysis of the media, 1982); *Samizdat Materials* no. 9 (1984) (A lexical-semantic analysis of political texts and the relaxing of international tensions, 1982).

58. Mark Reitman, "Mir i ne ot mira sego," 50–51; *Samizdat Materials* no. 21 (1983) (Mark Reitman, "An optimization model of disarmament with a controlled level of immigration," 1982).

59. HU OSA, 300-85-12/271 (Information on the Trust Group, 1982); *Samizdat Materials* nos. 23–24 (1987) (*Glasnost': The Informational Bulletin* no. 1, 1987).

60. HU OSA, 300-85-12/271 (Broadcast of May 23–24, 1983: "The Group for Establishing Trust . . . .").

61. Viacheslav A. Shuper, "Sovershennye i nesovershennye otkrytiia professora Medvedkova," *Demoskop Weekly*, February 18–March 2, 2008; HU OSA, 300-85-12/271 (The biography of Iurii Medvedkov, member of the Moscow group "For establishing trust between the USSR and the USA," geographer and refusenik, 1983); *Samizdat Materials* no. 26 (1986) (Iurii Medvedkov, "Letter to V. N. Eltsin, the First Secretary of the MGK KPSS," May 20, 1986).

62. *Samizdat Materials* nos. 23–24 (1987) (*Glasnost': The Informational Bulletin* no. 1, 1987).

63. Beck, Ulrich, *The Cosmopolitan Vision* (Cambridge: Polity Press, 2006), 2.

64. Cit. ex: Ul'rikh Bek, [Ulrich, Beck], *Chto takoe globalizatsiia? Oshibki globalizma—otvety na globalizatsiiu*, trans. A. Grigor'ev and V. Sedel'nik (Moscow: Progress-Traditsiia, 2001), 43.

65. Ibid., 74. Emphasis in the original.

66. Ibid., 80–81.

67. Kacper Szulecki, "'Freedom and Peace are Indivisible': On the Czechoslovak and Polish Dissident Input to the European Peace Movement, 1985–1989," in *Entangled Protest: Transnational Perspectives on Dissent and Opposition in Central and Eastern Europe*, ed. Robert Brier (Osnabrück: Fibre, 2012), 6.

68. Bek [Beck], *Chto takoe globalizatsiia*, 42–43.

69. Elena Zdravomyslova, "Kul'turnyi andergraund 1970-kh: Leningradskoe kafe 'Saigon' glazami zavsegdataia i issledovatelia," in Firsov, *Raznomyslie v SSSR i Rossii*, 136.

70. Ibid., 157. Art historian Stanislav Savitskii offers a similar assessment of Soviet bohemia and refers to the nonconformist culture of the USSR as a "culture of disenchantment," characterized by "negativity and a crisis of positive identification,"

and the "habit of "defining oneself negatively, in opposition." S. A. Savitskii, *Andergraund: Istoriia i mify leningradskoi neofitsial'noi literatury* (Moscow: Novoe Literaturnoe Obozrenie, 2002), 86, 114.

71. Aleksandr Vial'tsev, *Chelovek na doroge: Zapiski ob avtostope*, 2003, http://ponia1.narod.ru/roadbook.htm. Vial'tsev was also known as "Pessimist."

72. Aleksandr Ogorodnikov, "Kul'tura katakomb: K opytu pokoleniia," *Obshchina*, no. 2 (1978); Memorial Society Archive, file 169, d. 2.

73. Mata Khari [Mariia Remizova], *Puding iz promokashki: Khippi kak oni est'* (Moscow: FORUM, 2008), 104.

74. Ibid., 81.

75. A. O. Madison, "Anekdoty ob Andree Madisone," in A. O. Madison, *Sochineniia v dvukh tomakh*, vol. 2 (Saint Petersburg: Novoe kul'turnoe prostranstvo, 2009), 179–80.

76. The period from the mid-1970s to the mid-1980s saw the hippies' mass conversion to Christian Orthodoxy and other forms of Christianity and their intensive engagement with Asian religions and new religious movements and, to a lesser degree, indigenism, national-historical re-enactment, Tolkienism, and other similar utopian projects.

77. "Ideologiia sovetskikh khippi (1967–1987)," *Strana i mir* no. 6 (1987): 127.

78. Ibid., 140–41.

79. Ibid., 143.

80. David Satter, "The Soviets Freeze a Peace Worker," *The Wall Street Journal*, August 12, 1982.

81. Ibid.

82. Ibid.

83. S. Batovrin, "Kuda katit' zhernov egipetskogo kalendaria? Bespechnoe puteshestvie s gruppoi 'Volosy,'" *Slovo/Word* no. 80 (2013): 151–57, http://magazines.russ.ru/slovo/2013/80/17b.html.

84. HU OSA, 300-85 SA, no. 4761, 1.

85. Vasilii Boiarintsev, *My—khippi: Sbornik rasskazov* (Moscow: Lulu, 2001), 5–7; Sergei Pavlukhin, "Film 'Dom solntsa,'" *Izba-Chital'nia: Literaturno-khudozhestvennyi portal*, February 2, 2011, http://chitalnya.ru/work/289517/; Aleksandr Vial'tsev and Aleksei Ivanov, "Goroda i dorogi," in *Khippi u L'vovi: Almanakh*, ed. Ivan Banakh (L'viv: Triada plius, 2011), 282.

86. Iurii Burakov (1949–1992) was one of the best-known representatives of the first wave of the hippie movement in the USSR.

87. *Khronika tekushchikh sobytii*, no. 20 (July 2, 1971), http://www.memo.ru/history/diss/chr/.

88. Maksim Kapitanovskii, *Vo vsem vinovaty "Bitlz"* (Moscow: Vagrius, 2006), 222–26.

89. It is more likely that the demonstration was intended to emulate American hippies' rallies against the Vietnam war as well as the memories of the SMOG protest rally on April 14, 1965. SMOG was a nonconformist literary group. The acronym SMOG comes from the group's name: Smelost', Mysl', Obraz, Glubina—Courage, Thought, Image, Depth.

90. Aleksandr Vial'tsev, *Krug nepodvizhnykh zvezd: Roman*, in *Kontinent* no. 128 (2006), http://magazines.russ.ru/continent/2006/128/vial2.html.

91. R. Iashunskii, "Moi memuary (Fragmenty iz knigi)," in *Sumerki "Saigona,"* ed. Iuliia Valieva (Saint Petersburg: Samizdat, 2009), 454. I would like to thank the author for the opportunity to read the unpublished manuscript of his memoirs.

92. Aleksandr Lobachev, "Iz avtobiografii," in Banakh, *Khippi u L'vovi*, 159–64.

93. Georgii Meitin, "Ispoveduiu nenasilie," *Iasnaia Poliana* no. 10 (1988): 1; Georgii Meitin, "Dva leta," *Iasnaia Poliana* no. 11 (1989–1990).

94. Oskar Rabin, "Nasha zhizn' byla polna sobytiiami," in *Eti strannye semidesiatye, ili poteria nevinnosti: Esse, interv'iu, vospominaniia*, comp. Georgii Kizeval'ter (Moscow: Novoe Literaturnoe Obozrenie, 2010), 235–36.

95. Ibid., 237.

96. Bek [Beck], *Chto takoe globalizatsiia*, 119.

97. Iurii Levada, *Ishchem cheloveka: Sotsiologicheskie ocherki, 2000–2005* (Moscow: Novoe Izdatel'stvo, 2006), 265–66.

98. Ibid., 266.

99. Szulecki, "'Freedom and Peace are Indivisible,'" 6.

*Chapter 7*

# Dropping Out of Socialism with the Commodore 64

## *Polish Youth, Home Computers, and Social Identities*

Patryk Wasiak

This chapter discusses the ways in which Polish youth appropriated home computers as cultural artifacts, which helped them to build social identities shortly before and after 1989.[1] I argue that activities related to computer use significantly structured the everyday life and social identities of thousands of young Polish men at that time. During the 1980s, with the rise of a local computer market and the extensive support of communist youth organizations, home computers were widely appropriated by young people as cultural artifacts, that is, as objects that had meanings beyond those accruing to consumer goods. As I show, building an identity as a *komputerowiec* (computer user) was a strategy for "dropping out" of the normative model of computer use, which was shaped through the "computer literacy" program for young people.[2] However, it should be noted that state-sponsored computer clubs played a substantial role by providing young computer aficionados with the computer programming skills necessary to become a *komputerowiec*.

Looking at how young people appropriated home computers during the transition from communism to capitalism in Eastern Europe sheds light on the process of creating and reproducing "imaginary worlds."[3] Such worlds, especially those created by young people, were deeply influenced by the available knowledge about cultural currents in the West and the context of rapid socioeconomic changes in societies in transition. This case study provides empirical material that shows how young people actively constructed their identities in Eastern Europe of the 1980s and early 1990s. The notion of possibilities and constraints on expression of individual agency in late state socialism, which Alexei Yurchak discusses in depth, provides a stimulating framework for further studies of the last years of state socialism when individuals "dropped out" by structuring their own everyday lives as members of subcultures, scenes, or tribes, or as profit-driven entrepreneurs in the

157

informal economy.[4] However, Yurchak primarily offers an explanation of how dropping out was a general trend in Soviet society in the 1980s while dropping out done by small and distinctive groups, such as the *komputerowcy* discussed here, requires more explanation. A case study of young computer users can also shed some light on the rather neglected issue of the connection between practices of consumption and social identities during the transition from the socialist to the capitalist system in Eastern Europe.[5]

This chapter draws on sociological studies of "scenes" and brand communities and studies of the domestication of media technologies, which provide a useful theoretical framework for exploring cultural practices of computer use. British scholars influenced by the work of the Birmingham Centre for Cultural Studies have done important work on the "domestication" and cultural meanings of home computers in Western Europe in the 1980s.[6] In this case study, I explore patterns of computer domestication in the economic, social, and cultural context of Poland shortly before and after the process of political change in 1989. Margrethe Aune claims that the domestication of home computers is a two-sided process in which computer is "adapted to your everyday life, and your everyday life is adapted to this new and hitherto alien artifact."[7] On the one hand, individual computer owners influenced the rise of social structures such as brand communities as well as the economic structure of "computer fairs" (*giełdy komputerowe*). On the other hand, the availability of such structures exerted influence in both directions on the everyday lives of other young people who joined the ranks of computer users.

We usually think of drop-outs as unskilled young people who may be engaged in loitering, or drug abuse, or who may join one of the "usual" subcultures such as punks, metalheads, or skinheads. Of course, one can identify a substantial number of such drop-outs in the Polish social landscape of young people in the 1980s. However, here I shed light on a different kind of dropping out by investigating young people who used their high-level computer skills to build their social identities or even to build their own identities as devotees of particular computer brands.

In the first section of this chapter, I briefly outline how home computer use was framed in communist political ideology. The second section discusses how the concept of "scenes" used in sociological scholarship to explain several youth activities is a useful framework for discussing the social identities of Polish computer users in the context of system transition. Then, I discuss how participation in "computer fairs" and practices of software trading contributed to the rise of computer popularity during the period of economic and social changes growing out of the demise of the communist regime in Poland. Finally, I discuss how participation in particular "brand communities" such as Atari or Commodore 64 users became a primary identity for computer users at the time. This study is based on the analysis of computer journals, electronic zines, software artifacts, and interviews with members of Polish "computer scenes."

## COMPUTERS AND SOCIALIST VALUES

To understand the relevance of practices of computer use for a broader pattern of "dropping out of socialism" it is necessary to show how practices of young Polish computer users were considered both an example of "defragmentation of the social" and a challenge to the values of the communist computer literacy project.[8] In one of several articles on Polish youth, in a tone of moral panic, a columnist for the influential weekly news magazine *Polityka* described a cultural wasteland of young people who did not engage in activities organized by youth communist organizations and culture centers: "There is a no-man's-land between home and school. This land is inhabited by spontaneously established tribes that distinctly differentiate [themselves] from each other with clothing, customs and the rules of interaction. Some of them call themselves 'youth subculture' or 'alternative.'"[9]

Another article from the same year discusses one such tribe, here referred to as a "clan," in an unambiguously negative manner:

> Recently I became acquainted with a group of young people . . . who call themselves "computer underground [*komputerowy underground*] based on the Western model." Wealthy parents provided these pupils and students with those expensive toys . . . . They are simply swanking [*szpanować*]. The basic attributes of this swank are: overuse of technical jargon . . . spending several hours with a keyboard only to make more or less random "computer graphics." Apparently such graphics are based on Western software. This youth computer clan also developed its distinctive language. Its members are making simple graphic software [*programy rysunkowe*] which includes text messages, which they further copy on floppies.[10]

In the late 1980s in Poland, adolescent and young adult males interested in computer use began to be recognized as one of several "youth tribes." Earlier in the 1980s young computer users had been discussed in media discourse rather positively as a generation oriented toward the future with considerable technical skills that would contribute to the modernization of Polish industry. Several reports from that time described how children and adolescents eagerly participated in computer courses organized in clubs sponsored and supervised by the ZSMP (Związek Socjalistycznej Młodzieży Polskiej, or Association of Socialist Youth of Poland), a counterpart of the Komsomol.[11]

The ZSMP provided computer access for children and adolescents within its system of "centers for games and entertainment," a counterpart of the Komsomol's "youth recreation departments."[12]

The history of the social impact of computers, which mostly focuses on the US, emphasizes the role of countercultural movements as a social force that shaped the cultural meanings of computers.[13] The potential of computers to challenge oppressive social and political power structures is referred as the "Californian ideology."[14] Little has been written on the huge impact of Ronald Reagan's neoliberal political ideology of computer culture. It is worth remembering that in the 1980s home computers, with a range of spreadsheets, word processors, and databases, were widely disseminated among the American middle class as devices that enabled people to keep working at home after leaving the office, which allowed them to catch up in order to meet the requirements of a highly competitive job market.[15] Moreover, software targeted at small businesses also offered an opportunity to leave a salaried position and pursue a career as an entrepreneur running a small business, a hero of Reaganonomics.

In the context of the capitalist economy, the computer was recognized as an artifact that helps people achieve personal success and gain an advantage over less "computerized" competitors. In state socialism, political ideology framed the computer as a device which helped to achieve collective economic and social goals.[16] A propaganda piece in the journal *Magazyn Rodzinny* (*Family Magazine*) that promoted the ideology of communist youth organizations provides an excellent illustration of how the computer was framed in political ideology. In June 1986, shortly before the 10th Congress of the PZPR (Polska Zjednoczona Partia Robotnicza, or the Polish United Workers' Party) the magazine published an article entitled "Przed nami XXI wiek" ("The twenty-first century is before us"), which outlined recent successes in modernization and improvements in the standard of living. The article was illustrated with a collage of photographs of a heavy industry plant, harvesters on a field, a laboratory, a construction site, and a group of children next to a computer in a computer club.[17]

However, articles in the press about the computer underground reveal a more controversial way in which young people appropriated computers outside of official computer education programs.[18] Such warnings referred to an important trend in local computer culture that began around 1988, as membership in state computer clubs started to decline with the increase in privately owned computers and the formation of users' own milieus outside of the ZSMP-sponsored clubs. This is also an excellent picture of young people who "dropped out" from officially sanctioned "useful [*pożyteczny*] computer use" which was supposed to contribute to "the increase of the efficiency of work in society" (*wzrost społecznej wydajności pracy*).[19]

Generally, the mass media presented playing computer games and using computers for activities which did not contribute to the development and modernization of socialist Poland as an unwelcome domestication of computers in socialist society. Discussing Soviet computer literary projects, J. Nicholls Eastmond and Stephen T. Kerr  refer to an article from *Uchitel'skaia gazeta* written by a concerned teacher who explained the potential dangers of computer games: "they can turn children into hackers (*khakery*)."[20] Since, as this Russian teacher claimed, "every third student is a potential hacker" who "lacks social direction," such practices of computer use should be strongly discouraged. Such warnings had little impact. As we shall see, instead of "useful" computer use, Polish youth adopted their Commodore 64s and Ataris as meaningful objects in their everyday lives.

## HOME COMPUTERS AND "SCENES"

In the 1990s the usefulness of "subculture" as an analytic category for studies of youth culture was challenged by several categories that scholars put forward in the broader framework of "post-subculture studies." Chris Jenks points out that the historical process of the disintegration of the social world of youth includes the broad and complex emergence of "new communities, interest groups, scenes, assemblies, cults, fashions and style clusters," rather than the emergence of essentialist "subcultures."[21] Jim Riordan lists the activities of Soviet young people the late 1980s who are real-life counterparts of Jenks's abstract categories: "punks and hippies, night bikers and drug addicts, soccer hooligans and muggers, glue sniffers and prostitutes (male and female), vigilante gangs and skinheads . . ., Zen Buddhists and Hari Krishna followers, 'absurdists' and 'primitivists' even Swastika-sporting young fascists."[22]

One of the most influential approaches to such heterogeneous social structures is the concept of "scenes."[23] A "scene" refers to a group of individuals who share similar practices and establish a common social identity related to such practices. However, a scene is "something less" than a community. Holly Kruse notes in reference to Will Straw's work that her work on alternative music cultures focuses on, "the relationship between situated music practices and the construction of identity; and I use the word 'scene' to imply something less stable and historically rooted than a 'community.'"[24] The same remark is also relevant for studying the construction of identities related to practices of computer use.

Media domestication studies help to explain how computer scenes are constructed. In an essay which outlines the most significant concepts of the "media domestication" framework, Knut H. Sørensen suggests the themes that should be considered while discussing how a media technology artifact became "domesticated":

- The construction of a set of practices related to an artifact. This could mean routines in using an artifact, but also the establishment and development of institutions to support and regulate its use.
- The construction of meaning of the artefact, including the role the artefact eventually could play in relation to the production of identities of the actors involved.
- Cognitive processes related to learning of practice as well as meaning.[25]

Sørensen's outline provides a basic framework for understanding just how a scene of computer users is established by relevant actors and institutions. As I have shown in my previous work, in the mid-1980s the most significant institutions that supported and regulated computer use in Poland were state-sponsored computer clubs and the entry-level, popular computer magazine *Bajtek* (1985–1996), which was published under the auspices of the ZSMP.[26] (The cover of the first issue of *Bajtek*.) During the turnover of the 1980s and 1990s, social networks and "computer fairs" played the most significant roles in influencing practices of computer use. The testimony of an Atari computer user, known by the moniker of "Miker" in the Polish community of Atarians, powerfully shows this change:

> First I met Grzesiek . . . . It was in a computer club . . . where we started talking with each other. After a while we formed a group, at that time it was referred as a "firm" ["firma" in Polish]—G.M.S. Software . . . . Then it was renamed as ORBIT-Soft or something like that. At the beginning we were visiting each other and playing games together. Then we started doing something on our own. With Grzesiek we eagerly read *Bajtek*. From *Bajtek* we learned about the computer fair . . . in Warsaw. It was the beginning of the 1990s. First, I was astounded by the enormous number of people with computers in the same place. Further, I wanted more and more to copy something "new" at the fair.[27]

First, he attended courses organized by a state-sponsored computer club where he learned the basics of computer use and got to know his colleague Grzesiek. Together they "dropped out" and, instead of attending club courses, they started playing games without any supervision. Then, influenced by the rise of the "computer underground," they formed the "G.M.S. Software" group. At the same time they were still reading the ZSMP-sponsored magazine *Bajtek* from which they learned about the "computer fair" in Warsaw, which at that time was important as a site for copying software and making new, computer-related acquaintances. "Doing something on our own" in the computer jargon of that time referred not only to playing computer games but to a range of activities. Such activities could include gathering a library of software copied from colleagues, learning programming and experimenting with writing one's own programs, or creating computer graphics or music with the available editing software.[28] "Miker's" testimony shows a typical pattern of "dropping out" from the computer education program. This testimony is an expression of a process which is at the same time a peculiarity of late socialism in Poland and a trait of hacker culture. "Miker" described how he lost interest in participating in activities organized by a state-sponsored club and expressed his willingness to set up his own "firm," the business model of which, we may assume, was to commercially distribute pirated programs among his peers. At the same time, this testimony shows how a skilled computer user dropped out from a local computer club and sought out other computer users to help him improve his programming skills and find possibilities for applying those skills. Setting up a firm was popular among young people in Poland in the 1980s since many of them, while still in high school, were eager to become entrepreneurs by trading pirated video cassettes or music tapes at fairs or by becoming trade tourists. Finding sources of help to improve programming skills and ways to apply them were typical of computer hackers everywhere.[29]

Several testimonies with features similar to "Miker's" were elicited as part of two Polish retro-computing projects. One is part of the *Atari Online* website and the other can be found on the website of the *Commodore & Amiga Fan* magazine.[30] Similar testimonies can also be found in several disk magazines published by computer users in the early 1990s. For instance, as one of the prominent members of the C-64 scene with the moniker "Mosquito" explained, in the late 1980s he learned how to program in a state-sponsored computer club in Gdańsk and in 1990 he joined Slaves of Keyboard, one of the first groups of the "computer underground," as a programmer.[31]

Such activities, alongside the establishment of extensive personal networks, constituted the social world of the *komputerowiec* and provided him with a particular social identity. This was frequently accompanied by a moniker. In addition to "Miker," other monikers of popular Polish *komputerowcy* from the late 1980s include "Jetboy," "Silver Dream!," "Polonus," "Sky," "Mosquito," "Hi-Man," "Corpse," "Digger Metal," and "Mr. Mike." Anglophone monikers like these were similar to monikers used by members of the computer scene in Western Europe.[32] Examples of the first Polish computer demonstration programs (referred as "demos") to be preserved. These aimed to show a computer user's proficiency in programming and editing computer graphics. A digitized photo of members of the popular Luzers (in Polish *luz* means "at ease"), a group of the Commodore Amiga users established in 1990.

It is important to discuss the economic phenomenon of "firms" in the growing local computer market. In the 1980s, along with the booming informal economy, dozens of such "firms" were established, mostly by young entrepreneurs familiar with computers. These firms made profits in two ways. Firstly, they imported computer hardware from West Berlin, Dubai, or Singapore. Secondly, they traded in pirated software which was on offer at booths during "computer fairs" as is discussed below or was available in "computer studios." Such companies had colorful names like Videobit, Megabajt, Atari-Bajt, Computronix, Bonus, Macrosoft, or BIM, which used a logo that was very similar in design to the IBM logo. The small-scale, private entrepreneurs who started these companies were successful figures in the context of the transition economy. Computer users who were too young or lacked the resources to build their own companies trading in hardware imported semi-legally from the Far East were still eager to emulate such naming practices with names such as ORBIT Soft. They also used other naming conventions to emulate the computer scene in Western Europe with names such as The Housebreakers, Slaves of Keyboard, World Cracking Federation, Sex Instructors, or Colorado Squad.

It is also important to ask where exactly, outside of computer clubs, adolescents were able to interact with other potential or actual computer users and build their own identities as *komputerowcy*. Ray Oldenburg in his well-known study of communal spaces introduced the term "third places" for sites such as bars, coffee shops, beauty parlors, and parks, where it is possible to engage in social life outside the home, or school, or the workplace.[33] In an essay on the course of domestication of the home computer, Leslie Haddon emphasized the role of particular sites in such processes. As he pointed out, the "places where computer hackers meet and develop their individual and collective domestication strategies" significantly influence practices of technology use.[34] As Haddon discussed, computers were not domesticated by adolescents in the solitude of a bedroom, but rather, during time spent with peers interested in computers. Such conversations could take place in schools, or hangouts, or during visits to computer stores.

In Poland in the mid-1980s, computer clubs played this role for Polish adolescents. They were not only to able to learn how to operate a computer and write a program in BASIC, but they could also develop their social skills since the clubs were always crowded and usually one computer was operated not by a single user but rather a small group tasked, for instance, with writing a short program together. However, in the late 1980s such clubs began to be frequented less and less since Polish households owned many more computers. As an instructor in a computer club in Warsaw explained, the club, which acquired several ZX Spectrum computers the mid-1980s, could not attract young people by the late 1980s, when most of its target market was already familiar with the C-64, Atari XE/XL, or even the Commodore Amiga, which had superior graphic and sound capacities.[35] For young people who had their own computers at home, there was no need to visit computer clubs anymore, especially since computer club instructors did not allow them to play computer games. Moreover, the much more attractive "computer fairs," which were unofficial gatherings of local computer users, took over the role such clubs had played as "third places." "Miker's" testimony shows a typical pattern of "dropping out" from state clubs and the beginnings of interest in computer fairs.

The Polish computer fairs of the late 1980s originated from computer stalls at bazaars, which were the most important sites of the informal economy. At these stalls shoppers could not only privately purchase imported computers and peripherals but could also get pre-recorded cassettes, or floppy disks with software, or they could ask for a copy of software they selected on the spot. In 1985 one of Warsaw's computer clubs started to organize its own "computer fair" on weekends in a primary school on Grzybowska Street. The fair was supposed to be dedicated to non-commercial activities such as re-selling used hardware for a fair price or the exchange of public domain software on a non-profit basis. Its supposedly non-commercial character meant that *Bajtek* became the official sponsor of this initiative.[36] However, despite idealistic claims, this event instantly became a site of commercial and highly profitable trade in imported computer hardware and software.

Around 1988 some adolescent Commodore 64 software traders at the Grzybowska fair started adding their own loader screens onto software copied for clients. J. H., one of the most prominent software traders and an important figure from the C-64 scene, explained that he and his colleagues became familiar with such screens (referred to as "intros," or "crack intros" and which were popular in Western Europe) along with imported pirated computer games.[37] Polish software traders viewed such "intros" as an opportunity to advertise their business.[38]

The Grzybowska computer fair became known across Poland as the site where new computer software was available. As Adam Pokora, another software trader, claimed, the fair became a hub for local software traders from other cities: "At that time (1988–1990) I had several acquaintances from throughout Poland. They were visiting me regularly to bring me programs which were unavailable here and copied those which were unavailable in their cities. . . . The post office could easily destroy floppies sent in letters, thus the most reliable way to obtain software was a personal visit to Grzybowska in Warsaw."[39]

Pokora called his small enterprise Metal Software Service since as well as being a member of the computer scene at that time he was also a metalhead. The Warsaw computer fair played a significant role as a site where computer users could strike up acquaintances which led to the formation of computer scene groups. The first Polish C-64 group, Housebreakers, was established by Warsaw computer fair traders in 1988. As "Sky," one of the founders of the group, remembered, the group was established by a small circle of acquaintances from the Warsaw computer fair: "We started the Housebreakers . . . at that time we knew some people from the Grzybowska Street fair."[40] As Pokora

remembered, software traders were not only copying software but also playing games together: "The fair was not only [about] the software trade. Frequently we played Kick Off [a computer two-player soccer game] together
on the Amiga after the fair closed down . . . . A fair was also a site for social
gatherings of those who were fascinated by computers."[41]

Copying software during fairs was very profitable for teenagers. "Fiction,"
another well-known trader from the Grzybowska fair, revealed in an interview in a disk magazine how much he could earn from the software trade:
"Q: What you would say about your clients? How much money you were able
to get from them? A: I was able to make two average monthly salaries in one
week. Without any tax!!"[42]

Aside from the fair in Warsaw at least ten fairs of the same kind were
organized regularly in other big cities in Poland. Computer fairs in Poland
went on unchanged until the introduction of the copyright protection act of
1995, which made it possible to prosecute software pirates. This act allowed
the police to organize raids on the fairs and caused the subsequent demise of
this socioeconomic phenomenon which had its roots in the informal economy
of the 1980s. What is striking is that computer fairs had not changed much
during the intervening years. The only significant difference between fairs
in 1988–1989 and 1993–1994 were different hardware platforms, since the
Commodore Amiga and PC completely replaced the C-64 and Atari, but
the software traders were mostly the same. As we have seen, fairs played a
significant role as, to quote Sørensen, "institutions to support and regulate
computer use."[43] At the same time, they were important "third places" for
thousands of young computer users every weekend.

Computer use gave young Poles opportunities to both build their own attractive social identities and make substantial profits. In 1990 Polish sociologist
Lena Kolarska-Bobińska conducted research on a generation of young Poles
eager to "be on their own" (*być na swoim*) and to participate in the free market economy by opening their own businesses. As she claimed, many of them
considered opening a computer trade company one of the most appealing and
profitable business opportunities.[44] Recently Philipp Ther discussed the social
impact of the emergence of the free market economy in Eastern Europe.[45] The
economic aspect of the emergence of the computer scene in Poland during the
transition to capitalism shows the impact of this transition on Poles' everyday
lives and sheds light on how individuals co-constructed the new economy.
Adolescent *komputerowcy* were too young to participate in the hardware
market since it required personal travel to West Berlin or a flight to Dubai
or Singapore to import computer hardware worth several thousand dollars.
However, they could pursue their own careers as software traders which, as
traders explained in interviews, usually began with copying their own collection of games for profit. The practices of adolescent software traders show
how young Poles not only looked for profit-making opportunities, but also

how they symbolically attempted to became capitalist entrepreneurs by using Anglophone names that referred to the Western computer market such as "Robert King Corporation Ltd." or "G.M.S. Software."[46]

## HOME COMPUTERS AND BRAND COMMUNITIES

The Polish computer scene of the late 1980s and 1990s was divided into circles of users of particular hardware platforms such as the 8-bit Commodore 64, the ZX Spectrum, the Atari XE/XL, and the 16-bit Commodore Amiga and the Atari ST. The rise of particular "scenes" dedicated to hardware platforms was intertwined with the success or failure of manufacturers' marketing strategies. For instance, the British ZX Spectrum became popular only in the UK and continental Europe, while the Apple II, which was popular in the US, was virtually non-existent in Europe. The C-64 became highly popular in continental Europe and the UK because of successful marketing of the Commodore UK and the Commodore Deutschland.[47] In Poland in the mid 1980s, privately imported ZX Spectrums were popular only to be replaced by the C-64 and the Atari XE/XL which became the two dominant platforms during the period of system transition.

In Poland the C-64 gained popularity as one of the high-tech consumer electronics goods privately imported from West Germany. In a report on a ferry trip to Hamburg organized for trade tourists, we see a note on the popularity of the C-64: "Several of my travel companions are highly interested in home computers. My neighbor Ziutek bought the C-64 for no more than 600 DM and he is crazy with happiness."[48] The Atari became widely popular in Poland as a computer offered in Pewex, a hard currency chain store.[49] In 1986, while broadening its consumer electronics offerings, Pewex made a deal with a private joint venture company (*firma polonijna*), Karen, which not long before had become the official dealer of Atari computers in Poland. In the West Atari was mostly a market flop and definitely lost out in competition with the C-64, but in Poland it became widely popular because of Pewex's policy of offering it at a relatively low price.

From the beginning, the computer magazine *Bajtek* was divided into sections dedicated to the ZX Spectrum, the Atari, and the C-64, which were referred as "clans," for instance, "Klan Commodore." As well as publishing program listings and hints for computer users, such sections regularly included claims about the superiority of a particular platform in terms of technical capacities or the quality of the graphics and sound. At the same time, young computer users of both platforms became devoted to their hardware and started calling themselves "Atarowcy" and "Komodorowcy." Both communities are examples of "brand communities." In their influential paper, which brought the concept of the "brand community" to consumer culture scholarship, Albert Muniz and Thomas O'Guinn note that:

A brand community is a specialized, non-geographically bound community, based on a structured set of social relationships among admirers of a brand. It is specialized because at its center is a branded good or service. Like other communities, it is marked by a shared consciousness, rituals and traditions, and a sense of moral responsibility. Each of these qualities is, however, situated within a commercial and mass-mediated ethos, and has its own particular expression.[50]

Participation in one of the two aforementioned brand communities defined the social world of Polish computer users during the system transition. It is possible to learn just how particular brand communities were formed locally and how existing members reproduced them. I interviewed A. K., who founded what was probably the first informal club of Atari users, which he named Mr. Atari, in 1987 (when A. K. was sixteen years old). The club was founded in Kozienice, a small city with a population of about twenty thousand in the Mazovia region.[51] As A. K. explained, he founded his club to establish new contacts via correspondence with Atari users from other cities and to extend his software library through new contacts. In his small city, as A. K. told me, he and his colleagues not only supported actual Atari users with their software libraries and suggestions but also played the role of "warm experts" and convinced those who wanted to buy a computer that the Atari was the best possible choice.[52] They also assured potential users that they would support them with their own software libraries.

In his book on the history of the Commodore Amiga, Jimmy Maher discusses the rivalry between users of the Amiga and the Atari ST 16-bit computers and refers to this phenomenon as "platform nationalism."[53] During the turnover of the 1980s and 1990s, the competition between adolescent Atari and Commodore users became a struggle for dominance between two "platform nationalisms." The superiority of one or the other of those computers became a topic for discussion among thousands of adolescents who used offensive and derogative slogans to refer to members of the other "clan." For instance, one of the most popular slogans was "Atarowca wal z gumowca!" ("Kick an Atari user with your rubber boot!"). Using Muniz and O'Guinn's term, we can identify this social phenomenon as "an oppositional brand loyalty."[54]

One of the most interesting software artifacts made at that time was a C-64 demonstration program (or "demo") titled *Atari Syfff* (Atari Stinks).[55] It was simultaneously an expression of the C-64 community's "platform nationalism" and an advertisement for "Fiction," a prominent software trader from the Grzybowska Street computer fair who called his small enterprise Fiction Software Service (FSS). After being loaded into a computer's memory, the Atari *Syfff* demo displayed a high-quality, hand-drawn, color picture of Robocop (not made by "Fiction" but taken from one of several readily available computer graphics collections) which aimed to prove the superiority of the C-64 in terms of its graphic chip capacities. But next to the picture of Robocop, one of adolescent boys' favorite movie heroes in the late 1980s, there was a message: "Broken by FSS." In the computer jargon of that time, the statement "broken by [someone]" or "cracked by" added into a "crack intro" of a computer game was a claim that the game's copy protection had been removed by this individual hacker. Such a slogan was the customary claim of mastery of hacking skills, deviance, and manhood. But *Atari Syfff* was distributed independently, not as an intro for a game, so the "broken by" statement had only symbolic value. Moreover, it is worth noting that virtually all software imported to Poland had already been "broken" by hackers from Western Europe so Polish software traders just added this kind of a statement without doing any substantial software modification.[56] Below the "broken by" statement we can see an advertisement for his software business: "Warsaw. Poland. New Programs. 1989!" and a contact telephone and the name "Wojtek," which was "Fiction's" real first name. It was clear that he, an adolescent at that time, lived with his parents and a potential client was supposed to ask for Wojtek, not "Fiction,"if a parent answered the phone. *Atari Syfff* also included a scrolling text: "Hi computer maniacs! This is the maniac from Fiction Software Service. The best hacker in Poland! Atarians!!! [orig. "Atarowianie"—an intentionally awkward and probably offensive term for Atarians, who were usually referred as "Atarowcy"—P. W.] I challenge all of you to a programming duel. Try to program something like the piece you see here with your calculator."[57]

Pokora remembered that "Fiction," who was a popular figure at the Grzybowska Street fair, was approached by representatives of Karen Company shortly after *Atari Syfff* was released. "Karen representatives asked him to stop circulating this program because it had a negative impact on sales of Atari computers. Needless to say, such a rumor caused a great deal of joy and bursts of laughter among C-64 software traders at the fair."[58]

During computer fairs impressive "demos" were used by traders to attract clients to their stands and to perform a brand community ritual. A memoir of the computer fair in Wrocław shows how a proud owner of the Commodore Amiga performed this kind of ritual with *Walker Demo* (Imaginetics, 1988), a highly acclaimed animation which included digitized models of vehicles from the movie *The Empire Strikes Back*:

> The year 1988. Wrocław, Sunday, computer fair. There is only one stand with the Amiga computer and there is a crowd of viewers there. Everyone is watching. No one is copying software at the moment . . . . On the color monitor the imperial AT-AT walker slowly moves—this is Walker Demo. Two individuals are looking suspiciously. This is the competition which stands with the Atari ST . . . . They are simply starring in disbelief and anger.[59]

The sense of belonging to brand communities discussed above manifested itself in several ways, showing how computer users formed and expressed their social identities in available public space. This shows how adolescents "produced their own identities" as owners and advanced users of high-tech artifacts. Aside from rock music, jeans, and Marlboro cigarettes, the home computer was a key part of the material culture which enabled young people to access the "imaginary West."[60] Moreover, the evidence from the Wrocław fair shows how a computer could be used for showing off or swanking. Mentioned in Ewa Han's article about the computer underground quoted above,[61] the Polish term for swanking—*szpan*—was frequently used in the media discourse of the 1980s to describe contemporary nihilistic youth. According to several moral panic articles, young people of the late 1980s were more interested with making a decent entrance at discos with clothes from the Pewex hard currency stores and Marlboro cigarettes, rather than engaging in "social and political activities" (*aktywność społeczno-polityczna*) organized and supervised by the ZSMP. *Szpan* was highly unwelcome in the socialist value system since the aim of someone who made *szpan* was to distinguish him or herself from a supposedly egalitarian society by demonstrating high economic status, or access to the imaginary West. The Commodore Amiga was an excellent artifact for showing off in the cultural and economic context of Poland in 1988 since only a few dozen of this computer model were in Poland at that time and the only way to get the Amiga was to travel to Western Europe oneself to purchase it.

## CONCLUSION

This chapter has discussed how Polish young people shaped their social identities through practices of computer use in the context of the ongoing socioeconomic changes during Poland's transition from socialism to capitalism. Young computer aficionados, who became interested in computers by attending courses in clubs sponsored by communist youth organizations, dropped out from such clubs, formed the "computer underground" as an imagined community, and started making profits as traders in pirated software. It is remarkable to note that software trade during "computer fairs," an economic activity with a low entry barrier, gave adolescents an opportunity to make profits much greater than the salaries their parents earned. Needless to say, such easy profits contributed to the way young people assessed the values of older generations who built their careers as employees of state enterprises. I have also shown how brand communities, a phenomenon identified as an element of consumer capitalism, were also present in Eastern Europe during last years of state socialism.

This case study has shown how the consumption of imported commodities such as home computers gave inhabitants of Eastern Europe access to the imaginary West during the transition from socialism to capitalism. One of the most interesting yet overlooked social and cultural phenomena is the appropriation of several new artifacts by young people during the transition from socialism. Yurchak, Anna Pelka, and Ferenc Hammer have shown how young people in Eastern Europe appropriated jeans and denim clothing as meaningful objects.[62] Similarly, Gabriel Jderu has shown how the motorcycle became an artifact that helped to express individual agency among Romanian youth.[63] However, we know little about other artifacts that young people in Eastern Europe could make meaningful, while at the same time challenging the values promoted by socialist youth organizations. Recently a collection of essays in *Communism Unwrapped* presented several studies on the interdependence of the acquisition and consumption of particular goods and social identities in state socialism.[64] But the question of how patterns of consumption among young people changed in the last years of state socialism and the first years of the free market economy still remains to be answered. Becoming a *komputerowiec* in the late 1980s could be interpreted as "dropping out" of socialist computer clubs and the state's computer literacy program. But it was at the same time dropping into the international imaginary world of computer hackers and into a new economic order.

## ACKNOWLEDGMENTS

Research for this paper was supported with National Science Centre grant 2013/08/S/HS2/00267. I would like to express my gratitude to Juliane Fürst, Josie McLellan and an anonymous reviewer.

## NOTES

1. I discuss the rise in the popularity of computer use in the mid-1980s in an earlier paper. See Patryk Wasiak, "Playing and Copying: Social Practices of Home Computer Users in Poland during the 1980s," in *Hacking Europe: From Computer Cultures to Demoscenes*, ed. Gerard Alberts and Ruth Oldenziel (London: Springer, 2014). For other studies on the cultural role of home computers during late state socialism, see Bruno Jakić "Galaxy and the New Wave: Yugoslav Computer Culture in the 1980s," in Alberts and Oldenziel, *Hacking Europe*; Jaroslav Švelch, "Say It with a Computer Game: Hobby Computer Culture and the Non-Entertainment Uses of Homebrew Games in the 1980s Czechoslovakia," *Game Studies* 13, no. 20 (2013), http://gamestudies.org/1302/articles/svelch.

2. J. Nicholls Eastmond and Stephen T. Kerr, "French and Soviet Experiments in Computer Literacy: Parallels and Contrasts," *Educational Technology Research*

172 Patryk Wasiak

*and Development* 37, no. 4 (1989): 81–91; Richard W. Judy and Jane M. Lommel, "The New Soviet Computer Literacy Campaign," *Educational Communication and Technology* 34, no. 2 (1986): 108–23.

3. Alexei Yurchak, "Imaginary West: The Elsewhere of Late Socialism," ch. 5 in *Everything Was Forever, Until It Was No More: The Last Soviet Generation* [Princeton: Princeton University Press, 2005], Kindle edition.

4. Yurchak, "Late Socialism: An Eternal State," ch. 1 in *Everything Was Forever.*

5. For discussion on the interdependence of consumption and social identities, see Paul du Gay, *Consumption and Identity at Work* (London: SAGE, 1996).

6. See Thomas Berker, Maren Hartmann, Yves Punie, and Katie Ward, eds., *Domestication of Media and Technology* (Maidenhead: Open University Press, 2006); Leslie Haddon, *Information and Communication Technologies in Everyday Life: A Concise Introduction and Research Guide* (Oxford: Berg, 2004); Merete Lie and Knut H. Sørensen, eds., *Making Technology Our Own?* (Oslo: Scandinavian University Press, 1996).

7. Margrethe Aune, "The Computer in Everyday Life: Patterns of Domestication of a New Technology," in Lie and Sørensen, *Making Technology*, 91–120, here 91–92.

8. Chris Jenks, *Subculture: The Fragmentation of the Social* (London: SAGE, 2004).

9. Aldona Krajewska, "Plemiona ziemi niczyjej," *Polityka*, January 2, 1988, 1, 6, here 1.

10. Ewa Han, "Czy komputer zastąpi artystę," *Słowo Polskie*, September 21, 1988, 6. The author's awkward use of the terms "software" and "computer graphics" shows clearly that she was not familiar with computers.

11. For discussion of the rise of state-owned computer clubs supported by the ZSMP, see Wasiak, "Playing and Copying," 132–33.

12. Jim Riordan, "Soviet Youth: Pioneers of Change," *Soviet Studies* 40, no. 4 (1988): 556–72, here 558.

13. For instance, see Fred Turner, *From Counterculture to Cyberculture: Stewart Brand, the Whole Earth Network, and the Rise of Digital Utopianism* (Chicago: University of Chicago Press, 2006).

14. Richard Barbrook and Andy Cameron, "The Californian Ideology," *Alamut: Bastion of Peace and Information*, 1995, http://www.alamut.com/subj/ideologies/pessimism/califIdeo_I.html.

15. See Thomas Streeter, "Missing the Net: The 1980s, Microcomputer, and the Rise of Neoliberalism," ch. 3 in *The Net Effect: Romanticism, Capitalism, and the Internet* (New York: New York University Press, 2011).

16. For a discussion of computers and communist values, see Erik P. Hoffman, "Technology, Values and Political Power in the Soviet Union: Do Computers Matter?" in *Technology and Communist Culture: The Socio-Cultural Impact of Technology under Socialism*, ed. Frederic Fleron (New York: Praeger, 1977), 397–436. For a broader discussion of technology and communist values, see Paul Josephson, *Would Trotsky Wear a Bluetooth? Technological Utopianism under Socialism, 1917–1989* (Baltimore: Johns Hopkins University Press, 2009).

17. "Przed nami XXI wiek," *Magazyn Rodzinny*, June 1986, 1.

18. Han, "Czy komputer zastąpi artystę."

19. *Bajtek*, March 1989, 2. The linguistic practices that framed technical education for young people in the "authoritative discourse" reproduced through the activities of the ZSMP and popular science magazines such as *Młody Technik* (which was a counterpart of *Tekhnika Molodezhi*) call for a separate study. Cf. Yurchak, "Ideology Inside Out: Ethics and Poetics," ch. 3 in *Everything Was Forever*.

20. T. Kravtsova, "Aisbergi komp'iuterizatsii," *Uchitel'skaia gazeta*, January 19, 1988, 2, quoted in Eastmond and Kerr, "French and Soviet," 88.

21. Jenks, *Subculture*, ix.

22. Riordan, "Soviet Youth," 556.

23. See Paul Hodkinson and Wolfgang Deicke, eds., *Youth Cultures: Scenes, Subcultures and Tribes* (London: Routledge, 2007). See also Andy Bennett, and Keith Kahn-Harris, eds., *After Subculture: Critical Studies in Contemporary Youth Culture* (New York: Palgrave Macmillan, 2004); David Muggleton and Rupert Weinzierl, eds., *The Post-Subcultures Reader* (Oxford: Berg, 2003). On the historical use of the "scene" framework, see Michaela Pfadenhauer, "Ethnography of Scenes: Towards a Sociological Life-world Analysis of (Post-traditional) Community-building," *Forum: Qualitative Social Research* 6, no. 3 (2005), http://nbn-resolving.de/urn:nbn:de:0114-fqs0503430.

24. Will Straw, "Systems of Articulation, Logics of Change: Communities and Scenes in Popular Music," *Cultural Studies* 5, no. 3 (1991): 368–88, here, 373. The quotation is from Holly Kruse, "Subcultural Identity in Alternative Music Culture," *Popular Music* 12, no. 1 (1993): 33–41, here, 38.

25. Knut H. Sørensen, "Domestication: The Enactment of Technology," in Berker et al., *Domestication of Media and Technology*, 40–61, here 47.

26. For the role of *Bajtek*, see Wasiak, "Playing and Copying," 130–32.

27. Kaz, "Interview with Michał "Miker" Szpilowski," *Atari Online*, December 3, 2007, http://atarionline.pl/.

28. For the testimony of a Polish amateur computer graphics artist from that time, see "Interview with Carrion," *Vandalism News*, no. 51, 2009, *C-64* (electronic magazine), republished at http://www.atlantis-prophecy.org/recollection/?load=interviews&id_interview=24.

29. For more, see Douglas Thomas, *Hacker Culture* (Minneapolis: University of Minnesota Press, 2003).

30. *Atari Online*, http://atarionline.pl/; *Commodore & Amiga Fan*, http://cafan.pl/.

31. Interview with Mosquito, *Włócznia Wschodu* no. 3, 1990, C-64 electronic magazine (diskmag), available in the Commodore Scene Database, http://csdb.dk/release/?id=93171.

32. For a discussion of such monikers, see Patryk Wasiak, "Illegal Guys: A Cultural History of the First European Digital Subculture," *Zeithistorische Forschungen/Studies in Contemporary History* no. 2 (2012), http://www.zeithistorische-forschungen.de/.

33. Ray Oldenburg, *The Great Good Place: Cafes, Coffee Shops, Community Centers, Beauty Parlors, General Stores, Bars, Hangouts, and How They Get You Through the Day* (St. Paul, MN: Paragon House, 1989).

34. Leslie Haddon, "Empirical Studies Using the Domestication Framework," in Berker et al., *Domestication of Media and Technology*, 103–22, here 106–7. Cf. also T. Håpnes, "'Not in Their Machines': How Hackers Transform Computers into Subcultural Artefacts," in Lie and Sørensen, *Making Technology*, 121–50.

35. D. M. (former instructor in a computer club in Warsaw), interview with the author via e-mail, January 2013.

36. The discourse of computer culture in *Bajtek*, a discourse that was also articulated by computer club officials, shows that the official belief was that under state socialism the computer should only have "use value" and its "exchange value" should be as limited as possible. Cf. Serguei A. Oushakine, "'Against the Cult of Things': On Soviet Productivism, Storage Economy, and Commodities with No Destination," *Russian Review* 73, no. 2 (2014): 198. For the testimony of a Polish amateur computer graphics artist from that time, see "Interview with Carrion," *Vandalism News*, no. 51, 2009, *C-64* (electronic magazine), republished at http://www.atlantis-prophecy.org/recollection/?load=interviews&id_interview=24.236.

37. On the origins of such "intros," see Wasiak, "Illegal Guys."

38. J. H. (His moniker is "TG JSL"), interview with the author via e-mail, December 2012. The moniker stands for "The Great Jarek Software Limited." J. H. was one of the founders of the WCF (World Cracking Federation)—a computer underground group founded in 1989 by software traders from the Grzybowska computer fair.

39. "Rozmowa z Adamem Pokorą," *Commodore & Amiga Fan*, February 2013, 28–30, here 28, http://cafan.pl/.

40. Interview with "Sky," *Włócznia Wschodu* no. 4 (1991), *C-64* electronic magazine (diskmag), available in the Commodore Scene Database, http://csdb.dk/release/?id=93172.

41. "Rozmowa z Adamem Pokorą," 29.

42. Interview with "Fiction," *Włócznia Wschodu* no. 1 (1990), *C-64* electronic magazine (diskmag), available in the Commodore Scene Database, http://csdb.dk/release/?id=93169. This claim about profits is not an exaggeration. In 1989 the trade in pirated software and video movies was enormously profitable in comparison with salaries earned in the public sector.

43. Sørensen, "Domestication," in Berker et al., *Domestication of Media and Technology*, 47.

44. Interview with Lena Kolarska-Bobińska, Życie *Gospodarcze*, May 1991, 1, 4, here, 4.

45. Philipp Ther, *Die neue Ordnung auf dem alten Kontinent: Eine Geschichte des neoliberalen Europa* (Berlin: Suhrkamp, 2014).

46. For a discussion about the impact of the English language on everyday life in Central Europe during the transition from socialism, see Hermann Fink and Liane Fijas, eds., *America and Her Influence upon the Language and Culture of Post-Socialist Countries* (Frankfurt am Main: Peter Lang, 1998).

47. For a discussion of the successful international marketing of the Commodore, see Brian Bagnall, *Commodore: A Company on the Edge* [Winnipeg: Variant Press, 2011], Kindle edition.

48. Krzysztof Ptaszyński, "Brama świata," *Polityka*, May 4, 1985.

49. For a discussion of the cultural role of hard currency stores in state socialism, see Paulina Bren, "Tuzex and the Hustler: Living It Up in Czechoslovakia," in *Communism Unwrapped: Consumption in Cold War Europe*, ed. Paulina Bren and Mary Neuberger (New York: Oxford University Press, 2012), 27–48.

50. Albert Muniz and Thomas O'Guinn, "Brand Community," *Journal of Consumer Research* 27, no. 4 (2001): 412–32, here, 412.

51. A. K., interview with the author via e-mail, December 2012.

52. "Warm expert" is a term used by scholars who study the social impact of information technologies. For instance, Maria Bakardjieva uses this term in her study of the spread of Internet use to describe how relatives or friends with more knowledge teach less advanced users how to use a particular technology. Maria Bakardjieva, *Internet Society: The Internet in Everyday Life* (London: SAGE, 2005), 98–102.

53. Jimmy Maher, "The Scene," ch. 7 in *The Future Was Here: The Commodore Amiga* [Cambridge, MA: MIT Press, 2012], Kindle edition.

54. Muniz, and O'Guinn, "Brand Community": 420. The authors introduced this term to characterize, among other things, Mac users' derogative depiction of PC users as nerds. Cf. Russell W. Belk and Gülnur Tumbat, "The Cult of Macintosh," *Consumption, Markets & Culture* 8, no. 3 (2005): 205–17.

55. *Atari Syfff*, Fiction Software Service, February 21, 1989, C-64 one-file demo, available on the Commodore Scene Database, http://csdb.dk/release/?id=59773.

56. On practices of "breaking" or "cracking" games in Western Europe, see Wasiak, "Illegal Guys."

57. *Atari Syfff*. For the reception of action cinema of the 1980s by youth audiences in Eastern Europe, see Gabriel Bar-Haim, "Actions and Heroes: The Meaning of Western Pop Information for Eastern European Youth," *British Journal of Sociology* 40, no. 1 (1989): 22–45.

58. "Rozmowa z Adamem Pokorą," 28.

59. *Walker Demo*, *Fat Agnus* no. 2, 1991, Amiga electronic magazine, http://fat-magnus.ppa.pl/. *Walker Demo* footage is available on YouTube: *Walker Demo* (Imaginetics, 1988, Amiga ECS) HQ, https://www.youtube.com/watch?v=IyMpU0nMuzo.

60. Cf. Yurchak, ch. 5. See also György Péteri, ed., *Imagining the West in Eastern Europe and the Soviet Union* (Pittsburgh: University of Pittsburgh Press, 2010).

61. Han, "Czy computer."

62. Yurchak, ch. 5; Anna Pelka, *Teksas—land Moda młodzieżowa w PRL* (Warsaw: Wydawnictwo Trio, 2007); Ferenc Hammer, "The *Real One:* Western Brands and Competing Notions of Authenticity in Socialist Hungary," in *Cultures of Commodity Branding*, ed. Andrew Bevan and David Wengrow (Walnut Creek, CA: Left Coast Press, 2010), 131–54.

63. Gabriel Jderu, "Agency and Liberty: Motorcycle Riding and Freedom Figuration in Romania between 1950 and 1990" (paper presented at the "Dropping Out of Socialism: A Conference about the Hidden Side of Life in the Former Soviet Bloc" conference, Bristol, June 5–6, 2014).

64. Bren and Neuberger, *Communism Unwrapped.*

*Part III*

# DROPPING OUT IN STYLE

*Chapter 8*

# "We All Live in a Yellow Submarine"

## *Dropping Out in a Leningrad Commune*

### Juliane Fürst

An observant visitor to Leningrad in the late 1970s and early 1980s would have seen curious graffiti on the walls of the Kazan Cathedral on Nevskii Prospekt, the city's main thoroughfare.[1] It said "Long live the commune Yellow Submarine." For the uninitiated it was certainly puzzling. Were there communes in the land of Soviets and in a city that was bursting with *kommunalki*—communal apartments? Why was the commune named after a famous Beatles' song, a group that was officially banned in the Soviet Union? And how did the graffiti end up on the wall of Kazan Cathedral, once the symbol of Orthodox power and now the Museum of Atheism and Religion in the middle of socialist Leningrad? Yet to those in the know, it all made sense. In the short graffiti an entire parallel Soviet reality was embedded. It was a reality in which young people met and lived in communes that existed out of the free will of their inhabitants, not because of Leningrad's chronic shortage of living space. In this reality the Beatles reigned supreme and many of their songs served as shorthand for a complex set of emotions and experiences. And Kazan Cathedral was the place to go when you wanted to find this alternative sphere. It was here that Leningrad's "progressive" youth, and especially those who considered themselves part of the *sistema*, the all-Union hippie network, met. It was here that out-of-town visitors would go in order to find *svoi*—their own. Those in the know about Leningrad's alternative youth scene thus had an immediate set of keys at their disposal to decode the nature of both the graffiti and the commune it referred to: The Beatles song signaled that the commune was composed of young people who liked Western

Parts of this chapter were previously published Rebecca Clifford, Juliane Fürst, Robert Gildea et al., "Spaces," in *Europe's 1968: Voices of Revolt*, ed. Robert Gildea, James Mark, and Anette Waring (Oxford: Oxford University Press, 2013).

music and could not care less about what the party thought about their tastes. The location of the graffiti demonstrated that the Yellow Submarine was likely a commune of hippies or people close to them. Finally, the graffiti constituted a marker in itself. Like graffiti the world over, it had a whiff of underground. Official culture does not produce graffiti. Graffiti is the domain of those who see themselves as outside the mainstream.[2]

The commune Yellow Submarine was a product of its time and place. It came into existence in the summer of 1977 and dispersed in October 1978. It was permanently inhabited by a motley crew of seven to eight people, who differed in background, political outlook, and lifestyle but were united in their desire to live "differently" than late socialism envisioned and expected of them. In appearance, set-up, and underlying ideology it was part of the global counterculture of the 1960s and 1970s, to which it both explicitly and implicitly paid tribute. It also owed many (unacknowledged) intellectual and practical debts to its Soviet milieu, ranging from the communards of the post-revolutionary period to the more recent *turist* movement that saw youngsters travel in small groups to remote regions for weeks on end.[3] Yet it chiefly considered itself an obstinate outsider in a late Soviet world its members despised. It wanted to create a space and community that was non-Soviet, expressed their "true" selves, and allowed them to have fun, all at the same time. Just like its Western communal peers, it also wanted to be better than the "normal" world. "Going under" in the Yellow Submarine with its strawberry-adorned walls and Beatles' soundtrack was an avoidance tactic, a thrill, and an act of rebellion. Yet it was also firmly anchored in its socialist surroundings. Its members were students who studied at Soviet institutions of higher education—indeed mostly at Leningrad's prestigious State University. Their socialization had taken place in Soviet schools. Their stipends, their studies, and their voluntary work (some of them were even active in the Komsomol) tied them firmly to late Soviet reality. And, of course, the outside threat to their fragile community posed by Soviet officialdom served to give identity and create the special atmosphere that characterized life in the commune.

The commune's suspended state—living *in* late socialism, while desiring to be *outside* it—immediately evokes the concept of "living *vnye*," a term which Alexei Yurchak coined in his study of "the last Soviet generation." He describes the widespread phenomenon as a "style of living that [was] simultaneously inside and outside the system."[4] Indeed the Yellow Submarine belonged to the very same milieu that served as Yurchak's provider of primary material and while it does not appear in Yurchak's account as such, many of the people who do would have circulated in the wider orbit of the commune. It is thus justified to ask whether anything new can be learned from looking at the commune through the lens of "dropping out" rather than simply employing Yurchak's analysis. Or to ask, does the commune tell us anything original about life in late socialism at all?

It would be hard to claim representativeness for the commune. The number of people at its heart were less than a dozen and even, if one takes into account all the people who came through its door, this would at most add up to a few hundred. Rather, the more interesting angle is to look at the Yellow Submarine because of its extraordinariness: its interesting mix of inhabitants, its unusual set-up, and its peculiar dilemmas of identity. Not least, the Yellow Submarine is of interest, because it makes possible a wonderfully "thick" description and analysis of its brief existence through a variety of sources, ranging from interviews to its logbook and self-made posters, allowing a synchronic as well as a diachronic evaluation of the commune. Such an intense look at a relatively small and defined community highlights the value of the Yellow Submarine for a variety of debates.

Yurchak describes "living *vnye*" essentially as a static state of existence, held in place by the structural realities of late socialism. As will be shown in this chapter, the Yellow Submarine demonstrates that the simultaneous "living both inside and outside" of the Soviet context was a paradox that had to be re-negotiated every day and whose precise balance between "in" and "out" could oscillate significantly. The precise definition of what constituted "inside" and what "outside," degrees of alienation, and strategies of "making sense" were processes that had fluid outcomes and were subject to both internal and external dynamics. While there is no doubt that the Yellow Submarine was an almost perfect demonstration of "living *vnye*," within this framework its positioning vis-à-vis and within a vaguely defined "official" world changed not only over time but also depending on the subjective viewpoint of its various inhabitants. Further, Yurchak locates most of the concepts he has coined for the world of the "last Soviet generation" in a structural analysis of late socialism, turning its subjects' nonconformism into ciphers of the period rather than an act of agency. This neatly sidesteps the perennially tricky question of whether we can truly ever speak of resistance and opposition in a setting in which, as many historians have acknowledged, dissent and affirmation were tightly intertwined.[5] If Yurchak's alienated, indifferent crowd does not count as opposition, who then should count as a dissenter? Yet, it also means that the subjectivity of the late socialist subject fades from the picture. By looking at the Yellow Submarine through the prism of the term "dropping out," the subjectivity of its members is put center stage. The objective act of "dropping out" had to remain incomplete and hence is a permanent state of friction with the subjective reality of the act. The identity of the commune rested in its *perceived* remoteness from, distance to, and difference from the mainstream. Bringing back a subjective element allows both increased acknowledgment of personal "agency" to the analysis and greater differentiation within this alternative milieu. One of Yurchak's premises is that what he named "deterritorialized" milieus were apolitical and people in these milieus looked askance at political dissidents, whom they judged "abnormal."[6]

Yet going deep into the bowels of the Yellow Submarine, it becomes apparent that not only did the "apoliticals" frequently rub shoulders with more politically minded hotheads, but also that political thoughts were never far from peoples' minds, even when, or especially when, they listened to the Beatles or hung out in Leningrad's alternative cafes. And this was so precisely because "living *vnye*" was not a static state of mind, but was constantly debated, probed, and discussed.

This chapter is based on interviews with all but one of the commune members, a close reading of their "logbook," and an analysis of the art and literature they produced. Taken together, these sources create an unusually dense web of information. Rather than measuring its de facto distance to the mainstream, this chapter is interested in the conscious and unconscious mechanisms the commune employed to separate itself from the official world. It will thus carefully unpeel various layers of "dropping out" and examine its nature, function, and limits. Ultimately, this chapter will argue that the process of "dropping out" was achieved by the creation of insider knowledge, which ranged from simple things such as the existence and location of the commune to complex codes such as the half-serious, half parodistic self-testimonials the commune produced about itself. Yet while uniting against the outside world, the production of knowledge as a means of "dropping out" was also internally divisive, especially when it became clear that subjective views of what knowledge should be produced, who should be privy to it, and what it would entail differed significantly between members of the commune. The very same processes that once ensured the physical and spiritual existence of the commune also led to its destruction. Yet at the same time, the debates, conflicts, and alliances that ensued in the process provide a window on the late Soviet intelligentsia in quasi-laboratory conditions. The narrow confines of the commune allow a close examination of how in the late 1970s different strategies of how to deal with "actually existing socialism" existed side by side, sometimes mutually fertilizing each other, at other times competing for primacy, and at times violently opposed in their quest for survival.


## THE YELLOW SUBMARINE, ITS CREW, AND
## THE OCEAN OF LATE SOCIALISM

The home of the Yellow Submarine was an old wooden house on the then-outskirts of Leningrad. In August 1977, Feliks and Marina Vinogradov, sweethearts from school, newly married, and expecting a child, rented half of the house from an old lady. It consisted of two bedrooms downstairs with a small kitchen and two bedrooms upstairs with a much larger kitchen. The Vinogradovs moved into the upstairs part and were soon joined by

Marina's friend Tat'iana Komarova, and later by her boyfriend and soon-to-be husband Andrei Antonenko. Their common friend, political radical, and history student, Aleksandr Skobov, moved into one of the downstairs bedrooms and soon acquired the company of Igor Mal'skii, another history student from Leningrad State University. Feliks was born in Karelia to a family of party members and communist believers. He spent his formative years in Vorkuta, the site of the former GULAG, as the son of a high-ranking KGB official employed in border control. Feliks took to the newly fashionable hippie lifestyle with enthusiasm, first in Vorkuta, where his companions were, in his own words, longhaired and flower-shirted *gopniki* (hooligans) and criminals in the making. Later he socialized with the rebellious offspring of the Leningrad *nomenklatura*. After graduating from school, he enrolled at the history faculty of Leningrad State University. Marina was born in 1958 in Leningrad and came from a classic Leningrad intelligentsia family. She went to Special Mathematics School No. 121, just like her husband Feliks and her friends Aleksandr Skobov and Tat'iana Komarova. Marina shared both Feliks's dissatisfaction with the boredom of late socialist life and his taste in Western music and fashion. A soon-to-be young mother, she was less keen on the rock-and-roll lifestyle that developed in the commune, but she too wanted to live a life that was different than "normal" people's lives.[7] Tat'iana was also born in Leningrad in 1957, the child of secular Jewish parents who soon divorced. Despite an early dislike of the Soviet system—both her mother and grandmother passionately hated the Communist Party—she was, by her own account, a nice Soviet girl with excellent grades, who even fulfilled her duties in the Komsomol. She became a student at the Technological Institute and moved into the commune because she had fallen out with her mother. According to her, not much ideology was at play—neither political nor hippie—but she did concede that "if the revolution (meaning the anticommunist counterrevolution) had come, I would have participated, but doing it myself—never."[8] Her boyfriend Andrei straddled the border between the various factions of the house. He called himself a 25 percent hippie—based on the fact that he had walked down Nevskii Prospekt barefoot—yet he also sympathized with the more political stance of Skobov and his out-of-commune friends. Antonenko was also an active Komsomol member of the type who believed that on a very local level one could make a difference through involvement in the youth organization. However, during his time at the commune he ran into considerable difficulties at the university's history faculty because of an "inappropriate" joke in the wall newspaper for which he was responsible.[9]

The downstairs was both physically and mentally the realm of Aleksandr Skobov, often referred to by his upstairs friends as Ablativus. Skobov already possessed a colorful personal and KGB history. Born in 1957 in Leningrad to a single mother, he created his first neo-Marxist organization in eighth grade and was involved in the production and distribution of anti-Soviet flyers at the age of fourteen. Furiously intelligent, prone to drinking, and politically hotheaded, he was one of the ideological motors behind the commune.[10] Igor Mal'skii was the son of a government minister in the Moldovian Republic and had come to Leningrad to study history at the state university. Like Andrei Antonenko and Feliks Vinogradov, he actively participated in the creation of the wall newspaper that got Antonenko into so much trouble.[11] While being drawn into Skobov's activities by virtue of lodging downstairs, he also clearly felt a strong bond with the counterculture practices upstairs. In a short memory piece for the 1990s hippie publication *Khippilend*, he proudly showcases his fluency in "*sistema* slang."[12] Mal'skii died toward the end of the 1990s and is hence the only significant member of the commune who could not be interviewed. More temporary but nonetheless frequent residents were Skobov's old school friend and partner in political crime Andrei Reznikov, who had been arrested and sentenced to two years imprisonment over the flyer action, and his girlfriend Irina Feodorova.[13] Both were heavily engaged in the *turist* movement, a phenomenon that had taken off in the 1950s and 1960s among youth keen to carve out individual spaces. They started out within the Komsomol and its expedition program, but soon came to use official structures merely for permission and organization of their ambitious and daring outings into the more remote places of the Soviet Union. They went on long expeditions into the Siberian and northern wilderness and became adept at living in the wild for months on end. Their trips became less and less an official pastime and more and more escapes from Soviet mainstream life.[14] Skobov's other collaborator in all things political and dissident, Arkadii Tsurkov, and his girlfriend Irina Lopotukhina were frequent visitors to the commune. Of Jewish origins, Arkadii had failed to secure a place at the mathematics faculty in Leningrad and was therefore studying in Tartu where he attended Lotman's study circle. His ideological collaboration with Skobov linked him to the commune even though he disapproved of its hippie and rock-and-roll culture and had little belief in communal ideas as such. Irina was Arkadii's faithful childhood friend and came from a very observant Jewish family with many ties to the Jewish community in Riga.[15] She was not an ardent supporter of Skobov's and Tsurkov's neo-Marxism (despite helping them logistically), but in later years she became an outspoken activist in the human rights movement.

## KNOWLEDGE AS DISTANCE

In the eponymous Beatles film, the Yellow Submarine appears as a little boat that traverses a universe full of absurd creatures, pluckily making its way through this hilarious, yet dark world that seems both outlandish and ridiculous. None of the commune members ever saw the film, but they did know the song and its lyrics. (It is important to note here that, at best, the commune members had rudimentary English and their comprehension of the song was not one of minute dissection of the lyrics but an instinctive grasp of its significance and enjoyment of the poetics of the words rather than their content). The song perfectly embodied the commune's belief that the absurdity of the outside world is best answered by absurd responses, sidestepping rational engagement yet passing commentary nonetheless. The absurdity of the outside was countered with both rejection of facets of official life that seemed absurd and with exaggerated parodies of these very practices and rituals, thus creating a blanket of irony that shielded the commune from the outside world. The idea of everybody living in a yellow submarine was as ridiculous as the conflicts and hang-ups of the world outside—yet it was knowingly and purposefully absurd and thus superior to the unintended (and largely unrecognized)—absurdity of the "normal" people. Ultimately, both the Yellow Submarine of the Beatles song and the Yellow Submarine of Leningrad turned this idea of normality upside down. By virtue of superior awareness and knowledge and self-imposed exile from the official absurd, it was they who became "normal," while the "normal" people were the "weirdoes" stuck in an absurd world, ignorant of their situation.[16] Self-knowledge created distance from those who could not see.

At the beginning, the commune was both the escape from a corrupt world and the idea of creating a better world—a going under/away from hypocrisy and a life marred by petty coercions and a dip into a blissful existence in a watertight boat. Marina explained her motivation for the unusual step of spurning the relative comfort of her parents' apartment in Leningrad:

> I formed somehow a strong anti-communist outlook, maybe because all children comprehend lies at a certain level and for me it was that they said one thing in the radio and in school, but did everything differently. And this truth of life, which you can see and judge and all these lies around, made me feel like this [accompanied by a sign of sickness—J. F.]. I felt a strong desire to get away from my family and go into the commune—to a place that was free.[17]

Marina's friend Tat'iana concurred with this desire to get away from a life and society she disliked. In a world that had an enormous number of regulations and provided little agency to individuals, she wanted to build a social space in which she had control: "We said then that it was a kind of inner emigration. We could not leave the country. But we organized ourselves a society that was separate from general society. We lived by our laws and among our people and with the rest we only communicated as necessary, we went to the university and so on."[18] As their fictional author O. Mafin wrote in their logbook for

New Year 1978: "If you do not find a goal in life, make life itself the goal!"[19] Their life was to be their escape, their opposition, and their raison d'être. They did not want to attain some far-off goal but to live the life they desired.

They had had glimpses of what such an "independent" life could look like. Marina's uncle was an inhabitant of an illegal squat near the university which soon turned into a bohemian meeting place for hundreds of youngsters on the lookout for exactly what Marina and Tat'iana described: truth, authenticity, and distance from the regime. The squat, named Vorona Slobodka (after an infamous apartment in the famous Ilf and Petrov novel *The Golden Calf* and meaning "rookery"), was busted and the future crew of the Yellow Submarine took note.[20] Visibility was dangerous. It was not enough to be merely alternative. One had to disappear from view. One had to know more than the rest of society. One had to drop out of view. Hence the new commune had to offer privacy. This privacy was to be the counterpoint to the Soviet public sphere, but it was also to be the privacy of a mystical, more distant past, when life had been less intertwined with the state. This sentiment is apparent in the way its members stressed the special situation of their new home. Andrei Antonenko remembered: "And that house was literally the last private wooden house in the city: How did it survive all these times of nationalization?"[21] His girlfriend Tat'iana independently echoed his thoughts in her interview: "This was a private house, such a rarity, there were no private houses in Leningrad then."[22] The antiquated, private nature of the old, wooden house was to guarantee the way of life that corresponded to the age of the building: a bourgeois coziness of the past. In the context of Soviet norms where private matters were subject to official norms and judgment, this quest for bourgeois privacy was in itself quite rebellious.

In another reference to pre-revolutionary times, the commune members called their landlady *starushka-protsentshchitsa*, the term Raskolnikov uses in *Crime and Punishment* for his object of moral hatred and eventual murder victim.[23] Even though they admitted that the old lady was by no means an extorter of inflated rents, the nickname once again underlined that this transaction was not part of Soviet life but referred back to a time before the existence of government housing and Soviet bloc administration. But there is another moment here. By the late 1970s almost all such references, which the intelligentsia liberally bestowed on the world—literary, political, artistic—were pronounced with a twinkle in the eye or indeed a thinly disguised irony. The reference to such weighty matters such as Dostoevsky's great novel not only identified the commune members as members of the educated class. It was also simply an irreverent joke, another stone in the edifice of fun and parody that made up and defined the mental space of the Yellow Submarine. And in this double function as both sentimental evocation and ironic attribute it stands for the commune's main mechanism for creating distance.

Nicknaming the landlady created one layer of insider knowledge, while the correct understanding of how to decode the nickname added multiple others. From the very inception of the commune, its members busily shored up the remoteness and privacy of the physical space with numerous actions that generated a coded universe open only to those in the know.

## GENERATING INSIDER KNOWLEDGE

The first step toward creating the closed universe of the Yellow Submarine was the creation of a logbook. Feliks, Marina, Skobov, Andrei, and Tat'iana each marked their entry into the newly founded commune with a short note in the new *Vakhtenyi zhurnal*. The name itself was a play on association and a parody of its models. The term *Vakhtenyi zhurnal* was usually reserved for shipping journals and hence very apt for the voyage of the Yellow Submarine. Its very first page already sums up much of the commune's insider style: a heady mixture of referencing Western popular culture, parodying the peculiarities of Soviet life, and creating new symbols and rituals that drew on both of these spheres. The logbook hence served as both identity builder for the commune and differentiator from the outside.

The opening page of the logbook is made to look like the first page of a professionally printed book with a place and year of publication (Leningrad, 1977).[24] The name Yellow Submarine is written in English and supplemented by the newly created logo of the commune—a half eagle, half parrot creature sitting on top of a peace sign, looking half menacingly and half defensively to the left. It was a symbol of deviance and superiority, yet (purposefully) laughable in its shortcomings compared to its supposed model: the American eagle. On the left Feliks had drawn (probably at a slightly later date as the "Happy New Year" inscription seems to suggest) an impression of the upstairs kitchen, the heart of the commune. The walls were, of course, painted yellow with red strawberries as decorations, referring to another Beatles song, "Strawberry Fields Forever." A big sofa symbolizes coziness and community, a full washing line, domesticity. To the left of the sofa a record player is visible, reminding the viewer of the importance of the mostly English soundtrack that accompanied the commune. A sign in the window reads in English "Happy New Year," while another inscription in between the windows reads "Beware of the sleeping dog." The indebtedness to Western pop culture is obvious and explicit: the Beatles songs, the record player, the ambiance, and even the logo modeled on the American eagle. The persiflage of Soviet life is hinted at in the officious design of the title page and in the unmistakably Soviet look of the living room. And yet both the Western and Soviet references are rendered questionable as to their meaning

**Figure 8.1   First page of the communal log book.** *Source*: Archive Feliks and Marina Vinogradov.

by the obvious insincerity that permeates all of them. The eagle looks more like a parakeet and has the posture of a scarecrow. The pop art of the room is diminished by the depiction of the washed diapers (of Feliks and Marina's son) hanging across the room. The imitation of official publications jars with the hand-written and deliberately shabby style of the writing and drawing. The reference to the sleeping dog takes the coding to another level. There never was a dog in the commune.

This mixture of sincere referencing, parody, double parody, and humorous self-deprecation—not surprisingly late socialism knew a word for this, *stiob*[25]—is also visible in the written entries in the logbook. Before the commune even got off its feet its history was written, not necessarily for posterity at this stage, but for the commune members themselves. They were good students of the Soviet system. Revolution needs history. They could only be truly apart from the mainstream, if they documented how they achieved this distance. And to make perfectly clear from what they wanted to differ, they took the official Soviet world as a model. In the logbook the idea of the commune as a grand parody of the great socialist enterprise is continued and written down for legitimacy. The first lines of the logbook partly mimic the pomposity and convulsions of official language, while strewing the text with internal jokes and references to the West:

And here it is our commune . . . . We will try to answer some questions with regards to this, for our days, new form of social living by interviewing one of the personal staff members of our submarine.

Word is given to our speaker, F. V., who some bad tongues call the President or the House Administrator.

What has led you to here and why are you living in a commune?

F. In order to understand this correctly, one has to know the glorious history of the communal movement in our midst. It began a year ago in my kitchen, where I had a positive dialogue with the not-unknown Ablativus [Skobov's nickname] with regard to establishing a commune. I felt that I was not alone in my desires. I was so strongly taken by my idea, which could not be squashed, that they sent me directly to negotiations with an old lady at Lvinskii Bridge . . . . The new, energetic rise of the movement is inseparably connected with the so-called Vorona Slobodka [the aforementioned illegal squat] squashed by the Soviet police.[26]

Terms such as "glorious history," "communal movement," and "energetic" could not fail but to evoke revolutionary language, which, by the time of the creation of the commune, had petrified into rock-hard, pre-set phrases whose significance rested mainly in their performative aspect.[27] The pomposity of the language stands in stark contrast to what is actually described: a meeting in a kitchen—a place, which in itself had immediate resonance for late socialist people as a place for intimate, and often alcohol-fueled, conversations—and renting a house from an old lady.[28] Up to this point the text simply affirms the commune's temporal location in late socialism. Almost every Soviet citizen would have instantly understood the parody, which was biting, but harmless enough. The second part of the entry becomes both more risky and more exclusive. The invocation of the squat Vorona Slobodka narrows the comprehending audience to a certain part of Leningrad student youth, who knew and frequented the squat. At the same time by identifying a precursor—and especially a precursor that had been dispelled by the police—the commune started to enter more dangerous territory. It now identified as a movement—jokingly but nonetheless identified—and thus became a challenger to the only movement that was allowed to exist on Soviet soil—the communist movement. Aping the language employed to narrate revolutionary history had a dual effect: it elevated the Yellow Submarine to mythological status but also lowered the revolution to a level of humorous banality.

This short opening reveals another axis that was to dominate internal, communal discourse. Appropriations and twists of Soviet language were accompanied by more or less sophisticated handling of Western terms. The use of English interspersed in the texts establishes the mental space of the commune as outside the Soviet Union and inside the fabled West. At the same time, putting English terms on the same level as Soviet ones produces another level of irreverence, which essentially only leaves the submarine itself as the master of all irony. Feliks is described both as the "speaker and President" (which, given his self-professed love for the USA, can only be read as references to this country)[29] and as the "house administrator," which is an unveiled reference to all things connected to OVIR (the Soviet housing administration) and the myriad of regulations that ruled the Soviet housing question. Like OVIR, the yellow submarine is busy creating bureaucracy for the sake of bureaucracy. But unlike OVIR, the submarine is fully aware and in control of the uselessness of its official titles and papers and hence once again manages to "deterritorialize" itself from the Soviet space.[30] Andrei's entry picked up this idiosyncratic mixing of parody and references to Western pop culture. His text reads like a typically dense and incomprehensible Marxist treaty. (Andrei was a Komsomol organizer and editor of his faculty's wall newspaper after all.) "And a look at the commune as a regular step in the development of our micro-group returns to the question of this very micro-group . . .," while then suddenly concluding with a quotation from the Beatles song "Let It Be": "Let's come together." Skobov showcased his version of nonconformism by following other people's mocking, pseudo-Marxist tone and recounting the history of the commune as the history of the revolutionary movement. But rather than quoting the obligatory Western rock music, he concludes with Bulat Okudzhava: "Let's live in forgiveness for each other, especially since life is short (*Davaite zhit, vo vsem drug druga potakaia, tem bolee, chto zhizn korotkaia takaia*)." His preference for a Soviet bard over Western rock puts him in closer proximity to a cohort that was a bit older than the Yellow Submarine crew: the Thaw generation. It was not that no one else in the commune listened to the lyrical songs of the bards. But their Aesopian and melancholic songs were not young people's soundtrack in the late 1970s just as their open or veiled call for activism did not really resonate with this generation anymore.[31] From the very beginning the members of commune thus tap into two different reservoirs of knowledge to situate themselves vis-à-vis the Soviet system. Yet, most importantly, from the very beginning they cement their own peculiar reservoir of knowledge, which renders them distinct from the rest of the world.

Even though the logbook was only amended intermittently, it continued to be the depository of the commune's distinct knowledge, which grew exponentially as time went on, new events took place and were processed, and the commune became more and more complex in its own interactions. The commune not only existed in a simple one-dimensional reality, but relied on constant self-reflection and self-parody. At the end of the year Feliks called an "extraordinary congress" and presented a justificatory report to the commune committee, which was logged as being accompanied by "loud and continuous applause"—a phrase habitually used in the press to describe the response to

Brezhnev's speeches. Rivalries within the house were also transferred to this "fictional" level: Mal'skii at some point styled himself Speaker of the High Court of the Yellow Submarine and Skobov was censored in a mock-Komsomol assembly for his excessive drinking. Feliks, in protest at the behavior of some visitors, created the Fighter Organization under the Leadership of the Central Committee of the Icebreaker League (Boevaia organizatsiia pri TsK Aisbreakerskoi Ligi).[32] These usurpations of power and public criticisms were based on real-life conflicts and hence indicate that the boundary between life and autobiographical fiction was getting more and more blurred.

The culmination of this careful crafting of a second reality for the commune was the joint authorship by Igor', Feliks, and Andrei of a play about the life of a rock commune in the Soviet Union, which only thinly veiled the protagonists as the members of the Yellow Submarine. The authors' pseudonym O. Mafin, an acronym of the authors Mal'skii, Feliks, and Andrei, was well known to Soviet children as the name of a donkey in a famous children's novel. The reference to a children's book gave the whole enterprise a self-consciously infantile air, in line with the self-imposed childlikeness of the global hippie community, which liked to stress its spiritual proximity to the innocence and wisdom of children. (While none of the commune founders knew about the Soviet hippie *sistema* before the founding of the commune, very soon *sistema* hippies visited the commune, arriving in ever growing numbers and imprinting a certain hippie style on the community.) Yet the title of the play counteracts any assumed innocence. The play is called "Lazha"— a youth slang term, which roughly translates as "fancy tales," "lies" or, more bluntly, "bullshit."[33] The primary meaning here is the exposition of official untruths, yet it also implies a certain doubt about the veracity of the story itself, thus playing tricks on the audience's perception of what is real and what is not. As such it was perfectly in line with the messages conveyed in the logbook. Nothing was ever quite what it was made to look like. All that remains is the laughter of the insider. The play thus both cemented the separateness of the commune, which established its own history in the text, and stretched out a hand to a broader audience of like-minded youth. While the logbook had been a means of establishing internal cohesion and differentiation from the mainstream, the play added a missionary zeal to the commune's agenda (the play circulated widely in *samizdat* not only in Leningrad but also other Soviet towns). It was both a further step in "dropping out," not least because it represented uncensored, and hence, illegal literature, and a step to claiming an alternative public sphere and thus a certain opening up.

The Yellow Submarine also distinguished itself on a very visual level. Their house was different from the buildings that made up the typical Leningrad cityscape. Their walls were painted yellow and decorated with huge strawberries. And everywhere in the house Feliks's pop posters adorned the commune's walls. Like Christian iconography, they were loaded with symbolic references, understandable to their intended audience, yet intentionally incomprehensible to outsiders. Some of the visual clues are so much of their time and place that even Feliks himself could not decipher them thirty years later.[34] They range from political digs at the ruling Soviet class—Brezhnev as a tank, Stalin with a soft Dali clock—to Christian symbolism—a cross with the inscription "I do not believe in equality," St. John's head on an ashtray—to symbols of Western life—jeans, record players, the American flag and English or (badly translated) quotations from Beatles songs—to international, political references—1968 as the year of protests, 1972 as the year of the putsch against Salvador Allende. Interspersed in all of this are peace signs, American and Jewish stars (even though of the permanent commune members only Tat'iana was Jewish), personal photographs and internal jokes, slogans in a variety of languages—a huge jumble of serious allusions rendered playful and semi-ironic in their particular assemblage. While the posters were very much Feliks's depiction of the world, evidence suggests that other commune members, too, were not very discriminatory in their inspirations and references as long as the message conveyed an element of irreverence and deviance and/or lent itself to making a joke. A visitor to the commune described Skobov's room to the writer Vadim Nechaev, whose description of the commune made it into a report of Radio Free Europe's Information Department: "He (Skobov) pinned up homemade posters of Che Guevara and of Jesus Christ carrying a submachine gun. Behind Christ stood the Apostles, also armed to the teeth, and beneath them the caption, 'If you are hit on the right cheek, turn the left, but if they hit you on the left cheek too . . .!'"[35]

Skobov described his wall decorations in interview with me as nothing but a "childish game." But it was precisely in its childlike nature that the commune was running counter to the grain. The Soviet Union paid great attention to children and prided itself on its education. But the system was geared toward growing up. From the youngest ages children were encouraged to imitate adults in quasi-party organizations and with rituals taken from the adult world.[36] There was no space for infantilism in the Soviet system. A group of people who turned the Soviet demand for perfection in adulthood on its head, worshipping the age of childhood—Feliks even made his baby son the new President as soon as he was born—undermined one of the tenets of communist society: conscience (which came with age) was meant to guide life. Children, on the other hand, were guided by unfettered desire and emotions.

There certainly was no space for a community that in its quest for separation was prepared to supplement—or indeed substitute—reality with a layer of discursive reality that challenged Soviet reality. For the crew of the submarine the world of the commune, its long drinking and smoking sessions in the kitchen, its parodies of Soviet rituals, and its slogans derived from

Beatles songs were more "real" than their "real" lives: their studies at the university, their obligations to the *Voenkomat* (the military representative at every university), the life of their parents and other people outside the communal sphere. It was in the commune that they truly "lived." Their reality was theirs and theirs alone. In Soviet reality they went to university, they studied, they interacted with the Komsomol. In their reality they were a distinct entity complete with its own history, its own literary record, its own space, and its own aesthetics. No wonder that they were soon considered both highly attractive and highly suspicious.

## DROP-OUTS DIVIDED

The space of the commune was divided in two separate apartments. It soon became apparent that divisions ran deeper than just a staircase. They were agreed in their desire to create a space away from the mainstream. They all wanted to drop out from something somehow. But it soon became apparent that once they had taken the first steps toward establishing their submarine, they wanted to steer it in different directions. The upstairs was keener to lead a quiet life that shunned Soviet reality and did nothing to attract the attention of the authorities. Their self-imposed isolation from their "near outside" was compensated by an opening to the "far abroad"—the West or the way they imagined it. The downstairs—mainly in the persona of Skobov and his outside friends—was committed to using the commune as a launching pad for a struggle against the regime, relying on neo-Marxist rhetoric and tactics to formulate and advance their goal. Ironically, they also emerged as the more radical proponents of the "wild life," while the upstairs relied, in the creation of their sanctuary, on traditional values. Both floors wanted to be "free"—but it soon became apparent, in the reality they lived, that one version of freedom was endangering the other.

Both Feliks and Marina, and to a lesser degree Andrei Antonenko and his soon-to-be-wife Tat'iana Komarova, emphasized the idea of the submarine as an escape from a world of falsehood and lies. Their concern was to preserve the status quo of the commune as a place that attracted people from outside and that was characterized by conviviality, but which essentially was their place of retreat from a society they despised. This did not mean that their aims for this space were entirely devoid of more spiritual aspirations. Feliks tried to define his vision in the logbook after one of the first serious disagreements between the "upstairs" and the "downstairs":

> Let's remember that our goal was the multiple metamorphoses and foundation of a so-called "parallel society." . . . Are we in agreement or not that we differ significantly from "squares"? . . . and what our mutual relations are concerned.

> From time to time one feels some hostility based on nothing . . . and then remember that our common goal was self-perfection and education of oneself and those close to us. And also, if we differ from the masses, then one has to see this in our manner of behavior and in our external look. You can accuse me of "socialism" and [being] in pursuit of cheap popularity, but this is what we need.[37]

What is surprising is that here Feliks uses language straight from the Bolshevik—indeed, the Christian—canon of values and education without a hint of irony. Rather than stressing the hedonistic experience of the commune—a facet of the submarine's life that is more often mentioned in more recent interviews—at the time Feliks appealed to the joint desire to perfect oneself and lead by example. The commune was to have an educational mission. Yet for Feliks this mission was not one primarily of intellect. Rather, he saw a direct connection between exterior markers and an internal state of mind. More specifically he defended the significance of jeans and other insignia of a "non-square" lifestyle, which he considered essential to the commune's identity. Indeed, there is an almost messianic message in Feliks's pronouncements on fashion and lifestyle. The art of looking and living differently was to alter the mind. That was a belief that was not dissimilar from official Soviet doctrine, which firmly stated that social environment was the most important factor in shaping people's consciousness.[38]

Jeans in particular were central to Felik's self-perception. They appear again and again in the pop posters—both allegorically and expressively. In one there is a brain inhabiting a pair of jeans, while another has the heading "Only jeans and patches can save the world." Feliks also depicted his own "enlightenment" through listening to music. A lightbulb and kind of halo appear above his head when depicted next to a record player. He is dressed in a T-shirt with a peace sign, flared jeans, record player nearby, pipe in one hand, and a glass of something in the other. A big "Lee Rider" patch leaves no doubt that the poster was not referring to jeans from Poland or Latvia but that this was an enclave of Western enjoyment. On the walls it read "Drop out," while the inscription at the bottom declares: "This is our place—a temple for the squalid," thus drawing a definite distinction between the desired neatness of official culture and the "wilder" and "freer" space of the commune.[39] In other posters jeans are coupled with a victory sign. In all the pictures their luminous blue attracts the attention of the viewer. Blue was the color of jeans, America, and hence, freedom. Blue distinguished the cool from the gray masses. In another poster, Marina, Feliks, and Tat'iana are sitting in blue jeans in a bar sipping milkshakes. There is hardly any color in the drawing except the blue of the jeans. Marina gives expression to their view of the outside world by declaring: "I have had it with everything" (*mne do zhuti vse nadoeelo*).[40] Jeans were also the chosen attire for Tat'iana and Andrei Antonenko's wedding. The tension within commune members between more

**Figure 8.2 Drawing by Felisk Vinogradov: "I had enough of everything."** From left to right: Skobov, Feliks, Marina. *Source:* Archive Feliks and Marina Vinogradov.

traditional and mainstream values and a desire to break out is quite evident in this event. They got married—because this is what one does—yet they kept it secret, because, as Andrei declared, "it sort of jarred with the communal experiment."[41] Their jeans and jean jackets, however, came with them as an expression of their difference. They drew attention to the centrality of their attire by calling their wedding a "jeans wedding"—*dhinzovaia svadba*.[42]

Skobov was more skeptical about the importance of exterior attributes—and about the interpretation from "upstairs" of what it meant to make a difference: "By hippiedom they only understood the wearing of a standard prescribed uniform of jeans and certain attributes, and anyone who did not wear this, he [Feliks] called not a person, but a 'square.' As he then said: 'only jeans and money will bring us democracy.' By this definition I was not a hippie." Yet, he conceded that he too did not fit the expectation of the Soviet norm: "However, I also did not look like the way it was accepted among proper people."[43]

**Figure 8.3 Daily life and community in the commune.** *Source*: Archive Feliks and Marina Vinogradov.

Skobov's vision for the commune was not one that rested on visible markers nor was it one that envisaged caution or preservation of the status quo. In an interview Skobov laconically explained:

There was an idea of some kind of nonconformist lifestyle, which was understood quite differently by different people. Because I did everything to surround myself with critically-minded and more socially active people, in order to have at least some kind of perspective for some kind of collective action. And the majority was more inclined to the idea of dropping out from mainstream society in order to be less involved in society but also in order to have society less involved in them.[44]

Antonenko confirmed Skobov's assessment of the commune as staying out of political or public life, but at the same time validated Feliks's argument that the commune, as a visible beacon of difference, should serve as an educational location for perfecting oneself and others. There was an unavoidable tension in this simultaneous wish for change and personal revolution and the desire to be separate, undisturbed, and inward-looking. The private, commercial action ensured a sort of freedom, but it did not solve the question of what purpose this freedom was to have. Andrei put it like this:

Hence, I pay her [the landlady], and up to a certain point they could do nothing about what went on inside. It is a locking in from the inside—that was one step towards freedom. And this also guided all other actions—to be at least within the parameters of one's own group . . . . We felt simultaneously a sense of superiority and a sense of definite downfall . . . we tried to achieve the best possible self-perfection and character-building, yet declared our desire to build these in an introverted society. . . . Yet some like Skobov wanted to use this space of freedom to enlarge this freedom to cover the whole of the Soviet Union. That was inevitable.[45]

It was not that "upstairs" lacked missionizing zeal: after all, the upstairs had concocted the rock poem "Lazhi" and initiated its distribution via a network of friends. And in many ways wearing jeans was a more visible beacon than clandestine writing. But Skobov and his old school allies Reznikov and Tsurkov had more radical visions and tools in mind. Wearing jeans was not enough of an opposition. And it certainly did not satisfy Skobov's intellectual expectations. He veered in the direction of the New Left, yet when forced to choose between the evils of capitalism and socialism, he rated late Soviet reality worse.[46] The mere fact that the European Left could protest in the open filled him with envy: "Is there an alternative to the capitalist system? . . . I want to believe there is. How realistic that is and when it will come into existence—I cannot say now, but in my youth I believed very strongly that something better could happen tomorrow, the day after tomorrow . . . . And I believe until today that if you are not allowed to speak, you are allowed to shoot."[47]

Skobov and his friends never shot or even prepared to shoot. However, they began publishing an underground journal titled *Perspektivy* and went so far as to organize a clandestine "congress" of New Left groups in a forest. The other commune members knew about the journal and had various degrees of concern about such overt political activity. Mal'skii was a collaborator (possibly only because he lived downstairs with Skobov), Tat'iana helped Skobov to reproduce photographic copies of it in the bathtub, Andrei was worried but sympathetic and Marina and Feliks were outright opposed to such actions and tried to force Skobov to abandon what they thought would spell the end of the commune (and possibly rightly so).[48]

Antonenko was painfully aware that this disagreement opened up uncomfortable questions about the very nature of the space they had tried to create. The first floor acted in *loco imperii* to the ground floor: "Inside, we fulfilled the function of the state and were trying to rein in Skobov's desire for freedom. We tried to explain to him: this you can do and this you cannot."[49]

Skobov in turn was well aware that in many ways the desire to live together and be different was founded on a socialist notion of collectivism, which placed the value of the collective above that of the individual. One of his first logbook entries reads:

> You pride yourself in your independence from official ideology. But in reality you live imprisoned by the tenants of this ideology, in particular the Soviet idea of collectivism. Real collectivism, based on the need of the individual to live in association with other individuals, is only possible when the collective respects the right of all of its members, only then living together is not a burden.[50]

Antonenko saw fewer contradictions between the two strategies of being "un-Soviet": "Hippies, New Lefties, pop and Beatles fans were all boiled in the same pot, meaning they all belonged together in their refusal to live as was expected."[51] It was on that premise that the commune members first befriended each other and then agreed to dare the experiment of a commune. Moreover, it was not the 1950s anymore, when intellectual youth thought little of those following a hedonistic path,[52] and even convinced neo-Marxists like Skobov, Tsurkov, and Reznikov could not ignore that among youth the phenomenon of the nonconformist lifestyle was much more widespread—and in many ways much more successful in uniting large swathes of people—than revolutionary ideology. There was much discussion among them about if and how to integrate this section of society in the struggle for a better revolutionary order. Skobov argued that there was revolutionary potential within the movement of longhaired and music-loving youngsters who, to various degrees, linked themselves to the hippie movement and who clearly showed resistance in the face of official persecution. The mass riot on July 4, 1978 by a few thousand rock lovers who had been led to believe that Santana, Joan Baez, the Beach Boys, and Alla Pugacheva were about to play in Leningrad's Palace Square appeared to vindicate him:[53] "I got confirmation of my view.

Tsurkov and Reznikov were always skeptical about the hippie public,[54] that they would never produce anything and that they simply retreated into their own world and shied away from social problems. And there I said: 'See what they can do.'"[55] Consequently he dedicated some pages of the first number of *Perspektivy* to the "concert that never was."[56] Skobov, however, was unfair when he said that both Tsurkov and Reznikov dismissed hippies as potential allies. Tsurkov did indeed think little of the longhaired friends of his political collaborator. Reznikov, however, was decidedly interested in what hippies had to offer—possibly because he saw an affinity between his own expeditions with friends into the depths of Soviet nature and the hippies' love for the "untouched" and their custom of assembling in remote spots. Reznikov and his girlfriend Irina even went so far as to travel to a hippie festival in Lithuania in order to engage hippies in a dialogue. Unfortunately when they arrived the police had already disrupted the gathering and the remaining hippies fled when they saw people who did not look like their own. Reznikov recalls the absurdity of standing in the woods and shouting after the running hippies: "Stop, come back, we need to talk."[57]

## DROP-OUTS DESTRUCTED

In reality both floors realized that the life they had created had gotten a bit out of their hands. "Dropping out" was by no means their private matter anymore. While Skobov assembled his political friends downstairs and started stepping outside the borders of Soviet legality, the upstairs was mixed up by its own visitors. The *sistema*—the loose affiliation of Soviet hippies—soon discovered the commune as a hideout and turned it into a so-called *flet*—an apartment known on the Soviet hippie trail to welcome passing hippies and longer-staying guests. While the commune was hospitable and members still fondly remember some visitors (mostly those from the Baltic states), they soon felt overrun by "professional" hippies and their lifestyle. There was exasperation in Marina's voice when she declared: "We did not find the *sistema*. The *sistema* found us. And exploited us—as a *flet*."[58] The crew of the Yellow Submarine soon discovered that they were not quite ready for some of the more unconventional hippie values. Reznikov's camera was shamelessly and unremorsefully exchanged for some bottles of wine in a local store when visitors found themselves alone in the house. Drugs were left lying around. People were sleeping everywhere—alone, together, with each other. Antonenko expressed his increasing unease about life in the commune, using the communal cat as a proxy for the chaos that engulfed the house as time went on: "The fate of this cat was horrible, because on Saturdays it was fed wine from a teaspoon. She did not become an alcoholic, but she went a bit

crazy. . . . she jumped, ran, clawed . . . . Because there was a huge number of
people all the time and she did not know anymore, who her owner was . . . ."[59]

Six months after the commune was founded, Feliks and Marina had a baby
son, whose need for quiet and clean diapers (both of which infringed on the
space available for parties) drove an even larger wedge between the communal factions.[60] Mal'skii and Skobov at the same time started to experiment
with drugs and girls (even though Tat'iana's comment on Skobov's claim of
practicing free love was "in his dreams").[61] The "upstairs" worriedly observed
how the political discussions downstairs developed into ever more concrete
plans to proselytize. Tat'iana remembered:

> You know, we were always skeptical about Skobov as a revolutionary. Already
> because of his personal traits. You could not do revolution in the USSR as you
> did in France in 1968. This was only possible in the underground. Skobov
> thought he was an excellent conspirator, but in essence his skills were prosely-
> tizing and agitating. He would tell everybody in a beer bar about his plans. This
> would have been not so bad, except in every beer bar at least one person was
> an informer.[62]

If the upstairs observed the political underground developing in the downstairs with worry, the political underground also felt threatened by the commune and its attraction to a different type of underground. Irina Lopotukhina,
a collaborator on Skobov's underground paper, described her fears about what
was going on in the Yellow Submarine: "And these hippies and non-hippies
brought all sorts of dirty things, like drugs, not to speak of vodka and I did
not understand who they were—they only arrived last night and were drunk
on top . . . and here I am typing illegal stuff for which I can be imprisoned."[63]

Eighteen months after the commune was founded Feliks received a warn-
ing from his father that they were under observation. He and Marina left
the commune almost immediately as did Andrei Antonenko and Tat'iana.
Mal'skii had been expelled from university and had left long ago. Skobov
alone remained in the house—for lack of knowledge or lack of somewhere
to go. He was arrested in early October 1978. Arkadii Tsurkov was arrested
three weeks later. Reznikov went on the run and hid in the woods near
Leningrad for several months. His girlfriend Irina had to run to the train station to deflect the delegates of the "underground" congress of New Leftists
that had been called for those very days. When the matter of the underground
journal *Perspektivy* came to trial at the Leningrad city court, Tsurkov was sentenced to five years imprisonment for anti-Soviet agitation. Irina Lopotukhina
escaped arrest. She married Arkadii while he was in prison. Skobov was committed to a mental hospital for two years. It did not stop him from resuming
political activity during and after *perestroika*. Andrei and Tat'iana divorced

a few months later. They were interviewed many times about the Yellow Submarine by the KGB as were Marina and Feliks. A year after the "concert that did not happen" Feliks was arrested on Palace Square for wearing hippie-ish clothing. He was released without being charged, but the incident showed how jiggery the authorities felt in the late 1970s about the city's youth. Skobov was only released in June 1981. Andrei still feels guilty about having admitted that Skobov produced underground literature (even though the KGB likely knew this all along). Andrei concluded fatalistically: "It was clear in the end that this story was to end like this. The games were over and now someone had to pay for these games."[64]

## CONCLUSION

What does the rise and fall of the commune Yellow Submarine tell us about "dropping out" from socialism? What distinguished this commune from the many other communal experiments around the world which crashed due to inherent contradictions and internal strife? Was its type of "dropping out" in any way different because it happened under the tutelage of socialism? And indeed, was the commune really "dropping out"?

It would be easy to point out that the commune was neither very radical nor very unique on the global scene. Countercultural communes the world over had to realize in the heady 1960s and more sobering 1970s that living together was no easy matter just as many other communal experiments before them had.[65] It would also be easy to say that their type of "dropping out" in a remote house, listening to music, and smoking the occasional joint was very much a phenomenon of the time. Even their particular brand of parody had its Western equivalents in the street theater pranks organized by people such as the San Francisco Diggers or New York Yippies.[66] And finally, critics will be quick to point out that the Yellow Submarine's "dropping out" was very partial indeed. Its members were students at Leningrad State University and some of them were even members of the Komsomol. And yet these easy answers would not capture the essence of the Yellow Submarine. The Yellow Submarine was unique, not in a global setting, but in its very particular location in late socialism. From their subjective viewpoint they were a drop-out community. They desired escape from socialist normality so strongly that they created an entire alternative level of reality to cement their claim.

There were not many communes under socialism, mainly because the housing arrangements did not allow it. The sheer act of living together in a voluntary, private arrangement hence put the Yellow Submarine crew out of the mainstream. It is no surprise that they became famous all over town. Their space was different. Its hallmark was precisely that it was not Soviet.

By putting the bar for deviance so low, the Soviet system helped to no small
extent to create "drop-outs" in the first place and to make them so attractive in the second. Yet the Soviet system not only provided the background
to the Yellow Submarine's dropping out. It was an essential part of it. The
Yellow Submarine created its alternative sphere by parodying and caricatur-
ing the official system in which its members had been socialized. Indeed
it was the double knowledge of being able to decode the original model as
well as the joke that created the deep insider knowledge, which sustained the
community as a non-Soviet space and provided distance from the world they
mocked. Their spatial dropping out was significant, but not half as effective as
their rhetorical interpretation of this step and their subsequent practices as a
commune, all of which were constantly reflected back to them in words, pictures, and performance. The extensive discursive level in turn exponentially
increased the gulf between the "knowledge community" of the Yellow Submarine and its various outsiders. Outsiders constituted circles of knowledge,
ranging from fellow hippie or New Leftist visitors, who were privy to some
of the insider knowledge, all the way across the spectrum to KGB agents, who
snooped around but whose mental background prevented them from correctly
deciphering much of the codes that made up the Yellow Submarine. Rather
than "living *vnye*," the Yellow Submarine turned the tables, making itself the
"inside" that controlled access to its metaphysical space, even if it could not
safeguard its physical one.

However, the desire to be more than hedonistic youth—a shameful
occupation in the socialist world—was deeply engrained in the minds of
the various members and they drew different conclusions from it, drawing
on different models of behavior and virtue. The "upstairs" orientated itself
on a model that shunned political participation in favor of making lifestyle
statements, while the "downstairs" embraced an idea of change through
political reform or revolution. While in the West similar disagreements
generated practical and ideological variations on the 1960s counterculture,
in the socialist context it became an existential question. What seemed like
harmless child's play could suddenly turn into a question of life or prison.
Even the most modest drop-outs played for high stakes in the late socialist
context. The sword of Damocles that hung over all late socialist drop-out
cultures intensified the subjective experience of acts that in other societies
would not have carried an equivalent weight. Yet it also imposed a pressure
that ultimately made a lot of these cultures crack and scramble back to more
mainstream shores. None of the main members of the Yellow Submarine
lived in a commune ever again. None, except Marina and Feliks's son, who
was born into the Yellow Submarine, was its president for half a year, and
now lives in a commune in Berlin.

## NOTES

1. The author would like to thank Robert Gildea, Anette Warring and James Mark and OUP for permission to reuse some fragments of the article "Drop-outs," in Gildea, Warring, Mark, *Europe's 1968: Voices of Revolt* (Oxford: Oxford University Press), 2013.

2. On graffiti in the Soviet Union and Russia, see John Bushnell, *Moscow Graffiti: Language and Subculture* (Boston: Unwin Hyman, 1990). Several authors have recently turned to the phenomenon of alienated (but not oppositional) youth in this period, first and foremost, Alexei Yurchak, *Everything Was Forever, Until It Was No More: The Last Soviet Generation* (Princeton: Princeton University Press, 2006). See also William Risch, *The Ukrainian West: Culture and the Fate of Empire in Soviet Lviv* (Cambridge, MA: Harvard University Press, 2011), 237–46. Mark Swede, "All You Need is Lovebeads: Latvia's Hippies Undress for Success," in *Style and Socialism: Modernity and Material Culture in Post-War Eastern Europe*, ed. Susan Reid and David Crowley (Oxford: Berg, 2000), 189–208. Sergei Zhuk, *Rock and Roll in the Rocket City: The West, Identity, and Ideology in Soviet Dniepropetrovsk, 1960–1985* (Baltimore: Johns Hopkins University Press, 2010). For a participant-academic view of the *sistema*, especially as it existed in Leningrad in the 1980s, see Tat'iana Shepanskaia, *Sistema: Teksty i traditsii subkul'tury* (Moscow: OGI, 2004).

3. The communal idea was in the air in the 1960s and 1970s. See among others, Timothy Miller, *The 60s Communes: Hippies and Beyond* (New York: Syracuse University Press, 1999); Robert Gildea, James Mark, and Anette Warring, *Europe's 1968: Voices of Revolt* (Oxford: Oxford University Press, 2013); on post-revolutionary communes, see Andi Willimot, *Living the Revolution: Urban Communes and Soviet Socialism 1917–1932* (Oxford: Oxford University Press, 2016); On the *turist* movement, see Christian Noack, "Songs from the Wood, Love from the Fields: The Soviet Tourist Song Movement," in *The Socialist Sixties: Crossing Borders in the Second World*, ed. Ann Gorsuch and Diane Koenker (Bloomington: Indiana University Press, 2013), 167–92.

4. Alexei Yurchak, *Everything Was Forever*, 126–57, quotation from 128.

5. For a critique of Yurchak's refusal to evaluate his subjects vis-à-vis their relationship to the state and system, see Benjamin Nathans and Kevin Platt, "Socialist in Form, Indeterminate in Content: The Ins and Outs of Late Soviet Culture," *Ab Imperio* no. 2 (2011). On the close relationship between dissent and affirmation, especially in the late Stalinist and Khrushchev periods, see Juliane Fürst, "Prisoners of the Soviet Self? Political Youth Opposition in Late Stalinism," *Europe-Asia Studies* 54, no. 3 (2002): 353–75; Benjamin Nathans, "The Dictatorship of Reason: Aleksandr Vol'pin and the Idea of 'Rights' under Developed Socialism," *Slavic Review* 66, no. 4 (2007): 630–63. Benjamin Tromly, "Intelligentsia Self-fashioning in the Postwar Soviet Union: Revol't Pimenov's Political Struggle, 1949–57," *Kritika: Explorations in Russian and Eurasian History* 13, no. 1 (2012): 151–76.

6. Yurchak, *Everything Was Forever*, 129–30.

7. Marina and Feliks Vinogradov, interview with the author, St. Petersburg, June 8, 2009.

8. Tat'iana Komarova, interview with the author, Munich, May 2, 2011.

9. Anton Antonenko, interview with the author, St. Petersburg, June 10, 2009.

10. Aleksandr Skobov, interview with author, St. Petersburg, June 7, 2009. See also the extensive file on Aleksandr Skobov in the archive of Memorial, St. Petersburg. Also "Interviu s Marksistom," *Posev* no. 3 (1988): 50–54.

11. Antonenko.

12. Igor' Mal'skii, "Ne takaia eto lazha," *Khippilend* no. 3, unknown date of publication, 7.

13. Irina Feodorova is now better known as Irina Flige and serves as the director of the St. Petersburg Memorial society.

14. Andrei Reznikov, interview with the author, St. Petersburg, July 7, 2010; Irina Flige, interview with the author, St. Petersburg, July 5, 2010. On the *turist* movement in general, see Petr Vail' and Aleksandr Genis, *Mir sovetskogo cheloveka 60-e* (Moscow: Novoe Literaturnoe Obozrenie, 2001).

15. Arkadii Tsurkov, interview with the author, El Kfad, August 3, 2011; Irina Lopotukhina, interview with the author, El Kfad, August 3, 2011.

16. Yurchak, *Everything Was Forever*, 105–18; Juliane Fürst, "Where Did All the Normal People Go?: Another Look at the Soviet 1970s," review article, *Kritika: Explorations in Russian and Eurasian History* 14, no. 3 (2013), 621–40.

17. Marina and Feliks Vinogradov.

18. Komarova.

19. Logbook of the commune Yellow Submarine, private archive of Marina and Feliks Vinogradov.

20. Marina and Feliks Vinogradov.

21. Antonenko.

22. Komarova.

23. Marina and Feliks Vinogradov.

24. Logbook.

25. Yurchak also discussed *stiob* in relation to his notion of "living *vnye*." It was quite a common practice among critical youngsters at the time and served one function only: to create a layer of knowledge understandable only to insiders. Indeed, Yurchak discusses *stiob* with reference to two groups, one of which, the Mitki, were friendly with the Yellow Submarine's inhabitants. Yurchak, *Everything Was Forever*, 249–55. The related genre of what Yurchak calls "scary little poems," mutilated folk ditties with violent content, made headlines in the 1990s when former Yellow Submarine inhabitant Igor Mal'skii claimed that he had invented them during his time in the Yellow Submarine. See A. F. Belousov, "Vospominaniia Igoria Mal'skogo 'Krivoe zerkalo deistvitel'nosti': K voprosu o proiskhozhdenii 'sadistskikh stishkov,'" in *Lotmanovskii sbornik*, ed. M. L. Gasparov (Tartu: Garant, 1994), 681–91. However, it is much more likely that these poems were floating around in the milieu at the time, because they fitted the mood of alternative youngsters. Yet they were clearly very prevalent in the Yellow Submarine and every circle of friends coined their own scary ditties, thus cementing the creation of overlapping knowledge communities.

26. Logbook.

27. On the performative aspects of late socialist language, see Yurchak, *Everything Was Forever*, 47–50.

28. By late socialism, the "kitchen" had become shorthand for a space in which friends had frank conversations, saying things that were not meant for any space bigger than the tiny kitchens of postwar, Soviet-style apartments.

29. Feliks Vinogradov.

30. Yurchak, *Everything Was Forever*, 114–15.

31. Artemy Troitsky, *Back to the USSR: The True Story of Russian Rock* (London: Omnibus Press, 1987).

32. Logbook.

33. O. Mafin, "Lazha," unpublished manuscript, personal archive of Marina and Feliks Vinogradov.

34. Feliks Vinogradov.

35. Open Society Archives at Central European University, Budapest, Hungary (HU OSA), 300-80-1-45, Red Archive (Vadim Nechaev, "The Short-Lived Career of a 'New Left' Youth Commune in Leningrad," 1980).

36. Catriona Kelly, *Children's World: Growing Up in Russia, 1890–1991* (New Haven: Yale University Press, 2007); Lisa Kirschenbaum, *Small Comrades: Revolutionizing Childhood in Soviet Russia, 1917–1932* (London: Routledge, 2001).

37. Logbook.

38. Corinna Kuhr-Korolev, *Gezähmte Helden: Die Formierung der Sowjetjugend* (Essen: Klartext, 2005).

39. Pop poster "Eto nashe mesto," personal archive of Feliks Vinogradov.

40. Pop poster "Ia vse nadoela," personal archive of Feliks Vinogradov.

41. Antonenko.

42. Antonenko.

43. Skobov.

44. Skobov.

45. Antonenko.

46. On the New Left, see A. N. Tarasov, G. Iu. Cherkasov, and T. V. Shavshukova, *Levye v Rossii: Otumerennykh do ekstremistov* (Moscow: Center for Experimental Sociology, 1997), 13.

47. Ibid.

48. Mal'skii, *Khippilend*; Marina and Feliks Vinogradov; Antonenko; Komarova.

49. Antonenko.

50. Logbook.

51. Antonenko.

52. On this question, see for example, the memoirs of Iurii Ronkin, *Po smenam Dekabria prikhodit Ianvari: Vospominanie byvshego brigadmil'tsa i podpol'shchika i politzakliuchenego i dissidenta* (St. Petersburg: Memorial Zveniia, 2003).

53. On the "forbidden concert," see Nika Strizhak's documentary film, *Zapreshchennyi Kontsert: Nemusikal'naia Istoriia* (2006; Telekanal Rossiia). See also Gena Zaitsev, "Khronika Proshedshikh Sobytii," unpublished manuscript, 223–24, private archive of Gena Zaitsev.

54. De facto only a minority of the concert hopefuls were hippies, but a lot of young people shared their love of rock music, had longish hair, and wore jeans.

55. Skobov.

56. Aleksandr Skobov, "Perspektiva—Die Zeitschrift der Neuen Linken," in *Samizdat: Materialien der Konferenz "30 Jahre unabhängige Presse, 1950–80er Jahre,"* ed. V. Dolinin and B. Ivanov (St. Petersburg, Nauchno-informatsionnyi tsentr "Memorial," 1993), 121–22. In this article, Skobov is more negative about the revolutionary potential of the hippies, which he claimed they "massively over-estimated." But in 1992 too, he affirmed that his group actively collected materials written by them in order to unify different strands of opposition. Skobov, "Perspektiva," 122.

57. Tsurkov; Reznikov; Flige.

58. Marina and Feliks Vinogradov.

59. Antonenko.

60. Marina and Feliks Vinogradov; Antonenko.

61. Skobov; Komarova.

62. Antonenko.

63. Lopotukhina.

64. Antonenko.

65. The history of communal living is also a history of its repeated failure. See Bernard Lacroix, *L'utopie communitaire: Histoire sociale d'une revolte* (Paris: Presses universitaires de France, 1981); John Mercer, *Communes: A Social History and Guide* (Dorchester: Prism, 1984).

66. W. J. Rorabaugh, *American Hippies* (Cambridge: Cambridge University Press, 2015).

*Chapter 9*

# Ignoring Dictatorship? Punk Rock, Subculture, and Entanglement in the GDR

Jeff Hayton

Moritz Götze, graphic artist and member of the Halle-based punk band Größenwahn during the 1980s has claimed that during the final decade of the German Democratic Republic (GDR), the last generation of youth subcultures "ignored the GDR from the margins of the GDR."[1] What does it mean to ignore dictatorship? How is it possible to do so? Where do the margins of the GDR lie? In the following investigation I want to explore Götze's claim by examining the East German punk subculture. When it arrived from the West in the late 1970s, East German youths eagerly welcomed punk, set up thriving scenes in cities across the GDR, and connected with like-minded individuals across the Eastern bloc, especially in Warsaw, Prague, and Budapest. Playing in bands, gathering in local hangouts, and recording demo cassettes which then circulated throughout the country, punks sought to fashion more meaningful communities and alternative identities than those dictated to them by the Socialist Unity Party (Sozialistische Einheitspartei Deutschlands, SED). While in the West, punks cried "no future" to condemn (glorify?) the hopelessness of their generation, in the GDR young Easterners claimed instead they had "too much future" because their lives were mapped out in advance from school and the Free German Youth (Freie Deutsche Jugend, FDJ) to work and finally retirement. Instead, young Easterners wanted to experience difference and to escape a community ostensibly focused on uniformity and the collective, and they did so by mobilizing popular music to create a subculture that existed on the margins of officially tolerated society.

But the question remains: to what extent was this community based on imbrication rather than ignorance of dictatorship? In order to examine Götze's claim, I follow three threads. First, I elucidate the dimensions of the punk subculture in the GDR. Manufacturing scenes, DIY fashions, forming bands, performing at concerts—while officially punk did not exist in the GDR (the SED claimed socialist socioeconomic conditions precluded it), Eastern punks were nonetheless industrious in carving out spaces of alternative community that were often divorced from state-sponsored youth activities. Yet, at the same time, punk ideology and practice, whether expressed lyrically or in forms such as fashion, were virulently anti-state and thus constructed around a negation of many of those ideals upon which East German national identity was manufactured. Such intertwining thus raises an important question concerning the relationship of punk to the state: can an anti-state subculture ignore the state? The emphasis on the state in the construction of punk ideology and praxis points to the second thread, that is, the relationship between punk and the secret police (Ministerium für Staatssicherheits, MfS or Stasi). From very early on, the Stasi penetrated the subculture and co-opted many of its members to work for state authorities as informers (Inoffizielle Mitarbeiter, or IMs). While such cooperation never played out as the regime hoped since punks used their contacts with the Stasi mostly to further their own aims, the question remains: Can one ignore dictatorship while working for the dictatorship?

After repression failed to dislodge punk in the mid-1980s, the SED tried to incorporate the genre into the state as a means of diffusing its subversive qualities. To what extent then can punk ignore dictatorship if the subculture was taking advantage of the state music industry? Can one drop out when one is firmly integrated within? These questions point to the final thread of investigation, namely, the nature of Eastern punk memory which suggests how ignorance is perhaps more a construct of the present than of the past. Incorporation into state structures split the subculture, which is most evident in the exclusion of state bands from the "official" Eastern punk memory that has flourished since reunification. Thus, is ignoring dictatorship more a question of historical memory than past conduct? And if so, why and how? By examining the emergence, response, and memory of punk in the GDR, I want to explore how the subculture helps to better understand late socialist society and political culture, and especially the place of alternative cultures in these structures. By examining whether East German punks ignored the GDR, I want to shed light on the limits of dictatorship in order to reassess the degree to which punks contributed to the experience of "really existing socialism," both then and now. These threads and questions all center on a few deceptively simple questions which form the unifying theme of this volume: can one drop out of socialism? To what extent can one ignore the society in which one lives? The answers point to the difficulty of subversion within the Eastern bloc, and to what extent dropping out was possible under state socialism.

## "BETTER DEAD THAN UNIFORM": PUNK AND ITS IDEOLOGICAL IMBRICATION WITH THE DICTATORSHIP

Punk quickly arrived in Germany on the heels of its more famous relatives in the US and UK.[2] Having discovered it in the winter of 1976–1977, German youths responded to the new style and sound and hastily began imitating their Anglo-American elders.[3] By 1978 there were flourishing local scenes in Düsseldorf, Hamburg, Hanover, and West Berlin, and in the following year the genre crossed the Berlin Wall to the GDR. Learning about punk via the Western media, Eastern punks began carving out scenes in Erfurt, Weimar, Leipzig, and East Berlin.[4] Over the course of 1979, punk went national in West Germany with concerts, recordings, and publicity spreading the genre. Punks fashioned thriving scenes rooted in subcultural institutions like independent record stores, alternative clubs, and the fanzine press. By 1980–1981 one can likewise speak of a smaller but national scene in the GDR with membership hovering around a couple thousand, especially in the bigger cities. Attracting adherents tired of the uniformity of socialist society, bands played illegal shows in squatted apartments, basements, and attics, made music on cheap or self-made instruments and sang songs condemning the tyranny that ruled them.

One means of exploring whether punk "ignored dictatorship" is by examining some of the ideals and practices which helped constitute the subculture. Ideologically, Eastern punk was conceived in terms of freedom, of a striving toward independence, and a rebellion against the political order and its society. While anti-consumerism and the loss of independence associated with mass consumerism marked punk in the West, these considerations were of secondary concern for Eastern punks.[5] Rather, it was the authoritarian political system and corresponding societal conservatism under SED leader Erich Honecker (1971–1989) that drew youths to punk. In the East the entire political regime and state system was based on a series of falsehoods: the SED ruled in the name of the people; it was an anti-fascist state while West Germany was the continuation of Nazism; the GDR would surpass the West socially, economically, and morally; dissent was the work of wreckers and Western agitators, etc. Youths believed that punk could divorce them from the lies propagated by the SED by actively re-imagining a community that rejected oppression as a means of social and state organization. Punk music, lyrics, behavior, dress, and ideals were means of dramatizing dissatisfaction with the SED-dominated state and society. By engineering an alternative space to live their lives in ways they found to be authentic, individuals sought in punk cultural, social, and ideological emancipation from the oppression and conformity that they believed dominated the GDR under Honecker.

These concerns were manifested in punk rejection of the state and its ideology. As one Eastern punk explained in a rare pamphlet recording conversations with East Berlin youths from the early 1980s, punk was understood as a "type of protest" and a deliberate "rejection of the state, as it exists at the moment."[6] At the forefront, then, punk protested the misuse of power and criminal methods practiced by the SED state. What displeased punks most was the deceitfulness of a state that demanded obedience but would not or could not offer what youths wanted. As a member of the early East Berlin band Planlos complained, "I find it absolute nonsense that we always express our trust and they [the state] don't, and power is maintained through such deceitfulness."[7] While punk was but a small subculture, nonetheless, these beliefs were widespread among segments of the East German population by the 1980s: as scholars have elsewhere noted, youth disillusionment was less about socialism or living in the GDR than hatred of the SED and the way it ruled as the statement above—"as it exists at the moment"—suggests.[8]

In the West early punks cried "no future" because they lacked future prospects. But in the East youths instead complained of "too much future" because the future was seemingly set in stone: shuttled from school to work until retirement after decades of service to the state, youths in the GDR had very little time or space to strike out on their own.[9] Education policy in the GDR was designed to transform youths into "socialist personalities" who could then contribute to the historic victory of communism, with textbooks and teaching methods meant to inculcate East German patriotism, hatred of the Western enemy, and the superiority of socialism.[10] But for youths attracted to punk, school, the FDJ, and state youth culture were an enemy to be despised because of its state-controlled nature and demands for total conformity. As "Mike" explained to *Der Spiegel* in 1982, "This whole upbringing to become a machine . . . the whole state-run youth scene makes me sick. There is nothing there. So boring. When I think about our discotheques, I think: puke!"[11] The regimentation and uniformity pervading the GDR made punk appealing to those who thought or wanted to behave differently. Jörg Löffler, founder of the Dresden-based band Paranoia, later explained that discovering punk music on the radio was a release from the crush of the collective: "For me and a few of my schoolmates, the English program on RTL [Radio Luxembourg], that . . . was *the discovery.* At last, music that was acceptable. No pop, no Schlager, no disco, we didn't want to do the same as the other 90 percent of our class."[12] These comments point to how socialist modernity was a major impetus driving youths to punk, and are summed up in the punk slogan "Better dead than uniform" (*Lieber sterben als genormt sein*).[13]

The concern with individuality and rejection of the collective was expressed most visibly in punk couture. A crucial element of the punk subculture, appearances functioned as a means of reflecting one's attitude and authentic inner self.[14] As a member of Planlos explained, "Attitude and appearances go together; one cannot separate them from each other."[15] This belief in the unity of body and attitude was central to punk's dramatic appearances. So important was this belief that fashion became a barometer for one's commitment to the subculture as well as a means of policing the subculture: as another youth put it, "those who don't go around looking like that [like a punk] are not punks, and those who go around looking like a punk but somehow without having the correct attitude, then they are not punks either, everything has to really mesh together."[16] Early on, dressing in out-of-date clothes, and mixing and matching different styles were all attempts to shock the observer. Tight suits and outrageous shirts that mixed gender sensibilities were likewise all part of the program. Boots were often military. Clothes were ripped and torn with pins, patches, or chains sewn on. Shirts and pants could be colorful to separate the individual from the "normals" in society. Sometimes pants or shirts were adorned with strips of faux fur. Jackets could be denim but defaced, pierced with spikes and bits of metal and full of bands' names or slogans written in marker or paint across the back. Hair was cut short and rough to distinguish punks from hippies and workers. While Eastern punk fashions also succumbed to the ritualized look as conformity took over by the mid-1980s—leather or vinyl jackets, black jeans, and spiky hair—nonetheless, these styles set punks off from everyday East Germans and upset authorities who placed great stock in uniform collectivity.

"Too much future" was also a direct challenge to those ideals underwriting the GDR. Enshrined as the first article of the GDR constitution, work was both a goal and a responsibility of all GDR citizens, and "too much future" represented a clear negation of work as a central category of national identity and societal structure. As a key propaganda claim in the contest against Western capitalism, full employment levels in the GDR were often proclaimed in contrast to the millions of unemployed in the FRG. But by the late 1970s and 1980s, work had begun to lose its integrative hold on youths: to borrow Jonathan Zatlin's felicitous phrase, many felt they were "living to work, rather than working to live."[17] Contemporary East German studies likewise concluded that identification with work had been weakening among youths throughout the 1970s and 1980s.[18] That work was an obligation was a major stumbling block pushing some young people toward punk: as one East Berlin punk claimed, it was "not my goal to always work like that, to always live like that, of course, I go to work because it's practical for my needs, it's a necessity, I must earn money in order to live but I would like to be somehow more involved than simply this need."[19] In contrast, punk ideology stressed that there was more to life than simply working and should instead be rooted in singular experiential experiences and meaningful communal bonds. Despite living in a Marxist state that sought to ease the burdens of industrial labor, young punks expressed clear cases of alienation: as one youth observed, "When I go to work, there I have no goal that I am actually working for."[20] Band names similarly condemned the ideals and reality of the GDR work regime: Planlos ("no plan" or "without a plan") registered the overabundance of planning in the GDR and the gap between planning and actuality; Betonromantik ("concrete romance") was a compound-word critique of the SED's infatuation with concrete as a modern building material; and Papierkrieg ("red tape," literally: "paper war") claimed their name was an ironic aside about GDR bureaucracy and the amount of paper necessary to navigate "really existing socialism."[21]

It was not work itself which punks hated, but rather the specific kinds of work which the GDR favored and which to them entailed no personal growth or satisfaction or room for creativity. As a state whose authority stemmed directly from the proletariat, the SED (over)emphasized the industrial sector of the economy, which over the decades had difficulty competing with Western models and whose workers became less convinced of their role as the makers of history.[22] As one youth explained during the early 1980s, "If everyone had a job that they had fun at, then one couldn't say that one hates work."[23] What upset punks most about the work regime of the GDR was the belief that one's youth and individuality were being wasted working for the benefit of a state which gave nothing in return: as an East Berlin punk put it, succinctly highlighting where he put value during the day, "above all, one works and does everything and then one is still exhausted during free time."[24] The resignation and regret expressed in the Western slogan "no future" was likewise claimed by frustrated Easterners: "For the things that you somehow really want to achieve, you have no future, which is a fact, you won't achieve them as a matter of course. I understand 'no future' just the way it's said: that one really has no future for his things."[25] As another punk lamented, "I had so much to experience but I wasn't going to be able to do anything at all."[26]

Rejection of work took varied forms. Stasi reports on punks are replete with details about punks' questionable work ethics. One Dresden punk had his work discipline described as "poor" and he was labeled a "loafer."[27] Employed punks often skipped work and accusations (not necessarily unfounded) of sabotage were legion: a young East Berlin punk working in a grocery store was sent to prison for slipping pacifist poems into customer shopping bags.[28] Co-workers complained about their behavior or dress, and punks were often subject to disciplinary meetings.[29] Rejection of work went so far that punks who met at the Erlöserkirche in East Berlin used steel rods to break their pinkie fingers in order to spend eight weeks off work collecting insurance. Finger-breaking became so prevalent after 1983 that once the MfS got wind of the operation, it sentenced a number of youths to jail.[30]

When punks did work, they were often employed in jobs not directly linked to the planned socialist economy. Many punks, for example, found work in Evangelical churches as general workers or ushers.[31] Part-time work was desirable though, since working for a couple of hours a day allowed for considerable leisure time. And thanks to the generous subsidies of the socialist state, which guaranteed basic necessities such as shelter and food, youths could live adequately with only a minimum of work, leaving them time to engage in their subcultural activities, pointing to yet another way in which punk was helped by the socialist dictatorship.

The many ideas and practices that the subculture constituted itself around, suggest that dictatorship played an important role in the ideational and everyday world of Eastern punks. Whether it was clothing that sought to highlight conformity, activities that endeavored to break from the uniformed mass, or a rejection of work that clashed with the foundations of the state, the SED dictatorship was ever-present in shaping Eastern punk praxis. At the same time, punk was well suited to "really existing socialism." Its DIY aesthetic corresponded well sartorially with a society used to shortages, and the ample free time which the heavily subsidized state made possible allowed youths in the GDR to engage in subcultural goings-on. As Katherine Verdey has detailed about Romania, communist regimes sought to seize "time" from their citizens to prevent activity that might undermine state power.[32] This was likewise the case in East Germany where socialist volunteering such as the duties of the FDJ—meetings, awards, parades, etc.—were intended to occupy blocks of time and thereby prevent youngsters from engaging in any forms of youthful dalliances that might lead to dissent or active opposition.

But as just detailed, punks were also able to "seize" time from the regime in order to pursue activities frowned upon by the state. That punk individualism and spontaneity were in natural opposition to the extreme regimentation and uniformity that SED socialism sought to inculcate in its youth meant that punk was almost *a priori* an "enemy of the state." And such opposition was important for young punks because reaction was a significant component of the subculture with one East Berlin punk clearly remembering the transformation from conformist citizen to alternative outsider: "Then I cut my hair short and took one of my father's sweaters, cut it up and so on, and then put it on. . . . And at that time, I walked through the streets with real self-confidence even if people were staring at me."[33] Others too have recorded these feelings of exhilaration at being the object of observation: as Sven Marquardt has recorded, to be a punk and to be taken seriously and truthfully meant to engage in confrontation with the society in which one lived.[34] And yet at the same time, such confrontations, reactions, and the building of self-confidence could only possible in a society which was not "ignored."

## SUBCULTURE AND THE STASI: PUNK AND
## THE POLITICS OF ENTANGLEMENT

One of the more contentious aspects of the Eastern punk subculture was its relationship with the state security apparatus, the Stasi. As one of the dominant themes populating the genre's music, punks were incredibly critical of the security system in the GDR and especially the secret police, which formed the backbone of the repressive order.[35] In songs like Namenlos' "MfS-Lied," in which the Stasi were listening in on the singer's telephone call ("I phone my buddy—but there's someone else on the line!") before being compared with the Nazis ("Watch out, you're being watched—by the Mf Mf SS!"), punks spoke out about the oppressive tactics of the state security and its problematic continuity with German history. And yet, despite such criticism, from very early on, punk was completely penetrated by the Stasi with groups of youths containing one or more informers while bands were filled with members writing multiple reports from different angles about the same events, unbeknownst to one another. In a state in which one in seven members of the general population had some sort of link with the Stasi, the number is perhaps higher in the Eastern punk scene, and certainly in the illegal punk bands, the figure is closer to one in four.[36] But questions remain: does informing on your fellow citizens constitute state collaboration and thus imbrication? How can one ignore dictatorship if one is writing reports for it? But what we are going to see is that while the punk scene was almost wholly co-opted by the MfS, in peculiar ways many punks were able to keep the state at a distance, and in fact use Stasi collaboration to further subcultural ends, in many cases against the express desires and objectives of the state. This ambiguous process of push and pull makes any definitive conclusions about ignoring dictatorship difficult, but this shifting relationship nonetheless seems to have been the experience of alternative youths during the last decade of socialism in the GDR.

Punk was not the first musical subculture that the state had to come to terms with as the GDR had a long and fraught history with popular music. In the first two decades of the state's existence, the SED had sought to create its own socialist, popular music styles and dances in an effort to combat the penetration of Western rock'n'roll, which communist authorities deemed degenerate and subversive.[37] But by the early 1960s, the overwhelming popularity of Western rock'n'roll and the inability of socialists to develop a popular, alternative, socialist form, meant that the SED grudgingly pursued a partial acceptance of Beat bands—the name was meant to separate them from Western rock'n'roll—and began sponsoring them as part of its reconciliation with youth following the building of the Berlin Wall in 1961. However, the initiative backfired as the Beat bands became incredibly popular—and to socialist authorities quite disruptive—and when a Rolling Stones concert in West Berlin in 1965 ended in riots, Eastern hardliners moved to suppress the Beat movement. In October 1965 the SED Central Committee ruled to ban Beat groups and the Eastern media began attacking Beat bands and their fans for their decadent and Western-inspired activity.[38] In protest, on October 30, 1965 up to six hundred Beat musicians and fans took to the Leipzig streets only to be beaten and dispersed by police in the infamous Leipzig Beat Riots.[39] At the 11th Party Plenum of the SED in December 1965, future SED Party Chairman Erich Honecker famously condemned the "destructive tendencies" in that decade's East German art and throughout the 1970s Beat music and its outshoots like blues-rock were officially condemned and its fans criminalized.[40]

These methods of carrot and stick were likewise employed with punk. Officially, the regime publicly denied that the music genre could even exist in the GDR. In a series of official statements that appeared in the press toward the end of the 1970s, socialist authorities claimed that punk was the embodiment of capitalism's built-in inequalities: a manifestation of both the hopelessness experienced by those living in this society such as drug-use and of economic exploitation such as mass unemployment.[41] And since the GDR was a classless society built upon utopian equality and moral justice, punk could not exist in the "workers' and farmers' state." Any appearance of punk in the GDR, according to internal memoranda circulated by the Stasi, was considered "imitation" of Western styles and thinking, and a threat to the socialist order.[42] Of course, as we have just seen, much of what drove Eastern punk was specifically related to the conditions of "really existing socialism." But the use of the public press to condemn Western punk did not go as planned for the SED since young Easterners were often introduced to punk for the first time by articles appearing in *Junge Welt* and *Neues Leben*. Many punks remember these images and texts as their first taste of the subculture, encounters that produced fascination and allure which led to transformation, in fact conversion, which the dictatorship ultimately aided unwittingly.[43]

Yet behind the public façade of official denial, authorities were quickly compelled to account for punks who began appearing across the GDR in the late 1970s. At first, punks were undistinguishable from other forms of "negative-decadent youths," as the regime categorized all those who through appearances or behavior contradicted the norms of propriety for socialist society.[44] "Negative-decadent youths" included Blues fans, Gammlers, Trampers, hippies, the unemployed, alcoholics, rowdies, all those who were not contributing to the building of socialism in the proper manner and who were looked upon by regime authorities as asocials or subversives.[45] Thus, in the late 1970s it was predominately the criminal police who dealt with punks for a variety of usually petty infractions such as disturbing the socialist order.[46] But these violations and police attention were usually the result of individual acts (such as voicing anti-state statements), and not a result of belonging to the subculture per se, and it was only in the early 1980s, when the Eastern punk scene began to coalesce into a national entity, that the genre and its members became the focus of Stasi concern. Especially in late 1981, when punk was transferred to the Stasi division charged with combating the political opposition, a shift of authority broadening and increasing the dangerousness of the genre, did the subculture become the focus of heightened state concern.[47]

The shift of authority for combating punk meant not only increased danger for youths involved in the scene, but also the deep entangling of the subculture with the dictatorship. In the early 1980s the Eastern punk scene had expanded to a national entity with local scenes in various cities surrounding illegal bands (groups not officially registered with the authorities). Whereas previously concerts had taken place in practice spaces, squats, or attic spaces, in 1981 the first concerts began to occur in Protestant churches, as part of the latter's youth outreach programs. Soon, youths were traveling across the country to attend infrequent shows, or to meet in East Berlin on the weekends, especially at the Kulturpark, the amusement park in the Plänterwald. The emergence of such a public and oppositional subculture was greeted with alarm by state authorities. In 1983, after a series of newspaper reports appeared in the West on Eastern punk and several incendiary public punk shows took place, the East German state moved "Härte gegen Punk" (Hard against Punk) and tried to break the subculture, arresting prominent members of the scene, drafting others into the army, and forcibly shipping troublesome youths out of the country.[48] Meeting the growing subculture with force, state action against punk halved the number of adherents to slightly less than a thousand, marginalized members from existing public spaces and social relations, broke up a number of illegally existing bands, and penetrated local scenes with informers.[49]

In this context of heightened public prominence, the Stasi began to recruit members of the punk scene to act as informers (IMs), and over the course of the decade the MfS was able to fully penetrate the East German punk scene with dozens if not hundreds of spies. As a number of internal Stasi memorandum made clear, the use of informers would allow the state to neutralize any potential threat which punk might present by taking "preventative measures" to curb any manifestation of anti-socialist behavior or anti-state activity.[50] Especially targeted by the Stasi were the so-called "härte Kern" (hardcore) of the subculture which meant leaders in local scenes ("Rädelführer"), and members of the illegal punk bands. In this endeavor the Stasi was incredibly successful in infiltrating Eastern punk groups: reading the list of bands with at least one member working for the Stasi at one time or another reads like a who's who of East German punk. Organizers and important members of the more political punk scenes—such as those youths who were a part of the AlösA group that met at the Erlöserkirche in East Berlin Rummelsburg or those involved with the Jugend-Gemeinde (church youth group) Stadtmitte in Jena—were similarly targeted as the various Stasi circulars on punk suggest.

As with all informers, a variety of motives help to explain why some worked for the Stasi, and for punks, they can generally be broken down into three categories. First and foremost, fear must be foregrounded as one of the primary reasons for collaboration. Young and usually threatened with arrest, punks were pressured by Stasi officers with threats of future difficulties if they did not agree to work with the state. IM "Biafra" is a case in point. Coming into view of the MfS after being arrested along with other punks in Halle-Neustadt for listening publicly to anti-state punk songs, a search of his bedroom at his parents' house turned up nearly two dozen illegal cassettes. Receiving probation instead of jail time, "Biafra" was shaken by his narrow escape, as indicated by his nearly complete break with punks following his arrest. Afterwards, the Stasi worked to bring "Biafra" into the fold. During a series of contact meetings with MfS officers, his arrest and the cassettes were raised a number of times during their conversations and while the threats remained unspoken, they were nonetheless implicit. Yielding to the intimidation, "Biafra" agreed to work with the MfS and to spy on Halle-based punks.[51]

Others were motivated by ideological beliefs, convictions nurtured expertly by Stasi handlers. IM "Berry," perhaps the longest-running informer in the East Berlin punk scene is an eminent example here. Interrogated after attempting to travel illegally to Prague for a motorcycle race, "Berry" began reporting on his fellow East Berlin punks in 1982. Considered "reliable and honest" by the Stasi, "Berry" had a "fundamentally positive attitude toward the social conditions in the GDR" and the trust built up between him and his MfS contact was strong.[52] According to his file, "Berry" worked with the MfS because of "conviction," and was "pleased about the conversations," asking only "whether it will always be like that, that he ['Berry'] can address all of his problems" to his Stasi contacts.[53] The MfS in turn stoked "Berry's" fears about emerging nationalism within the punk subculture. Outlining their concerns to "Berry," the Stasi convinced him that the enemy was trying to build a Skinhead opposition movement in the GDR through the use of the Western mass media.[54] Recognizing the uncertainty in "Berry," his doubts about punk and state motives, the Stasi exploited them to the hilt: "His motives are mainly the prevention of hostile political activities, [and] he showed an absolute rejection against Skinheads and Nazi-punks."[55] In subsequent meetings, the MfS hammered home the state's ideological position, discussing with "Berry" the pros and cons of socialism, and the necessity of vigilance and collaboration against any form of nationalist activity to overcome his occasional hesitancy.[56] Throughout the rest of the 1980s "Berry" would report on his fellow scene members.

Does the deep imbrication of various punks and the Stasi mean that youths felt oppressed by their cooperation with the state security? This complex question cuts to the heart of the complexities of ignoring dictatorship and the difficulty of dropping out of socialism because it points to the third motive behind punk's relationship with the state: for many youths, the MfS was a means of acquiring privileges as they used the MfS to secure benefits that otherwise were unobtainable. Nearly every punk IM received money or favors from the Stasi and the state security office became an important source of income for the subculture—at 50 or 100 marks at a time these sums were significant for teenagers.[57] IM "Michael Müller," for example, less a punk than a free jazz musician whose apartment became a central meeting place for the alternative scene in Dresden, had thousands of marks worth of musical equipment bought for him by the MfS.[58] "Biafra" was given blank cassettes in exchange for his cooperation.[59] IM "Käpt'n" used subversion to destroy Wutanfall in exchange for support from the Stasi in acquiring an apartment.[60] IM "Dominique" sought to emigrate from the GDR and believed that working for the MfS would help his application.[61] Using cooperation with the Stasi as a means of securing privileges, punks actively sought to use state fear of the subculture to make gains, a reversal suggesting that manipulating the dictatorship played as much a role in the creation of the Eastern punk scene as ignoring it.

Involvement with the Stasi, moreover, was not set in stone, as punk informers were a constant thorn in the side of the state security. Punks would continually miss meetings with their officers, tell others that they were now informers, and ignore specific instructions, all of which defeated the purpose and power of silent subversion.[62] While a number of bands were broken up, new bands were formed almost immediately, often from members of the recently disbanded group.[63] In fact, being IMs did not seem to stop youths from playing in punk bands or trying to release music, write articles for Western fanzines, or engage in other subversive activities. Dieter "Otze" Ehrlich from Schleim-Keim, for example, was an IM for the Stasi at various points during the 1980s, though his intractable behavior (releasing GDR punk in the West) and demands for money (his primary motive), meant the state received next to nothing from its investment in him.[64] The behavior of punks toward their Stasi controllers and the steady exasperation of the MfS toward their charges indicate that the security apparatus recognized the limited advantages gained by punk IMs. Even as loyal an informer as "Berry" needed continuous reinforcement by his MfS controllers in order to, "build up the political motivation for his actions."[65] In fact, some did not even think about the Stasi despite our present-day assumptions about the pervasiveness of MfS surveillance that narratives of the GDR as a "Stasiland" seem to suggest.[66]

Nor does persecution or the heavy hand of the security apparatus—when it was deployed against youths—seem to have been experienced entirely oppressively: in fact, there is some evidence that suggests a certain amount of ambiguity (understanding?) felt by some punks toward the repressive mechanisms of the state and perhaps even a little pleasure as well. While certainly many youths did not enjoy the frequent violence visited upon them by the police or the GDR citizenry, some nonetheless seem to have enjoyed their "outsider status" even embracing the martyrdom which accompanied the status of a "negative-decadent youth": as one East Berlin punk explained disapprovingly, "A martyr role has spread very widely among the punks, to rush headlong into disaster, and that is bullshit."[67] For others, punk was a game to be played with the state, in which youths took on the role of the oppressed while seeking to outwit the oppressors: as Mike Göde, former singer from the East Berlin band Reasors Exzess, remembered with a grin in the documentary film *ostPUNK!*, a weekend without an encounter with the police meant an uneventful weekend.[68] In certain ways punk enabled youths to strike back at the state, an act of defiance which separated them from the docile and conformist crowd they condemned. Marquardt, for example, has remembered that perhaps because they were not involved in any serious acts of subversion (though some punks were and did spend significant time in jail), they viewed police action against them with a certain amount of casualness.[69] And as Peter "Flake" Lorenz, keyboardist for Feeling B and later famously of Rammstein, reminded us—pointing to the politics of authenticity at work within the punk subculture—in the East, one wanted to be taken seriously by the Stasi.[70] So while Eastern punks railed against the East German state, some nonetheless enjoyed their pariah status and took pleasure in their combative relationship with the dictatorship. Indeed, punk's move to legality slightly prior to the collapse of East Germany caused considerable disorientation among Eastern punks both before and after reunification.

While "Härte gegen Punk" had a devastating effect on the Eastern scene, it also produced a number of unexpected outcomes that in fact worked against the objectives of the SED.[71] Most consequentially, "Härte gegen Punk" drove Eastern punks into the Evangelical churches where youth outreach programs provided them with a measure of protection against coercive state action.[72] Once ensconced under the roofs of Protestant churches, punks were socialized into the oppositional politics of the burgeoning dissident groups then gathering there, and began participating in the various ventures—human rights concerns, environmentalism, social justice, women's issues, pacifism—that members of the small GDR opposition were pursuing in an attempt to undermine the political legitimacy of the SED. Recognizing the danger which their policies had created and the pressing need to rethink state youth policies in the wake of youth violence at the end of 1987, the SED reworked its strategy against punk.[73] Thus, in February 1988, in an effort to use popular music to prop up its crumbling regime, the SED abruptly reversed its position and began supporting a host of new alternative groups called "die anderen Bands" (the other bands). Integrating punk into the state music industry, the SED hoped to blunt punk criticisms by flooding the market with this new music while also shoring up its waning political legitimacy through cultural bribes.

Playing on the radio, appearing in print and on screen, recording on the state record label Amiga, and playing live in FDJ-Jugendklubs (youth clubs), punk surged into the East German music industry after years of exclusion. Predictably, bands such as Hard Pop, Die Vision, Feeling B, Sandow, and Die Skeptiker became the sights and sounds of late GDR and Wende-era popular music for Easterners and former Easterners. Through inclusion the SED hoped to depoliticize the subculture while at the same time mobilize popular music to generate support for its increasingly unpopular regime. By adding the carrot to the stick, the SED leadership hoped that linking punk to the state would facilitate some measure of control over the previously independent scene that coercion had failed to break. Permitting punks to play in FDJ-Jugendklubs also meant drawing strength away from the churches and it was hoped that state integration would dull anti-state criticism. For Eastern punks, integration signaled opportunities to record, play live, expand fan bases, and, in several cases, even tour in the West. But opportunity also meant compromise: if Eastern punk was inspired ideologically by a hatred of the state, could Eastern punks remain critical while playing on state radio, performing on state stages, recording in state studios, or collecting a state salary?

As this question suggests, the emergence of "die anderen Bands" produced a crisis for East German punk. Could an anti-state subculture accept support from the state? Ideologically constructed on regime hatred, state integration meant that the subculture faced charges of hypocrisy. Some youths responded with outrage. Tainted by association with the hated regime, "die anderen Bands" were viewed by some as opportunists and tarred with the brush of inauthenticity. Nor was it clear whether the SED gained any cache from supporting "die anderen Bands." Bands like Die Skeptiker continued to lambast the SED in sarcastic and subversive lyrics, such as the band's celebration of the avant-garde that challenged convention in its song "Dada in Berlin" but which also could be (and was) read as an attack on the socialist project: "As it once was/so it could not remain the same/They wanted to violently drive/the society ever forwards." As Patricia Anne Simpson has argued, these bands were crucial in eroding the political legitimacy of the SED from within state structures because they carved out space from which to criticize the dictatorship.[74] Did punks allowed to scream subversive lyrics ten times more often in FDJ-Jugendklubs than in churches constitute dropping out? Was recording on the state record label Amiga an act of "ignoring dictatorship"? Or was "ignoring dictatorship" less the work of those in the past than Götze would have it and more the work of those in the present?

## PUNK ARCHIVES: "DIE ANDEREN BANDS" AND USEABLE MEMORY IN REUNIFIED GERMANY

These questions highlight an important conundrum involved in dropping out: can subcultures ignore the society into which they are embedded? And what we will see is that Moritz Götze's formulation speaks to efforts at controlling Eastern punk memory in the post-reunification era rather than being an explanation of the period that they purport to describe. Since the fall of the Berlin Wall, the memory of punk in Germany has grown by leaps and bounds. Through these endeavors to archive the genre, young Germans (and now not-so-young Germans), use punk as a means of making sense of their burdensome pasts, uncertain presents, and complicated futures. Overwhelmingly, punk memory focuses on the first few years of the subculture in the GDR, as punk is remembered in glowing terms, with punks as "good Germans" in the face of a corrupt and compromised society, a subculture that retained its authenticity and uncompromised character. In documenting punk as a form of political opposition, former Easterners attempt to recuperate the genre as a resisting movement even after it had been tainted by revelations that a number of punks worked for the secret police as informers. As such, it is the first generation of punks who are the gatekeepers of punk memory and who work assiduously to deny entities—such as "die anderen Bands"—who might disrupt such straightforward narratives. These efforts complicate Götze's suggestion, or, at any rate, suggest that "ignoring dictatorship" is more the work of the present than the past.

The fall of the Berlin Wall provoked mixed reactions among Eastern punks.[75] Some had been committed participants in the mass protests and welcomed their newly fought-for freedom. Others were less interested in the historic events.[76] With an ideology rooted in anti-capitalism, quite a few punks considered the Federal Republic to be more or less the same as the GDR; different discrimination, but intolerance and inequality nonetheless. Many crossed the previously shut border after 1989 to receive the *Begrüßungsgeld* (welcome money) offered by Western authorities to newly arrived Germans, which they promptly spent on records, sound systems, and equipment they had been unable to acquire in the GDR.[77] However, these tourists rarely settled in the West and many punks who did move to West Germany often returned to the former East. A number felt that they did not belong in the old Western portions of the now reunited Germany and believed that their interests were better understood among former Easterners.[78]

Much more interesting to former Eastern punks were the musical opportunities that arose with the collapse of the Eastern state. Anglo-American
and West German outfits suddenly had seventeen million more potential
fans who had waited patiently for years to see them play, and Western bands
poured across the former border; symbolic was Roger Waters' epic staging
of *The Wall* on the former "no-man's land" where the Berlin Wall had stood
between Potsdamer Platz and the Brandenburg Gate, attended by close to
half a million people on July 21, 1990.[79] Eastern punk bands likewise took
advantage of the dense West German touring circuit, appearing in clubs and
independent youth centers in front of audiences that had never seen or heard
Ostpunk before.[80] West German record labels such as HöhNIE Records and
Nasty Vinyl started recording Eastern punk bands such as Schleim Keim and
Müllstation.[81] And an explosion of fanzines and music magazines erupted
in the former Eastern states long denied such freedom of expression. The
confusion surrounding national and municipal authority in the immediate
post-Wall period meant that squats and illegal concert spaces were set up in
Friedrichshain and Prenzlauer Berg in Berlin or in the Connewitz neighborhood in Leipzig.[82]

But the East-West punk exchange, like other East-West exchanges during this period, was unequal to say the least. Backed by Western money,
equipment, marketing, and production, Western outfits were able to dominate the former Eastern music scene. Moreover, the collapse of the state
was disorienting for those Eastern bands that had relied on it since, as state
employees, musicians now no longer received their salaries. Amiga, the only
East German record label, for example, was bought by BMG (now part of
Sony) along with the entire back catalog in 1991. Perhaps most crucial was
the inability of Eastern bands and Western audiences to communicate with
one another. The lyrical themes that Eastern bands emphasized in their songs
were difficult for Western audiences to relate to: in the West, for example,
criticism of the SED, obviously, did not have the same resonance. And since
Eastern bands had understood themselves in opposition to the state and constructed their identities around this antagonism, the sudden disappearance of
the state was confusing. As "Flake" told *Der Spiegel* recently, "In the years
after the Wall everything was dead. Due to the regime change, we somehow
no longer had an enemy and thus no orientation."[83] This uncertainty affected
many former Easterners who could not reconcile their past identities with
their present circumstances.

Compounding these issues were the damaging revelations emerging from
the archives of the former East German state, especially from the secret
police files.[84] As a number of influential politicians, church officials, and dissidents turned out to be informants, so too did a number of prominent punks.
The Stasi had wholly penetrated the East German punk scene and bands as

we have seen. Nor were they marginal figures but individuals central to the scene. Sascha Anderson, who had helped record the *DDR von unten/eNDe* album (one of the only GDR punk albums ever recorded during the 1980s) and smuggle it west, was unmasked as a long-time informer.[85] Singer Tatjana Besson and keyboardist Frank Tröger from Die Firma, an influential band during the 1989 revolution, were (unbeknownst to each other) both reporting on the band.[86] And IM "Dominique," the crown jewel of punk informers, turned out to be Imad Abdul Majid in Leipzig, a musician in L'Attentat, and perhaps the most connected punk in the whole GDR.[87]

Revelations of the widespread collaboration with the MfS was a tremendous blow to the authority and integrity of the East German punk scene.[88] Those tarnished by the Stasi brush were condemned and ostracized and the feeling was that the subculture had been betrayed from within. As a resistant subculture priding itself on opposition to the state, the fraud perpetrated by those within the scene was immense and the rancor consuming punk was reflective of wider uncertainty over German reunification, as former Easterners and Westerners questioned whether national reunion had been a good idea. The colonization of the Eastern scene compounded matters. Whereas Western bands had little difficulty in playing in the former East or selling their products to newly enfranchised consumers, the opposite was simply not the case.[89] Most East German punk bands retreated to the former East or broke up and, as the Berlin Republic reasserted control temporarily ceded during the post-Wall era, specific Ostpunk sites such as the influential club der Eimer (Garbage Can) on Rosenthalerstraße in Berlin disappeared.[90] The feeling of loss was expressed perhaps best with a series of compilation albums featuring classics of the East German punk scene released by HöhNIE Records beginning in 1992. The title of this series—*Sicher Gibt Es Bessere Zeiten, Doch Diese War Die Unsere* (Surely There Were Better Times, But These Were Ours)—reflects a bygone era. The fact that a West German record label was needed to record Eastern punk classics however is telling. As the Feeling B song "Ich such' die DDR" (I'm Searching for the GDR) put it so well ("I'm searching for the GDR and no one knows, where it is/It's such a shame that I've forgotten it so quickly"), the quick demise of the nation that youths and bands had called home was sudden and disorienting.

Into this context of betrayal and acrimony, a vibrant East German punk memory culture has emerged. As the fireworks over the Stasi revelations from the early 1990s died down and many of the Ostpunk bands broke up, at the end of the decade and gathering strength in the new millennium, a number of important books, films, and exhibitions have appeared in an effort to rescue punk from the dustbin of history. In 1999 former GDR journalist and radio DJ Ronald Galenza and musician Heinz Havemeister published *Wir wollen immer artig sein . . .* (We were always so well behaved . . .), a landmark collection on the independent alternative scene in the GDR during the 1980s.[91] Featuring chapters written by participants and scholars as well as interviews, and detailing the many city scenes, the book generated significant press, and an expanded version was released several years later.[92] *Wir wollen immer artig sein . . .* was the first of many books that have been published in recent years on East German punk ranging from the biographies of individual punks or bands to depictions of more personal experiences of the Ostpunk scene such as the memoirs by Angela "China" Kowalczyk.[93]

In the new millennium these efforts were redoubled. In 2005 the large exhibition *ostPunk!/Too Much Future* was held in Berlin in an old factory in Prenzlauer Berg, and later iterations appeared in the city museums of Dresden, Halle, Jena, and elsewhere. Like the amount of interest in *Wir wollen immer artig sein . . .*, extraordinary numbers of people visited the exhibition. At the Berlin exhibit, 2,500 people were at the opening and more than 5,000 visited in the first two weeks. The exhibit catalog was sold out on the opening night prompting a revised and extended edition that was translated into several languages.[94] Organized by former Eastern punks Michael Boehlke and Henryk Gericke, the goal of the exhibition was to show the German public a glimpse of subcultural life in the GDR. In 2007 a cinematic version *ostPUNK!/too much future* that mixed talking heads, photos, and rare Super 8 clips from films recorded in the early 1980s was released to critical acclaim.[95] The resonance these retrospectives have generated has been vast and convinced a number of former Eastern bands such as Müllstation and Sandow to reform and release records.[96] Nor do these efforts appear to be slowing down: in November 2012 the Staatsgalerie Prenzlauer Berg hosted an exhibition on Eastern punk photography featuring amateurs and professionals called East End: Punks in the GDR, and in July 2015 an exhibition on fan culture in popular music opened at the Künstlerhaus Bethanien featuring a number of ex-GDR punk artists.[97]

## CONCLUSIONS

While the GDR punk scene never had more than two thousand members, demand for Ostpunk in reunited Germany remains high. How to explain the widespread appeal of Eastern punk? How does this mass appeal relate to "ignoring dictatorship"? In line with other cultural phenomena such as films, cookbooks, or fashion shows that are grouped under the phenomenon of *Ostalgie*, Ostpunk is part of a large wave of sensibilities and material culture that looks back nostalgically on the GDR and celebrates a way of life now gone.[98] The appeal of East German punk in this instance is that it represents a different East Germany, a resistant East Germany, an East Germany that remains uncorrupted by collaboration and is most defiantly not "a footnote in world history."[99] Crucial here is the complete exclusion from this memory culture of "die anderen Bands," those state-supported bands from the final hours of the GDR, because by relegating punk to the pre-"Härte gegen Punk" era, Eastern punk memory is able to retain an oppositional character which "die anderen Bands" threaten. In proclaiming the death of punk in 1983, this memory culture is able to avoid uncomfortable questions about Stasi complicity or state salaries. The politics of authenticity are essential in this respect. After "Härte gegen Punk," "real punk" died and "die anderen Bands" are not "genuine" since they worked with the hated state that Eastern punk ideology denied. It remains to be seen how long Ostpunk memory will be able to exclude "die anderen Bands" from its story. But at a time when much of the GDR—its experiences, successes, goods, architecture, ways of life—is disparaged in reunified Germany and the very traces of the former state are rapidly disappearing, the memory of Ostpunk as an uncorrupted subculture and alternative East Germany acts as an essential ballast for those with an unsteady gait.[100] As "Flake" comments above about the uncertainty of Ostpunk without the state to which it devoted its opposition suggest, Götze's claim that the last generation of East German subcultures "ignored dictatorship" perhaps misses the mark. But the memory of East German punk in many ways tells us more about the politics of memory in the Berlin Republic and about the efforts of former Easterners trying to integrate elements of their pasts into an unforgiving present than it does about the 1970s and 1980s in the German Democratic Republic.

## NOTES

1. Cited in Paul Kaiser, "Wutanfälle und Flugversuche: Wie die DDR zu einer richtigen Boheme im falschen Land kam," in *Die DDR wird 50: Texte und Fotografien*, ed. Volker Handloik and Harald Hauswald (Berlin: Aufbau-Verlag, 1998), 174.

2. On UK punk, see John Robb, *Punk Rock: An Oral History* (Oakland: PM Press, 2012); Clinton Heylin, *Babylon's Burning: From Punk to Grunge* (London: Viking, 2007); and Jon Savage, *England's Dreaming: Anarchy, Sex Pistols, Punk Rock, and Beyond*, rev. ed. (New York: St. Martin's Griffin, 2002). On US punk, see Clinton Heylin, *From the Velvets to the Voidoids: The Birth of American Punk Rock*, updated ed. (Chicago: Chicago Review Press, 2005); Steven Blush, *American Hardcore: A Tribal History* (Los Angeles: Feral House, 2001); and Legs McNeil and Gillian McCain, eds., *Please Kill Me: The Uncensored Oral History of Punk* (London: Abacus, 1997).

3. On West German punk, see Hollow Skai, *Alles nur geträumt: Fluch und Segen der Neuen Deutschen Welle* (Innsbruck: Hannibal, 2009); Frank A. Schneider, *Als die Welt noch unterging: Von Punk zu NDW* (Mainz: Ventil Verlag, 2007); Ulrike Groos,

Peter Gorschlüter, and Jürgen Teipel, eds., *Zurück zum Beton: Die Anfänge von Punk und New Wave in Deutschland 1977–'82* (Cologne: Walther König, 2002); and Jürgen Teipel, *Verschwende Deine Jugend: Ein Doku-Roman über den deutschen Punk und New Wave* (Frankfurt am Main: Suhrkamp, 2001).

    4. On East German punk, see Frank Willmann, ed., *Leck mich am Leben: Punk im Osten* (Berlin: Neues Leben, 2012); Anne Hahn and Frank Willmann, *Satan, kannst du mir noch mal verzeihen: Otze Ehrlich, Schleimkeim und der ganze Rest* (Mainz: Ventil Verlag, 2008); Michael Boehlke and Henryk Gericke, eds., *too much future—Punk in der DDR* (Berlin: Verbrecher Verlag, 2007); Bernd Lindner and Mark M. Westhusen, *Von Müllstation zu Grössenwahn: Punk in der Halleschen Provinz* (Halle: Hasen Verlag, 2007); and Ronald Galenza and Heinz Havemeister, eds., *Wir wollen immer artig sein . . .: Punk, New Wave, HipHop und Independent-Szene in der DDR 1980–1990* (Berlin: Schwarzkopf & Schwarzkopf, 2005).

    5. See Alan O'Connor, *Punk Record Labels and the Struggle for Autonomy: The Emergence of DIY* (Lanham, MD: Lexington Books, 2008); and Stacy Thompson, *Punk Productions: Unfinished Business* (Albany: State University of New York Press, 2004).

    6. Bundesbeauftragte für die Unterlagen des Staatssicherheitsdienstes der ehemaligen DDR (hereafter BStU), Ministerium für Staatssicherheit (hereafter MfS), Hauptabteilung (hereafter HA) XXII, Nr.17742, Erinnerung an eine Jugendbewegung: P U N K, n.d., 2.

    7. BStU, MfS, HA XXII, Nr.17742, Erinnerung an eine Jugendbewegung: P U N K, n.d., 2.

    8. See Anna Saunders, *Honecker's Children: Youth and Patriotism in East(ern) Germany, 1979–2002* (Manchester: Manchester University Press, 2007); and Alan McDougall, *Youth Politics in East Germany: The Free German Youth Movement 1946–1968* (Oxford: Clarendon Press, 2004).

    9. Boehlke and Gericke, *too much future*, 13.

    10. See Saunders, *Honecker's Children*; Benita Blessing, *The Antifascist Classroom: Denazification in Soviet-occupied Germany, 1945–1949* (New York: Palgrave Macmillan, 2006); and John Rodden, *Repainting the Little Red Schoolhouse: A History of Eastern German Education, 1945–1995* (Oxford: Oxford University Press, 2002).

    11. "Auf die Sahne," *Der Spiegel*, June 14, 1982, 59.

    12. Harald Heusner, "Jörg Löffler—ein Punk-pionier aus der DDR," *Trust* no. 77 (1999): n.p.

    13. BStU, MfS, HA XXII, Nr.17742, Erinnerung an eine Jugendbewegung: P U N K, n.d., 11.

    14. On punk fashion, see especially Dick Hebdige, *Subculture: The Meaning of Style* (London: Routledge, 1979). On its Eastern inflections, see Kate Gerrard, "From London to the GDR: Symbols and Clothing in East German Punk," *United Academics Journal of Social Sciences* no. 11 (2012): 56–70.

    15. BStU, MfS, HA XXII, Nr.17742, Erinnerung an eine Jugendbewegung: P U N K, n.d., 9.

    16. BStU, MfS, HA XXII, Nr.17742, Erinnerung an eine Jugendbewegung: P U N K, n.d., 9.

17. Jonathan R. Zatlin, *The Currency of Socialism: Money and Political Culture in East Germany* (London: Cambridge University Press, 2007), 5.

18. See Stiftung Archiv der Parteien und Massenorganisationen der DDR im Bundesarchiv Berlin [hereafter SAPMO-BAB], DY 30/IV 2/2.039/246, Bericht. Zur Lage der Jugend 1988, June 1988.

19. BStU, MfS, HA XXII, Nr.17742, Erinnerung an eine Jugendbewegung: P U N K, n.d., 3.

20. BStU, MfS, HA XXII, Nr.17742, Erinnerung an eine Jugendbewegung: P U N K, n.d., 14.

21. *Atroma*, no. 3 (1989): 17.

22. See for example, Linda Fuller, *Where Was the Working Class? Revolution in Eastern Germany* (Urbana-Champaign: University of Illinois Press, 1999).

23. BStU, MfS, HA XXII, Nr.17742, Erinnerung an eine Jugendbewegung: P U N K, n.d., 14.

24. BStU, MfS, HA XXII, Nr.17742, Erinnerung an eine Jugendbewegung: P U N K, n.d., 14.

25. BStU, MfS, HA XXII, Nr.17742, Erinnerung an eine Jugendbewegung: P U N K, n.d., 13.

26. BStU, MfS, HA XXII, Nr.17742, Erinnerung an eine Jugendbewegung: P U N K, n.d., 14.

27. BStU, MfS, BV Dresden, AIM 2399/89, Bd. I/1, Information, February 25, 1983, 38.

28. Angela Kowalczyk, *Punk in Pankow: Stasi-"Sieg": 16jährige Pazifistin verhaftet!* (Berlin: Anita Tykve Verlag, 1996).

29. BStU, MfS, BV Erfurt, AOP 772/85, Bd. V/1, OV "Blauköpfe," Eröffnungsbericht zum Anlegen des Operativ-Vorganges "Blauköpfe," Reg.-Nr. IX 1412/81 auf der Grundlage des Straftatbestandes der staatsfeindlichen Hetze gemäß § 106 StGB, November 19, 1981, 32–33.

30. See the numerous charges in BStU, MfS, HA IX, Nr. 9828, Urteil Im Namen des Volkes!, 1985, 1–18.

31. Galenza and Heinz Havemeister, *Wir wollen immer artig sein . . .*, 506.

32. See Katherine Verdey, *What Was Socialism, and What Comes Next?* (Princeton: Princeton University Press, 1996), 39–57.

33. BStU, MfS, HA XXII, Nr. 17742, Erinnerung an eine Jugendbewegung: P U N K, n.d., 8.

34. Sven Marquardt with Judka Strittmatter, *Die Nacht ist Leben: Autobiographie* (Berlin: Ullstein, 2014), 92.

35. See Gary Bruce, *The Firm: The Inside Story of the Stasi* (Oxford: Oxford University Press, 2010).

36. John O. Koehler, *Stasi: The Untold Story of the East German Secret Police* (Boulder, CO: Westview Press, 1999), 9.

37. See Wiebke Janssen, *Halbstarke in der DDR: Verfolgung und Kriminalisierung einer Jugendkultur* (Berlin: Links, 2010); Mark Fenemore, *Sex, Thugs and Rock 'n' Roll: Teenage Rebels in Cold-War East Germany* (New York: Berghahn Books, 2009); Toby Thacker, "The Fifth Column: Dance Music in the Early German

Democratic Republic," in *The Workers' and Peasants' State: Communism and Society in East Germany under Ulbricht, 1945–1971*, ed. Patrick Major and Jonathan Osmond (Manchester: Manchester University Press, 2002), 227–43; and Uta Poiger, *Jazz, Rock, and Rebels: Cold War Politics and American Culture in a Divided Germany* (Berkeley: University of California Press, 2000).

38. ZK (Central Committee) decision on October 11, 1965, "Zu einigen Fragen der Jugendarbeit und dem Auftreten der Rowdygruppen." See Bernd Lindner, *DDR: Rock & Pop* (Cologne: Komet Verlag, 2008), 52–53.

39. Lindner, *DDR: Rock & Pop*, 56–57; Michael Rauhut, *Rock in der DDR, 1964 bis 1989* (Bonn: Bundeszentrale für politische Bildung, 2002), 34–36; Mark Fenemore, "The Limits of Repression and Reform: Youth Policy in the Early 1960s," in Major and Osmond, *The Workers' and Peasants' State*, 183–84; Dorothee Wierling, "Youth as Internal Enemy: Conflicts in the Education Dictatorship of the 1960s," in *Socialist Modern: East German Everyday Culture and Politics*, ed. Katherine Pence and Paul Betts (Ann Arbor: University of Michigan Press, 2008), 163.

40. Michael Rauhut and Thomas Kochan, eds., *Bye Bye, Lübben City: Bluesfreaks, Tramps und Hippies in der DDR,* expanded edn. (Berlin: Schwarzkopf & Schwarzkopf, 2009); Günter Agde, ed., *Kahlschalg. Das 11. Plenum des ZK der SED 1965: Studien und Dokumente*, expanded edn. (Berlin: Aufbau, 2000); and Michael Rauhut, *Beat in der Grauzone: DDR-Rock, 1964 bis 1972: Politik und Alltag* (Berlin: BasicDruck, 1993).

41. Jeff Hayton, "'Härte gegen Punk': Popular Music, Western Media, and State Responses in the German Democratic Republic," *German History* 31, no. 4 (2013): 535–42.

42. BStU, MfS, ZAIG 3366, Information über beachtenswerte Erscheinungen unter negativ-dekadenten Jugendlichen in der DDR, May 18, 1984.

43. Boehlke and Gericke, *too much future*, 13–15, and 33.

44. BStU, MfS, ZAIG 3366, Information über beachtenswerte Erscheinungen unter negativ-dekadenten Jugendlichen in der DDR, May 18, 1984.

45. See Sven Korzilius, *'Asoziale' und 'Parasiten' im Recht der SBZ/DDR: Randgruppen im Sozialismus zwischen Repression und Ausgrenzung* (Cologne: Böhlau, 2005), Thomas Lindenberger, *Volkspolizei: Herrschaftspraxis und öffentliche Ordnung im SED-Staat 1952–1968* (Cologne: Böhlau, 2003); and Matthias Zeng, *'Asoziale' in der DDR: Transformationen einer moralischen Kategorie* (Münster: LIT, 2000).

46. For an example, see Marquandt, *Die Nacht ist Leben*, 94–95.

47. Galenza and Havemeister, *Wir wollen immer artig sein . . .*, 40–43 and 140–45.

48. See Hayton, "'Härte gegen Punk,'" 523–49.

49. BStU, MfS, ZAIG 3366, Information über beachtenswerte Erscheinungen unter negativ-dekadenten Jugendlichen in der DDR, May 18, 1984, 4.

50. BStU, MfS, BdL/Dok. 008323, Erscheinungsformen gesellschaftswidrigen Auftretens und Verhaltens negative-dekadenter Jugendlicher, besonders sogenannter Punker, innerhalb der DDR und Maßnahmen zur politisch-operativen Bearbeitung dieses Personenkreises, July 7, 1986, 5.

51. See BStU, MfS, BV Halle, Abt. XX VIII 2003/86, Bd.I/1 and II/1.

52. BStU, MfS, BV Berlin AIM 3772/89, Bd.I/1, Auskunftsbericht, October 27, 1983, 14.

53. BStU, MfS, BV Berlin AIM 3772/89, Bd.I/1, Auskunftsbericht, October 27, 1983, 17; and BStU, MfS, BV Berlin AIM 3772/89, Bd.I/1, Bericht zum zweiten Kontaktgespräch, August 31, 1982, 86.

54. BStU, MfS, BV Berlin AIM 3772/89, Bd.I/1, Bericht über die Kontaktaufnahme zu einem Punk-Fan im Rahmen der Vorbeugungsmaßnahmen zu den Motorrad WM in Brno/CSSR, August 26, 1982, 83–84.

55. BStU, MfS, BV Berlin AIM 3772/89, Bd.I/1, Bericht über die Kontaktaufnahme zu einem Punk-Fan im Rahmen der Vorbeugungsmaßnahmen zu den Motorrad WM in Brno/CSSR, August 26, 1982, 84.

56. BStU, MfS, BV Berlin AIM 3772/89, Bd.I/1, Bericht über die Kontaktaufnahme zu einem Punk-Fan im Rahmen der Vorbeugungsmaßnahmen zu den Motorrad WM in Brno/CSSR, August 26, 1982, 85.

57. See BStU, MfS, BV Leipzig, AIM 2017/88, Bd.I/1, Quittungen über ausgezahlte Beträge und geleistete Sachwerte, n.d., 182.

58. See BStU, MfS, BV Dresden, AIM 392/90, Bd.I/1, Quittung, June 29, 1983, 183.

59. BStU, MfS, BV Halle, Abt.XX VIII 2003/86, Bericht über das 7. Kontaktgesprach, January 27, 1988, 164.

60. BStU, MfS, BV Leipzig, AIM 643/86, Bd.I/1, Vorschlag zur Werbung eines IM im Sicherungsbereich negative-dekadente Jugendliche/Gruppierungen/Punker, July 30, 1983, 115.

61. See BStU, MfS, BV Leipzig, AIM 2017/88, Bd.I/1, Information, August 26, 1988, 203–5.

62. See the repeated breaches in BStU, MfS, BV Leipzig, AIM 2017/88, Bds.I/1 and II/1.

63. For example, after the bassist from Ernst F. All was arrested and jailed for avoiding military service in 1982, the other members of the band went on to form O.T.Z.E. in 1983. See Galenza and Havemeister, *Wir wollen immer artig sein . . .*, 316–18.

64. See Hahn and Willmann, *Satan*, 28–29, 55, and 134–38.

65. BStU, MfS, BV Berlin, AIM 3772.89, Bd.I/1, Bericht über die Kontaktaufnahme zu einem Punk-Fan im Rahmen der Vorbeugungsmaßnahmen zu den Motorrad WM in Brno/CSSR, August 26, 1982, 84.

66. Marquardt, *Die Nacht ist Leben*, 89–91. The term was coined by Anna Funder in her book of the same name: Anna Funder, *Stasiland: Stories from Behind the Berlin Wall* (London: Granta, 2003). For a critique of such a conceptualization, see Hester Vaizey, *Born in the GDR: Living in the Shadow of the Wall* (Oxford: Oxford University Press, 2014).

67. BStU, MfS, HA XXII, Nr.17742, Erinnerung an eine Jugendbewegung: P U N K, n.d., 4.

68. *ostPUNK! Too much future*, DVD, directed by Carsten Fiebeler and Michael Boehlke (Berlin: Good!Movies, 2006).

69. Marquardt, *Die Nacht ist Leben*, 95–98.

70. Thomas Winkler, "Das Herz ist noch das alte," *tageszeitung*, November 7, 2007, 25.

71. See Detlef Pollack, "Modernization and Modernization Blockages in GDR Society" and Ralph Jessen, "Mobility and Blockage during the 1970s," in *Dictatorship as Experience: Towards a Socio-Cultural History of the GDR*, ed. Konrad H. Jarausch, trans. Eve Duffy (New York: Berghahn Books, 2006), 27–45 and 341–60.

72. On punk and the churches, see Kirche von Unten, *Wunder gibt es immer wieder—das Chaos ist aufgebraucht, es war die schönste Zeit: Fragmente zur Geschichte der Offenen Arbeit Berlin und der Kirche von Unten* (Berlin: Eigenverlag, 1997).

73. Jeff Hayton, "Krawall in der Zionskirche: Skinhead Violence and Political Legitimacy in the GDR," *European History Quarterly* 45, no. 2 (2015): 336–56.

74. Patricia Anne Simpson, "Born in the 'Bakschischrepublik': Anthems of the Late GDR," in *Transformations of the New Germany*, ed. Ruth A. Starkman (New York: Palgrave Macmillan, 2006), 89–111.

75. On the events surrounding the fall of the Berlin Wall, see Ilko-Sascha Kowalczuk, *Endspiel: Die Revolution von 1989 in der DDR* (Munich: C. H. Beck, 2009).

76. Hahn and Willmann, *Satan*, 100, and 111–12.

77. See "No Reissbrett: Punk in der DDR," *Ox-Fanzine*, June–July 2007, 121–22.

78. See Thomas Winkler, "Interview with Flake," *Frankfurter Rundschau*, November 9, 2007.

79. See *The Wall: Live in Berlin*, DVD, directed by Ken O'Neill and Roger Waters (1990: New York: Universal Music International, 2004).

80. See *Zap*, October 1990, 3–8.

81. Hahn and Willmann, *Satan*, 80–90.

82. See Ulrich Gutmair, *Die ersten Tage von Berlin: Der Sound der Wende* (Stuttgart: Tropen Bei Klett-Cotta, 2013); Patricia Anne Simpson, "Soundtracks: GDR Music from 'Revolution' to 'Reunification,'" in *The Power of Intellectuals in Contemporary Germany*, ed. Michael Geyer (Chicago: University of Chicago Press, 2001), 227–48; and Connie Remath and Ray Schneider, *Haare auf Krawall: Jugendsubkultur in Leipzig, 1980 bis 1991* (Leipzig: Connewitzer Verlagsbuchhandlung, 1999).

83. Christian "Flake" Lorenz, "Mir fehlt die DDR," *Einestages*, June 13, 2008, n.p.

84. On the history of the Stasi files in post-unification Germany, see Alison Lewis, *Die Kunst des Verrats: Der Prenzlauer Berg und die Staatssicherheit* (Würzburg: Königshausen & Neumann, 2003); Matthias Wagner, *Das Stasi-Syndrom: Über den Umgang mit den Akten des MfS in den 90er Jahren* (Berlin: Edition Ost im Verlag Das Neue Berlin, 2001); and Klaus Michael and Peter Böthig, eds., *MachtSpiele: Literatur und Staatssicherheit im Fokus Prenzlauer Berg* (Leipzig: Reclam, 1993). See also Andrew H. Beattie, *Playing Politics with History: The Bundestag Inquiries into East Germany* (New York: Berghahn Books, 2008).

85. See Konstantin Hanke, "Ostpunk auf Schallplatte," *Ox-Fanzine*, August–September 2007, 120; and Sascha Anderson, "Zwitschermaschine," in *Spannung*.

*Leistung. Widerstand: Magnetband-Kultur in der DDR, 1979–1990*, ed. Alexander Pehlemann and Ronald Galenza (Berlin: Verbrecher Verlag, 1999), 42–51.

86. Galenza and Havemeister, *Wir wollen immer artig sein . . .*, 174–77.

87. See *Zap*, August 1994, 7–8; Interview with Bernd Stracke, *Kalpa Vriksche*, no.1 (n.d.): n.p.; and *Zap*, October 1990, 4–7.

88. Former Easterners are now more understanding of collaboration with the Stasi than they were in the 1990s. See Konstantin Hanke, "Ostpunk auf Schallplatte," 120–21; and "No Reissbrett: Punk in der DDR," 122–23.

89. See *Zap*, October 1990, 3–8.

90. See Simpson, "Soundtracks," 227–48.

91. Galenza and Havemeister, eds., *Wir wollen immer artig sein . . . .*

92. See Edo Reents, "Die Nase blutig, der Rücken staubig," *Süddeutsche Zeitung*, February 5–6, 2000; and Torten Wahl, "Der Sound einer Szene," *Berliner Zeitung*, September 16, 1999.

93. See Marquardt, *Die Nacht ist Leben*; Hahn and Willmann, *Satan*; Ronald Galenza and Heinz Havemeister, *Mix mir einen Drink: Feeling B: Das Ende einer Legende* (Berlin: Schwarzkopf & Schwarzkopf, 2002); and Kowalczyk, *Punk in Pankow*.

94. Boehlke and Gericke, *too much future*.

95. *ostPUNK! too much future*.

96. See Andreas Hartmann, "Dekadente Westerscheinung," *Frankfurter Rundschau*, September 23, 2006; Jörn Luther, "Virulent, kraß, geladen," *Scheinschlag: Berliner Stadtzeitung*, September 1–29, 2005, 9; "Meine grundeigene Renitenz," *Neues Deutschland*, September 24–25, 2005; Markus Ströhlein, "Genosse Punk," *Jungle World*, September 21, 2005, 22; Ingo Arend, "Aufstand gegen das Reißbrett," *Freitag*, September 9, 2005, 16; Claus Löser, "Subversion im Hier und Jetzt," *tageszeitung*, August 31, 2005, 25; and "Wir standen mit einem Bein im Knast," *Tagesspiegel*, August 26, 2005, 23.

97. See "'Passion' im Künstlerhaus Bethanien," *tipBerlin*, July 15, 2015; and Boris Pofalla, "Ratte heißt wieder Maik," *Frankfurter Allgemeine Sonntagszeitung*, November 11, 2012.

98. On *Ostalgie*, see Dominic Boyer, "*Ostalgie* and the Politics of the Future in Eastern Germany," *Public Culture* 18, no. 2 (2006): 361–81; Paul Cooke, *Representing East Germany since Unification: From Colonization to Nostalgia* (Oxford: Berg, 2005); Paul Betts, "The Twilight of the Idols: East German Memory and Material Culture," *Journal of Modern History* 72, no. 3 (2000): 731–65; Martin Blum, "Remaking the East German Past: *Ostalgie*, Identity, and Material Culture," *Journal of Popular Culture* 34, no. 3 (2000): 229–53; and Daphne Berdahl, "'(N)Ostalgie' for the Present: Memory, Longing, and East German Things," in *Ethnos* 64, no. 2 (1999): 192–211.

99. Hans Ulrich Wehler sparked controversy when he quoted East German dissident writer Stefan Heym who said in March 1990 that the "GDR will be nothing more than a footnote in world history" in his magisterial, five-volume history of Germany. See Donna Harsch, "Footnote or Footprint? The German Democratic Republic in History," *Bulletin of the German Historical Institute* no. 46 (2010): 9–25; and Thomas

Lindenberger, "What's in This Footnote? World History!" *Bulletin of the German Historical Institute* no. 46 (2010): 27–31.

100. Witness the decision to tear down the Palast der Republik and restore the former Berliner Stadtschloss in its place. See John V. Maciuika, "Whose Schloss-platz? Architecture and the 'Materialization' of German Identities in Berlin's Historic Center, 1945–2009," in "East German Material Culture and the Power of Memory," supplement 7, *Bulletin of the German Historical Institute* (2011): 15–28.

## Chapter 10

# "Under Any Form of Government, I Am Partisan"

## *The Siberian Underground from Anti-Soviet to National-Bolshevist Provocation*

### Evgenyi Kazakov [Ewgeniy Kasakow]

The history of rock music on post-Soviet territory has distinct regional specificities. The Ural region was, for instance, a stronghold of New Wave, and Leningrad/St. Petersburg was the birthplace of Russian Ska. In the 1980s, far from from the centers, on the outskirts, an independent trend that is sometimes called Siberian suicide-punk and sometimes Siberian underground appeared. The variety of the many bands and solo performers from different cities became an antithesis to the rock clubs in Moscow and Leningrad that were gaining increasing acceptance, even official acceptance, and had a long-term influence that has extended to the politicized music scene in present-day Russia.

In order to gain some breathing room, the rock scene in most of the USSR always tried to deny its obvious political attitude, even if it was present. Most Soviet rock musicians did not want the authorities to associate them with staunch opponents of the Soviet regime like the dissidents.[1]

The Siberian scene chose the opposite path. In 1982 the first band project from this region gave itself a provocative name, Posev, which was the name of a famous anti-communist publishing house. Although sympathy for the conservative publishing house can hardly be heard in the cryptic texts of the young group from Omsk, it surely attracted the attention of the repressive regime. The members of the Siberian underground who grew up during the Brezhnev era were forced to react to a new situation in which their methods of shocking and offending were rapidly losing their effectiveness. And, unlike the generations of their parents and grandparents, their generation did not go through anything "heroic" like wars or revolutions.[2]

This chapter is dedicated to the emergence and development of the "Siberian punk phenomenon" and is based on the memoirs of the participants, publications in rock *samizdat* and fanzines as well as such open sources as articles in the Soviet mass media.

233

## THE BIRTH OF PUNK-*"TUSOVKA"* IN SOVIET SIBERIA

The key figure of Siberian punk was Igor "Egor" Letov (1964–2008). Egor Letov's parents were a doctor and a World War II veteran.[3] Egor was a sickly child and spent a lot of time in hospitals so instead of a school-leaving certificate he only received a confirmation that he had "attended the secondary school course." With this document it was impossible to get into a vocational school or university. Egor went to Moscow where for some time he was enrolled in a vocational school for the building trades. However, he was soon expelled for non-attendance.[4] At that time he was living with his brother in the suburb of Liubertsy, the city that later became famous for "the Liubers," members of its aggressive anti-rock and anti-West subculture.[5]

His elder brother was saxophonist Sergei Letov (b. 1956), who later became famous. While living in Moscow Sergei became well acquainted with the rock scene in the capital, took part in Pop-Mekhanika, the experimental group led by Sergei Kurekhin,[6] and also worked with DK, a group led by Sergei Zharikov (b. 1956), which is often called a precursor of Soviet punk.[7] Musically, DK has very little resemblance to punk. It was more like *stiob*, a phenomenon Alexei Yurchak analyzed as a relationship of "inside-outsideness" (*vnenakhodimost'*) to official as well as oppositional discourses.[8] Zharikov himself admitted later that the group's irony was aimed at both Soviet pop music and the "serious" groups with their pathos.[9] Sergei Letov remembers that at the beginning his brother loved Soviet rock groups like Voskresenie and Mashina Vremeni. Thanks to his brother he also became familiar with *samizdat* and *tamizdat*.[10] For somebody from a Siberian province, Letov knew a great deal about music and had connections and quite a bit of practical experience.

The choice of the group's name reflected the decision not to agree to any deals and it was a frontal attack on the authorities, who had the power to permit or to prohibit. In 1985 Posev became Grazhdanskaia Oborona, which means "civil defense" (its abbreviation was GrOb, which means "coffin"). Repressions soon followed. Soviet rock musicians were occasionally prosecuted for illegal concerts and business practices, something the *militsiia* (police) dealt with. But the musicians from Omsk were—as Letov remembers—accused of terrorism and thus it became a case for the KGB.[11] Already at the end of the Brezhnev era, after a period of relative quiet, the state security service began to pay close attention to youth subcultures again.[12] In 1982 a special branch of the KGB was created to deal with youth subculture.[13] In the Andropov years certain activities were still tolerated, but during Chernenko's rule the last big offensive against rock music in the USSR took place.[14] In fact, Chernenko launched the campaign with his speech at the TsK plenum on June 14, 1983.[15] Although the speech was about official Soviet pop music and did not mention rock music as such, repressions against both the so-called vocal-instrumental ensembles (VIA) and the rock groups began.[16]

The repressions carried out against the Siberian punks reflected this new policy. Egor Letov, the founder of the band, was put into a closed psychiatric clinic after a series of suicide attempts. He remained there for three months, treatment usually reserved for political opponents of the Soviet system, dissidents, and sometimes the most active members of the hippie subculture. Egor Letov insisted that he was forcibly "cured" by Neuroleptil, but his brother Sergei says that their mother used her medical connections to ensure that he would not be subjected to any rough treatment.[17]

Despite heart disease, the bass player Kuzia UO (Konstantin Riabinov, b. 1964) was drafted and—as he remembers it—he had to serve in Baikonur which was the site of the famous center for launching space missions.[18] However, this only interrupted music production for a short time because Letov recorded many albums on his own. Afterwards, he started playing with the Lishchenko brothers' band, which was called Pik Klakson.[19]

Siberian rock musicians' cooperation culminated in the first Novosibirsk rock festival, which took place in April 1987. An indication of the new policy of *perestroika*, many rock festivals took place in the spring of 1987. They were officially tolerated but looked upon with suspicion. The Novosibirsk festival witnessed the birth of the so-called Siberian school. There Letov met some kindred spirits from Novosibirsk, for instance Oleg "Manager" Sudakov (b. 1962), with whom he had become acquainted earlier, the band Spinki Menta[20] (later Chernyi Lukich) led by Vadim "Dima" Kuz'min (1964–2012), and the songwriter Iana "Ianka" Diagileva (1966–1991).

Letov performed with the Lishchenko brothers but their joint performance only took place because two famous bands cancelled their performances, which created a gap in the program. Onstage, Letov and Lishchenko announced themselves as the band Adolf Hitler and played songs with provocative political lyrics that, despite the band's name, were anti-fascist. The chorus of one of the songs went: "Read *Mein Kampf!*" with which the excited audience began to sing along, adding to the shocking effect. Although in the following line the Führer's book was called a "textbook for sadists and scumbags," an outside observer might easily have mistaken the concert for a genuine neo-Nazi gathering.[21] With their performance, the punks got in the way of the educational/propagandistic function of the festival, which was supposed to be the main function of every public event in the USSR under the Komsomol's patronage.[22]

In this respect, Grazhdanskaia Oborona had much in common with the kind of provocations that West German groups Deutsch-Amerikanische Freundschaft and Fehlfarben were famous for in the early 1980s. The use of Nazi symbols, which contrasted with the song lyrics, was confusing for listeners. There are also obvious analogies with the aesthetic strategy of the group Laibach.[23]

The group's performance at the Novosibirsk festival can be seen as an example of the ironic attitude of "inside-outsideness" (as Alexei Yurchak calls it) that appeared under the new conditions created by *perestroika*. Yurchak separates the term "inside-outsideness" from any expression of political opposition; this term is relevant here because the Siberian punks, who had already collided with the KGB, could not, strictly speaking, be called an opposition.[24] In fact, the musicians from Omsk did not advocate an "anti-Soviet" agenda of any kind. Their main means of expression was the use of forbidden symbols out of context (the name "Posev," Nazi slogans, or names of anti-heroes like Hitler or General Vlasov) However, at that time no traces of real sympathy toward the dissidents or any other anti-Soviet movements (except frequent references to Solzhenitsyn) could be found among the Siberian punks.

Less than half an hour later, the show was interrupted. The scandal was perfect—Letov had to flee the festival as soon as possible because of his impending arrest. Together with Ianka, who from that moment on was his girlfriend, he was on the run across a USSR that was churned up by *perestroika*.[25] The legendary couple of Soviet rock history performed in conspiracy-like conditions and they left a significant trace in the form of audio recordings that were quickly distributed.

## PUNK OF ALL-UNION SIGNIFICANCE

The Letov-Diagileva journey drew the entire rock scene's attention to the remote Siberian province. The actual founding of a Siberian punk network took place in Simferopol in Crimea at a rock festival in August 1987 where Letov and Diagileva met other protagonists of the Siberian scene, including the group Instruktsiia po Vyzhivaniiu (IPV or Instructions for Survival) from Tiumen'.[26] Like Letov and his GrOb, IPV outraged the authorities in their city.

Gusel' Nemirova (née Savalatova, b. 1960), one of the key figures of the Tiumen' scene, remembers that back then Tiumen's distinguishing feature was a high percentage of young people. There were five universities for 480,000 people, twenty science centers, fifteen vocational schools, and after the discovery of oil, an enormous number of new people, many of them young, came to the city. There was a great deal of demand for recreational venues for young people. At the beginning it was not easy to organize these with the help of Komsomol. As an employee of the newspaper *Tiumenskii Komsomolets*, Savalatova kept in touch with rock groups in the neighboring cities as well as with influential people in the Komsomol organizations.[27]

Young people in Tiumen' had more opportunities for experimenting and developing subcultures than their peers in neighboring Omsk.

The group around schoolteacher and poet Miroslav Nemirov (1961–2016) was initially officially registered as the local university's rock club. On April 12, 1985 they gave a performance and were immediately accused of propagandizing fascism, homosexuality, and drugs. One of the participants, Arkadii Kuznetsov (b. 1969), remembers:

> Nemirov wrote the script. All this looked like a play, exposing bourgeois mass culture, all about a certain musician, Iggy Jivetone, who is being harassed in every way by the sharks of show business. Throughout the play we presented every possible rock music style, beginning with rock-and-roll and ending of course with punk and New Wave . . . .
>
> Neumoev played the capitalist show business shark, Mr. Drumych, with a top hat on.[28]

This indicates that in playing different genres of Western music Tiumen's punks found a link between the Western underground and Soviet propaganda: the condemnation of commercial music under capitalism.

Another famous Tiumen' band called Kooperativ Nishtiak founded in 1983 by Kirill Rybiakov (b. 1968), soon changed its aesthetic from punk to "gothic." Kooperativ Nishtiak often turned to forbidden subjects such as esoterica and the culture of the Third Reich.[29] Although the lyrics were an obvious mixture of irony and parody and they took their ideas about the Nazis from postwar mass culture, unlike Letov, they never explicitly distanced themselves from fascism. Where Grazhdanskaia Oborona hinted at similarities between fascism and Soviet society, Kooperativ Nishtiak just poked fun at fascism. Rybiakov liked to take on the role of the enemy. He used the German alias "Doktor Karl Fisher" and called his 1987 parallel project Al Jihad al Islam.

In the beginning, the rock scene in Tiumen' had no scruples about using Komsomol structures for its own purposes. However, the participants were expelled from the Komsomol and the university and drafted into the army. As happened to Letov, the KGB intervened.[30] No doubt the fact that some of the members of the rock scene, including Roman Neumoev (b. 1963), worked at some of the city's many defense industries also played a role.[31] While rockers from Moscow and Leningrad were mostly prosecuted for illegal concerts, the Siberian bands became a case for the state security apparatus and they saw themselves as enemies of the state. Arkadii Kuznetsov remembered how, "as evidence against him, one of the participants was presented with the *Bhagavat Gita*, which was forbidden, the Krishnaite literature was forbidden. You could go to prison for this. They knew that they couldn't get you for the music.

But everybody had something they could get you for."[32] At first, the Tiumen' punks did not intend to provoke the authorities. On the contrary, the repressions against them gave them a chance to see themselves as "real heroes."

Some members of the Siberian underground began their career outside Siberia. The singer Nikolai Kuntsevich, "Nick Rock-n-Roll" (b. 1960), joined the clique of Siberian exiles in Simferopol. The son of a professor, until then he had been trying unsuccessfully to put together a punk group. His behavior onstage earned him the title of the Russian Iggy Pop. Nick also had experienced confinement in a psychiatric clinic.[33] In Simferopol Kuntsevich founded his group, Vtoroi Echelon. What Kuntsevich had in common with punk was his behavior on the stage, for example, cutting himself with a piece of broken glass during a performance.[34]

With Letov's and Diagileva's return to Siberia, the regional underground's so-called golden times began. Cooperation between the musicians from Omsk, Tiumen', and Novosibirsk involved more and more local bands and individual artists. People shared not only rooms and equipment but also song lyrics. For instance, GrOb and IPV swapped lyrics many times. Miroslav Nemirov, who could neither play nor sing, mostly wrote the lyrics for both groups. Some musicians simultaneously belonged to more than one group. The Siberian punks did not perform in the city of Omsk itself. GrOb's first albums were recorded there but to perform in public the musicians went to places where they were less well known by the authorities.[35]

The popularity of Siberian punk grew continuously, helped by an increasingly liberal policy toward young people. At the same time, the differences between the Siberian scene and the rest of the growing rock community in the Soviet Union were becoming more pronounced.


## *PERESTROIKA:* ROCK UNDER NEW CONDITIONS

*Perestroika* brought about a considerable loosening of censorship and the media began to speak favorably about rock music as well.[36] The leading bands from Leningrad, Moscow, and Sverdlovsk rock clubs became known outside of the rock music subculture. Rebellious young people were considered allies of *perestroika* in the war against "fossilized structures," "bureaucracy," and other so-called "isolated problems" of Soviet society. The trick that the successful bands had to pull off was to convince the state and the party that they would not betray their remaining trust but at the same time they had to remain trustworthy in the eyes of their fans. For instance, Viktor Tsoi, the leader of the Leningrad band Kino, played in *The Needle* (1988), a film that combined action elements with an anti-drugs message. His famous song "We Want Changes" was used in the film *Assa* (1987) and the Soviet mass media styled this song the anthem of *perestroika*. Reflecting the spirit of change, the experts were now suggesting that rock music should be professionalized to restrain the "underground's" bad influence.[37]

For the Siberian band this attitude was unthinkable. They did not want to avoid conflict. When Letov and his friends began to call themselves punks, they were breaking a taboo, since punk was depicted in Soviet propaganda as a particularly dangerous style of rock music, which was already viewed with suspicion. In 1982 a major newspaper, *Komsomol'skaia Pravda*, published an article that declared that punks in the West were being trained to become fascist militants.[38] Artemy Troitsky, the pioneer of Soviet rock journalism remembers: "About the punks you knew only one thing: they were fascists. That's how our correspondent in England always described them. The attempts not to equate the punks with the National Front didn't succeed. Even quotations from the English *Morning Star* [a communist paper—E. K.] or excerpts from The Clash's lyrics didn't help."[39] In 1986 the new First Secretary of the Komsomol, Viktor Mironenko, was compelled to respond to readers of *Komsomol'skaia Pravda* who were asking how it could happen that those punks grew up in families of war veterans. The head of the Komsomol responded that there were no real punks in the USSR, only young people who were trying to imitate them,[40] which shows that the punks were considered the most socially dangerous and anti-Soviet subculture.

According to Troitsky, music collectors and rock musicians also shared this negative view.[41] This was the result of provocation caused by Posev and Adolf Hitler. In 1988–1989 Letov and Oleg "Manager" Sudakov created a joint band project called Armiia Vlasova, named after the Russian collaborator's army in World War II. Even if Sudakov's lyrics, inspired by reading Solzhenitsyn's *GULAG Archipelago*, were cryptic, the determination to be worthy of the image created by Soviet propaganda was there.[42] Solzhenitsyn, who was the canonical anti-hero of Soviet propaganda, became a real object of worship for those who considered themselves anti-Soviet.[43]

The Siberian punks did not want to convince the authorities that they were harmless. On the contrary, by using "forbidden words" alone they wanted to frighten them. In Tiumen' the Nemirov and IPV circle put out a fanzine with the politically provocative name of *Anarkhiia*. Various legal rock clubs were denounced in it for having a pernicious influence.[44] The first festival of alternative and left-radical music took place in Tiumen' in 1988.[45] If the scene in Omsk and Tiumen' in those days expressed their political opinions, it was always about anarchism, even if there is no evidence that there were any debates about any practical political implementation of anarchism outside of the subculture.

A deep mistrust of *perestroika* was also typical of the Siberian underground. Letov sang, "The cycle is over/Back to where we were/the spiral of *perestroika* is slowing down/Out of our sight a new 1937 is being prepared."[46] (This song is on the 1988 album *So the Steel Was Hardened*).[47] Miroslav Nemirov already saw the foundation of a new personality cult in the so-called new thinking: "Oh, punish them Comrade Gorbachev! Oh, take their houses and dachas!/Take away their confident look! . . . punish them father!/Set your KGB on them/oh, set on them your evil cops (in *Nochnoi Bit*, 1986)."[48] The author uses the tactics of hyper-affirmation and hyper-identification. The appeal to "Comrade Gorbachev," who was called on to punish the bad bureaucrats, seems to be an appeal to young people to actively participate in *perestroika* and take up an active position as citizens.

As usual one did not hold oneself back—Letov's work of the 1980s is positively full of hostilities: "Parallel to communism flows a blood-red river" (*Fight Incentive*, 1988);[49] "I hate the color red, destroy those like me" (*Pearl Game in front of the Pigs*, 1986);[50] and "The rusty bunker is my freedom/ sweetmeat has dried a long time ago / . . . We have killed the state in us" (*Everything Goes According to Plan*, 1988).[51]

Vadim Kuz'min's Spinki Menta was more likely to attack elements of the official ideology head-on, for example, going after the image of the security forces (*The Erection of Lieutenant Kireev*, 1988) or public holidays such as May 1 and November 7 (in the concert album *Concert in Egor's Apartment*, 1987).

Although more and more rockers started to express themselves politically in 1988, the Siberian punk scene was probably the most radical music scene in the USSR. It is striking that in work written by opinion-shaping experts who, in effect, formed a canon during this time (Artemy Troitsky, Il'ia Smirnov)[52] the Siberian school is hardly mentioned. Punks seem to be the marginal among the marginal.[53] The reservations of the periphery about the center therefore were reinforced within the scene. Siberian punks openly prided themselves on being prosecuted by the police and the KGB. Siberia, a traditional place of exile where others feared to be sent, was their homeland.

What Siberian punk had in common with its Western counterpart was disbelief in the future.[54] Siberian punk rockers differed from Russian rockers in feeling that their punk rebellion was authentic.[55] If not an open assault on the regime, their "dropping out" seemed to them at least preparation for an assault. In collaborative work with the Tiumen' punk rockers it looked like this:

We're descending into basements
We're escaping to underground flats
We're becoming the illegals
And this is our rock-n-roll front
You are blind, you are ridiculous for teenagers and wives
You are a dangerous temptation

Suspiciously alive, you're probably a kike
A psycho, a dissident, a homo
Your friends are in the penal battalions
On the floor of student hostels, in nuthouses
They know what KGB is
They know what it is—metallic fear[56]

When the term "punk" was used in the Soviet Union, it did not necessarily connote great musical proximity to Western punk. Rock in the USSR was fixated on the lyrics—often at the expense of the music. In the West the public did not understand any of GrOb's texts and musically GrOb and other Siberian punk bands were difficult to categorize. Because of its neglect of musical perfection for the sake of the lyrics, Russian rock failed to find Western audiences. Moreover, the musicians rarely had access to good instruments and recording technology. This was an even bigger problem in the provinces than in Moscow and Leningrad.

As the discussion above suggests, Soviet rock music was shaped by the songwriters' (*bardy*) scene. Siberian punks were seen as punks in the first place because of their lyrics, not their music. External attributes such as Mohawks were unusual and much of the music is reminiscent of garage rock. Letov despised The Exploited and the Dead Kennedys, because in his opinion punk should not restrict itself to external stylistics.[57] That is why "native" influences such as Russian Futurism were important. Nemirov wrote a tribute to the Futurist poet Aleksei Kruchenykh. Letov's lyrics often refer to Vladimir Mayakovsky. In addition, Andrei Platonov's works, the performance art of the Moscow conceptualist left, and the poems of the avant-garde collective of musicians, writers, and visual artists of the late 1920s and early 1930s, OBERIU (Ob"edinenie Real'nogo Iskusstva or Union of Real Art) left significant traces in the Siberian underground.[58] Like OBERIU, who used to play with political terminology, calling their art "real" and their performance "left" without specifying the exact meaning of the words, the Siberian punks made reference to anarchism, anti-Soviet dissidents, and the Soviet heroic tradition. In order to understand their real attitude to all these things, the public had to listen to the lyrics very attentively, but the lyrics also left you confused. Like those who read Platonov, the audience for Siberian punk asked themselves if there was any ironical distance in the lyrics, and if there was, where did it begin? What for instance were they to think about such lyrics as this: "The Pamiat' Society and the Red Regime/A shot in the back and the down in the soul/The honeyed sweetness of bloody porridge/ Headfirst into the muddy spring . . . . The reddened dawn lights the wounds Proud tribe, rise for the battle!/We call you with cross and sword: 'Hang the kikes and save Russia!'"[59]

The first signs of crisis began to show up in 1988. In the late *perestroika* period many normally far more cautious actors from the rock scene started to pounce on political events. Thus, Siberian punk lost its special status. The protagonists were willing to act politically when political action was constituted as breaking a taboo. Direct intervention in politics when taboos were being removed did not interest them until the late 1980s. Mass demonstrations in Omsk on the eve of the 19th Party Congress in the summer of 1988 apparently left no impression on the rock scene.[60] The "political" anarchists who emerged in those years in the USSR disliked the punks and the youth subculture. They thought that exaggerated attempts to shock would cast a negative light on real anarchism.[61] The informal movement presented many political programs during *perestroika*,[62] but there is no indication that these were debated in any way in the punk scene.

At the same time, the Stalinist past played an important role in the work of Siberian punks during the 1980s. For instance, the studio project Kommunizm (Communism) created by Letov, Sudakov, and Diagileva in 1988 combined eulogies to Stalin written by Dagestani poet Suleiman Stalskii not only with punk and industrial music but also with the sounds of Big Beat and Easy Listening. In Kommunizm's albums one finds a mixture of quotes from writer, journalist, and poet Varlam Shalamov and Solzhenitsyn, children's folklore, and poems of semi-official Soviet poets. The creators of such collages would not provide any indication of whether they were mocking the Soviet way of life or being nostalgic about it. Of course, Kommunizm's cryptic songs could not compete with Grazhdanskaia Oborona, whose songs were known all over the country by the end of *perestroika*.

Studio experiments with new music genres, such as industrial, noise, free jazz, Letov's project Kommunizm, Kuz'min's Muzhskoi Tanets (Men's Dance),[63] or Promyshlennaia Arkhitektura (Industrial Architecture) from GrOb guitarist Dmitrii Selivanov (1964–1989) met with little response although the Siberian school had developed a new approach to policy and provocation—for example, original recordings of official Soviet music were mixed with its own work. An infinite game with the multiple contexts in which they were making music developed, which did not allow the authors to define a political position, but at the same time allowed them to point out the political dimension of seemingly innocuous Soviet popular music. The Siberians did not want to pander to what many of the new fans wanted. When terms such as "Suicidal Siberian (post) punk" or "existential Underground" came up, a "Punk label" hardly enabled a consensus in the network connecting Omsk, Tiumen', and Novosibirsk.

On April 22, 1989 Dmitrii Selivanov hung himself. Ianka Diagileva died in mysterious circumstances in May 1991. Both of these deaths fit with the image of the Siberian underground as self-destructive and gloomy, but they were also signals of its decline. During this time, suicides and other "unnatural" deaths accumulated throughout the entire Soviet rock scene: In February 1988 the rock "bard" Aleksandr Bashlachev, who had had a great deal of influence on Diagileva, fell out of an eighth-story window. In August 1990 Viktor Tsoi died in a car accident and in August 1991 the legendary Leningrad musician Mikhail "Mike" Naumenko died after a head injury of unknown origin.

The initial optimism of the subcultures was significantly diminished. For many bands, a new era had just started. It was the era of commercial exploitation of its own underground image.[64] In this situation, GrOb, the flagship of the Siberian scene, dissolved after a farewell concert in Tallinn on April 13, 1990. Letov was becoming increasingly fascinated by the mythological, the fairytale, and the mystical.[65] Socialism ended, but the punks' "dropping out" did not.[66] After Diagileva's death, Letov pulled himself back. There were wild rumors circulating about him. The actual era of Siberian punk was over but the story about it was just beginning.

## IN OPPOSITION TO THE NEW POWER

A revival of the Siberian underground began in 1993 but this time in a highly politicized version. When President Yeltsin took up arms in October 1993 against the insurgency of the parliamentary majority of nationalists and communists, Letov announced a reunion of GrOb. Now he saw himself as a radical, leftwing opponent of Yeltsin's market reforms and a Soviet patriot. The following year he became a member of the National Bolshevik Party (NBP).[67] From the very beginning, the party created by Eduard Limonov recruited nonconformist artists and some of them responded.[68] With Neumoev's IPV, "Manager" Sudakov's new band Rodina (Homeland) and bands from Belarus he founded the Russkii Proryv (Russian Breakthrough) movement, a nationalist and communist rock movement. These artists saw their task as the mobilization of a joint anti-Western movement of the Left and the Right.

IPV quickly shifted their direction. Although Miroslav Nemirov was the founder and a leading writer of lyrics for IPV, he did not play any instrument and could not sing. In 1988 Roman Neumoev became the band's leader. Neumoev had been the first to turn to a scene that combined Christianity and nationalism. He campaigned for anti-Semitic conspiracy theories and made contact with rightwing organizations. In April 1991 IPV caused a scandal at a festival in Moscow. An old text of Nemirov's, namely "kill a bull, to collect his gun" was modified by Neumoev. From now on, IPV's most famous text ran thus: "kill a kike,/to buy a gun/to kill a kike to be armed/The people who have the guns are practically invincible/The people who have the gun cannot be made into the flock."[69] Nemirov, who did not share Neumoev's views, finally distanced himself from IPV.[70] Today Neumoev lives near a monastery and still plays concerts occasionally in cooperation with the ecclesiastical authorities. He sees his task as advertising for the faith with music and he pays homage to the monarchy.[71] When Neumoev cooperated with Letov in Russkii Proryv, they had a poor relationship. Neumoev quarreled with Letov about his leftwing and pro-Soviet attitude and offended him.[72] Today IPV's website shows a montage of Red Army soldiers riding into the sunset (from the Soviet movie *The Elusive Avengers*) and a portrait of Nicholas II with the following text: "And so he is going, the hundred-year-old raging lout [Ham]/ And the White Kingdom is being rebuilt again, the kingdom in which there is a Tsar."[73] A more obvious illustration of the shared roots between Soviet and anti-Soviet romanticism is hard to imagine.

Nick Rock-n-Roll, who had had a final falling-out with Letov after Ianka's death, was perhaps the first to openly declare his opposition to Yeltsin. During the August coup, he was trying to declare his support for the GKChP (Gosudarstvennyi komitet po chrezvychainomu polozheniiu or State Committee on the State of Emergency) on Tiumen' radio.[74] This stance surprised and disgusted many former fans. Henceforth, Siberian punks joined forces with the former thugs who previously had prevented their concerts from taking place,[75] with "village prosaics" who would have loved to prohibit their rock music,[76] and fascistic Pamiat' activists who were among the archenemies of subculture youth since its inception during the *perestroika* period.[77]

Almost everybody from the earlier Siberian scene found themselves in the nationalist, anti-Yeltsin camp during the 1990s. The band Kooperativ Nishtiak later became popular among the "serious" Right, and worked with Alexander Dugin's Eurasian Youth Union during the 2000s.[78] This included bands that were enthusiastic about Christianity and monarchism such as Vtoroi Echelon and Kulturnaia Revoliutsiia, which was founded and led by Artur Strukov (b. 1963) from Tiumen',[79] as well as Teplaia Trassa (Warm Line) from Barnaul, which associated itself with the Tiumen' scene.[80] Strukov was a member of the militant rightwing organization Union of Orthodox Banner-Bearers. The Barnaul "Bard" Aleksandr Podorozhnyi (b. 1966), however, preached Slavic neo-paganism and discovered in his Christian colleagues a harmful influence, which he characterized as "Jewish."[81]

## THEIR PARENTS' CHILDREN

Explanations of this phenomenon are still debated today. It is striking that many of the Siberian underground's protagonists came from the families of senior party officials. For example, the poet Vladimir Bogomiakov

(b. 1955), who played a major role in the Tiumen' scene, is the son of Gennadii Bogomiakov, who was the First Secretary of the CPSU in the Tiumen' region.[82] Bogomiakov senior was removed from his post in 1990 after harsh criticism from below for stagnation.[83] The father of Igor "Jeff" Zhevtun (b. 1967), a member of GrOb, IPV, and countless side projects, was the deputy head of the Tiumen' city administration.[84] The First Secretary of the city's party organization also had a son who was active in the scene, Iurii Shapovalov (1964–2009), who was part of the environment of IPV.[85]

Letov's father is a former army officer and member of the CPSU who joined the Communist Party of the Russian Federation in the 1990s and actively participated in the National Salvation Front. There were victims of the purges on his mother's side. Letov's grandmother, who spent a lot of time with her grandsons, was from a merchant's family. Not only did she express gratitude to Khrushchev, but she also used to rave about the *Domostroi* and life in a merchant household before the revolution.[86] Vadim "Dmitrii" Kuz'min's father worked in the defense industry and became unemployed after 1991 like many of his colleagues. The milieu from which these scene activists came was a fertile ground for opposition to Yeltsin.[87]

However, this is hardly a sufficient explanation for the behavior of a subculture that stood for a break with their parents' lives. The Siberian punks also saw how fast the criticism of Soviet reality became a legitimating ideology of the new regime.

## . . . AND CONSEQUENT REBELS

Siberian punks had even less sympathy for the new Russia than they had for the former Soviet Union. The adjusted behavior of most rockers and the crisis of rock music, which had been displaced mercilessly by pop after the initial "hype," had something to do with their change of heart.[88] Letov's attitude also played an important role. Early on, he announced in his songs: "I'll always be against it" (in the 1989 album *Pes'ni radostii schastiia* or *Songs of Happiness and Joy*) or "under any form of government, I am a partisan, under any regime, I am an anarchist" (in the 1989 album *Tak zakalialas stal* or *So the Steel Was Tempered*). The Soviet system could be best provoked by references to Vlasov or Solzhenitsyn. Now democratic Russia was provoked by constant preaching of the theory of totalitarianism with reference to the RAF or Stalin. If anti-Western prejudices became part of the state's ideology during the last period of the Soviet Union, then, by 1990, as Vladimir Sorgin says, pro-Western attitudes reached their peak, so that later the democratic mass media had to constantly resist growing disappointment.[89] Yesterday's provoking slogans became today's official jargon. Artemii Magun says that "the democratic revolution" was winning with the slogan that revolutions were impossible and unacceptable.[90] The history of Siberian punk shows that consistent nonconformism is absolutely indifferent to content. Such noncon-formists can change sides at any moment depending on whatever opinions predominate at that moment. To be in opposition to the dominant opinion is considered an inherently worthy stance. From the very beginning, the Siberian underground was following the traditions of the Russian and the global avant-garde. Next to the official negative attitude toward the avant-garde tradition it might have looked like a staunch "anti-totalitarian" movement. However, both the Marxist Mikhail Lifshitz and the postmodernist Boris Groys noted a close affinity between the aesthetic and political ideas of the avant-garde and totalitarianism.[91] By the end of 1990s, Letov was openly saying that in his opinion a totalitarian society was an ideal environment for artists. "When a man knows that he can be persecuted for what he does, then his actions are worth something. When he knows that for this film or for this word he will be shot, then this man is really worth something! But when he can say anything, everywhere, then it's all just empty chatter."[92] About the same time, the critic Vladimir Kotov, who himself used to write for rock *samizdat*, wrote about the Soviet punk phenomenon that, "Essentially, post-Soviet punk is the mental-ity of the Brezhnev period," and he pointed out that, "the same doublethink, utter indifference to the meaning of words that are used only as a sound ("free the punks!"), the same aggressive cult of mediocrity, aversion to creativity, fear of any individual expression, total mutual control" had sunk into the collective unconscious.[93]

If for older Russian nationalists rock music was one of the most odi-ous examples of rotten Western culture,[94] young people discerned in many Western subcultures a protest against Western values.[95] Soon supporters of a more discerning approach to rock music appeared—in the Russian Orthodox Church.[96]

Even if Letov's immediate political commitment did not last very long, he was discredited in the eyes of many punks and anarchists. In Russia, a new generation of punk bands developed which was mainly based on the Western scene's trends: Hardcore, DIY, veganism and straight edge, and skate punk.[97] They were keen to let their music really sound like punk in the modern West-ern understanding of this concept. Therefore, they rejected the tradition of the Siberian school. Other bands such as Az, Purgen, and Chudo-Iudo were more akin to the "anti-social" image of punk.

Numerous successors (and imitators) of the Siberian school have been active in the environment of the NBP and the Eurasian Youth Movement up to the present, although Letov turned his back on them in the 1990s.[98] This camp in particular claims the Siberian school for itself as an example of authentic Russian punk that did not allow itself to be taken over by the

Western punk subculture. "Political correctness" was and is frowned upon by the adepts of the Siberian underground. And even in these bands, which claim anarchy for themselves, there are few inhibitions about taking part in various cross-front projects.

# NOTES

1. Alexei Yurchak, *Everything Was Forever, Until It Was No More: The Last Soviet Generation* (Princeton: Princeton University Press, 2005), 146–47.

2. Mikhail Rozhanskii, "Pokoleniia sovetskikh idealistov," *60 parallel'* 35, no. 4 (2009): 20–27.

3. "Otets Letova: Sin byl ochen' talantliv. No slishkom mnogo pil," *Komsomol'skaia Pravda*, February 20, 2008.

4. Sergei Letov, letter to the author, February 26, 2015.

5. Dmitrii Gromov, "Liuberetskie ulichnye molodezhnye kompanii 1980-kh godov: Subkul'tura na pereput'e istorii," *Etnograficheskoe obozrenie* no. 4 (2006): 23–38.

6. "Letov, brat Letova," Sergei Letov interviewed by Aleksei Rosovetskii," *RockYou*, http://rockyou.com.ua/rumors?id=1484; Vladimir Marochkin, *Moskva rok-n-roll'naia: Cherez pesni—ob istorii strany: Rok-muzyka v stolitse: paroli, iavki, traditsii, moda* (Moscow; Tsentropoligraf, 2014), 490–97; According to some sources, Egor also participated in the performances of Pop-Mekhanika. See also Aleksei Koblov and Boris Akimov, "Egor Letov: 'Nasha rok-tsena udruchaet: opiat' liamku samomu tianut' prikhoditsia,'" *Rolling Stone Russia* no. 4 (2004). On Kurekhin, see Alexei Yurchak, "A Parasite from Outer Space: How Sergei Kurekhin Proved that Lenin was a Mushroom," *Slavic Review* 70 no. 2 (2011): 307–33.

7. Andrei Sidel'nikov, "Zarozhdenie pank-kul'tury v SSSR," *Diletant: Istoricheskii zhurnal dlia vsekh*, September 12, 2012, http://diletant.ru/articles/5144022/?sphrase_id=394733.

8. Alexei Yurchak, *Everything Was Forever*, 250, 278.

9. "Russkii rok v litsakh: Gruppa DK," *Stolica FM* website, September 19, 2010, http://stolica.fm/archive-view/3060/2/.

10. For instance, Sergei Letov had a copy of Bulgakov's novel *The Master and Margarita* which was published by Posev. See Sergei Letov.

11. Egor Letov, "Konets nastupaet togda, kogda unichtozhaetsiia zhivaia energiia tvorchestva," *Periferiinaia nervnaia sistema* [fanzine] no. 2 (1990).

12. Nikolai Mitrokhin, *Russkaia partiia: Dvizhenie russkikh natsionalistov v SSSR, 1953–1985* (Moscow: Novoe Literaturnoe Obozrenie, 2003), 542.

13. Oleg Kalugin, *Proshchai, Lubianka! (XX vek glazami ochevidtsev)* (Moscow: Olimp, 1995), 273–74; Aleksandr Smykalin, "Ideologicheskii kontrol' i Piatoe upravlenie KGB SSSR v 1967–1989," *Voprosy istorii* no. 8 (2011): 38.

14. Aleksandr Kushnir, *Zolotoe podpol'e: Polnaia illlustrirovannaia entsiklopediia rok-samizdata 1967–1994: Istoriia-Antologiia-Bibliografiia* (Moscow: AGRAF, 2003), 39–44.

248          *Evgenyi Kazakov [Ewgeniy Kasakow]*

15. Konstantin Chernenko, "Aktual'nye voprosy ideologicheskoi, massovo-politicheskoi raboty partii," *Pravda*, June 15, 1983. See also Paul Easton, "The Rock Community," in *Soviet Youth Culture*, ed. Jim Riordan (Bloomington: Indiana University Press, 1989), 45–82, here 56; Ewgeniy Kasakow, "Das lange Jahr 1984: Ein Krisenabschnitt der sowjetischen Rockszene," in *1984! Block am Block: Subkulturen in Orwell-Jahr*, cd. Alexander Pehlemann, Bert Papenfuß, and Robert Mießner (Mainz: Ventil Verlag, 2015), 267–70.

16. Dirk Krechmar [Kretzschmar], *Politika i kul'tura pri Brezhneve, Andropove i Chernenko* (Moscow: AIRO-XX, 1997), 179; Artemy Troitsky, *Back in the USSR: The True Story of Rock in Russia* (London: Omnibus. 1987), 89–93.

17. Il'ia Stogov, *Revoliutsiia seichas! Dokumental'nyi roman* (St. Petersburg: Amfora, 2001), 148–49; Sergei Letov, *Kandidat v Buddy* (St. Petersburg: Amfora, 2014), 91.

18. Egor Letov, "Grob-khroniki," *Kontr KulturUr'a* 3 (1991): 20–21.

19. Arsentii Bukintsov, "Daleko nepolnaia istoriia gruppy 'Pik Klakson,'" *Music. lib.ru*, http://music.lib.ru/p/pikklakson/about.shtml.

20. A play on words, consisting of "spinki mintaia" (fillets of Alaska pollock but "spinka" can also mean spine), a famous tinned fish, and "ment," a derogatory term for a policeman, that is, "cop," so the translation is roughly "fillet of cop" or "a cop's spine."

21. A. I. Mazurova, "Pank—alternativa vnutri alternativy," in *Po nepisanym zakonam ulitsy . . .*, ed. K. E. Igoshev and G. M. Minkovskii (Moscow: Iuridicheskaia literatura, 1991), 218–38, here 233.

22. Gabor T. Rittersporn, Malte Rolf, and Jan C. Behrends, eds., "Von Schichten, Räumen und Sphären: Gibt es eine sowjetische Ordnung von Öffentlichkeiten? Einige Überlegungen in komparativer Perspektive," in *Sphären von Öffentlichkeit in Gesellschaften sowjetischen Typs: Zwischen partei-staatlicher Selbstinszenierung und kirchlichen Gegenwelten*, ed. Gabor T. Rittersporn, Malte Rolf, and Jan C. Behrends (Frankfurt am Main: Peter Lang, 2003), 389–421.

23. Alexei Monroe, *Laibach und NSK: Die Inquisitionsmaschine im Kreuzverhör* (Mainz: Ventil Verlag, 2014).

24. Yurchak, *Everything Was Forever*, 133–34.

25. Anthony Qualin, "Marginal Notes: The Poetic World of Yana Diagileva," *Canadian Slavonic Papers* 45, nos. 3–4 (2003): 295–306.

26. Aleksei Rybin, *Anarkhiia v RF: Pervaia polnaia istoriia russkogo panka* (Moscow: Amfora, 2007), 110–11.

27. Vladimir Kozlov, "Interv'iu Guzeli Nemirovoi dlia filma *Sledy na snegu*," Moscow, November 2013, YouTube video, 26:06, published December 6, 2014, www.youtube.com/watch?v=hK2nJCY3QZo. Vladimir Kozlov directed *Sledy na snegu* (2014). The interview with Nemirova was not included in the film. See also D. A. Fedorova, "Dosug gorozhan v 1964–1985 gg. (na materialakh Tiumeni)," *Gumanitarnye nauki v Sibiri* 2 (2014): 97–100.

28. Ella Katsmel'bogen [pseud.], "Instruktsiia po Vyzhivaniiu: Interv'iu s Arkashei Kuznetsovym," 1997, http://imperium.lenin.ru/LENIN/10/ipv.html.

29. Andrei Smirnov, "Kooperativ Nishtiak (Vozvrashenie titanov)," *Zavtra* 49 (2000).

30. Roman Neumoev, "KGB-ROK, ROK-KGB . . .," ch. 3 in *Mifologiia*, vol. 2 (n.d.), at *Instruktsiia po Vyzhivaniiu: Ofitsial'nyi Sait*, http://www.neumoev.ru/chapter3_b2.phtml.

31. Roman Neumoev, "KGB vdeika," ch. 6 in *Mifologiia*, vol. 2 (n.d.), at *Instruktsiia po Vyzhivaniiu: Ofitsial'nyi Sait*, http://neumoev.ru/chapter6_b2.phtml.

32. Katsmel'bogen, "Instruktsiia po Vyzhivaniiu."

33. Aleksandr Alekseev, *Kto est' kto v rossiiskoi rok-muzyke?* (Moscow: AST, 2009), 353–55.

34. Dmitrii Desiaterik, "Pank," in *Al'ternativnaia kul'tura: Entsiklopediia*, comp. Dmitrii Desiaterik (Ekaterinburg: Ultra.Kul'tura, 2005), 121–25, 125.

35. Evgenii Gruzdov and Anton Sveshnikov, "'Khozhdenie v narod'—2: Iz opyta raboty nad 'Slovarem mifologii Omska,'" *Novoe literaturnoe obozrenie* 74 (2005): 431–45.

36. Polly McMichael, "Prehistories and Afterlives: The Packaging and Repackaging of Soviet Rock," *Popular Music and Society* 32, no. 3 (2009): 331–50.

37. Andrei Gromov and Oleg Kuzin, *Neformaly: Kto est' kto?* (Moscow: Mysl', 1990), 60–71.

38. A. Efremov, "Panki—svastiki na zatylke," *Komsomol'skaia Pravda*, September 16, 1982.

39. Troitsky, *Back in the USSR*, 43.

40. "Davai rabotat' vmeste," *Komsomol'skaia Pravda*, September 7, 1986.

41. Troitsky, *Back in the USSR*, 43.

42. Olga Aksiutina, *Pank-virus v Rossii* (Moscow: Lean Format, 1999), 190.

43. On Solzhenitsyn's role in anti-Soviet mythology, see Birgit Menzel, "Entmythisierung in der russischen Literatur am Beispiel von A. I. Solschenizyn," in *Osteuropa im Umbruch: Alte und neue Mythen*, ed. Clemens Friedrich and Birgit Menzel (Frankfurt am Main: Peter Lang, 1994), 109–23.

44. Aleksandr Kushnir, *Zolotoe podpol'e*, 190.

45. Viktor Shchegolev, "Festval 'razrushitelei ili Pank-rok-festival' v Tiumeni," *Tiumenskii Komsomolets*, July 17, 1988.

46. Nineteen thirty-seven was considered the height of the Stalinist purges.

47. Egor Letov, "Novyi 37-i," *Tak zakalialas' stal'* (GrOb Recordz, 1988), www.gr-oborona.ru/pub/discography/tak_zakaljalas_stal.html.

48. Roman Neumoev, "Tovarishch Gorbachev," *Nochnoi Bit* ("Natsional'nyi Tsifrovoi Agregator," 1986), www.gr-oborona.ru/texts/1056963028.html.

49. Egor Letov, "Zaebis'!," *Boevoi stimul* (GrOb Recordz, 1988), Track 13, www.gr-oborona.ru/pub/discography/boevoj_stimul.html.

50. Egor Letov, "Nenavizhu krasnyi svet," *Igra v biser pered svin'iami* (GrOb Recordz, 1986), Track 9, www.gr-oborona.ru/pub/discography/igra_v_biser_pered_svinjami.html.

51. Egor Letov, "Gosudarstvo," *Vse idet po planu* (GrOb Recordz, 1988), side 3, track 2, www.gr-oborona.ru/pub/discography/vse_idet_po_planu.html.

52. Il'ia Smirnov, *Vremia kolokol'chikov: Zhizn' i smert' russkogo roka* (Moscow: INTO, 1994).

53. During this time, the only thing Western audiences could learn about Soviet punk was about the son of famous ballet master Valerii Panov, Andrei "Svin" Panov, who founded the band Avtomaticheskie Udovletvoriteli (AU or Automatic Satisfiers) in 1979 in Leningrad. The fact that AU sang about an "antisocial alcoholic's existence" contrasted with the Siberian understanding of punk as an intellectual movement. See Troitsky, *Back in the USSR*, 62–64; Kushnir, *Zolotoe podpol'e*, 294–96; Ivan Gololobov and Yngvar B. Steinholt, "The Evolution of Punk in Russia," in *Punk in Russia: Cultural Mutation from the "Useless" to the "Moronic,"* ed. Ivan Gololobov, Hilary Pilkington, and Yngvar B. Steinholt (New York: Routledge, 2014), 22–48.

54. Frank Apunkt Schneider, *Als die Welt noch unterging: Von Punk zu NDW* (Mainz: Ventil Verlag, 2007).

55. On the conflict of generations between punk and rock, see also Alexa Geisthövel, "Auf der Tonspur: Musik als zeitgeschichtliche Quelle," in *Die Kunst der Geschichte: Historiographie, Ästhetik, Erzählung*, ed. Martin Baumeister, Moritz Föllmer, and Philipp Müller (Göttingen: Vandenhoeck & Ruprecht, 2009), 157–68, 162.

56. Roman Neumoev, Kirill Rybiakov, and Iurii Kryllov, "Rok-n-roll'nyi front," *Instruktsiia po vyzhivaniiu* (GrOb Recordz, 1986).

57. On genesis of the punk aesthetic, see also Alexa Geisthövel, "Böse reden, fröhlich leiden: Ästhetische Strategien der punkaffinen Intelligenz um 1980," in *Das schöne Selbst: Zur Genealogie des modernen Subjekts zwischen Ethik und Ästhetik*, ed. Jens Elberfeld and Marcus Otto (Bielefeld: transcript Verlag, 2009) 367–99.

58. Aleksei Cherniakov and Tat'iana Tsvigun, "Poeziia E. Letova na fone traditsii russkogo avangarda (aspekt iazykovogo vzaimodeistviia)," in *Russkaia rok-poeziia: Tekst i kontekst* no. 2 (1999): 96–104; Matvei Iankelevich, "Sredi zarazhnego logikoi mira," in *Aleksandr Vvedenskii v kontekste mirovogo avangarda*, ed. Egor Letov and Aleksandr Vvedenskii (Moscow: Gileia, 2006), 238–59; Danila Davydov, "Dadaizm vnutri: smysly Egora Letova," *Arion* no. 4 (2014): 41–46.

59. Egor Letov, "Obshchestvo Pamiat'," *Vse idet po planu* (GrOb Recordz, 1988). See also Evgenyi Kazakov, "Models of 'Taboo Breaking' in Russian Rock Music: The Ambivalence of the 'Politically Incorrect,'" *Kultura: Russian Cultural Review* no. 4 (2009): 20.

60. Andrei Pral'nikov, "Govorite!" *Moskovskie Novosti*, June 6, 1988.

61. Aleksandr Shubin, *Predannaia demokratiia: Neformaly i perestroika (1986–1989)* (Moscow: Evropa, 2006), 174–75.

62. Hans Asenbaum, *Demokratie im Umbruch: Alternative Gesellschaftsentwürfe der russischen Perestroika-Bewegung* (Vienna: New Academic Press, 2013).

63. See for example, the official website, *Lukich*, www.lukich.info/album/25/.

64. Andrei Kotov, "Kontrkul'tura," *Panorama* no. 17 (1990); Ulli Hufen, "Rock in der Sowjetunion: Von der Perestroika in die Bedeutungslosigkeit," in *Mainstream der Minderheiten: Pop in der Kontrollgesellschaft*, ed. Tom Holert and Mark Terkessidis (Berlin: Edition ID-Archiv, 1996), 72–86.

65. Sergei Gur'ev, "The Matrix: Ochishchenie iadom," *KontrKul'tUra* 13 (2002).

66. Grigorii Durnovo, "Orientatsiia v plastelinovoi vselennoi: (Ne)sovetskii rok 1990 goda," *Novoe literaturnoe obozrenie* no. 1 (2007): 685–98.

67. Eduard Limonov, *Moia politicheskaia biografiia* (St. Petersburg: Amfora, 2002), 120–21; Markus Mathyl, "The National-Bolshevik Party and Arctogaia: Two

Neofascist Groupuscules in the Post-Soviet Political Space," *Patterns of Prejudice* 36, no. 3 (2002): 62–76.

68. Il'ia Kukulin, "Revolutsiia oblezlykh drakonov: ultrapravaia ideia kak imitatsiia nonkonformizma," *polit.ru*, April 8, 2007, http://polit.ru/article/2007/04/08/kukproh/; Andrei Rogatchevski and Yngvar B. Steinholt, "Pussy Riot's Musical Precursors? The National Bolshevik Party Bands, 1994–2007," *Popular Music and Society*, DOI 10.1080/03007766.2015.1088287 (posted online October 2015), http://dx.doi.org/10.1080/03007766.2015.1088287.

69. For more about this song and IPV, see Sergei Gur'ev, "Tsivilizatsiia postroila aprel': Mify Romana Neumoeva," *Okorok* no. 8 (1992): 1–3, 8; Kazakov, "Models of 'Taboo Breaking.'"

70. Misha Verbitskii, "'Ubit' zhida' Romana Neumoeva (Vmesto retsenzii na al'bom *Smertnoe*)," *Legkaia muzyka dlia nemnogo oglokhshikh* no. 22, July 26, 2000, on *LENIN* site, http://imperium.lenin.ru/LENIN/22lmdg/22lmdg.html.

71. Petr Silaev, "Pank vo Khriste: Sotsialnyi protest mozhet privesti k vere," *NG Religiia*, January 19, 2005.

72. "Roman Neumoev [interview]: Pevets nemnogikh dush," *Politicheskii zhurnal* nos. 17–18 (2007): 117–19. On Letov's Soviet patriotism, see Anatolii Korchinskii, "Obiazatel'naia voina Egora Letova: Istoricheskaia pamiat', ideologiia, mif," in *Russkii avangard i voina: Sbornik nauchnykh trudov*, ed. Korneliia Ichin (Belgrade: Filologicheskii fakultet v Belgrada, 2014), 304–23.

73. See the home page, *Instruktsiia po vyzhivaniiu*, www.neumoev.ru.

74. Nik Rock-n-Roll, "Ia podderzhal GKChP," *Den'*, October 1992.

75. Jim Riordan, "Teenage Gangs, 'Afgantsy' and Neofascists," in Riordan, *Soviet Youth Culture*, 122–42.

76. Iurii Bondarev, Vasilii Belov, and Valentin Rasputin, "'Legko li byt' molodym?': Priglashaem k razgovoru," *Pravda*, November 10, 1987; Fedor Uglov, *Lomechuzy* (Leningrad: LIO Redaktor, 1991); Vasilii Belov, *Vnemli sebe: Zapiski smutnogo vremeni* (Moscow: Skify, 1993), 27; See also Alexandra Mey, *Russische Schriftsteller und Nationalismus, 1986–1995: Vladimir Solouchin, Valentin Rasputin, Aleksandr Prochanov, Eduard Limonov* (Bochum: Projekt, 2004); Anna Razuvalova, *Pisateli-"derevenshchiki": Literatura i konservativnaia ideologiia 1970-kh godov* (Moscow: Novoe Literaturnoe Obozrenie, 2015).

77. "Mimo fashizma: Beseda s Sergeem Gur'evym," *Panorama* no. 1 (1993); Wayne Allensworth, *The Russian Question: Nationalism, Modernization, and Post-Communist Russia* (Lanham, MD: Rowman and Littlefield, 1998), 231–33, 277.

78. Mikhail Pozharskii, "Krestostrel Evraziiskoi Polnochi: O poeticheskoi 'sviashchennoi voine' na vosem' frontov govorili na vechere Evraziiskogo soiuza molodezhi," *Lenta Novostei*, August 19, 2005, reprinted on credo.ru, http://www.portal-credo.ru/site/?act=news&id=35902.

79. Olga Rakhimova-Nadeikina, "Tiumen': Kulturnaia revolutsiia (Golos virtual'nogo kontinenta)," *Zavtra*, January 1, 2001; Roman Neumoev, "Muzyka bunta," *Zavtra*, January 22, 2001; Aleksandr Oblomov, "Teploi trassy [interview with Vadim Makashenets]," *Zavtra*, November 6, 2007.

80. Daniil Toropov, "Vzyskanie neba," *Zavtra*, July 22, 2003.

81. See Podorozhnyi's personal website, *Antidualizm*, http://antidualizm.narod.ru.

82. Miroslav Nemirov, "Vse o poezii 52" [re: Vladimir Bogomiakov], column in *Russkii zhurnal*, July 18, 2001, http://old.russ.ru/krug/20010718n.html.

83. Maksim V. Kotliarov, "Kadrovaia politika KPSS v partiinykh organizatsiiakh Zapadnoi Sibiri v period perestroika," *Gumanitarnye nauki v Sibiri* no. 2 (2009): 105–8, 107.

84. Roman Neumoev, "My rozhdeny, chtob Kafku sdelat' byl'iu," ch. 7 in *Mifologiia*, vol. 2 (n.d.), at *Instruktsiia po Vyzhivaniiu: Ofitsial'nyi Sait*, http://www.neumoev.ru/chapter7_b2.phtml.

85. Miroslav Nemirov, "Iurii Shapovalov—Chelovek-katalizator," June 6, 2005, Miroslav Nemirov's blog, http://nemiroff.livejournal.com/560907.html.

86. Sergei Letov, *Kandidat v Buddy*, 7–11.

87. Hans-Henning Schröder, "Die Verlierer der Perestrojka: Das Militär und die Rüstungsindustrie," in *Revolution in Moskau: Der Putsch und das Ende der Sowjetunion*, ed. Eduard Schewardnadse et al. (Reinbek bei Hamburg: Rowohlt, 1991), 156–75.

88. "Zapovednik—Konturkul'tura: Interv'iu Sergeia Gur'eva," *Panorama* no. 3 (1992).

89. Vladimir Sogrin, *Politicheskaia istoriia sovremennoi Rossii, 1985–2001: Ot Gorbacheva do Putina* (Moscow: INFRA-M, 2001), 65–67.

90. Artemii Magun, "Perestroika kak konservativnaia revoliutsiia?" *Neprikosnovennyi zapas* no. 6 (2010): 231–49. On the role of historical fatalism, see also Nancy Ries, *Russian Talk: Culture and Conversation during Perestroika* (Ithaca: Cornell University Press, 1997).

91. Mikhail Lifshits, "Pochemu ia ne modernist?" *Literaturnaia gazeta*, October 8, 1966; Boris Groys, *Gesamtkunstwerk Stalin: Die gespaltene Kultur in der Sowjetunion* (Munich: C. Hanser, 1988). See also Philippe Sers, *Totalitarisme et avantgardes: Au seuil de la transcendance* (Paris: Belles Lettres, 2001); Felix Klopotek, "Eine Übung in Orthodoxie: Mitteilungen über Leben und Werk Michail Lifschitz," in *Politik der Gemeinschaft: Zur Konstitution des Politischen in der Gegenwart*, ed. Janine Böckelmann and Claas Morgenroth (Bielefeld: transcript Verlag, 2008), 197–216. See also Evgenyi Kazakov, "Die Fantasie von der Macht fernhalten: Michail Lifschitz—Westmarxist im Osten," in *Ästhetik ohne Widerstand: Texte zu reaktionären Tendenzen in der Kunst*, ed. Annette Emde and Radek Krolczyk (Mainz: Ventil Verlag, 2013), 37–52.

92. Aksiutina, *Pank-virus*, 265.

93. Vladimir Kotov, "Levaia, pravaia gde storona," *Panorama* no. 41 (1998).

94. Kseniia Mialo, *Vremia vybora: Molodezh i obshchestvo v poiskakh alternativy* (Moscow: Izdatel'stvo politicheskoi literatury, 1991), 29–43.

95. Aleksandr Nepomniashchii, "Pravoslavie i rock-muzyka: vozmozhen li chelovecheskii dialog?" *Sobranie*, February 2–13, 2002, reprinted in *Sobranie* no. 9 (2007), www.sobranie.org/archives/9/5.shtml.

96. Andrei Kuraev, *Rok i missionerstvo: Beseda s bogoslovom* (Moscow: EKSMO-Iauza, 2004); Ieromonakh Grigorii (Vadim Lur'e), "Ia znaiu, gde zhivet Sid Barett," June 16, 2004, www.russ.ru/pole/YA-znayu-gde-zhivet-Sid-Barrett.

97. See Olga Aksiutina, *"Esli ia ne mogu tantsevat', eto ne moia revoliutsiia!"— DIY pank/hardkor stsena v Rossii* (Moscow: Nota-R2, 2008).

98. Viacheslav Likhachev, *Natsizm v Rossii* (Moscow: Panorama, 2002), 32–34.

*Part IV*

# DROPPING OUT ECONOMICS

## Chapter 11

# Living in the Material World

## *Money in the Soviet Rock Underground*

### Anna Kan

Existing studies of the Soviet rock music underground of 1970s and 1980s, even those that explore its "material" aspects (recording and distribution of tape albums, *samizdat* fanzines, semi-legal and apartment-based concerts) usually do not touch upon the financial component of these and other similar activities.[1] One could get the impression that the entire multifaceted and developed infrastructure was driven by pure enthusiasm. True, it was indeed mostly enthusiasm and a passionate desire for the newborn songs to reach their audience that was fundamental to the wide range of activities with and around music, the enthusiasm of musicians as well as their fans and supporters.

Money, however, was an extremely important factor. True, underground musicians lived lives that in many ways were different from those of their ordinary fellow countrymen, yet they were by no means detached from the economy of the late socialist society. In this chapter, I will discuss this increasingly forgotten element in the underground artists' lives—the economy of the underground rock community.

Various forms of music production, distribution, and consumption that ran parallel to the existing official Soviet system began to emerge in the 1960s and reached the peak of their development in the 1980s. In these alternative economic channels money was a factor no less important and instrumental in dropping out of socialist economic realities than Western-inspired music and culture were in dropping out of socialist ideological and cultural dogmas.

Dropping *into* socialism for officially recognized writers, artists, and musicians meant not only being able to publish, exhibit, or perform their works, but also being financially compensated for their creative endeavors. If the Soviet system did not recognize an artist officially, he or she would not be allowed to sell their paintings, be paid for their performances, or receive any honoraria for their works. Thus, the state system itself defined art and artists through their ability/inability to be financially rewarded for their work. Elaborate and diversified tariff rates in publishing, music performance, theatre, and cinema reflected the hierarchy of official recognition just as much as the coveted state awards and titles of Merited or People's Artist. Any and every aspiring artist not accepted into the official creative unions of writers, artists, and composers, and not a staff member of state-run concert organizations would automatically be deemed an "amateur." Amateurs were supposed to have a different source of income and be doing art only as a leisure pastime within the framework of an amateur group.

Deprived of opportunities to "drop into socialism," underground artists were forced to "drop out of it" and start looking for ways to pursue their cultural activities through previously existing or newly established alternative channels for production, distribution, and consumption of their cultural products. Artists, writers, and musicians all had their channels but the system created by rock musicians and rock community in the 1970s–1980s proved to be the best developed and most efficient.

In this chapter I will show what was free and, if payment was necessary, what one had to pay for, who the paying consumers were, and how the proceeds were distributed among artists, manufacturers, and distributors of the artistic and/or media product. I will also look at the role money played in underground rock musicians' efforts to make it into "official" Soviet culture.

## THE ECONOMICS OF SEMI-OFFICIAL AND UNDERGROUND CONCERTS IN THE 1960s–1970s

A wide and well organized network of semi-official concert managers and promoters had existed long before the rock explosion. They used all sorts of cunning schemes involving official concert organizations in remote places to put on performances in a small venue—a trade union, or students' club or, even in a cinema. These concerts were certainly not officially approved or sanctioned, but ways to make them happen could always be found. Between the mid-1960s and the early 1980s, rock groups that could not or did not even attempt to acquire an official status with one of state regional concert organization used complicated, semi-legal schemes for organizing concerts. The schemes were much more popular in Moscow than they were in Leningrad and to a large extent they were implemented not by musicians themselves but by their shadow promoters, who received the lion's share of the profit but, on the other hand, they also took most of the risk.

One of these schemes, according to Moscow music writers and promoters Artemy Troitsky and Il'ia Smirnov, Moscow music journalist and Zvuki Mu group bass player Aleksandr Lipnitskii, and others, was first used as early as in the mid-1960s and consisted of renting a café for a private event: a birthday party or a wedding.[2] Officially, tickets to such event could not be sold; people who could afford five rubles per ticket were invited through private channels.

The very first such concert, a concert of the group Sokol in 1965, attracted eighty paying audience members. The ticket cost five rubles. According to the group's director, Iurii Aizenshpis, "1.5 out of this five went to the group. The remaining 3.5 paid for food and drinks for the audience: a bottle of vodka or wine for a table of four, a salad, a main course, ice cream, and tea. Our 1.5 rubles were shared equally after all expenses."[3] Within a year the group moved to a much larger café with 500–600 seats, and then to palaces of culture with 1,000 seats. There a ticket officially cost two to three rubles, but of course without any food or drinks. Only part of the 2,000–3,000 rubles per concert went to musicians. Formally, the organizers rented out the hall for a film screening, and at the last moment a concert was substituted for the film. The ubiquitous touts were reselling tickets right before the concert at a much higher price. Even though the whole scheme was illegal there were no problems with the authorities: the organizers shared their profits with the police as well as with the directors of clubs or palaces of culture.

According to Troitsky, groups played almost every weekend. The fee was between fifty and one hundred rubles but that included expenses. Troitsky thinks the organizers of these concerts made very decent money:

A concert in the Tushino Palace of Culture attracted 300–400 people. Tickets cost at least three rubles, so even subtracting the (often very long) guest list the "door" was around 1,000 rubles. Even the trendiest group would not receive more than 300 rubles, more often much less. Yes, something had to be given to the administration of the Palace of Culture. Say, one hundred rubles. Even after that the profit was quite substantial and all the talk about altruistic enthusiasm here is just for the naïve.[4]

Troitsky and Smirnov remember that this system existed in Moscow throughout the 1970s all the way up to 1983 when all concerts of non-professional groups were banned outright.[5]

In Leningrad, according to Vladimir Rekshan, Troitsky, and Lipnitskii, the situation in the 1970s was only partially similar to that in Moscow. The lower average standard of living in Leningrad reduced this kind of concert organizing to the bare minimum.[6] Troitsky and Lipnitskii both agree that the main difference was that Moscow was the capital. There is always more money and a higher-paid and more influential bureaucracy in the capital.[7] Troitsky says that the many more temptations that Moscow could and did offer largely defined the difference between the rock scenes in the two cities. Moscow had many more "business people" with a great deal of experience in making money out of entertainment; they adapted old-fashioned schemes that had worked effectively for a long time in other types of show business and they worked equally successfully in organizing semi-official and underground concerts in a newly emerged genre—rock music.

If the groups of the late 1960s and early 1970s in Leningrad had some instruments and a primitive PA system that was barely sufficient for a concert in a student hostel, the groups of the late 1970s and early 1980s had no PA system of their own whatsoever. In the course of ten years only a few concerts could be organized through the "café rental" scheme described above. But even those brought hardly any profit to musicians or organizers.[8] In the late 1960s and early 1970s there was a brief period when groups could regularly play at dance functions outside Leningrad, in student clubs or university dormitories. This period, however, ended in 1973–1974: there were constant, money-based conflicts between musicians and so called "black managers." Quite often these "managers" were just petty crooks.[9]

Between the mid-1970s and early 1980s Leningrad groups lived through a period of *seishns*. This word, obviously derived from English (session), meant concerts that were either free or the entrance charge was alcohol. Musicians Vladimir Rekshan, Boris Grebenshikov, and Iurii Stepanov all claim that in the early 1970s "sessions" were regular occurrences.[10] They were mostly concerts in the universities' clubs with access limited primarily to students. Musicians brought their own PA system which was much inferior to the PA systems of the Moscow bands. Some groups played at dancing functions outside the city but these opportunities were few and far between.

Rekshan, on the other hand, says that throughout his group Sankt-Peterburg's existence (until 1973), along with their student stipends the money they received for these rare events was the main source of income for him and his musicians.[11]

The notion of "a rock manager" already existed. These "managers," however, were mostly amateurish music fans rather than show business professionals.[12] More often than not they were owners of a PA system. Unlike the situation in Moscow, where every group tried to own its own PA system (it was called an *apparat*) the *apparat* owners (*apparatchiks*) in Leningrad were indispensable and therefore very important and influential.

## MONEY AND THE ROCK COMMUNITY IN LENINGRAD IN THE 1970s–1980s

Troitsky, Lipnitskii, and music critic and producer Aleksandr Kan note that the other difference between Moscow and Leningrad that strongly influenced the entire further development of the musical underground was the existence in Leningrad, unlike Moscow, of its own well-developed rock community.[13] Troitsky and Lipnitskii explain the absence of a rock community in Moscow by the fact that Moscow was too big; there were too many unrelated and unconnected professional and social communities and groupings, each with its own interests. "When people are poor and do not really aspire to compete financially it brings them together and creates an atmosphere of trust and friendship. In ever-affluent Moscow things were very different. If the scene in Leningrad was like a shopping bag with a huge watermelon, in Moscow it was more like a shopping bag with fifty oranges."[14]

From the period when it emerged in the late 1960s and in the 1970s, the Leningrad rock community tried to organize a rock club that could produce concerts and—ideally—have a venue of its own. In Moscow there were no attempts of the sort until *perestroika*.

Independent of these efforts, in 1979 a permanently active and officially permitted music club—the first of its kind in Leningrad and, as far as is known, in the country—was organized. It was called the Contemporary Music Club (CMC) and it existed on the premises and under the aegis of a trade union leisure center, the Lensovet Palace of Culture. The CMC existed for three years. Rock music and rock concerts were not in the club's original remit. Its members' main areas of interest were avant-garde jazz, contemporary classical music, and free improvisation. The venue was there, the Palace of Culture even paid for printing posters, and tickets were officially sold but all the proceeds had to go to the box office. Even though musicians never received any fees, the money however was badly needed: to rent the PA system, taxis for a double bass or a harp, and train tickets or airfare for visiting musicians. Aleksandr Kan, the CMC President, remembers that the Club activists came up with a scheme that was not very legal but simple and very effective. They received officially issued tickets and were allowed to sell them among friends and acquaintances. So each ticket went through three or four rounds of circulation: the necessary payments were duly made to the box office and the remainder paid for all the necessary expenses. The entrance was controlled by Club activists and if you had paid for the ticket you were admitted and your ticket was resold. Rock was the Club's only marginal activity, the amounts were miniscule, the annual turnover was in the lower hundreds of rubles, and when the CMC was eventually banned in 1982, it was for ideological rather than financial reasons.[15]

In March 1981 the first rock club in the USSR was opened on the premises and under the aegis of the Leningrad Inter-Union House of Amateur Creative Activity (Leningradskii Mezhsoiuznyi Dom Samodeiatel'nogo Tvorchestva, LMDST). Like the CMC it was a grassroots initiative but it was financially supported by the trade unions. Trade unions existed on membership dues and they had their own leisure and entertainment centers, houses and palaces of culture whose job was to organize "cultural activities" for the trade unions' constituents. "Cultural activities" was a very broad concept which included children's workshops, various educational courses (from knitting and sewing to foreign languages and radio engineering), nonprofessional photography, and film studios—the range was enormous. The opening of the Leningrad Rock Club (Leningradskii rok-klub) was a part of a wider program of creating a KGB-curated network of "cultural reservations" for the underground art community in Leningrad. At the same time that the Rock Club opened, writers were allowed to open their Klub-81 and visual artists received permission to form the Association for Experimental Visual Arts (Tovarishchestvo Eksperimental'nogo Izobrazitel'nogo Iskusstva, TEII).[16]

LMDST had a small hall with a PA system where it was possible to have regular (originally, monthly) concerts. Tickets were free and were distributed among the musicians (one each), members of the board, photographers, and special guests. Musicians performing in a given concert were entitled to two tickets but received no fees for performances.

Inna Volkova from the group Kolibri observes that there was a certain period when any group that was granted a Rock Club membership—irrespective of the quality of its music—immediately rose in status, reputation, recognition, and commercial potential.[17]

Journalist Vladislav Bachurov remembers that there were groups which aspired to become Rock Club members with one and only one purpose—to be eligible for the Rock Club concert tickets. They hardly ever played but never missed a concert. On the other hand, there were those who never attended other groups' concerts and were therefore a reliable source of tickets for a concert they did not play. Sometimes unneeded tickets were sold before the concerts—not for the money as such, just to buy some booze for the after-party.[18] Olga Slobodskaia, the Rock Club secretary in the late 1980s, remembers that tickets were indeed sold: "For special occasions (the opening of the season or the festival) the tickets could fetch up to five rubles. Once I was asked to sell a few tickets that had been allocated to our technical team—they needed money to buy cables, jacks, and other necessary stuff. I was told to get a fiver for each ticket. But generally the tout culture did not really exist. It was only occasionally that you could find a ticket sold."[19] Artist Andrei Stolypin remembers that a full set of tickets for the 1986 rock festival cost forty rubles.[20] But Dem'ian Kudriavtsev, at the time a high school student without any connections to the scene, remembers that young fans like him had to pay between ten and twenty-five rubles per ticket. On the day of the concert an outsider could consider himself extraordinarily lucky if he could find a ticket for five rubles.[21]

Vsevolod Grach, the director of Zoopark, remembers that people with influence and connections within the Rock Club hierarchy could be a source of concert tickets:

The *Roksi* [magazine] editor Sasha Startsev had a regular clientele from other cities that came specifically for the festival. Unlike our penniless bohemians, these people had money and were prepared to pay a hefty price for the access to a concert. If the set of tickets to the 1986 festival at the Nevskii Palace of Culture did indeed cost forty rubles, a year later, after Akvarium had played official concerts at a sports arena and was regularly featured on TV, the same set already cost seventy rubles. Often musicians asked friends to sell their unneeded tickets—to do it themselves would be below their dignity. If the concert was taking place elsewhere, comp tickets would be an alternative source of income. Musicians and/or owners of the PA system equipment were sometimes paid in comp tickets. Say at a concert in the Lenin or Krupskaia Palace of Culture, a top group could receive up to one hundred comp tickets. Their starting resale price was three rubles. The system was not unlike that in the 1970s when everybody who could sell ten tickets got himself a free comp ticket. But if in the 1970s one in four or five concerts ended with a police raid, after the Rock Club was opened the raids stopped even though there 500–600 unaccounted for rubles around each concert.[22]

Between March 1981 and April 1982 the Leningrad Rock Club and the Contemporary Music Club existed in parallel but in April 1982 the CMC was closed.[23] The most likely reason for the ban was the desire of the city authorities responsible for ideological control in the cultural sphere to localize and concentrate the entire music underground under one roof, that of the Rock Club. The CMC was an alternative venue which required additional efforts and resources to control. The idea of mono-reservations in the cultural underground prevailed.[24]

## TOURING MOSCOW: THE ECONOMICS OF THE LENINGRAD GROUPS' SEMI-OFFICIAL CONCERTS IN THE CAPITAL IN THE EARLY 1980s

The system of club-based "reservations" for the former cultural underground that was set up in Leningrad on the basis of trade unions economically and organizationally placed them on par with numerous other amateur cultural groups and societies who were allowed to practice their art in their free time without any financial remuneration. True, the opportunity to play more or less regularly without having to be concerned with finding a venue or the

necessary PA system was a significant step forward: it gave the groups access
to an audience and a chance to somehow find a way into official, professional
Soviet entertainment system. What it did not offer was money. Money, however, was badly needed: unlike their Moscow counterparts Leningrad rock
musicians of the early 1980s did not play in VIAs, in restaurants, or at dance
soirées. Most of them however were nearing thirty; many had families or
lived with a partner rather than with their parents. Most had an "official" day
job elsewhere. In most cases this job had nothing to do with music, and was
unrelated to their education (finished or unfinished). Salaries ranged between
seventy to one hundred and forty rubles a month. This money could be sufficient to live the relatively "normal" life of an average Leningrad resident,
especially if your wife or girlfriend had a job paying similar wages, but it was
certainly not enough to invest in and sustain the existence of a group. Being a
rock musician meant buying instruments and maintaining a "rock lifestyle":
owning new releases of Western music, and maintaining your clothing and
overall appearance in accordance with certain standards accepted within the
rock community.

The best opportunity to make money was by touring, first and foremost in
Moscow. The earliest Moscow concerts of Leningrad groups were organized
almost exclusively by Troitsky.[25] In organizing these concerts, he combined
two missions: enlightenment and "soft intrusion." He organized Akvarium
concerts in small venues for a very select and very narrow audience of influential culture and media people in order to introduce them to the new wave
of Leningrad rock. He did not have any ambition to make money out of this.
Nor did he think the groups should aim to make money. He tried to obtain
what he called "mixed funding." For instance, he arranged for Akvarium
to participate in the Central TV youth program "Veselye Rebiata" in 1981.
Central TV paid for their train fare, accommodations, and food, and Troitsky
organized a few concerts on the side—but without receiving any fee for
himself or the group.[26] He also organized "home concerts" for the cultural
elite in huge professorial or *nomenklatura* apartments which could hold up to
one hundred people.[27] At Troitsky's instigation the new wave of Leningrad
rock—Akvarium, Zoopark, and Kino—was seen by the new Moscow "managers." This new managerial generation consisted largely of rock fans, most
of them still students. For them, as much as for Troitsky, this activity was
more a matter of proselytizing than business.

A niche for organizing such concerts was found in the gray zone of vaguely
defined administrative subordination of several cinemas and houses of culture. Like Leningrad and every other Soviet city, Moscow had a number of
houses of culture which belonged to local trade unions and sometimes were
even directly connected to a factory or an institute. Managers picked up these
venues, which were mostly on a small scale, for the new wave of rock concerts. They began with local bands of the new generation and a few of the

surviving groups from the 1970s. Soon, however, they switched to Leningrad groups that were enjoying much more popularity. Troitsky condemns these concerts as "too commercial,"[28] although Il'ia Smirnov, one of the new promoters, insists they were hardly any different from those organized by Troitsky himself: all the money that they made went to cover the expenses of bringing musicians from Leningrad and their fees.[29] In any case, this new frenzy of concert activity could not go unnoticed by the authorities. Since these concerts were beyond any system, virtually any branch of state power could impose restrictions or ban them outright.

From 1981 on various governmental and administrative bodies in Moscow issued a number of executive orders and regulations aimed at regulating concerts and tours, music played in discotheques, and similar music-related activities.[30] Most of these decisions and regulations remained largely unnoticed by rock promoters. The authorities were trying, again and again, to regulate the work of the same orchestras or ensembles that were officially registered at trade union houses of culture. There were very few of those among the new generation of Moscow groups, while Leningrad groups were beyond Moscow's local jurisdiction altogether.

In 1983 the Moscow City Committee of the Komsomol, the City Government Departments of Culture, the People's Education and Professional Education, and the Moscow Council of Trade Unions issued a joint decree. It was called "On Measures for Regulating the Activities of Amateur Variety Musical Collectives in the City of Moscow." This decree finally managed to fill in the interdepartmental crack that allowed unofficial rock concerts to be organized at various venues. Control of "amateur musical collectives" (i.e., rock groups) was delegated to the so-called Scientific and Methodical Centers of Folk Creativity.

According to this decree, industrial enterprises, educational institutions, and Komsomol organizations were no longer allowed to organize dance events without special permission from the District Department of Culture. Trade union organizations were no longer allowed to their own PA systems and instruments without special permission.[31]

In August 1983 the leader of Voskresen'e, Aleksei Romanov, and the group's sound engineer, Aleksandr Arutiunov, were arrested and charged with private entrepreneurship that consisted of selling tickets to one of the group's own concerts. Even though they were not tried until May 1984,[32] right after their arrest all concert activity in the city virtually stopped. Any attempt to organize a concert invariably resulted in a police raid and no possibility of potential earnings could encourage musicians to take that risk. The very limited concert activity that remained was kept absolutely secret and was finally terminated in the spring of 1984 after the police raided a Bravo concert and the group's singer, Zhanna Aguzarova, was arrested for the use of a false passport.[33]

## THE ECONOMICS OF THE APARTMENT
## CONCERTS (*KVARTIRNIKI*) IN MOSCOW

The Romanov and Aguzarova cases signaled the end of the era of semi-legal concerts and the beginning of the era of apartment concerts. After the ban on rock concerts in Moscow, the same managers who had organized events in clubs and cinemas moved to a system of apartment concerts. However, they switched almost exclusively from organizing events for Moscow groups to organizing concerts for groups from Leningrad who mostly had small-scale chamber programs, did not require PA systems or electric instruments, and could play acoustic ("unplugged") in apartments.[34]

Il'ia Smirnov, who organized the lion's share of these concerts, remembers that the entrance charge for an apartment concert was one-and-a-half to two rubles, very rarely three. He claims he and his fellow organizers were very strict in charging no more than what was necessary to cover expenses. The entrance price was calculated with simple arithmetic: the band's fee, plus the cost of the hired equipment divided by the capacity of the listening area in the apartment. Anyone entrusted with selling tickets and caught overcharging was immediately dismissed.[35] Smirnov adds: "The entrance fee to apartment concerts was the same as it had previously been for clubs and cinemas. Expenses, however, were immeasurably smaller."[36] Troitsky disagrees. He thinks that rock managers who were deprived of their income at semi-legal café and cinema events transformed the apartment concerts that had been originally put on for pure enlightenment, entertainment, and fun into a money-oriented business. He remembers that "prices far exceeded the old one-and-a-half to three rubles and went as high as five or even ten rubles."[37]

These two different approaches to organizing concerts and different ways of understanding the purpose of these concerts resulted in a serious conflict between two groups of rock managers even though both were genuine rock enthusiasts. Troitsky, as mentioned above, pursued the line of a gradual and, as he believed, potentially possible integration of Leningrad rock groups into the official culture. To achieve his objective he used (mostly apartment) concerts as a means of convincing those with influence that this new wave of rock presented no threat to members of the official Composers Union or any other state institution. With that purpose in mind, Troitsky believed that these groups should by no means be in conflict with the law. Therefore he abstained from receiving any fees and remained firmly in legal territory. Apartment concerts as such were not illegal, but charging entrance fees for them was. Troitsky, along with his influential friends, feared that musicians could find themselves in the dock not for concerts as such but for being paid for playing in them.

Troitsky admits that his position, reasonable as it was, was not entirely welcomed by Leningrad musicians. Akvarium, Kino, and Zoopark as well as their respective leaders Grebenshikov, Tsoi, and Naumenko as "solo artists" saw these concerts primarily as a source of income and, in spite of Troitsky's warnings, they continued to accept invitations to play at for-fee apartment concerts. This was hardly surprising: according to Smirnov, Akvarium's fee could reach 200–400 rubles per concert, depending on the number of musicians playing.[38] Just one such concert paid more than musicians earned in a month at their jobs as night watchmen, street cleaners, or boiler room operators. No wonder it was hard for Leningrad musicians to resist the temptation to play at for-fee concerts. They maneuvered between the influential Troitsky and financially efficient managers skillfully and quite successfully, accepting invitations from both camps and ignoring Moscow infighting. In one place they made money, in the other they tried to find a way into the official scene.

Musicians' fees for apartment concerts in the 1980s varied greatly and depended on the band's status and reputation as well as the size of the apartment. Aleksei Rybin from the early incarnation of Kino remembers that the fees for apartment concerts were quite fixed. The audience was charged three or five rubles, and the musicians usually received fifty rubles. Mike Naumenko established a fixed rate for his Moscow concerts: one ruble per minute: "He would start his concerts by smoking his pipe and telling jokes. In the meantime, the clock was ticking . . . ."[39]

## THE ECONOMICS OF THE APARTMENT CONCERTS (*KVARTIRNIKI*) IN LENINGRAD

The wave of apartment concerts in Leningrad began at about the same time as it did in Moscow. Apartment concerts in their own city gave musicians a chance to earn additional income as well as to try out new songs in front of an audience. Initially these concerts were organized by someone from the musicians' close circle of friends who had a relatively large apartment and peaceful or friendly neighbors.[40] In the mid-1980s *kvartirniki* were organized with increasing frequency by enterprising fans who were not necessarily from the musicians' close circles. Rock journalist Vladislav Bachurov, a teenage schoolboy in those days, remembers that the entrance charge to an apartment concert was one ruble plus something for the alcohol if there was only one musician—Mike solo for instance. If the artists were in a duo—Viktor Tsoi with his guitarist Iurii Kasparian—the price doubled, plus of course something for the wine that the entire audience and the musicians shared.[41]

Andrei Stolypin, the designer of the Alisa rock group, remembers that the entrance charges for different artists varied. "Grebenshikov—alone or with one or two musicians—cost two rubles plus something for the booze. Mike or Tsoi in the same apartment cost less."[42]

Inna Volkova from the female band Kolibri remembers that sometimes concerts were organized with hardly any financial incentive. "After a Viktor Tsoi concert the audience was very gently encouraged to contribute as much as they could. All the proceeds were immediately spent on booze."[43]

How did people find out about these concerts? Andrei Temkin, who regularly organized Grebenshikov's apartment concerts in the 1980s, remembers:

Before my first concert I went to the RIM (an unofficial name for a popular student café), and told all my friends. I also told a few people from the Saigon (another café, with an equally unofficial name). About thirty people crammed into my friend's tiny studio. I charged three rubles apiece and gave the entire amount to the last kopek to Grebenshikov and his bass player Titov. It turned out to be even more than their pre-agreed fee. I never kept a penny for myself. It was a pleasure and a privilege anyway. Then a friend tells me: I want to do one, put me in touch with the maestro.[44]

Temkin continues: "He organized a huge event in a spacious old apartment in Petrogradskaia. There were more than one hundred people. The entrance charge was ten rubles. I did not organize the concert so I did not count the money but I know that the musicians received only 10 percent of the door. My friend, however, made quite a bit of money and bought himself an expensive twelve-string guitar."[45]

Vsevolod Grach explains that the pay for the apartment concerts as well as their duration largely depended on musicians' character and how they felt on a given day:

[Alisa's leader and songwriter] Kostia Kinchev when inspired could sing for hours for people he hardly knew. Mike Naumenko, on the other hand, treated performing live as a very serious business. He was often reluctant to sing, played only for close friends and colleagues. As for the entrance charge to a *kvartirnik*, it varied from one ruble to three. Very rarely did it reach five plus the contribution for the booze, of course. As a personal friend of musicians, I never paid. But I always brought people who never whined about paying and always had plenty of booze with them. That was my contribution to the business. The number of [people in] the audience usually varied between fifteen and fifty. Quite often there would be a really wealthy member of the audience, mostly someone from Moscow, and during the painful process of collecting money for the booze they could just throw in a note of twenty-five or fifty rubles and that would resolve the issue.[46]

Apartment concerts went on in Leningrad and Moscow until the late 1980s. In the late 1980s, the entrance charge to a *kvartirnik* was often considerably higher than what it cost to go to a large concert, but people were prepared to pay for exclusivity, intimacy, and a chance to talk to and share a drink with the artist.

## *MAGNITIZDAT* AND HOW IT MADE MONEY

*Magnitizdat*[47] as a phenomenon was not invented by rock musicians. Like semi-legal concerts and *kvartirniki*, it had existed since the very early 1960s and was mostly associated with the bard movement. With the artist's permission, a bard concert was taped by the organizers or by members of the audience and the tape was consequently reproduced.[48] Mass distribution of such tapes became possible when tape recorders became widely available in the USSR in the late 1950s. The very first models cost a prohibitive 300 rubles but only a few years later the 1960 Chaika' cost 105 rubles which was about an average monthly wage at the time. A good quality tape recorder cost about 200 rubles which was quite affordable for many families.

There were two systems of distribution: free if you copied a recording from friends or relatives and for money when duplicating tapes was turned into a business. For free taping people used household tape recorders and record players; the business system was concentrated in the sound recording kiosks that operated in all the major cities.

Officially these kiosks existed so that you could tape a vinyl record released by the state label Melodiia or records released in Eastern European countries and licensed in the USSR. However, in these very kiosks you could find tape recordings of Vysotsky and, with the advent of the rock boom, reels with Western rock music. The kiosks qualified as "personal services" and for a long time their work and the music they offered were not regulated in any way.

Rock *magnitizdat* in Leningrad grew directly out of the underground concert activity of the late 1970s.[49] Andrei Tropillo, who recorded all the most important and significant albums of Leningrad rock, began as semi-legal concert organizer. Tropillo's official job was teaching children the basics of recording engineering at a Young Pioneers club. A small, but decently equipped recording studio was almost entirely at his disposal. Always trying to combine his creative ideas with commerce, Tropillo began by duplicating the recordings that Mashina Vremeni brought along from Moscow. Soon he thought, however, that those recordings were neither technically nor conceptually satisfactory:

> I realized there had to be an album form. The album, I believed, was the
> ideal self-generating form of communication. I just took the recordings that

[Mashina Vremeni leader Andrei] Makarevich brought along and tweaked them the way I thought was better on my quite lousy equipment. So I made a collection of songs, called them *Den' Rozhdeniia* (Birthday), took some photographs, made 200 copies of the reel and released them through my friends and contacts into the city. I did not really try to make any money. I was just curious: what on earth would happen? So it all happened.[50]

Tropillo never charged musicians for using "his" recording facilities at the Young Pioneer Club studio. Aleksei Vishnia, one of his students who later set up a makeshift studio in his own apartment and recorded a few Kino albums, remembers that Tropillo strictly forbade him to charge musicians for using the studio as well as selling tape albums: "As soon as you start doing it," as Vishnia recollects Tropillo's words, "OBKHSS [the economic police–AK] will come to you as a regular client with a test purchase and you will have very serious problems"[51]

Vishnia admits, however, that Tropillo was far from altruistic even though he loved the process of recording and enjoyed beating the system. In the mid-1980s he encouraged his student to record as many Rock Club groups as possible: a time would come, he said, when all these recordings would be in high demand, capitalism would arrive, and the owners of the original master tapes would become millionaires.[52]

Now, when asked, Tropillo cannot quite understand what his confidence that the Soviet system would collapse sometime soon was based on. He admits though that his predictions turned out to be much too optimistic: when proper record labels did arrive in the 1990s, the biggest royalties for the proper releases of the original tapes of albums went to songwriters rather than the owners of the master tapes.[53]

One of the initial sources of "commercial" distribution of taped albums—like sales of tickets to the Rock Club concerts—were the musicians themselves. The musicians' immediate circle of friends could count on receiving copies for free, "friends of friends," however, not only had to supply a blank tape but had to pay for the recording as well. A 525m reel of Soviet-made Tasma or Svema tape cost seven rubles, imported ORWO or Scotch tape cost eighteen to twenty rubles.[54] Imported tapes were used to record off original Western vinyl. Russian magnetic albums were recorded onto Soviet-made tapes. Bass player Aleksandr Titov remembers selling audio tapes with Akvarium and Kino albums he played on for ten rubles apiece. Tropillo gave him studio-made copies of the original masters as well as a semi-professional MELZ tape recorder. Grebenshikov gave him his Mayak-205 tape recorder. With these two machines he could manufacture multiple copies. He bought Soviet-made blank tapes in shops. The photographer Andrei "Willy" Usov charged him one ruble for a print of his original photograph. Titov's profit was two rubles from every tape. Among his clients were friends of friends as well as people he did not know at all who had come from other cities in search of new recordings and had been given his phone number at the Saigon.[55]

Albums were usually sold as 250-meter reels so that each side of the tape ran for about twenty to twenty-five minutes to be as close as possible in duration to an average LP. Track lists were divided into Side A and Side B. All this was done to make the listening experience as close as possible to listening to an original Western LP album. Mike Naumenko emphasized the deliberateness of the effort by screaming at the top of his lungs at the end of Side A of a Zoopark album: "Turn it over!"

Producer and sound engineer Igor "Punker" Gudkov also remembers that leading musicians were selling their albums: "I paid Boris Grebenshikov six rubles for the *Brothers and Sisters* album. I also remember selling a reel with Mike's *LV* album for twelve rubles. The proceeds were split with the artist."[56] The *Brothers and Sisters* album is a very early (1977) recording. As Andrei Temkin recalled, in the mid-1980s, with the popularity of domestic rock growing, prices for tape albums skyrocketed. "In 1985–1986, I bought tapes directly from Grebenshikov and paid fifteen rubles for an album. For this price you also got the prints of Willy Usov's photographs and you were supposed to glue them on the packages DIY." He also remembers that he paid fifteen rubles for a Zoopark album: "The seller did not look particularly trustworthy, some punk who I accidentally met outside the Zvezdnaia underground station. However, Zoopark was there as it should have been, and the other side was filled with a Deep Purple album. Both were recorded at top sound quality."[57]

Kino co-founder Aleksei Rybin says the group's musicians were selling their albums for ten rubles an album.[58] Aleksei Vishnia sold the tapes not only to fans but to wholesale dealers: "I glued the prints with Usov's photographs onto the packages and sold the tapes with one album at ten rubles apiece," he remembers. Andrei Temkin and Aleksandr Senin from the group Coffee rightly observe that "prices varied greatly." They depended on the quality of the photoprint on the cover and the city of purchase (Moscow, Leningrad, or further out in the provinces) and ranged between ten and twenty-five rubles.[59] Lithuanian journalist and promoter Mark Shliamovich confirms that outside Leningrad tape and/or cassette albums cost much more. In Vilnius in the mid-1980s a cassette with two albums cost at least ten and more often fifteen rubles. Sometimes the price could reach twenty-five rubles.[60] Vsevolod Grach gives a more elaborate and detailed picture:

> The starting price (when bought directly from a musician) for a packaged tape album was around ten rubles but eventually it could reach twenty-five especially in other cities. Quite often DJs from Kazan, Kharkov, or other cities bought just

recordings without packaging and paid two to three rubles for an album (on top of the price of a blank tape of course). But they demanded top-notch sound quality. Close friends, members of the *tusovka* received new recording mostly for free—at worst for a bottle of alcohol for joint, friendly consumption. Duplication was not as easy or accessible as it may look—hardly anybody owned decent equipment for the purpose. Sergey "Firik" Firsov, the main distributor of recordings in the city, owned an Aiwa double cassette deck. This wonderful Japanese miracle cost absolutely improbable 1,500 rubles. Having invested such a fortune in your equipment, charging distant acquaintances or DJs from other cities two to three rubles per album seemed a fair price. Every year I was going to a ski resort on the Elbrus Mountain, in the Caucasus. Local bartenders and DJs always asked me to bring along tapes with new music. There were strict requirements however: the music had to be NEW, the recording had to be a first-generation copy off an original LP for the Western music or off an original tape for the Soviet rock groups. They paid twenty rubles for a cassette with two albums. The blank cassette cost nine rubles so the margin was well worth the effort. Four or five sleepless nights earned me a pair of skis with boots—Western-made, impossible to find in any store. On top of that I could use the chairlifts for free and was treated to complimentary drinks at the bar—after all it was MY music that sounded throughout the resort.

Russian rock with good sound quality was a very commercial proposition. Sasha Startsev, the editor of the *samizdat* rock magazine *Roksi*, had a well-developed network of DJ clients in various cities, from Kharkov to Vladivostok:

> They were decent, educated guys with a mission to spread new music in their regions. At the same time, they were quite affluent and prepared to pay a good price for quality. I'm sure they could return their investments quite easily in their own cities. A bit later, with the cooperative movement starting, these guys opened their own private recording salons and studios. They had played a huge role in spreading the word and once the underground rock musicians were allowed to perform, fifty posters would be enough to fill a stadium for a concert of a leading group.[61]

## HOW MOSCOW "WRITERS" MADE MONEY ON *MAGNITIZDAT*

With or without an exchange of money, Leningrad-made albums on tape were spread by musicians further and further out into the provinces along the routes described by Grach. In Moscow, the situation was, however, quite different. Moscow groups were not nearly as active in recording albums as their Leningrad counterparts and until the mid-1980s it was primarily Leningrad groups' albums that were circulating in the capital. Smirnov, Troitsky, Lipnitskii, and others remember that original, fully packaged albums with proper photoprint covers hardly ever reached Moscow and only very few personal friends of musicians were privileged to receive them as personal gifts.[62] Tape duplication was the business of the so-called *pisateli.* The word literally means writers. The reason they were called writers lies in the etymology: the word *zapisyvat'* (to record) has the same linguistic root as *pisat'* (to write). A "writer" had at least ten tape (and later cassette) recorders in his apartment, and in the hottest period (when a new Akvarium album had just come out) they worked around the clock.[63] Like those friends of Grach who came to Leningrad to purchase tapes, "writers" had business partners all over the country: they were either local "writers" or worked in small retail kiosks. It was a labor-intensive but highly profitable business but its scope, volume, and monetary value are very difficult to estimate.

Initially the "writers" worked independently of each other. In the early 1980s, however, they formed a "writers' union." It was a very elaborate and complicated structure that split the country into "spheres of influence." So "writers" worked in Moscow and their distributors went out as traveling salesmen to their allocated regions with boxes of tapes. Moscow "writer" Andrei Lukinov remembers that several writers contributed to the purchase of the master original that cost fifty to two hundred rubles, depending on the expected demand. The money earned was invested in developing the business: acquiring high-quality tape recorders and tapes.[64] Moscow "writers" even went as far as investing money in rare recordings of Moscow-based groups. Troitsky remembers how Viktor Alisov, who was one of the best-known "writers," funded studio recordings of Alliance and Primus. He got a return on his investments by duplicating and selling cassette copies of the recorded albums.[65]

No Leningrad musician, member of the *tusovka,* or recording engineer ever had any problems with the *militsiia* (police) or the KGB for recording and distributing their tapes. This could be explained by the fact that apart from the above-mentioned Sergei "Firik" Firsov there were no "writers" as such in Leningrad. In Moscow, however, the situation was quite different. The first restrictions appeared in 1984 when, on the basis of the Ministerial Decree, the All-Union Scientific and Methodological Center of the USSR Ministry of Culture recommended a ban on reproducing and displaying vinyl records, cassettes, video-recordings, posters, and other products that reflected activities of certain groups, Western as well as Soviet. This ban was recommended for commercial activities around records, cassettes, and related products in the city of Moscow. The recommendation was issued as a follow-up to the decree that ordered a thorough inspection of the repertoire of discotheques and audio-recording kiosks. The order resulted not just in inspection but in an attempt to shut down the distribution network and its center in Moscow. Several "writers" were charged with unlawful entrepreneurship although none of them were tried and convicted.[66]

Troitsky believes that pressure upon "writers" was not as strong as it could have been because by that time the focus of ideological and financial control had shifted to fighting "video-writers."[67] Duplication of video films that was evolving virtually simultaneously with music was much more important and serious, for two reasons: the legal ramifications and the financial turnover. "Video-writers," as Troitsky and Lipnitskii note, were busy reproducing either erotic films, which were subject to anti-pornography legislation, or films like *Rocky* which could be qualified as anti-Soviet and therefore subject to the corresponding, strictly enforced articles of the Penal Code.[68] Many "video-writers" were arrested and jailed, but they were sentenced mainly on the basis of the two provisions of the Penal Code mentioned above. On the other hand, Troitsky does not exclude the fact that "writers" had their own "business" relations with the *militsiia*'s economic departments: "They made very serious money and I have no doubt that they shared their profits with the *militsiia*." At a later stage, Troitsky reminds us, some "writers" in Moscow were fully legalized and did their job quite officially under the auspices of the Rock Laboratory that was established in Moscow in 1987.[69]

By the mid-1980s both kiosks and "writers" switched from reel-to-reel tapes to cassettes: Soviet-made and imported cassette-recorders as well as cassettes were widely popular and replaced outdated reel-to-reel tapes. Evgenii Pavlenko, then a student in Leningrad, remembers that in the mid-1980s a Soviet MK-60 cassette cost four rubles and an imported C-90 cost nine rubles.[70] Soviet-made cassettes were of a very poor quality: the tape fell apart in flakes, was often "chewed up" by the cassette-player, and damaged the recording heads of the cassette-recorder. Also, the duration of a standard rock album was forty-five minutes so for two albums you needed either one imported cassette for nine rubles or two Soviet-made cassettes at four rubles apiece. Of course music fans preferred imported cassettes. Still, they were expensive and, as Dem'ian Kudriavtsev remembers, there was a market for used cassettes that you could buy at second-hand shops or from a second-hand dealer at schools or universities.[71] Moscow journalist Aleksei Pevchev remembers that in the late 1980s the prices charged by "writers" and at audio kiosks were about the same: it cost four rubles to record a side of a cassette (one album).[72]

The culture of recording and reproducing magnetic albums existed for years after the collapse of the USSR. The first CDs with reissued classic Akvarium albums were only released in 1995. For another few years (until 1998), only newly recorded albums were released as CDs and the old catalogs were very slowly reissued. In the last years of the "cassette culture" albums were no longer recorded in audio kiosks but were bought and sold in the music shops that mushroomed all over the former USSR.

## CONCLUSION

Recording and packaging tape albums, establishing the Leningrad Rock Club, organizing semi-official concerts, tours and festivals, publishing *samizdat* rock magazines, Soviet rock musicians and the rock community conceived and created an alternative rock "industry" in the 1970s–1980s. Their efforts in creating a microcosm of their own were enormously important as a means of creative self-realization. At the same time, this alternative and independent infrastructure provided musicians with additional sources of income from reproducing and selling tape albums, re-selling concert tickets, and playing apartment and semi-legal concerts.

The very existence of these alternative channels for both underground musicians and their managers to make money means that the Soviet system had room for many possibilities for engaging in unofficial commerce. The underground developed a sophisticated economic system, which exploited the weaknesses of the official one. This alternative economy played a key role in spreading rock culture across the USSR. Even though the main agents were shadow businessmen driven primarily by commercial interests, music reached much wider audiences through their "business" than it could have if distributed gratis from friend to friend.

Having emerged and functioning largely in a situation of "dropping out of socialism," the Soviet musical underground replicated much of the official system. As was the case in the "normal world," there was an unwritten hierarchy of pricing among the groups, which reflected their as yet unofficial popularity, recognition, and status. As was usual in every other sphere of Soviet life, *blat* or connections played a crucial role: they gave free or cheap access to things that any outsider had to buy at a full market price.

## NOTES

1. Thomas Cushman, *Notes From Underground: Rock Music Counterculture in Russia* (Albany: State University of New York Press, 1995); Paul Easton, "The Rock Music Community," in *Soviet Youth Culture*, ed. James Riordan (Bloomington: Indiana University Press, 1989); Polly McMichael, "'After All, You're a Rock and Roll Star (At Least, That's What They Say)': Roksi and the Creation of the Soviet Rock Musician," *Slavonic and East European Review* 83, no. 4 (2005): 664–84; Polly McMichael, "The Making of the Soviet Rock Star, Leningrad, 1972–1987" (PhD diss., University of Cambridge, 2007); Polly McMichael, "'A Room-Sized Ocean': Apartments in the Practice and Mythology of Leningrad's Rock Music," in *Youth and Rock in the Soviet Bloc: Youth Cultures, Music, and the State in Russia and Eastern Europe*, ed. William Jay Risch (Lanham, MD: Lexington Books, 2015); Sabrina P. Ramet, *Rocking The State: Rock Music and Politics in Eastern Europe and Russia* (Boulder, CO: Westview Press, 1994); Timothy W. Ryback, *Rock Around the*

*Bloc: A History of Rock Music in Eastern Europe and the Soviet Union* (New York: Oxford University Press, 1990); Yngvar B. Steinholt, *Rock in the Reservation: Songs from the Leningrad Rock-Club 1981–86* (New York: Mass Media Music Scholars' Press, 2004); Artemy Troitsky, *Back in the USSR: The True Story of Rock in Russia* (London: Omnibus Press, 1987).

2. Artemy Troitsky (b. 1955), interview with the author, London, May 2014; Il'ia Smirnov (b. 1958), interview with the author, Moscow, July 2013; Aleksandr Lipnitskii (b. 1952), interview with the author, London, November 2012.

3. Iurii Aizenshpis, *Ot fartsovshika do prodiusera: Delovye liudi v SSSR* (Moscow: Algoritm, 2014).

4. Troitsky.

5. Troitsky; Smirnov.

6. Vladimir Rekshan, *Kaif polnyi* (St. Petersburg: Amfora, 2006); Aleksandr Ustinov, *Etot russkii rock-n-roll* (St. Petersburg: Amfora, 2009), Troitsky; Lipnitskii.

7. Troitsky.

8. Diusha Romanov, *Istoriia Akvariuma: Kniga fleitista* (Moscow: Olma-Press, 2001); author's interviews with the musicians of Akvarium: Boris Grebenshikov (b. 1953), interview with the author, London, August 2012; Diusha Romanov (1956–2000), interview with the author, St. Petersburg, 1996; Mikhail Fainshtein (1953–2013), interview with the author, St. Petersburg, 1996.

9. Vladimir Rekshan (b. 1950), interviews with the author, St. Petersburg 1996.

10. Rekshan; Grebenshikov; Iurii Stepanov (1951–2010), interview with the author, London, 2007.

11. Rekshan, *Kaif polnyi*.

12. Romanov, *Istoriia Akvariuma*; Steinholt, *Rock in the Reservation*.

13. Troitsky; Lipnitskii; Aleksandr Kan (b. 1954), interview with the author, London, 2012.

14. Troitsky.

15. See more about the Contemporary Music Club in Aleksandr Kan, *Poka ne nachalsia Jazz* (St. Petersburg: Amfora, 2008).

16. Nataliia Veselova (b. 1958, Leningrad Rock Club curator from LMDST in 1984–1989), interview with the author, St. Petersburg, 2015; underground culture curator from the KGB in early 1980s (who asked to remain anonymous), interview with the author, St. Petersburg, 2015.

17. Inna Volkova (b. 1964), interview with the author, St. Petersburg, 2013.

18. Vladislav Bachurov (b. 1965), interview with the author, St. Petersburg, 2013.

19. Olga Slobodskaia (b. 1966), interview with the author, St. Petersburg, 2013.

20. Andrei Stolypin (b. 1963), interview with the author, St. Petersburg, 2013.

21. Dem'ian Kudryavtsev (b. 1971) interview with the author, London, 2013.

22. Vsevolod Grach (b. 1951), interview with the author, St. Petersburg, 2013.

23. Kan.

24. Kan, *Poka ne nachalsia jazz*.

25. Troitsky; Grebenshikov; Lipnitskii.

26. Troitsky.

27. Lipnitskii.

28. Troitsky.

29. Smirnov.

30. Reshenie Ispolkoma Mossoveta "Ob usilenii kontrolia za provedeniem kontsertnoi raboty v g. Moskve," no. 3828, December 26, 1980; Reshenie Ispolkoma Mossoveta "O merakh po sovershenstvovaniiu konsertnoi raboty v g. Moskve i gastrolnoi deiatel'nosti Moskontserta," no. 558, March 10, 1981; Reshenie Ispolkoma Mossoveta i Prezidiuma MGSPS "O merakh po vypolneniiu postanovleniia Soveta Ministrov RSFSR 'Ob uluchshenii praktiki organizatsii khudozhestvennoi samodeiatelnosti v RSFS,'" no. 3720, December 31, 1981; Reshenie Ispolkoma Mossoveta i kollegii Minkultury SSSR "O sozdanii Koordinatsionnogo soveta po organizatsii konsertnoi deiatel'nosti v Moskve," no. 1453-91, May 31, 1982; Reshenie Ispolkoma Mossoveta, Prezidiuma MGSPS i Buro MGK VLKSM "O merakh po povysheniiu ideino-khudozhestvennogo urovnia raboty diskotek g. Moskvy," no. 3115, November 3, 1982.

31. Quoted by Il'ia Smirnov in *Vremia kolokolchikov* (Moscow: INTO, 1994), 108–9.

32. Romanov was sentenced to a three-year suspended sentence and confiscation of all his possessions. Arutiunov was sentenced to three years in a labor camp.

33. See more about the Romanov and Aguzarova cases in Smirnov, *Vremia kolokolchikov*.

34. Troitsky; Lipnitskii; Smirnov.

35. Smirnov.

36. Smirnov.

37. Troitsky.

38. Smirnov.

39. Alexei Ribin (b. 1960), interview with the author, St. Petersburg, 2013.

40. See more about this kind of *kvartirniki* in McMichael, "'A Room-Sized Ocean.'"

41. Bachurov.

42. Stolypin.

43. Volkova.

44. Andrei Temkin, Facebook chat with the author, September 2013.

45. Temkin.

46. Grach.

47. *Magnitizdat*, from *magnitofon* (tape recorder) and *izdavat'* (to publish), a word that appeared as a musical analogy to *samizdat*, was a system for self-production and self-publication of underground rock albums. Different researchers use the term to denote different phenomena, ranging from copying original Western records onto other sound media (x-ray film, reel-to-reel tapes, audio cassettes) to creating original recordings at home or in professional studios for distributing them through further copying outside officially existing channels.

48. See more about bards and *magnitizdat* in Martin J. Daughtry, "Magnitizdat as Cultural Practice" (paper prepared for the conference "Samizdat and Underground Culture in the Soviet Bloc Countries," University of Pennsylvania, Philadelphia, April 6–7, 2006); Rosette C. Lamont, "Horace's Heirs: Beyond Censorship in the Soviet

Songs of the Magnitizdat," *World Literature Today* 53, no. 2 (1979): 220–27; Rachel Platonov, *Singing the Self: Guitar Poetry, Community, and Identity in the Post-Stalin Period* (Evanston, IL: Northwestern University Press, 2012); Peter Steiner, "On Samizdat, Tamizdat, Magnizdat, and Other Strange Words That Are Difficult to Pronounce," *Poetics Today* 29, no. 4 (2008).

49. See more about early Leningrad *magnitizdat* artist Iurii Morozov in Cushman, *Notes From Underground.*

50. Andrei Tropillo (b. 1951), interview with the author, St. Petersburg, 2008.

51. Aleksei Vishnia (b. 1964), interview with the author, St. Petersburg, 2015.

52. Vishnia.

53. Tropillo.

54. Vishnia.

55. Aleksandr Titov (b. 1957), interview with the author, London, 2013.

56. Igor Gudkov (b. 1960), interview with the author, St. Petersburg, 2013.

57. Temkin.

58. Rybin.

59. Vishnia.

60. Mark Shliamovich, interview with the author, Vilnius, 2013.

61. Grach.

62. Smirnov; Troitsky; Lipnitskii.

63. Troitsky.

64. Andrei Lukinov in Aleksandr Kushnir, *100 magnitoal'bomov sovetskogo roka 1977–1991: 15 let podpol'noi zvukozapisi* (Moscow: Lean, 1999), 36.

65. Troitsky.

66. See more in Kushnir, *100 magnitoal'bomov.*

67. Troitsky.

68. Lipnitskii; Troitsky.

69. Troitsky.

70. Evgenii Pavlenko, interview with the author, St. Petersburg, 2013.

71. Kudriavtsev.

72. Aleksei Pevchev (b. 1972), interview with the author, Moscow, 2013.

*Chapter 12*

# Socialism's Empty Promise

## *Housing Vacancy and Squatting in the German Democratic Republic*

### Peter Angus Mitchell

"Without schnapps you'd freeze your arse off here," said Johnny, a squatter in one of East Berlin's rundown, inner city districts. Sporting a beard, shoulder-length hair, and dressed in jeans and a parka, Johnny had recently left his family home in the provinces and moved to the East German capital. After two days searching, he found an empty apartment in a *Hinterhaus* (back house) of a dilapidated tenement building, consisting of a room and kitchen, and heated by a coal-burning oven. Johnny's was one of several thousand apartments that had been squatted in the eastern half of the city and, though he had moved into the property without the prior knowledge or permission of officials in the local housing organs, he did not seem particularly concerned about being forced out. "*Biste erst mal drin*," he explained, "*bleibste auch drin*."[1]

This chapter explores the history of squatting in the German Democratic Republic (GDR), that is, the illegal occupation of apartments and buildings without the prior permission of the relevant state authorities.[2] Although it has thus far received little scholarly attention, squatting proved relatively wide-spread and enduring in East German towns and cities in the 1970s and 1980s.[3] Whereas a number of influential top-down studies paint the East German party-state as an ultra-centralized, streamlined, and even "totalitarian" entity, the case study of squatting demonstrates that everyday life in the GDR was often saturated by a complex network of implicit, unwritten, and negotiable rules which helped to sustain the social edifice.[4] Indeed, in the context of an acute housing shortage—as late as 1990, some 89,000 families and 382,000 individuals in East Germany were still without accommodation of their own[5]—a parallel economy reality was made possible through circumventing official regulations.

During the period of late socialism in the GDR, squatting could and did serve as an alternative housing strategy, an undertaking which was in many cases tacitly tolerated by officials in the local housing organs, its illegality notwithstanding. This practice not only eroded the party-state's control over the housing stock; it also undermined the ruling party's political and ideological hegemony. Perhaps the most obvious attestation of the subversive potential of squatting was its popularity among East Germans who identified with various non-state-sanctioned urban subcultures or who were attempting to pursue alternative lifestyles within state socialism. And, indeed, the historical contours of squatting in the GDR and those of East Germany's urban subcultures were, as this chapter argues, closely intertwined. But squatting, moreover, undermined state control to the extent that it could break, if only temporarily, an asymmetric relationship of dependency between the ruling party and ordinary private citizens which characterized so many facets of everyday life in the GDR. Still, although squatters subverted the party-state's all-embracing claims, the illegal occupation of empty apartments could at the same time prove beneficial to the organs at the local level. Indeed, in this practice we can detect the fundamental ambiguity that characterized so many manifestations of "oppositional behavior" in state socialism, for the boundaries between conformity and nonconformity were often fluid and rarely clear-cut.[6] Indeed, as an unconventional means, this chapter argues, squatting could serve various ends, allowing people not only to "drop out" of the socialist mainstream but also to integrate more fully into socialist society.

## SQUATTING AS AN ALTERNATIVE HOUSING STRATEGY

Housing in the GDR, as Mary Fulbrook reminds us, "was a truly political matter."[7] During the Honecker era (1971–1989), the provision of good quality housing was *the* major social priority in the GDR and housing policy was elevated to the "centerpiece" of the ruling SED's sociopolitical program.[8] The right to housing was anchored in the East German constitution and the East German Code of Civil Law explicitly stated that "the Socialist state guarantees all citizens and their families the right to housing."[9] The ruling Socialist Unity Party (SED) claimed for itself an unprecedented responsibility not only for the construction and maintenance of the housing stock, but also for the allocation of apartments and living space. In East Berlin, for example, the state-controlled Kommunale Wohnungsverwaltung (Communal Housing Association, hereafter KWV) was responsible for administering 359,000—or 72 percent—of the capital's 500,000 individual properties. A further 77,000 apartment units were classed as workers' cooperative housing, belonging to the large state enterprises which were based in the city. Only 14 percent of the housing stock was in private hands.[10] But even this latter category fell under the purview of the party-state's control as, irrespective of whether the property belonged to the KWV, a workers' cooperative, or a private individual, only after first obtaining written consent from their local state housing organ were citizens legally permitted to take up residence at a particular address.[11]

Through controlling the provision of housing in the GDR, the authorities hoped to bind citizens in a relationship of dependency to the East German state and—by extension—to the ruling party, the SED. Squatting provided a means to circumvent this relationship of dependency, its illegality notwithstanding. It was a practice made possible due to high levels of empty housing as an ever-increasing proportion of the country's prewar, tenement-housing stock stood vacant, having fallen into various states of disrepair. Over the course of the 1970s and 1980s the highly centralized East German construction industry constructed millions of new dwellings in the ubiquitous satellite estates that sprang up across the GDR. However, for every two new homes built under Honecker, one older property fell into dereliction. Levels of vacancy in the GDR in fact doubled during the 1970s and by 1981 some 200,000 apartments, or 3.1 percent of East Germany's total housing stock, were standing empty, either scheduled for demolition or awaiting essential repairs.[12] "In an afternoon," explained one seasoned squatter, "you [could] find a dozen empty apartments in [the East Berlin district of] Prenzlauer Berg" alone.[13]

In their documentation of everyday life in East Berlin—which was banned by the East German authorities, though it nevertheless achieved cult status in the GDR—Harald Hauswald and Lutz Rathenow describe how their friends "doggedly climb[ed] stairwells, the side-wings of buildings, wander[ed] through back courtyards," knocked on doors and talked to residents in their search to find empty apartments.[14] When walking along the streets in the older tenement quarters, prospective squatters would keep their eyes peeled for windows without curtains—apparently a sure sign that the apartment was uninhabited. "That's how I found the flat I moved into," explained one East Berlin squatter on being questioned by the Volkspolizei (People's Police).[15] On moving from Magdeburg to East Berlin, the writer Annett Gröschner and her husband had nowhere in the capital to live so they "did what was usual [and] set off with a skeleton key and searched for [unoccupied] apartments."[16] Upon finding a suitable property, some squatters might simply break in. After being alerted to one suspected instance of illegal squatting in the Friedrichshain district of East Berlin, the local authorities noted that "Frau S. forcefully broke open the lock and proceeded to occupy the apartment."[17] Another squatter, Dirk Moldt, recalls opting for a more cunning approach. Dirk was informed by an acquaintance that an apartment in Friedrichshain's Samariterstraße had been standing empty for some time. The apartment itself was in good condition, and was bright and airy with a balcony facing out onto the street. Instead of breaking in, Dirk dressed himself in blue workman's overalls and went to the local KWV office, purporting to be a tenant in the same building. He complained that a pipe had burst in the flat above him (the one he intended to squat in) and that water was seeping into his apartment. He requested access to the property, stating that he was a plumber by trade and would be willing to fix the problem himself in order to prevent any further water damage. His masquerade proved successful, and a grateful official lent him the key. Dirk squatted in the property in 1986 and lived there, illegally and without an official contract, until the party-state's collapse in 1989.[18]

Squatting was practiced in urban centers across the GDR, from the port cities on the Baltic coast to the industrial heartlands of Saxony in the south. In 1988 the security organs in Rostock, for instance, reported that in the city's old town there had emerged a "concentration" of students from the local university who had illegally squatted in buildings in the district.[19] Even small, provincial towns, such as Fürstenwalde, were not immune to the phenomenon.[20] It was, however, in East Berlin where squatting was most widespread and by the early 1980s around a thousand incidences of illegal squatting were being registered in the GDR capital per annum.[21] Here, in the crumbling labyrinth of the turn-of-the-century tenement quarters, the state's oversight of the housing stock was particularly weak. Already in the late 1960s the Magistrate of East Berlin was warned that the "relevant state organs are completely incapable of maintaining order and control" over the assignment and allocation of housing in the city.[22] In 1971 the Mayor of East Berlin, Erhard Krack, was informed that a "substantial number" of letters and citizens' petitions directed toward the civic authorities in the previous six months had concerned themselves with "the illegal occupation of dwellings."[23] Subsequent reports noted that the number of such cases was "rising" and referred to an "intensification" in the practice of illegal squatting in the city.[24] In March 1978 a commission charged with inspecting the empty housing stock reported back to Konrad Neumann, Politburo member and First Secretary of the SED in Berlin. It identified some 893 properties that had either been illegally occupied or where the tenancies were "unclear."[25]

Although it is difficult to build up a detailed picture, the majority of East German squatters were probably young, single adults.[26] This was due to the fact that, in the context of the socialist shortage economy, such individuals and their housing needs were not considered as a priority by the local housing organs.[27] Especially among the younger population, there was a widespread loss of confidence in the state's ability to deliver on its social promises and in particular its promise to deliver good quality housing for all. As officials in East Berlin admitted, "young people are critical of the fact that the resolutions passed by the party and regime [with respect to solving the housing question in the capital] do not affect them."[28] East Germans who had engaged in dissident behavior, moreover, or who had not displayed the requisite amount of political conformity, often found themselves at the bottom of the housing waiting lists and discriminated against when attempting to secure accommodation through the official channels. On submitting a request for improved housing, Ulrike Poppe, a founding member of the dissident organization Frauen für den Frieden (Women for Peace), was told: "[I] should first have a child, and this child had better have asthma or TBC, then I might have a chance of being allocated a new apartment."[29] For those whose housing needs were not considered as priority cases, therefore, the parallel economic reality presented by squatting offered an effective means of self-help.

Squatting was not a practice that was restricted to young adults and the GDR's marginalized outsiders, however, as the housing shortage in the GDR affected a broad section of the population during the period of late socialism. At the beginning of the 1970s there were 600,000 individuals on the official housing waiting lists, and by the decade's end the average waiting time to obtain an apartment in East Berlin still stood at between six and eight years.[30] In the context of this acute housing shortage even those whose housing needs were deemed a priority by the housing organs could face difficulties. In 1981, for instance, Honecker was informed that for newly married workers in Rostock's Neptune shipyard, "the waiting time before being assigned an apartment was circa four years."[31] In East Berlin the authorities recorded cases of illegal squatting undertaken by individuals from a variety of occupational backgrounds including mechanics and machine workers and employees of the postal service and other large state enterprises. Many were students, though there were also cases of middle-aged and middle-class squatters, such as Dr. G. and his wife Frau S. who "illegally squatted in the ruined side wing" of a building in East Berlin's Schliemanstraße.[32] Squatting was a tactic, moreover, that was practiced by couples and young families who were desperate to find a place together, as well as by those whose relationship had come to an end and who were looking to part. "We have unlawfully moved into an empty apartment," explained one young family in a letter to the SED leadership in Berlin in 1979. Not having a home of their own, they argued, their condition apart had become "intolerable."[33] In a separate case, Frau S. informed the local officials in Berlin-Friedrichshain that she had resorted to squatting in an empty property because "life together with her ex-husband [in her old apartment] had become unbearable."[34]

Although squatting was illegal, eviction rates in the GDR were surprisingly low, especially in the larger urban centers. Indeed, the difficulty in obtaining a forced eviction could serve to empower individual citizens and provide them with leverage when confronted by the housing authorities. From the 218 instances of illegal occupations registered in the district of Berlin-Lichtenberg in 1981 and 1982, local officials reported that only in forty-one cases they succeeded in "restoring order" through forcing the squatters to leave.[35] Only eighty-eight forced evictions were carried through in East Berlin in 1983, despite the fact that there were 954 recorded cases of illegal squatting recorded in the city that year.[36] And, while 130 instances of squatting were brought to the attention of the housing officials in Berlin-Friedrichshain in the first nine months of 1984, as of September 30, only a single squatter had been evicted in the district.[37] In most cases, therefore, squatters' chances of remaining in the property they had occupied were reasonably high.

There were a number of reasons for this. Firstly, many months could pass before an instance of illegal squatting was detected in the GDR. As the Arbeitsgruppe Wohnungspolitik (a working group tasked, among other things, with combating illegal squatting) noted: "It is often the case that a long time passes before such a manipulation [*sic*] is first noticed by the housing organs."[38] Such delays in detecting cases of squatting made it all the more difficult for the authorities to counteract this illegal practice. The old adage of possession being nine-tenths of the law may not have been legally binding in the East German dictatorship. Nevertheless, duration in the GDR was a conferrer of legitimacy, de facto if not de jure. By the time squatters were uncovered, they may have already transferred several months' rent into the KWV's account. Most would have moved their furniture into the apartment, or perhaps decorated and carried out repairs. Some might have been co-habiting with their partner, or even expecting a child. Those who had used squatting as a means to move from the provinces to Berlin could have found a job in the city, meaning that a forced return home would affect their employers. Others would have obtained a police registration in the property (an *Anmeldung*) further complicating matters. The trick, Dirk Moldt recalls, "was to play the different bureaucracies off against each other."[39]

What is more, the squatters often occupied properties that were primitive in the extreme and in such a state of disrepair that they could no longer be assigned to legitimate tenants. One squatter, for example, recalled occupying what she described as a "rundown pigsty" which had been standing empty for five years—ever since the previous tenant had passed away.[40] In another instance, an East Berlin squatter told of how he occupied "a damp, uncomfortable" building, which had been boarded up by the hygiene inspectors.[41] He proceeded to dry out the walls with an electric heater; he plastered the apartment and fixed the heating and plumbing, after which he was duly presented with a legal tenancy contract for the property.[42] In such cases, unless the property in question was scheduled for immediate renovation or demolition, allowing squatters to remain in an apartment that would otherwise have stood empty not only eased pressure on the waiting lists, but also helped maintain the integrity of the building structure. What is more, squatters also demonstrated a considerable degree of initiative and resourcefulness in their ability to carry out maintenance work and repairs—qualities that were often lacking among those staffing the housing organs in the GDR's dilapidated inner city districts. The authorities in Prenzlauer Berg in East Berlin, for instance, were not able to meet their renovation targets in 1982 due to a shortage of 3,200 ovens, 1,300 bathtubs, and 700 toilet bowls. A shortfall of skilled laborers and tradesmen, in particular bricklayers, chimneysweeps, locksmiths, joiners, and plumbers, was also noted.[43]

The extent to which illegal squatting was tolerated out of practical considerations varied from region to region. Whereas in smaller towns and also in certain cities the local authorities were committed to evicting squatters, noted one report, "in the capital Berlin, for instance, citizens who act unlawfully are for the most part only confronted with fines of up to 300 marks."[44] A similar tacit toleration of squatters was practiced in other urban centers. One Stasi report revealed that in Dresden in 1984, the housing officials were known to grant temporary contracts to squatters, so long as they agreed to undertake and finance necessary renovation work.[45] In 1988 such customs were still evident in Rostock, where the local authorities largely turned a blind eye to illegal occupations in the city's old town, being of the opinion that "as long as these buildings remain occupied, they won't fall completely into ruin, and value will be preserved."[46]

Tacit toleration of squatters was not always on account of the local authorities' pragmatism or benevolence, however, but rather due to the fact that their room for maneuver was circumscribed by socialism's social contract. Upon inquiring as to what measures could be taken against illegal squatters in Dresden, one local official was informed by the housing department's legal council that a substitute property would first have to be made available before the courts could issue an eviction warrant.[47] Similarly, in East Berlin, a report filed to the Mayor's office in 1980 noted that "an eviction is not possible in the majority of cases, because these citizens [the squatters] do not possess a home of their own."[48] While officials could attempt to force squatters to move back to a previous address, such as the family home, it was possible for squatters to counter with various reasons as to why this was not feasible. In Berlin-Prenzlauer Berg, for example, officials noted that their attempts to evict one squatter "cannot be carried through," because his parents, to whom he was instructed to return, "are not willing to take their son back in again."[49] The authorities at the grassroots level, it seems, were often sensitive to the fact that a forced eviction could lead to further problems down the line, either in the form of complaints and appeals from the squatters and their families, or through the attraction of unwanted attention from their superiors in the party-state apparatus. As one report commissioned by the Council of Ministers in 1982 concluded: "In most cases, the local organs are inclined to retroactively sanction this practice as . . . forced evictions are largely avoided."[50]

As a form of *private* protest, therefore, squatting could prove effective, enabling a number of East Germans to lay claim to their right to housing—a right that the East German state promised its citizens, yet one which it was unable to guarantee universally. Squatters were often assertive, openly stating that they had illegally occupied an empty apartment. One family, for example, appeared at the local Mayor of Berlin-Prenzlauer Berg's office hours to notify him that they had squatted a three-bedroom property in the district, adding that they were not prepared to freely return to their previous one-room apartment.[51] At the same time, however, squatters could also strike a conciliatory tone, accompanying their petitions to the authorities with professions of support for the wider socialist polity as a whole—a tried and tested technique adopted in East Germany and elsewhere in the Soviet bloc when dealing with the state. In a letter to the SED leadership in East Berlin in 1979, for instance, one couple stated: "we have unlawfully moved into an empty apartment that has been standing empty since 1970/71." Although they had a young child and were married, the couple had been forced to live separately for the previous four years and, in desperation, resorted to illegal squatting. The couple hoped, they added, to be able to live together in dignified conditions, "so that we can devote our energy to the construction of *our* state and provide our child with a happy future."[52]

Though the right to housing was anchored in the East German constitution, obtaining a dwelling or an apartment, as Hannsjörg Buck puts it in the standard work on housing in the GDR, was ultimately, "an act of state indulgence."[53] Squatting, it is argued here, provided a means to circumvent this relationship of dependency, its illegality notwithstanding. In their efforts to secure a place of their own, many East German squatters were simply staking claim to a right guaranteed to them as citizens of the socialist state, and in this sense, the reason for squatting was not so much motivated by a desire to subvert state power but instead by the more mundane wish to live an ordinary life in the GDR. Due to the imperfections in the East German economy and the state's inability to resolve the "housing question," which was the main sociopolitical priority during the Honecker era, squatting became an increasingly common practice during the 1970s and 1980s, with individuals from a range of occupational backgrounds resorting to this tactic in towns and cities across the GDR. Indeed, and somewhat paradoxically, circumventing official regulations and committing this legal transgression often provided a novel means for securing a basic need and therefore for integrating more fully into socialist society.

## ALTERNATIVE LIFESTYLES

Squatting not only served as an alternative housing strategy but also offered opportunities for those who sought to pursue alternative lifestyles that deviated from that of the average East German denizen. To be sure, the existence of alternative cultures in the GDR was not wholly dependent on squatting and their trajectories were influenced by other important developments, such as the emergence of youth cultures in the West. Rural guesthouses, private apartments, the Protestant Church and even state-run youth clubs all contributed to the infrastructure of the various East German alternative cultures in the 1970s and 1980s.[54] Nevertheless, contemporaries have stressed the important link between squatting and alternative lifestyles in the GDR, particularly in an urban context. For Wolfgang Rüddenklau, an opposition and environmental activist, the "islands of squatted apartments and buildings helped to forge an alternative society, affirming a self-determined way of life."[55]

"[S]ocialist space," both in the GDR and in other polities in Eastern Europe, as a recent publication argues, constituted a "contested aspect of life in the [Soviet] Bloc."[56] One way in which socialist space was contested was through the emergence of "micromilieus" in certain districts, that is "a conglomerate of individuals, groups, places . . . and infrastructures who, through their physical and symbolic presence, mark a particular space (Raum)."[57] During the 1970s and the 1980s, small but nevertheless vibrant alternative milieus emerged in towns and cities across the GDR, including in Leipzig, Dresden, Potsdam, Halle, and Magdeburg. Their presence, which was facilitated by the practice of illegal squatting, arguably impacted on everyday experiences of the "the urban," serving to construct a "sense of place" from below and associated "imagined geographies" in the socialist city.[58]

In 1983, an investigation carried out in East Berlin's Prenzlauer Berg identified some 800 illegally occupied apartments in the district.[59] The neighborhood of Prenzlauer Berg was of course associated with the GDR's avant-garde. "If the East German capital had a Greenwich Village or a Haight Ashbury," writes David Clay Large in his biography of the city, "this was it."[60] Here, squatters often belonged to what one historian and contemporary has termed an East German "parallel society."[61] Some had opted not to complete military service and had found that the prospect of a university place and a career was now barred. Others simply found the idea of an apprenticeship and full-time work unappealing, opting instead to get by through doing odd jobs here and there. One unemployed squatter, for instance, earned his money modeling and sewing jackets.[62] Trading in homemade jewelry and knick-knacks to tourists was another common means for East German drop-outs to earn enough to get by.[63] Such individuals may have dropped out of the socialist mainstream, but they nevertheless had to negotiate their place within and in relationship to the wider polity, being unable—and often, unwilling—to leave the geographical confines of socialism.

Illegal squatting played a role in establishing the niches and spaces in which this alternative culture could operate, with empty apartments being used variously as makeshift galleries, exhibition venues, and meeting places.

"Through squatting in empty buildings," as the squatters' contemporary, Roland Galenza, puts it, "a lively sub-cultural infrastructure" could emerge and take root.[64] In October 1987, for instance, the security organs in East Berlin noted that an "illegal youth club" was operating out of the basement of a derelict building in Lichtenberg's Kaskelstraße and was frequented by a "multitude of predominantly young people (aged between seventeen and twenty two) of both sexes." Other boarded-up apartments in the building, the intelligence report noted, were being used as drinking dens, walls of which, it was noted disapprovingly, were covered with subversive slogans and graffiti.[65] In July 1980, to provide another example, the local authorities in Berlin's Prenzlauer Berg were notified that one squatter, after breaking into an apartment that had long been standing empty in the district's Wichertstraße, proceeded to knock down the interior walls and established a "photograph laboratory" in the property.[66] The East German artist Jürgen Schweinebraden, the founder of East Berlin's EP Gallery, resorted to similar means. Schweinebraden had been provided with a modest apartment in Prenzlauer Berg's Dunkerstraße, measuring around forty square meters. He required more space for his "private" gallery, however, and acquired it through squatting a further two neighboring properties in the building, which he then converted into one single unit. The gallery was first established in 1974 and operated until 1980, when it was shut down by the Stasi. One of the most important independent exhibition spaces in the city, it showcased not only the work of "Western" artists but also contemporary Eastern European art.[67]

Although the closure of the EP Gallery and similar venues was a blow to the independent artist scene in the GDR, other ad hoc exhibition spaces sprang up in their place.[68] In 1986 the twenty-two-year-old D. started holding various "provocative art" events, which took place in his apartment in East Berlin's Prenzlauer Berg. Located in a rundown building off Schönhauser Allee, a busy thoroughfare to the north of Alexanderplatz, entry to the "gallery" was obtained via a junk-filled courtyard and then through a dilapidated stairwell in the building's side-wing.[69] "I have not been to New York, but the short way from the street to the exhibition space is how I imagine Brooklyn," recalled one artist who showcased his work there.[70] The apartment itself, including the floorboards, was painted completely white, and illuminated with spotlights. The only piece of furniture was a raised platform next to the window, which was used alternatively as a stage during the exhibitions and as a makeshift bed.[71]

D.'s apartment hosted its first event in September 1986, showcasing the work of an artist from the University of Applied Arts in Dresden. Some fourteen additional such exhibitions were held in D.'s apartment between this point and April 1988.[72] The exhibitions usually took place on the first weekend of the month and displayed work of artists from both sides of the German divide, including artists based in West Berlin's Kunsthaus Bethanien.[73] Indeed, the Stasi noted that D.'s contacts in the West appeared to be "inspired" by his work.[74] According to one source, the opening nights of new exhibitions in D.'s makeshift gallery were considered "highlights" among East Berlin's bohemian milieu.[75] Those present, a Stasi informant noted, had "the outward appearance of avant-garde intellectuals."[76] Such events were normally attended by between twenty and thirty guests, although one exhibition of punk graffiti and slogans attracted some one hundred visitors.[77] The evenings usually included film showings and readings, and were rounded off with dancing and revelry. One tenant in the building explained to Stasi Lieutenant Kubis that, on several occasions, she had witnessed the guests engaged in "bare-chested gyrating" to what she described as "primitive African jungle music."[78] This resident, who used a set of binoculars to spy on her neighbors, suspected that not only alcohol was consumed at these gatherings, but other intoxicants too.[79] Her suspicions were in fact well founded, as D. was known to supply his visitors with homegrown marijuana, which he cultivated on his father's allotment.[80]

One subculture in particular that benefitted from illegal squatting was the GDR's punk scene.[81] Illustrative of the fact that youth culture in Cold War Europe recognized no borders, the sound and aesthetic of punk rock, born in the United Kingdom and exported to the GDR via the Federal Republic, grew in popularity in East Germany in the 1980s. The aggressive nihilism of punk music scene and its harsh aesthetic arguably presented more of a challenge to the official cultural politics of the socialist polity than the rock and hippy music of the seventies had done. Groups with names such as Wutanfall (Fit of Rage), Zorn (Wrath), Zwecklos (Pointless), and Skeptiker (Skeptic) expressed a visceral aversion to socialist everyday life. Most of these bands were officially prohibited from performing, though "in Prenzlauer Berg," as Torsten Preuß, a member of the punk band Namenlos recalls, there were sometimes opportunities to hold "concerts in squatted apartments, hidden cellars or back-courtyards."[82]

One squatter involved in this subculture was a young man whose Stasi case file was appropriately titled "Besetzer" (squatter).[83] A "hardcore punk," he sported "fire-red" hair and was often seen wearing a leather jacket with the words "beat the fascists wherever you see them" written on the back.[84] "Besetzer" originally belonged to a "loose grouping" of punks, most of whom were in their late teens or early twenties, who gathered in various youth clubs in Bernau, a small city just north of the GDR capital. Numbering around thirty to forty individuals, the punks from Bernau were regarded by the security organs as having a "politically negative" attitude toward the GDR while they "celebrated western 'punk-ideology.'" Within this looser grouping, the Stasi identified a "hard core" of seven individuals, with "Besetzer" as their "ringleader."[85]

"Besetzer" himself was twenty years old and had begun an apprentice-ship in the VEB Kombinat Landtechnik at the age of seventeen. Repeatedly disciplined for "skiving," he broke off his traineeship in February 1988.[86] For the next six months he had no official employment, earning money instead through selling clothes, stolen electrical goods, and fake Swiss watches, which he received from contacts in the West.[87] A punk and unemployed wheeler and dealer of Western contraband, "Besetzer" was the prototype of an East German juvenile delinquent. He reportedly consumed alcohol in excess and engaged in street brawls with neo-Nazi youth gangs. In one altercation, "Besetzer" and his fellow punks from Bernau ambushed a group of neo-Nazis, leaving one victim lying bloodied and unconscious on Berlin-Lichtenberg's Storkower Straße.[88] According to his Stasi file, he was known to have an "absolutely negative attitude toward [the] socialist state."[89]

In 1988, "Besetzer" and five of his friends moved to East Berlin, squatting in a number of apartments in Berlin's Prenzlauer Berg. "Besetzer" found a "nice" apartment in the Schliemannstraße. A number of other punks from his hometown had already squatted in this neighborhood, while another punk from Zepernick, a suburb of Bernau, had illegally occupied the apart-ment directly below—an indication of the importance of informal networks through which information about empty properties could be spread.[90] In the GDR capital the squatters from Bernau established contacts with local punks who gathered in Prenzlauer Berg's Zionskirche, and who engaged in a number of breaches of public order that coincided with sensitive political events in the capital. These, included a "solidarity action" in support of West Berlin squat-ters who, on July 1, 1988, were evicted from a small strip of erstwhile East German territory that lay on the western side of the Berlin Wall.[91] "Besetzer" and the punks from Bernau were also under investigation in connection with subversive graffiti that had been sprayed on a number of buildings in East Berlin, including the slogans "I like Gorbi" (written in English), "Glasnost,'" and "SED: Traitors of Communism."[92]

By the late 1980s, there were a number of connections between the local punk scene in Prenzlauer Berg, to which "Besetzer" now belonged, and the organized domestic opposition. A case in point is the Umweltbibliothek, an environmental opposition network that operated out of the Zionskirche.[93] The co-founders of the oppositional network Umweltbibliothek, Wolfgang Rüddenklau and Carlo Jordan, who also edited the *samizdat* publication *Umweltblätter*, lived nearby in a tenement building in Fehrbellinerstraße in East Berlin's Prenzlauer Berg, which served as a "meeting place for politi-cally negative individuals."[94] "With the exception of two to three tenants," the security organs noted, all the other residents in this building were thought to have occupied their apartments "illegally."[95] A number of "punk music groups" rehearsed in the squat in the Fehrbellinerstrasse, while members of the punk bands Freygang and Feeling B lived in this building.[96]

Although concrete political action was largely organized under the protective auspices of the Protestant Church, rather than in private homes and illegally occupied apartments, squatting was nevertheless intertwined with the history of the GDR's domestic opposition and its patterns of nonconformity. Squatting served not only as a strategy for securing a roof over one's head but was also exploited to expand the infrastructure of various urban subcultures, with illegally occupied apartments serving as makeshift galleries, meeting places, and underground music venues. The presence of these urban alternative milieus, a development that was facilitated by the practice of illegal squatting, contrasted with official representations of the socialist city and concepts of the urban and arguably contributed to a rereading of the socialist city's symbolic meaning.

## SQUATTERS AND THE SED-STATE

Whether resorted to as an apolitical housing strategy, motivated by the search for alternative lifestyles, or indeed a combination of both, squatting presented an unwelcome development from the perspective of SED hierarchy. For a start, squatting undermined the principles of "order, discipline, and security" to which the GDR's elites were so attached.[97] What is more, the emergence of alternative lifestyles in East German cities—a process which itself was facilitated by illegal squatting—proved a far cry from what the East German authorities would have thought constituted a socialist *Wohnkultur*, or way of life. Squatting led to an erosion of control in this crucially important sphere of domestic policy, thus presenting a political and ideological challenge to the SED-state. For, in contrast to Karl Marx, in whose name and in accordance to whose principles the East German regime purported to govern, it was inconceivable to the GDR's rulers that state control should even fray around the edges, let alone wither away.

Strategies to counter squatting were discussed by the highest *state* authority in the GDR, including the Council of Ministers and its subsidiary department, the Abteilung für Staats- und Rechtsfragen (Department for State and Legal Affairs). Squatting was a matter that also concerned the *party* leadership, particularly at the *Bezirk* level. In the GDR capital individuals such as Konrad Neumann, First Secretary of the SED in East Berlin and Politburo member, and his successor, Egon Krenz, were keen to see illegal squatting stamped out. While it is true that squatters in the GDR did not become the targets of mass repression, the authorities at the higher echelons were not indifferent to this practice. Throughout the 1970s and particularly in the 1980s, measures to tackle squatting were discussed, debated, and written into law. In 1980, the Chairman of the Council of Ministers, Willi Stoph, passed a strongly worded resolution calling for correct procedures in the allocation of housing to be "strictly enforced."[98] To this end, a special commission, the Arbeitsgruppe Wohnungspolitik, was established in 1982, under the direct control of the Council of Ministers. A central aspect of the commission's remit was to devise strategies for countering the growing trend in illegal squatting that was being registered republic-wide.[99] In 1985, after several years of deliberation and consultation with local party and municipal leaders, the legislation governing the distribution of housing (the *Wohnraumlenkungsverordnung*) was modified, providing greater powers to the local housing authorities. "In cases where living space is occupied without (official) permission," explained the introductory preamble to the legislation, "the eviction process is to be simplified and [made] more effective."[100] Fines for illegal squatting were also increased.

In the East German capital the authorities responsible for devising strategies for tackling illegal squatting included the SED *Bezirksleiter*, the city's mayor, and the Stadtrat für Wohnungspolitik. In 1983, with as many as 1,000 cases of squatting being recorded per annum, discussions involving all three—Konrad Neumann, Erhard Krack, and Wolfgang Bein—focused on the potential for new legislative powers to assist "the fight against (and prevention of) the illegal occupation of apartments."[101] That same year, East Berlin's SED-party leadership passed a resolution calling for "a more energetic application of the [current] legal measures available to combat the unlawful occupation of properties."[102] Not to be outdone, Mayor Krack even ventured to advocate using the state-controlled press organs to "mobilize public opinion against the illegal occupation of living space," though there is no evidence to indicate whether his somewhat implausible suggestion, which would have entailed a public admission of the problem, was ever seriously considered practical.[103] More pragmatically, the housing authorities resolved to decrease the time apartments were vacant, noting that properties that stood empty for an extended period served to "encourage" citizens to move in illegally.[104] Moreover, buildings that were, in the view of the hygiene inspectors, not fit for human habitation, were also to be secured and their utilities cut off in order to prevent "unauthorized entry or use."[105] In addition to adopting a tougher approach toward illegal squatters, the practice of squatting itself, the authorities hoped, would become a more difficult enterprise to undertake in the first place. However, the impact of these measures proved minimal. Although the number of cases of squatting recorded in East Berlin in 1985 dropped from a high of 1,251 the previous year, "870 illegal occupations clearly indicate," one report noted, that more had to be done.[106]

In "totalitarian" polities, power is regarded as radiating out smoothly from the center, encountering few hurdles and little resistance. However, one problem faced by the SED hierarchy in their attempts to tackle illegal squatting was that the new powers provided to the local organs were not effectively utilized.

Contrary to the wishes of those at the higher echelons of the party-state apparatus, officials at the local level did not consistently respond to cases of illegal squatting in the disciplined manner in which they were supposed to act. In 1987, two years after the new legislation had become operative, the Akademie für Staats- und Rechtswissenschaft (Academy for State Jurisprudence) commented that the "differentiated exertion of influence" furnished by the new legislation "is not being sufficiently applied."[107] At the grassroots level there was little perceptible change in mentality. The local organs continued to respond to cases of squatting only "hesitantly, or not at all."[108]

A closer examination of the organ directly responsible for housing in the GDR, the Communal Housing Association (KWV), reveals the difficulties with which the SED-state was confronted at the grassroots. Over 10,000 staff worked in the East Berlin KWV, which had a central office as well as sub-departments in each district. The organization was responsible for managing almost half a million individual apartments in the capital. Given that the KWV impacted on the everyday lives of almost all of East Berlin's denizens, ensuring its "efficiency," as one local party official noted, was a "foremost political priority."[109] Quite simply, the KWV counted among "the most important organizations" in the city.[110]

Even a cursory analysis of citizens' petitions, however, indicates the frustration felt by many with the KWV. The KWV's staff were constantly criticized for their "bureaucratic mind-set" and their "cold-heartedness," both by private citizens and by those within the party-state apparatus.[111] To be sure, many of the problems associated with the KWV ran much deeper than the bureaucracy itself and were rather the product of entrenched structural weaknesses in the command economy. Nevertheless, as the Council of Ministers itself concluded in 1977, those staffing the KWV were often "technically and politically under-qualified" for the job and the responsibilities that it entailed—sentiments which were echoed in reports coming from the *Bezirk* and *Kreis* levels.[112] In 1980, for instance, those staffing the KWV in Friedrichshain were described as suffering from "inadequate typing skills, insufficient qualifications and an underdeveloped sense of responsibility."[113] Republic-wide, only one in ten of the KWV's staff possessed higher education qualifications, and only a small minority of officials, some 15 percent in total, were SED party members.[114] Internal memoranda from the 1970s and 1980s indicate that those employed in the housing organs suffered from a "heavy psychological and physical burden," which led to "untenably high" levels of staff turnover, in particular in inner city districts where the housing conditions were the worst and the pressure on officials highest.[115] In Prenzlauer Berg, for instance, the annual turnover rate in the district's Department for Housing was 35 percent.[116] Such high rates of fluctuation, as party investigations and reports noted, not only impacted negatively on the effectiveness of the bureaucracy as a whole, it also "made an effective prevention of legal transgressions," such as squatting, "more difficult."[117]

Because of the magnitude of the housing shortage, and the difficulties that it presented, officials and local organs were hesitant to tackle the problem head-on, seeking instead to prevaricate or delegate responsibility elsewhere. Its social importance notwithstanding, the housing question was often treated as a "hot potato," as one report from the 1960s put it, with the responsibility for addressing the fundamental material needs of the population being passed on from one department to the next.[118] Such tendencies were exacerbated by the surprising absence of a central ministry, subdepartment, or even an individual responsible for coordinating the regime's housing policy on the national level. While central ministries played an important role in overseeing housing con-struction and urban planning—initially through the Ministry for Reconstruc-tion, and, from 1958, through the newly established Ministry for Building and Construction—there was no such framework for managing the *existing* housing stock.[119] From an early stage in the GDR's history, the administration of the GDR's housing stock found itself in an institutional and conceptual "no-man's land," as Jay Rowell puts it.[120] This continued to be the case in the 1970s and 1980s, despite the elevation of the housing question to the center-piece of the SED's sociopolitical policy.[121]

With the absence of a central organization, it was often left to the local authorities at the *Bezirk* level to coordinate and devise their own strategies for allocating and distributing housing, the result being a lack of coherence and unity in policy.[122] The Council of Ministers had been informed in 1977 that the administration at the *Bezirk*, *Kreis*, and municipal levels failed to work together to ensure a unified policy.[123] In 1980, moreover, the Chairman of the Council of Ministers could note that "leading comrades" in the localities were continually bringing attention to the fact that, "in such a politically important area such as housing policy . . . which impacted on the everyday life of citi-zens in every city and community, there existed no unified central leadership vis-à-vis the local organs [*Bezirke*]."[124] Indeed, in the authorities' response to illegal squatting differences manifested themselves not only at a regional or city-by-city level, but could also vary between the organs in neighboring local districts in the GDR's towns and cities as well.

This was nowhere more evident than in the East German capital, where the local authorities in neighboring districts could adopt completely differ-ent approaches in response to the same problem. Not only did the number of cases of squatting vary across the city, as one report to the Magistrate of East Berlin noted, but there was also a "clear distinction . . . between the ways in which the different municipal districts respond[ed]" to such transgressions.[125] In 1984, for instance, squatters were granted legal contracts in just over half of 311 recorded cases in Prenzlauer Berg. In Weissensee, however, this figure was 75 percent. In Pankow and Mitte, on the other hand, only one in five squatters were able to legalize their tenancies retroactively. Yet in neither of these two districts were any squatters evicted. In Pankow only three of its 104 squatters were issued with fines. In Treptow, by contrast, the authorities evicted a quarter of the district's squatters and issued fines in 96 percent of cases. In Köpenick 90 percent of the district squatters were fined; yet none of the eighty-seven illegally occupied apartments had been evicted.[126] With little direction from above, and needing to respond to pressures from below, the local authorities acted with a degree of autonomy, often choosing to follow the path of least resistance. The authorities' often—and perhaps surprisingly—mild reaction to squatting stemmed from deep-rooted structural problems in the command economy and the party-state. The consequence thereof was that, after four decades of communist rule, the party-state at the grassroots was considerably less rigid than a number of top-down accounts which focus on the surveillance state and its apparatus of repression would suggest.

It should be pointed out here that the Stasi was well aware of the problematic of squatting. Indeed, on reading one report on the city's empty housing stock in 1978, General Major Schwanitz, the Stasi chief in East Berlin, stressed that "it must not be permitted that asocial and hostile elements are able to find shelter in such objects."[127] The party's "sword and shield" served as the intelligence nerve center of the East German state and it received information about this practice not only through its network of informants but also from the other bureaucracies that constituted the SED state. In its forty-year history the East German security organs collected some 178 kilometers of files, maintained records on six million individuals, gathered over one million photographs and negatives, and stored thousands of human scents in glass jars.[128] By 1989 the behemoth had 91,000 full-time operatives and 174,000 unofficial informants, or IMs. Its agents were much thicker on the ground than the Gestapo's, which had 31,000 in active service covering the whole of the *Reich* in 1944.[129] Indeed, much of material on which this chapter draws stems from the security organs files.

A number of squatters found themselves caught in the crosshairs of the Stasi. One such individual was Carsten P., who illegally squatted a flat in Prenzlauer Berg's Christinenstraße on June 18, 1982, using a ratchet to break open the door.[130] The MfS identified Carsten's squat as an "illegal meeting place of various punks from the capital [East Berlin] and the rest of the GDR."[131] According to one neighbor, Carsten's apartment was regularly frequented by around twenty punks, who were "strikingly dressed." One of them, she added, sported a "strip of hair" on his head that was "dyed green in the middle."[132] On searching the property the Stasi noted that "the entire apartment is unkempt and dirty."[133] The interior walls were covered with incriminating graffiti and slogans, varying from the openly hostile "better dead than red" to the face-tious "half-wobbled anarchist underground organization [of the] GDR."[134] Next to a portrait of the East German leader Erich Honecker, Carsten had scribbled the slogan "anarchy is possible"[135]—an example of *détournement*, the Situationist-inspired tactic of appropriating and changing the meaning of official symbols, being applied in the context of late socialism.

It was not the illegal occupation of his apartment that triggered the MfS's interest in Carsten and his friends, however. Rather, the security organs' atten-tion was initially aroused through his contact with West German journalists who were researching the GDR punk scene. Following a chance meeting, the journalists had visited Carsten's apartment, where they interviewed him and his friends and took photographs of them posing outside the squat—photo-graphs that were later published in articles in West Germany's *Konkret* and *Tip* magazines. Carsten was subsequently arrested and, after several months of interrogation, was sentenced to fifteen months in prison, on charges of forging illegal contacts with enemies of the GDR and slandering the social-ist state.[136] Following his conviction, the Stasi's case file concluded that his "apartment and its use as a meeting place for decadent youths and citizens from non-socialist countries" had been "liquidated."[137]

In these particular cases the Stasi noted the illegal occupations in their files in their efforts to build up an incriminating case against their targets and to underscore their negative character. Yet, while a number of squatters did fall under the crosshairs of the Stasi, the security organs did not instigate a witch-hunt against the milieu as a whole.[138] Individuals squatters attracted the attention of the security apparatus primarily on account of their perceived "asocial" behavior and hostility toward the socialist state, or for having con-tacts in the West, rather than for the fact that they had illegally squatted in the apartments they were living. Indeed, it is perhaps worth noting that the phe-nomenon of squatting first emerged and then spread in the very decades—the 1970s and 1980s—in which size of the Stasi bureaucracy itself ballooned.

## CONCLUSION

This chapter has explored the practice of squatting in East Germany—a practice that proved enduring during the 1970s and 1980s and which belongs to the history of everyday dissidence and nonconformity in late socialism. Through creating niches for the GDR's subcultures to take root, squatting played an important role in establishing an alternative "topography" in the GDR, especially in larger cities such as East Berlin, Dresden, and Leipzig. However, squatting was not only practiced by those who belonged to the GDR's "parallel society," but also, in light of East Germany's chronic housing shortage, by an increasing number of citizens who resorted to the tactic as an alternative housing strategy. While it could provide space for urban subcultures and for those looking to "drop out" of the socialist mainstream, squatting could also be used to secure the basic housing needs of citizens hoping to carve out an ordinary life for themselves within the parameters imposed by the socialist polity.

Although squatting served to corrode state control over the housing stock, and in turn the relationship of dependency between the authorities and private citizens, the regime proved unable to stamp out the practice. Indeed, illegal squatting proved an enduring phenomenon in the GDR, continuing right up to the Peaceful Revolution and beyond. This was in part, as we have seen, due to the fact that squatting was undertaken covertly and was often difficult to detect. However, it was also a result of the nature of the polity itself, whose space for action was constrained by the promise of socialism's social contract which guaranteed citizens the right to housing, on the one hand, and the state's inability to universally fulfill this pledge, on the other. Squatting often served to ease pressure on the official waiting lists through providing an outlet for enterprising citizens to practice a form of self-help which circumvented the official housing allocation process. And because squatting could often prove beneficial to the housing organs, the authorities at the local level at times responded to this novel tactic in ways unforeseen by the party-state hierarchy. That is to say, it was not only squatters who opted to transgress official regulations and to engage in this parallel economic reality: confronted by the practice of illegal squatting, at the grassroots level the SED-state also reacted at times to this manifestation of nonconformist behavior in unconventional ways.

## NOTES

1. "[O]nce you're in, you're in." See Dieter Bub, "'Stern' Bericht," reproduced in *Instandbesetzer Post*, June 19, 1981.

2. In the GDR the practice was often referred to as "*schwarzwohnen*"—a term that does not lend itself readily to translation, but which is redolent of "*schwarzfahren*" (fare dodging) or "*Schwarzmarkt*"(the black market). Not all GDR squatters were happy with this expression and its apolitical connotations, however. Indeed, in East Berlin, the term most often used was "*wohnungsbesetzen*" (apartment squatting). See Udo Grashoff, *Schwarzwohnen: Die Unterwanderung der staatlichen Wohnruumlenkung in der DDR* (Göttingen: V&R Unipress, 2011), 11–12.

3. As far as this author is aware, the existing academic literature on the subject is restricted to the contributions by Dieter Rink and the excellent introduction to the subject provided by Udo Grashoff. See Grashoff, *Schwarzwohnen*; Udo Grashoff, *Leben im Abriss: Schwarzwohnen in Halle an der Saale* (Halle: Hasenverlag, 2011);

Dieter Rink, "Der Traum ist aus? Hausbesetzer in Leipzig-Connewitz in der 90er Jahren," in *Jugendkulturen, Politik und Protest: Vom Widerstand zum Kommerz?* ed. Roland Roth and Dieter Rucht (Opladen: Leske + Budrich, 2000).

4. For interpretations that adopt a "totalitarian" interpretation, see Klaus Schroeder, *Der SED-Staat: Partei, Staat und Gesellschaft, 1949–1990* (Munich: Carl Hanser Verlag, 1998); Armin Mitter and Stefan Wolle, *Untergang auf Raten: Unbekannte Kapitel der DDR-Geschichte* (Munich: Bertelsmann, 1993). In his history of postwar Germany Hans-Ulrich Wehler contends "in terms of its claims . . . and its political praxis, the GDR embodied the regime typology of a left-totalitarian dictatorship." Hans-Ulrich Wehler, *Deutsche Gesellschaftsgeschichte: Bundesrepublik und DDR* (Munich: Beck, 2008), 414. For a critique of the "totalitarian" interpretation, see Mary Fulbrook, "The Limits of Totalitarianism: God, State and Society in the GDR," *Transactions of the Royal Historical Society* (Sixth Series) 7 (1997).

5. Hannsjörg F. Buck, *Mit hohem Anspruch gescheitert: Die Wohnungspolitik der DDR* (Münster: Lit Verlag, 2004), 383.

6. For a discussion on the various manifestations of "oppositional behavior" in the GDR, see Ilko-Sascha Kowalczuk, "Von der Freiheit, Ich zu sagen: Widerständiges Verhalten in der DDR," in *Zwischen Selbstbehauptung und Anpassung: Formen des Widerstandes und der Opposition der DDR*, ed. Ulrike Poppe, Ilko-Sascha Kowalczuk, and Rainer Eckert (Berlin: Links, 1995).

7. Mary Fulbrook, *The People's State: East German Society from Hitler to Honecker* (New Haven: Yale University Press, 2005), 50.

8. For the SED's housing policy in the Honecker era, see Jay Rowell, "Wohnungspolitik 1971–89," in *Geschichte der Sozialpolitik in Deutschland seit 1945, Deutsche Demokratische Republik 1971–1989: Bewegung in der Sozialpolitik, Erstarrung und Niedergang*, ed. Christoph Boyer (Baden-Baden: Nomos, 2008).

9. Buck, *Mit hohem Anspruch gescheitert*, 7.

10. Landesarchiv Berlin (hereafter LAB), C Rep. 100-05, Nr. 1894/2, "Leistungsentwicklung der VEB KWV für die Wohnrauminstandhaltung und Maßnahmen zur weiteren Verbesserung der Führungstätigkeit des Magistrats und der Räte der Stadtbezirke," 11.08.1982, Anlage 1.

11. Buck, *Mit hohem Anspruch gescheitert*, 363.

12. Stiftung Archiv der Parteien und Massenorganisationen der DDR im Bundesarchiv (hereafter SAPMO), DY 30/IV 2/2.039, Büro Ergon Krenz, Akademie für Gesellschaftswissenschaften beim Zentralkomitee der SED Institut für Marxistisch-Leninistische Soziologie, "Studie zur Lösung der Wohnungsfrage als soziales Problem bis 1990 in der Deutschen Demokratischen Republik," Juni 1985, fol. 111.

13. Dieter Bub, "Hausbesetzer Ost," *Instandbesetzer Post*, June 19, 1981.

14. Harald Hauswald and Lutz Rathenow, *Ost-Berlin: Leben vor dem Mauerfall*, 4th edn. (Berlin: Jaron Verlag, 2008), 31–34.

15. Bundesbeauftragten für die Unterlagen des Staatssicherheitsdienstes der ehemaligen Deutschen DemokratischenRepublik (hereafter BStU), MfS, HA IX, Nr. 301, fol. 108.

16. Barbara Felsmann and Annett Gröschner, eds., *Durchgangszimmer Prenzlauer Berg: Eine Berliner Künstlersozialgeschichte in Selbstauskünften* (Berlin: Lukas Verlag, 1999), 532.

17. LAB, C Rep. 135-02-02, Nr. 1186, Rat des Stadtbezirks Friedrichshain, Ratssitzung am 1. Feb. 1979, "Zustimmung zur Räumung von Wohnungen auf dem Verwaltungswege gemäß §23 Verordnung Wohnraumlenkung (12/79)."

18. Dirk Moldt, interview with the author, Berlin, September 2, 2013.

19. BStU, MfS, BV Rostock, Abt. XX, Nr. 1633, fol. 3.

20. BStU, MfS, HA XXII, Nr. 21940, fol. 6.

21. LAB, C Rep. 111, Nr. 57, "Stellvertreter des Oberbürgermeisters für Wohnungspolitik: Information über die Eingaben während der Vorbereitung der Wahlen am 6. Mai 1984," "Ungesetzliche Bezüge im I. Halbjahr 1984"; LAB, C Rep. 100-05, Nr. 1996, Magistrat von Berlin, Büro des Magistrats, "Stand der Erfüllung der Wohnraumvergabepläne der Räte der Stadtbezirke per 21. Aug. 1985," October 2, 1985.

22. LAB, C Rep. 100-05, Nr. 1397, Magistrat von Berlin, Büro des Magistrats, Sitzung des Magistrats am 5. März 1969, "Analyse über die Verwirklichung des Erlasses des Staatsrates der DDR 'Über die Eingaben der Bürger und die Bearbeitung durch die Staatsorgane' durch die örtlichen Staatsorgane in Berlin im Jahre 1968."

23. LAB, C Rep. 100-05, Nr. 1472, Magistrat von Berlin, Büro des Magistrats, Sitzung des Magistrats am 29. Sept. 1971, "Eingabenbearbeitung 1. Halbjahr 1971."

24. LAB, C Rep. 100-05, Nr. 1500, Magistrat von Berlin, Büro des Magistrats, Sitzung des Magistrats am 13. Sept. 1972, "Analyse über die Bearbeitung der Eingaben der Bürger im 1. Halbjahr 1972"; LAB, C Rep. 100-05, Nr. 1578, Magistrat von Berlin, Büro des Magistrats, Sitzung des Magistrats am 13. Nov. 1974, "Analyse über die Bearbeitung der Eingaben der Bürger im III. Quartal 1974."

25. LAB, C Rep. 902, Nr. 4320, "Information zur Kontrolle der Leitungstätigkeit zur Erfassung und schnellen Vergabe leerstehender Wohnungen in der Hauptstadt," May 22, 1978, 8.

26. Grashoff, *Schwarzwohnen*, 72.

27. Ibid., 72.

28. LAB, C Rep. 100-05, Nr. 1578, Magistrat von Berlin, Büro des Magistrats, "Analyse über die Bearbeitung der Eingaben der Bürger im III. Quartal 1974," November 13, 1974.

29. Felsmann and Gröschner, *Durchgangszimmer*, 362.

30. Hartmut Häussermann and Walher Siebel, *Soziologie des Wohnens: Eine Einführung in Wandel und Ausdifferenzierung des Wohnens* (Weinheim: Juventa Verlag, 1996), 169; SAPMO, DY 30/2201–Informationen an Erich Honecker über regionale Probleme in den Monatsberichten des Ersten Bezirkssekretärs der SED in Berlin (Bd 4: 1978–1979), fol. 30.

31. SAPMO, DC 20/12744, "Sekretariat des Ministerrates: Information über die Eingabenarbeit im 1. Halbjahr 1981," fol. 5.

32. LAB, C Rep. 135-02-02, Nr. 1250, Rat des Stadtbezirks Friedrichshain, Ratssitzung am 18. December 1980, "Zustimmung zur Räumung von Wohnungen auf dem Verwaltungswegegemäß § 23 der Verordnung über Lenkung des Wohnraums (268/80)"; Robert Havemann Gesellschaft e.V. Archiv der DDR Opposition, HAV-WSi 01, 3.

33. LAB, C Rep. 902, Nr. 4899, Bezirksleitung der SED, "Eingabenbearbeitung durch die Arbeitsgruppe für Staats- und Rechtsfragen beim 1. Sekretär

der Bezirksleitung der SED, Legalisierung eines illegalen Bezuges," 12.7.79, unpaginated.

34. LAB, C Rep. 135-02-02, Nr. 1186, Rat des Stadtbezirks Friedrichshain, Ratsitzung am 1. Feb. 1979, "Zustimmung zur Räumung von Wohnungen auf dem Verwaltungswege gemäß §23 Verordnung Wohnraumlenkung" (12/79).

35. LAB, Berlin C Rep. 100-05, Nr. 1919, Magistrat von Berlin, Büro des Magistrats, Ratsitzung des Magistrats am 27. April 1983, "Erfahrungen des Rates des Stadtbezirkes Berlin-Lichtenberg bei der Wahrnehmung der Verantwortung für die Wohnraumlenkung und für die effektive Nutzung des Wohnungfonds."

36. LAB, C Rep. 100-05, Nr. 1945/1, "Eingabeanalyse 1983," 7–8.

37. LAB, C Rep. 902, Nr. 6050, Bezirksleitung Berlin der SED, Information zur Eingabenbearbeitung, "Einschätzung über der Stand der Abarbeitung der Eingaben der Bürger an die Partei- und Staatsorgane im I. Halbjahr 1984," 4.

38. BAB, DP 1/20292, "Information über Probleme und Hinweise aus Wohnungseingaben zur Wohnraumlenkungsverordnung," unpaginated.

39. Moldt.

40. Felsmann and Gröschner, *Durchgangszimmer*, 11–12.

41. Bub, "Hausbesetzer Ost."

42. Ibid.

43. LAB, C Rep. 143-02-02, Nr. 1251, Ratbeschlüsse Prenzlauerberg, Ratsitzungen am 24.2.1982, "Information über den erreichten Stand in der Arbeit mit Hausreparatur plänen in der Wohnraumwertverhaltung," unpaginated.

44. Bundesarchiv Berlin (hereafter BAB), DP 1/20292, "Information über Probleme und Hinweise aus Wohnungseingaben zur Wohnraumlenkungsverordnung," unpaginated.

45. BStU, MfS, BV Dresden, AKG Nr. 10070, fol. 10.

46. BStU, MfS, BV Rostock, Abt XX, Nr. 1633, fol. 3.

47. BStU, MfS, BV Dresden, AKG Nr. 10070, fol. 10.

48. LAB, C Rep. 100-05, Nr. 1837, Magistrat von Berlin, Büro des Magistrats, "Maßnahmen zur Senkung der Leerstandzeiten von Wohnungen," September 24, 1980.

49. LAB, C Rep. 134-02-02, Nr. 1319, Rat des Stadtbezirkes Prenzlauer Berg, Ratsitzung am 23. 5. 1984, "Räumung auf dem Verwaltungsweg von Herr H.," unpaginated.

50. SAPMO, DY 30/22388, "Beschluss zur weiteren Verwirklichung der sozialistischen Wohnungspolitik und zur Erhöhung der Effektivität der Wohnungswirtschaft" 2.2.1982, 5.

51. LAB, C Rep. 134-02-02, Nr. 1180, Rat des Stadtbezirks Prenzlauer Berg, Ratsitzung am 24. Mai 1979, "Räumungen auf dem Verwaltungswege" (146/79; 157/79; 148/79).

52 LAB, C Rep. 902, Nr. 4899, Bezirksleitung der SED, Eingabenbearbeitung durch die Arbeitsgruppe für Staats- und Rechtsfragen beim 1. Sekretär der Bezirksleitung der SED, "Legalisierung eines illegalen Bezuges," 12.7.79, unpaginated, emphasis mine.

53. Buck, *Mit hohem Anspruch gescheitert*, 169.

54. See Michael Rauhut, Thomas Kochan, and Christoph Dieckmann, eds., *Bye Bye, Lübben City: Bluesfreaks, Tramps und Hippies in der DDR* (Berlin: Schwarzkopf & Schwarzkopf, 2004).

55. Wolfgang Rüddenklau, "Vorwort," in *mOAning star: Eine Ostberliner Unter-grundpublikation, 1985–89*, ed. Dirk Moldt (Berlin: 2005), 7.

56. David Crowley and Susan E. Reid, "Socialist Spaces: Sites of Everyday Life in the Eastern Bloc," in *Socialist Spaces: Sites of Everyday Life in the Eastern Bloc*, ed. David Crowley and Susan E. Reid (Oxford: Berg, 2002), 4.

57. See Dieter Rucht, "Das alternative Milieu in der Bundesrepublik: Ursprünge, Infrastruktur und Nachwirkungen," in *Das Alternative Milieu: Antibürgerlicher Lebensstil und linke Politik in der Bundesrepublik Deutschland und Europa 1968–1983*, ed. Sven Reichardt and Detlef Siegfried (Göttingen: Wallstein Verlag, 2010), 65.

58. I borrow the terminology from Sabin Bieri's article on Swiss squatters and urban culture. See Sabin Bieri, "Contested Places: Squatting and the Construction of 'the Urban' in Swiss Cities," *GeoJournal* 58, no. 2–3 (2002): 207.

59. SAPMO, DY 30/22387, "Abschlussbericht des Verfassungs- und Rechtsau-schusses der Volkskammer der DDR über die Arbeitsgruppen Einsätze zur Kontrolle der Wirksamkeit der Rechtsvorschriften zur Verhütung und Bekämpfung von Ordnungswidrigkeiten," May 1983, 10.

60. David Clay Large, *Berlin* (New York: Basic Books, 2000), 514.

61. Dirk Moldt, "Parallelgesellschaft in der DDR: Ein gelebtes Ausstiegsmodell in den 80er Jahren in Ostberlin," *Horch und Guck: Zeitschrift zur kritischen Aufarbeitung der SED-Diktatur* no. 52 (2005).

62. BStU, MfS, AOP 1071/91 (1/3), fols. 118–19.

63. Moldt, "Parallelgesellschaft in der DDR," 1.

64. Roland Galenza, "Wimpelgrab & Gegentanz: Berlin," in *Wir wollen immer artig sein . . .: Punk, New Wave, HipHop und Independent-Szene in der DDR 1980–1990*, ed. Roland Galenza and Heinz Havemeister (Berlin: Schwarzkopf & Schwarzkopf, 1999), 263.

65. BStU, MfS, BV Berlin, AKG Nr. 4368, fol. 3.

66. LAB, C Rep. 134-02-02, Rat des Stadtbezirks Prenzlauer Berg, Ratssitzung am 7. Juli 1980, "Hinweise, Kritiken und Eingaben aus den V. Wahlkreisaktivberatung."

67. "Die EP Gallerie Jürgen Schweinebraden," *bpb: Bundeszentrale für politische Bildung*, http://www.bpb.de/geschichte/deutsche-geschichte/autonome-kunst-in-der-ddr/55803/ep-galerie-schweinebraden.

68. See "Dossier Autonome Kunst in der DDR," *bpb: Bundeszentrale für politische Bildung*, http://www.bpb.de/geschichte/deutsche-geschichte/autonome-kunst-in-der-ddr/55795/berlin.

69. BStU, MfS, AOP 1071/91 (1/3), fol. 28; BStU, MfS, AOP 1071/91 (1/3), fol. 231.

70. "Lesung an der Wand: und danach party," in BStU, MfS, AOP 1071/91 (1/3), fol. 231.

71. BStU, MfS, AOP 1071/91 (1/3), fol. 67, 235.

72. Ibid., fol. 235.

73. Ibid., fol. 236.

74. Ibid., fol. 105.

75. Ibid., fol. 236.

76. Ibid., fol. 67.

77. Ibid., fol. 58.

78. Ibid., fol. 144.

79. Ibid., fol. 144.

80. Ibid., fol. 116.

81. For a history of the East German punk scene, see Jeff Hayton, "'Härte gegen Punk': Popular Music, Western Media, and State Responses in the German Democratic Republic," *German History* 31, no. 4 (2013).

82. Torsten Preuß, "Stasi, Spaß und E-Gitarren: Die Geschichte der Berliner Punkband Namenlos," in Galenza and Havemeister, *Wir wollen immer artig sein . . .*, 52.

83. BStU, MfS, BV Berlin, 16816/84 (6).

84. Ibid., fol. 22.

85. Ibid., fols. 67–70.

86. Ibid., fol. 6.

87. Ibid., fol. 3.

88. Ibid., fol. 42.

89. Ibid., fol. 22.

90. Ibid., fols. 7, 42.

91. Ibid,. fol. 70.

92. Ibid., fol. 119.

93. Ibid., fols. 70–71.

94. BStU, MfS, AOP Nr. 9610/83, fol. 173.

95. BStU, MfS, AOP Nr. 16816/84, fol. 136.

96. BStU, MfS, AOP Nr. 9610/83, fol. 173; Michael Horschig, "In der DDR hat es nie Punks gegeben," in Galenza and Havemeister, *Wir wollen immer artig sein . . .*, 34–36.

97. In 1980, for example, the Council of Ministers instructed the local authorities at the *Bezirk* level to ensure "eine straffe Leitung der staatlichen Wohnungspolitik . . . und dafür zu sorgen, dass *die Prinzipien von Ordnung, Disziplin und Sicherheit bei der Vergabe von Wohnungen konsequent beachtet werden.*" SAPMO, DC 20/25332-Ministerrat der DDR, Sekretariat des Ministerrates, "Beschluß über Maßnahmen zur Erhöhung der Verantwortung der örtlichen Räte auf dem Gebiet der Wohnraumlenkung," 1980, fol. 4, emphasis mine.

98. See SAPMO, DC 20/25332, Ministerrat der DDR, Sekretariat des Ministerrates, "Beschluß über Maßnahmen zur Erhöhung der Verantwortung der örtlichen Räte auf dem Gebiet der Wohnraumlenkung," 1980, fol. 4.

99. SAPMO, DY 30/22388, "Information über die Tätigkeit der Arbeitsgruppe Wohnungspolitik und Wohnungswirtschaft beim Ministerrat," 1.

100. Ibid., "Neue Verordnung über die Wohnraumlenkung," 1985, 4.

101. SAPMO, DY 30/22387, "Sektor Staatsorgane: Vorschläge zur Durchführung des von Genossen Konrad Neumann angeregten Gespräche mit den Genossen Erhard Krack und Genossen Bein . . . über den Beschluß des Sekretariats der Bezirksleitung Berlin vom 21.3.1983."

102. Ibid., "Bezirksleitung Berlin der SED, Büro des Sekretariats: Beschluss des Sekretariats der Bezirksleitung Berlin der SED 0-7/83-31-vom 21.3.1983," 5.

103. SAPMO, DY 30/22387, "Magistrat von Berlin, Der Oberbürgermeister: Dienstanweisung zur Bekämpfung des ungesetzlichen Bezuges von Wohnraum in Berlin," April 20, 1983.

104. LAB, C Rep. 100-05, Nr. 1847, Magistrat von Berlin, Büro des Magistrats: "Maßnahmen zur Senkung der Leerstandzeiten von Wohnungen," January 21, 1981.

105. "Über die Volkspolizei-Inspektion Berlin-Friedrichshain ist wiederholt zu kontrollieren, dass die gesperrten Häuser, Gebäudeteile und Konzentrationen gesperrter Wohnungen entsprechend gesichert sind und nicht durch Unbefugte betreten oder genutzt warden." LAB, C Rep. 135-02-02, Nr. 1126 Rat des Stadtbezirks Friedrichshain, Ratsitzungen am 9. June 1977, "Maßnahmen zur Erfassung von leerstehendem Wohnraum (0138/77)"; "Leerstehende Wohnungen sind so zu sichern, dass eine unbefugte Nutzung verhindert wird, werden ganze Stränge oder Gebäudeteile nicht mehr bewohnt, ist sofort die Medienversorgung zu unterbrechen." LAB, C Rep. 143-02-02, Nr. 1387, Ratbeschlüsse Prenzlauerberg Ratsitzung am 27.11.1986, "Sperrung von Wohnungen und Nebengebäuden," unpaginated.

106. LAB, C Rep. 100-05, Nr. 2007, "Einschätzung über den Stand der Arbeit mit den Eingaben der Bürger in den Staatsorganen im Jahre 1985 sowie mit den Eingaben zu den Wahlen 1981 und 1984," January 20, 1986, 9.

107. SAPMO, DY 30/22388, Akademie für Staats- und Rechtswissenschaft der DDR, "Information über Erfahrungen bei der Anwendung und zur Wirksamkeit der Verordnung über die Lenkung des Wohnraumes vom 16. Oktober 1985" (January 1987), 7.

108. Ibid., 7.

109. SAPMO, DY 30/22386, Abteilung Staats- und Rechtsfragen, "Einschätzung des Standes der Verwirklichung des Beschlusses der Stadtverordnetenversammlung Berlin zur Entwicklung der VEB KWV," October 25, 1979, 4.

110. Ibid., 4.

111. See for example, LAB, C Rep. 100-05, Nr. 1458, Magistrat von Berlin, Büro des Magistrats, "Eingabenbearbeitung 2. Halbjahr 1970," March 17, 1971, 8–10.

112. SAPMO, DC 20/22820, Ministerrat: "Analyse: zur Vorlage: Vorschläge zur besseren Gewährleistung der Verwaltung und Erhaltung des Wohnungfonds," 1977, fol. 26.

113. LAB, C Rep. 135-02-02, Nr. 1246, Rat des Stadtbezirks Friedrichshain, Ratsitzungen am 23. Okt. 1980, "Bericht über die Ergebnisse bei der Durchsetzung der gemeinsamen Arbeitsanweisung des Rates zur Arbeit mit Wohnungsleerstand zur Erschliessung von Wohnraumreserven durch den VEB KWV," 6.

114. BAB, DC 20/11272, "Analyse und Schlussfolgerungen zur Erhöhung der Leistungsfähigkeit und Effektivität . . . der KWV . . .," 14.

115. SAPMO, DC 20-I/4/6260, "ABI Bericht über die Kontrolle zur Erhöhung der Wirksamkeit der VEB Gebäudewirtschaft/KWV für die Verwaltung und Erhaltung des Wohnungsbestandes," fol. 13; SAPMO, DC 20/22820, Ministerrat: "Analyse: zur Vorlage: Vorschläge zur besseren Gewährleistung der Verwaltung und Erhaltung des Wohnungfonds," 1977, fol. 26.

116. SAPMO, DY 30/22387, "Abschlussbericht des Verfassungs- und Rechtsausschusses der Volkskammer der DDR über die Arbeitsgruppeneinsätze zur Kontrolle der Wirksamkeit der Rechtsvorschriften zur Verhütung und Bekämpfung von Ordnungswidrigkeiten," May 10, 1983.

117. Ibid., 10.

118. LAB, C Rep. 307 Nr. 7, "ABI Bericht über der Durchführung des Staatsratserlasses vom 2.7.1965."

119. Jay Rowell, "Wohnungspolitik 1949–61," in *Geschichte der Sozialpolitik in Deutschland seit 1945, Deutsche Demokratische Republik 1949–1961: Im Zeichen des Aufbaus des Sozialismus*, ed. Dierk Hoffmann and Michael Schwartz (Baden-Baden: Nomos, 2004), 703.

120. Ibid., 709.

121. Rowell, "Wohnungspolitik 1971–89," 683.

122. Rowell, "Wohnungspolitik 1949–61," 711–12.

123. SAPMO, DC 20/22820, Ministerrat, "Analyse: zur Vorlage: Vorschläge zur besseren Gewährleistung der Verwaltung und Erhaltung des Wohnungfonds," 1977, fol. 10.

124. Ibid., Ministerrat der DDR, Sekretariat des Ministerrates, "Die Erhöhung der Verantwortung der örtlichen Räte auf dem Gebiet der Wohnraumlenkung," April 1, 1980, unpaginated.

125. LAB, C Rep. 100-05, Nr. 1968, Magistrat von Berlin, Büro des Magistrats, Sitzung am 7. Nov. 1984, "Stand der Erfüllung der namentlichen Wohnraumvergabepläne 1984 und der Vorbereitung 1985 sowie Erfahrungen in der Arbeit der Räte der Stadtbezirke." This document included: "Information über eine Untersuchung ausgewählter Aufgaben auf dem Gebiet der Wohnungspolitik," November 13, 1984.

126. Ibid.

127. BStU, MfS, BV Berlin, Abteilung VIII, 271. fol. 1.

128. Catherine Epstein, "The Stasi: New Research on the East German Ministry of State Security," *Kritika: Explorations in Russian and Eurasian History* 5, no. 2 (2004): 322.

129. A point made by Gieske. See Christian Semler, "1968 im Westen—was ging uns die DDR an?" *Aus Politik und Zeitgeschichte* 45 (2003): 106.

130. BStU, MfS AOP Nr. 9610/83 (1/3), fol. 20, 40, 41.

131. Ibid., fol. 20, 26.

132. BStU, MfS AOP Nr. 9610/83 (2/3), fol. 9.

133. BStU, MfS AOP Nr. 9610/83 (1/3), fol. 46.

134. Ibid., fol. 179.

135. Ibid., fol. 42.

136. BStU, MfS AOP Nr. 9610/83 (3/3), fol. 144.

137. Ibid., fol. 144.

138. Grashoff, *Schwarzwohnen*, 24.

# Conclusion

## *Dropping Out of Socialism?*
## *A Western Perspective*

### Joachim C. Häberlen

To learn about an author's intellectual background, one usually turns to the list of contributors of an edited volume like this. Yet, it may be useful to outline my scholarly background here to explain my perspective on "dropping out of socialism." Indeed, I came to this project—and the very stimulating conference this volume draws on—as an outsider: I am, first and foremost, a historian of Western Europe, primarily the Federal Republic of Germany.[1] While I teach about politics of protest in the postwar period across the bloc boundaries, socialist Eastern Europe is not my area of expertise. What I have to say about the chapters assembled in this volume thus comes from a deeply Western perspective; it is informed by knowledge of the history and historiography of somewhat similar phenomena in the West. Given that the volume seeks to challenge the Cold War notion of the Communist East and the Capitalist West as two entirely separate entities, such a perspective from the West on the East might indeed be helpful (and I should add that I do not know of any reverse perspective, that is, scholars of Eastern Europe commenting on phenomena in the West through an Eastern lens, as it were—something that is perhaps telling about the state of the profession).

For a historian of Western Europe, both the conference on which this volume is based, and the contributions included in this book are highly stimulating. We learn about punks, hippies, yogis, squatters, Islamic students, and "mad" artists, all phenomena that existed in Western Europe as well. Given that it is a volume about Eastern Europe, what we learn here looks strangely familiar. It challenges any notion of peculiar Western developments, and requires us to explore and conceptualize the history of post-1968 Europe across bloc boundaries.

In what follows, I will, in all brevity, outline how historians of West Germany—and I should note already here that I will draw on a mostly

Germanophone discussion—conceptualize protests in the long 1970s. I will then use this to inquire about what looking at Eastern Europe with such a Western perspective in mind might yield, thereby engaging in a discussion of two key terms of this volume: "socialism," and "dropping out." Since Western and Eastern drop-outs framed their social critiques and their goals and visions in surprisingly similar terms, and engaged in similar practices to accomplish their "dropping out," we need to question the Cold War division of the world into a capitalist West and socialist East. Neither were Western-ers dropping out of *capitalism* nor were Easterners dropping out of *socialism*, I propose. Building on an issue raised already in the introduction, I then want to inquire about the notion of "dropping out," emphasizing the productive quality of what various groups did.

Scholars of postwar Western Europe have discussed various protest and countercultural movements that emerged in the wake of 1968 more or less since the events themselves, often putting them into a narrative of political democratization and cultural liberalization.[2] Recently, however, scholars such as Joachim Scharloth and Sven Reichardt have challenged this inter-pretative framework. In particular, Reichardt's 2014 study *Authentizität und Gemeinschaft* (Authenticity and Community) is conceptually innovative by providing an interpretative framework that might be helpful for looking at Eastern Europe as well. Unlike most scholars who focus on the protests around 1968, Reichardt analyzes the "alternative milieu" that emerged in West Germany during the 1970s as an attempt to create an "authentic" sub-jectivity in a world activists deemed deeply inauthentic. Drawing on Michel Foucault's work, Reichardt interprets the alternative milieu as a "regime of subjectification, in which self-shaping [*Selbstmodellierung*] was turned into life-politics [*Lebenspolitik*]." Reichardt analyzes a variety of practices, such as expressing emotions, exploring the body, or living communally, alterna-tives used to "performatively create themselves" as "authentic." He asks, in other words, what leftists had to do in order to be recognized by themselves and others as "authentic." In that sense Reichardt explores a regime of subjec-tivity that was anything but simply liberating, and was, in fact, highly norma-tive and restrictive.[3] Reichardt's work is part of a broader debate in German historiography that addresses changing subjectivities in the post-1968 era.[4] One aspect of this debate is particularly noteworthy here: the peculiar regime of subjectification that characterizes neoliberal capitalism, and how a "neo-liberal" self began to emerge in the protest movements around 1968. In neo-liberal capitalism subjects are required to take responsibility for themselves, to be creative and flexible, to take care of their own health and happiness, for their own sakes, but also for society's sake. With the help of a plethora of guidance literature and personal coaches, people have to constantly work on their selves and observe themselves.[5] Practices of self-determination have thus become part of a regime of governmentality. As Thomas Lemke, Susanne Krasmann, and Ulrich Bröckling note, "in the context of neoliberal governmentality, self-determination, responsibility, and freedom of choice do not signal the limits of governing [*Regierungshandeln*], but are themselves an instrument and medium [*Vehikel*] to change how subjects relate to themselves and to others."[6] This emergence of a neoliberal subject can be tied to a change in capitalism itself, as Luc Boltanski and Eve Chiapello have claimed. The "new spirit of capitalism" Boltanski and Chiapello examine relies less on external forces, and more on internalized self-control, on ideals of autonomy, self-realization, and self-improvement. Ironically, then, the very ideals of the protagonists of 1968 and the subsequently developing New Left contributed to a transformation of capitalism rather than to its weakening.[7]

For a discussion of "dropping out of socialism," three issues that emerge from this literature are pertinent: first, the critique of an inauthentic society common among Western activists. Western activists criticized the world they were living in as gray and monotone, splitting up bodies and personalities according to criteria of efficiency and productivity; in their minds, the capitalist world did not allow for any genuine feelings (and their expression), nor for a positive relationship to the whole body. Did activists on the other side of the Iron Curtain develop a similar critique of the (socialist) world they were living in, and if so, how much sense does it make to characterize this as a critique of *socialism*? Second, the focus on practices many authors share is of interest. They explore bodily, emotional, and communicative practices, such as doing yoga or mediating in the context of New Ageism, which activists used to shape their authentic self, or, put differently, to *be* authentic.[8] The interest in the practical creation of an alternative and authentic self reveals activists as tremendously productive: they produced a new form of subjectivity. Can we observe a similar productivity among Eastern European activists? And if so, what precisely did they "produce," and how did they do so? Did a similar kind of (perhaps alternative) subjectivity develop across the Iron Curtain? Finally, the arguments Western scholars have made regarding the transformation of capitalism and the emergence of a neoliberal self should stir up our interest. If the "drop-outs" in socialist Eastern Europe were similarly interested in autonomy and self-improvement, issues that observers of changes in Western Europe have interpreted in terms of a neoliberal self and a transformation of capitalism, how might this fit into a socialist context? These are, I suggest, challenging questions that force us to rethink the division of postwar European history into East and West. The chapters in this volume provide fascinating first answers to those questions, and we may look forward to more detailed studies exploring them further.

For me as a historian of Western Europe, it is indeed striking how much the people who populate the pages of this volume resemble their counterparts in the West. Estonian hippie Vladimir, for example, recalls: "We couldn't protest against capitalism, because we didn't have it here. But we had the same bureaucrats, rednecks, and just very box-headed people."[9] In a few words Vladimir invokes a peculiar critique of the modern world that, in his mind, Western and Eastern hippies shared. Vladimir formulated, it seems to me, a critique that is much more specific than a general critique of the "established order," be it "rigid ideas about race, gender, class hierarchies," and so on, in the United States, or be it "authoritative discourse, morals, militarism," and so on, in the East.[10] In fact, his brief comment suggests that, in his mind, capitalist and socialist societies resembled each other, because bureaucrats and rednecks were governing them—what Theodor Adorno and other thinkers of the Frankfurt School had called the "totally administered world."[11] According to this line of critique, the individual had no freedom of choice in a world that was utterly regulated and predetermined by bureaucratic rules that governed life on both sides of the Iron Curtain.

To take another example: yogi Gregorian Bivolaru's critique of prudish sexual norms in Romania is very much reminiscent of critiques Western activists made. And while Western followers of New Age religions were deeply skeptical of scientific rationalism, Bivolaru was hostile, or so the regime thought, to Romania's official "scientific atheism."[12] East German punk Mike, whom Jeff Hayton discusses, provides a final example. What Mike told a journalist from the West German magazine *Der Spiegel* could very well have been said by a West German punk, perhaps with the exception of the reference to the "state-run youth scene": "This whole upbringing to become a machine . . . the whole state-run youth scene makes me sick. There is nothing there. So boring. When I think about our discotheques, I think: puke!"[13] And Western activists would have understood that a band name like Betonromantik entailed a critique of boring, gray, and monotonous cities that were hostile to feelings, senses, and bodies—though one wonders whether punks were not also playing with this critique of modern urbanity and instead celebrated it.[14]

All these examples point to a more or less explicit critique of socialism among Eastern "drop-outs" that is remarkably similar to the critique of modern capitalism we find in the West. Just like their counterparts on the other side of the Iron Curtain, hippies, yogis, and punks (though they should not, of course, simply be confused) saw themselves living in a deeply boring world that was governed by bureaucrats and scientific rationality, but remained hostile to bodies, senses, and the imagination; it was a "spiritually void" world, as a pacifist discussed by Irina Gordeeva put it, though he also criticized hippies for not filling this void.[15] It would be interesting to know whether Eastern activists, too, perceived this world as lacking authenticity.

If there indeed was a rather similar critique (and by highlighting similarities, I do of course not want to suggest that it was the *same* critique, but similarities are more interesting because they allow us to question the Cold War divide) of capitalism and socialism across the Iron Curtain, then we might wonder whether "socialism" (and, for that matter, "capitalism") are the most useful analytical categories, unless we want to use them in a simply descriptive way referring to "the West" and "the East," respectively. Did Eastern "drop-outs" really drop out, if they did, of *socialism* (and their Western counterparts of *capitalism*)? Would it be more appropriate, if also more clumsy, to say that they dropped out of rational, industrial modernity? Perhaps. In any case, the critique these drop-outs formulated indicates, I would like to suggest, the need to think about terms that allow us to conceptualize the post-1968 world, or at least Europe and the United States, across the Cold War divide.

But did these people really "drop out"? The terms we pick generate certain questions, they push the analysis into a certain direction. "Dropping out" implies spatiality: people drop out of somewhere, and they drop in somewhere else. But was it actually possible to drop out of socialism? Jeff Hayton's discussion of East German punks who claimed to ignore the socialist states indicates that, despite claims to the contrary, this was never possible. Many other authors make similar points; indeed, as Peter Mitchell shows, drop-outs simultaneously participated in the socialist state.[16] The term also implies that people "drop in" somewhere (unless they get lost in permanent movement): into the imaginary worlds of hippies that Terje Toomistu and Juliane Fürst discuss, the borderless cosmopolitanism of pacifists that populate Irina Gordeeva's chapter, an imaginary West, as in the case of the Polish hackers Patryk Wasiak writes about, the worlds of punk (and rock music in general) discussed by Evgenyi Kazakov, Anna Kan, and Jeff Hayton, into global Islam, as Madigan Fichter shows, or into a squatted apartment, as Peter Mitchell's contribution notes. But the spatial register of "dropping out," or "dropping in" does not mean that the worlds people were dropping out from and dropping in to simply existed; as the introduction emphasizes, especially the spaces into which people could drop had to be constructed. Elaborating on this point, I want in what follows to stress the productivity and creativity of various "drop-outs."

What, then, did those drop-outs create? Scholars of Western Europe have drawn on Michel Foucault and his notion of "technologies of the self" to analyze a great variety of practices common among West European "drop-outs." In Foucault's famous definition, "technologies of the self" are practices "which permit individuals to effect by their own means or with the help of others a certain number of operations on their own bodies and souls, thoughts, conduct, and way of being, so as to transform themselves in order to attain a certain state of happiness, purity, wisdom, perfection, or immortality."[17] Working on the self, that is, produces a peculiar subjectivity. In his study of the West German alternative left, Sven Reichardt has suggested that by engaging in a variety of spiritual, emotional, bodily, and communicative practices, leftists created an "authentic" subjectivity. Given that we can see a somewhat similar critique of a boring and inauthentic world in Eastern Europe, does it make sense to interpret what activists did in a similar way as attempts to produce authentic experiences and to shape an authentic self? Not least, inquiring about practices in multiple ways may help us historicize bodies and feelings without turning to ultimately ahistorical theories of affect.[18] Importantly, pursuing such a praxeological approach also means that we need to avoid asking how genuinely "authentic" people's experiences were; instead, we need to inquire about how authenticity was produced, and according to which rules and norms.

The chapters in this volume suggest that such an interpretation might indeed be fruitful. What the people who populate the pages of this volume did resembles in many ways the practices that historians of Western activism will be familiar with. In West Germany alternative leftists constantly referred to their "damaged personalities," which they tried to "fix," as it were, in countless therapy and encounter groups.[19] Eastern activists, too, described a personal self-transformation as one of their major goals, though I wonder if they shared the sense common among Westerners that their self was "damaged." As a member of the Yellow Submarine commune discussed in Juliane Fürst's chapter wrote: "Remember that our common goal was self-perfection and education of oneself and those close to us." Another former commune member said: "We tried to achieve the best possible self-perfection and character-building, yet declared our desire to build these in an introverted society."[20] While Fürst notes that self-improvement was part of a Soviet tradition, we should not forget that working on the (damaged) self was also an essential aspect of Western alternative cultures; perhaps this may explain why such alternative cultures could flourish on both sides of the Iron Curtain. Even official Romanian psychology considered exercises like "meditation, deep breathing, hypnosis, and other forms of relaxation as methods of improving cognitive capacities and promoting healing," as Irina Costache writes.[21] The yogis she discusses shared this desire for a personal transformation. Similarly, "mad" artists like Ştefan Bertalan described their artistic work as "self-therapy," as a means to "cure myself." "They want to transform our spirits into slaves," he charged, and hence spiritual resistance and healing would be necessary.[22] We can observe a similar goal among the Estonian hippies Toomistu discusses. In their case resistance against a rational and scientific world involved creating "altered states of consciousness," the recovery of "dreams, fantasies, and spiritual quests," a language reminiscent of Western leftists who celebrated feelings, dreams, insanity, and excesses as subversive forces in a rational world.[23] For Estonian hippies, reaching the spheres of an altered consciousness, dreams, and fantasies was not an escape from reality, but an entry into a more "real" world. If only "for a few seconds," they could be "completely awake," one hippie claimed. It created a "feeling of personal freedom, being free like God."[24] Similar to their Western counterparts, hippies longed for more authentically "real" experiences that they missed in the normal life of socialism. Whereas yogis like Bivolaru sought to reach a "higher plane of consciousness," Toomistu interprets the hippies' "self-formation process" as an "indefinite becoming."

Many "drop-outs" were, it seems, engaged in some project of self-transformation, but what exactly this project should achieve was anything but clear—whether there was any "goal," so to speak, like a higher sphere of consciousness, or whether the process itself was the goal. In analyzing such projects of self-transformation, however, we need to be careful to pay attention to the historicity of the analytical concepts we use. By describing hippies as a "rhizomatic" community with "no sense of place," for example, Toomistu turns to a rhetoric and to authors, Gilles Deleuze and Felix Guattari, who were very much part of the historical moment she is describing.[25] In West Germany activists described their "scene" as a "rhizome," and indeed tried to create "rhizomatic" structures, so to speak;[26] I wonder how much Estonian hippies, too, even without using this term, styled themselves in such a fashion (and, for that matter, I wonder about the influence of Western authors such as the Beat poets and their idealization of constant movement for their endeavor).

Activists sought to achieve this self-transformation in multiple ways. They engaged in what might be described as spiritual or mental, bodily, and spatial practices that would transform the self and create the conditions for successful self-transformations. Aleksandr Ogordonikov, a hippie who organized underground religious seminars in the 1970s, as Irina Gordeeva writes, believed in the creation of a "second culture" that would touch "all spheres of human activity (literature, philosophy, history, art, and so on)." Where Western activists in February 1978 wanted to "sail to the beaches of Tunix" to escape from the "model Germany," Ogordonikov imagined "island communities" that would "carry a radically new spirituality and are capable of molding people with a non-Soviet consciousness and mode of action." "Love and freedom" would structure the "topographic universe of this new spirituality," and "art is its lifeblood."[27] But how exactly did this "new spirituality" work? What did people do (with their bodies, feelings, and minds) to develop a "non-Soviet consciousness"? While the chapters hint at practices, we need more thick descriptions of various practices to answer such questions. Maria-Alina Asavei makes a similar point about the artists she studies, who did not seek a new "spirituality," but chose to be mad, as it were, to distance themselves from the regime; they chose, she notes, "existence in a state of mind of perpetual immaturity in which they rejected the adult *status quo*"; they chose "dreamlike" and "self-induced euphoric states of mind" as a way to escape from socialist reality.[28] Along somewhat similar lines, the commune members Juliane Fürst studies celebrated "childish games" in a society that had no place for infantilism.[29] It would be worthwhile to know more about exactly what a "state of mind of perpetual immaturity" implied, how "self-induced euphoric states of mind" could be achieved. Was there a desire to be, to feel (rather than think) like children that we can observe among Western activists?[30] But also in a completely different context, namely that of the Islamic revival in Yugoslavia discussed by Madigan Fichter, prayers and other spiritual practices played a crucial role for changing the self in a way that made it part of a global Islamic community.[31] Again, it would be interesting to know more about exactly how praying as a bodily and spiritual practice could facilitate such a self-transformation, if sources can provide answers to such a question.

In many instances, bodies and what people did with their bodies played a crucial role for transforming the self. Indeed, the body had to be changed as part of the self-transformation drop-outs engaged in. Estonia's hippies, for example, not only wanted to create a community of permanent becoming, Toomistu tells us, but also to "open their bodies for perpetual becoming."[32] How did this work? Obviously, bodily practices like dressing in a particular style set activists apart from mainstream socialist society. But these practices also facilitated specific experiences that were lacking, according to activists, in "normal" society. The East German punks Jeff Hayton and Peter Mitchell discuss, for example, wore colorful clothes and had "fire-red hair"; Hayton notes that those attributes separated individuals from the "normals" in society, but it would be worthwhile to ask if dressing and grooming oneself like that were not also ways to bring color into a world perceived as gray and monotonous, something that Soviet hippies tried to do by wearing blue jeans (blue being the color of freedom) in distinction from the gray masses in the Soviet Union.[33] Interestingly, Hayton emphasizes that for punks, appearance and attitude went hand in hand: an authentic punk attitude required a specific appearance.

The hippies Toomistu discusses listened to "the mesmerizing sound of rock," a sensual experience that gave them a sense of "internal dreamscapes." Music could, as one of her interviewees noted, get listeners into the "right mindset."[34] Given the importance of sounds for punk cultures too, one does indeed wonder how music could affect listeners and help them either "drop out" or reach an altered state mind, in particular if considered in combination with dancing at punk concerts, an issue neither Hayton nor Evgenyi Kazakov nor Anna Kan really touch upon.[35] Western activists, for example, reported how excessive collective dancing during concerts could disrupt the "bodily armor" that alienated people from their own bodies as well as others. A woman from West Berlin, to give just one example, reported that collective dancing was "insane, in a way liberating, feeling the body and all that."[36] Toomistu hints at similar experiences when she quotes a claim made by one of her interlocutors that, "the whole crowd was breathing together that night" during a concert. Not surprisingly, drug consumption had similar effects. Rather than concealing the truth, it was under the influence of drugs that, "you understand everything, the whole truth about the world," a hippie told Toomistu.[37] Drugs, that is, facilitated a truthful and authentic experience in an inauthentic world. Yoga, meditation, specific diets, and breathing exercises were further techniques that would help hippies in Estonia and yogis in Romania to transform themselves. Yoga guru Bivolaru, for example, claimed to "use the representation of nude women to practice Tantric yoga." Looking at their pictures enabled him to channel his "sexual energies toward the achievement of a higher plane of consciousness."[38]

Last but not least, creating imaginary or, perhaps even more importantly, real spaces was crucial for creating a different subjectivity. In the West, activists established communes and youth centers as a means to overcome the monotony and isolation that, in their minds, characterized capitalist society. They colorfully painted gray walls to beautify the monotonous city and to encourage communication between neighbors.[39] We find something similar in the East. For the inhabitants of Leningrad's Yellow Submarine commune, moving into the "last private wooden house" on the city's outskirts meant entering "a place that was free." Decorating the house, painting the walls in yellow with huge strawberries, and putting up posters of Western pop icons made the place special. Colors and subversive or ironic posters created a space in which a "wilder" and "freer" life seemed possible. Yet Fürst also highlights that spatial or sensual practices like painting walls in yellow did not in themselves create "wilderness," as it were; for this to happen, a "rhetorical interpretation" was necessary. Practices function, this indicates, only in conjunction with a knowledge about what these practices might yield.[40] In East Germany, we learn from Peter Mitchell, squatted apartments provided a ground for alternative lifestyles, for underground exhibitions and concerts.[41] Yet, we learn little about what squatters did with these spaces, how they rearranged and recreated spatial settings. Did they, like their Western counterparts, tear down walls and doors to overcome isolation? Did they paint walls to counter the gray monotony of concrete, as Soviet hippies had done? We learn that squatters left their apartments dirty and that anarchists sprayed graffiti at the walls, but why did this matter for dropping out of socialism?

Space mattered also in other contexts. "Mad" artists studied by Asavei, for example, needed asylums so they could "create" their own world through "fantasies."[42] The yogi followers of "Guru Grig" assembled at a "remote beach,"

Costache writes, because practicing yoga at a beach created a "direct connection of bodies and the therapeutic effects of the sun."[43] One wonders in
this context what kind of clothes the yogis wore to expose their bodies to the
sun.[44] In Estonia, hippies decorated the stage for a concert with candles and
filled the hall with balloons. Was this, I wonder, a means to bring color and
sensual experiences into a gray world? But activists not only (re-)arranged
spaces, they also moved through spaces. Just like their Western counterparts,
hippies in Estonia hitchhiked through the country and gathered for festivals;
their bodies were in constant movement through space, refusing any fixation.
It was another way of practically opening bodies to a "perpetual becoming."[45]
The Polish hackers Patryk Wasiak discusses used computers to escape into an
(imagined) West.[46] And of course, as Irina Gordeeva reminds us, physically
leaving the Soviet Union by emigrating was the most straightforward step for
"dropping out" of socialism.[47] But cosmopolitanism and a desire to dissolve
national boundaries, which were common among Western activists as well,[48]
also challenged the ideological foundations of communism. In the absence
of borders that separate nations and human beings, love would bring people
together, a Soviet hippie remarked. Only this might facilitate a true community, based on "equality and brotherhood." Even hippies had to overcome
their loneliness, the authors of the "Free Initiative" manifesto wrote.[49]

All these were practices we can also find in the West. If we interpret
those practices as "technologies of the self" that shape a historically specific
subjectivity, then the fact that those practices spread across the Iron Curtain
indicates, I would like to suggest, the emergence of a common culture of
subjectivity. The question is how to frame this subjectivity. Scholars of West
Germany have emphasized the desire for self-improvement, but also desires
for autonomy and creativity, which suggests, as I have noted above, that a
"neoliberal" self emerged that went hand in hand with a transformation of
capitalism. Strikingly, we find evidence for similar developments in some of
the contributions to this volume. The East German squatters Peter Mitchell
discusses, for example, "demonstrated a considerable degree of initiative"
while at the same time refusing to work regular jobs.[50] They longed, it seems,
for more "autonomous" work. Similarly, the punks studied by Jeff Hayton
wanted, just as West German punks did, to work to live, and not to live to
work.[51] Most interestingly, the Polish computer aficionados whom Patryk
Wasiak discusses wanted "to be one's own" by setting up their own semi-
legal businesses outside the official state economy of the state. In a striking
similarity to the new "creative" professions in the West that Luc Boltanski
and Eve Chiapello discuss in their work on the "new spirit of capitalism,"[52]
these young Poles longed for the possibility of doing something "on their
own"; they longed for autonomy and creativity in the sphere of work, something they found through a range of practices related to computers. Of course,

more research is needed in this regard. But it would be a fascinating and highly counterintuitive outcome if we could find, amidst a socialist society, evidence for something that looks akin to the transformation of capitalism Boltanski and Chiapello have described for the West. Not least, this might shed a new light on "neoliberal" developments in post-1989 Eastern Europe.[53] Tellingly, Wasiak emphasizes that the informal computer economy that emerged in the mid- to late 1980 survived until the mid-1990s and contributed to the neoliberal transformation of Poland.

Alternatively, we might interpret these technologies of the self across the Iron Curtain in terms of authenticity. Rather than assessing how genuinely authentic activists were, we need to inquire what people did to feel authentically in a world that seemed sterile and unreal. By practicing yoga, meditating, or consuming drugs, people tried to have the "real" and "meaningful" bodily experiences they were otherwise missing. In that sense, people practically created their authentic self. While there is something to be said for such a perspective, it seems difficult to square this interpretation with the theatricality and playfulness we find among some "drop-outs" like the Siberian punks that Evgenyi Kazakov describes.[54] Like West German bands such as Deutsch-Amerikanische Freundschaft that sang "Dance the Mussolini, dance the Adolf Hitler, dance the Jesus Christ" (*Tanz den Mussolini, tanz den Adolf Hitler, tanz den Jesus Christus*), these bands mocked their audience.[55] Rather than longing for more "real" experiences, they seem to have denied the reality of anything and any experience. The "necrorealists" that Maria-Alina Asavei explores, also seem to have refused any stable identity. Naked men running around aimlessly, impersonations of cruelty, or "clown-like hooliganism" were hardly a means to be "authentic." The "madness" of these performances was not "more real," it seems, but absurd. Perhaps these artistic performances mocked the very search for authenticity we can observe among other protagonists. Necrorealists challenged, as Asavei argues, the "Soviet regime of discipline and representation"; but they hardly offered a more "authentic" alternative, as perhaps Estonian hippies, Islamic students in Yugoslavia, or Romanian yogis did.[56]

Finally, this raises the question of how political "dropping out" was, an issue that many contributions raise. Toomistu, for example, stresses that hippies, while not openly protesting against the Soviet regime, nevertheless were political by questioning the norms of Soviet society through forms of self-expression.[57] Other activists more openly rebelled against the political system, like East German punks. The crucial issue is that a new form of political struggle developed that resembled, once again, what we can find in the West. In a famous essay on the "Subject and Power," Michel Foucault has noted the development of a new kind of struggle which he characterized as "struggles against the 'government of individualization'"; these were struggles "against that which ties the individual to himself and submits him to others in this way (struggles against subjection, against forms of subjectivity and submission)."[58] In the 1970s the place of politics moved, as it were, to the subject. Foucault's analysis quite aptly describes the struggles the protagonists of this volume were involved in. Simply asking whether these were indeed *political* struggles is, then, perhaps asking the wrong question, because such a question might operate with an ahistorical understanding of what politics is. Rather, across the Iron Curtain, we can observe the development of a new understanding of the political (and Foucault, for that matter, contributed to this understanding as much as he analyzed it). We need, that is, to understand the internalization of the political as a historical process. One problem of the socialist regimes might have been that they failed to understand this form of political challenge. Toomistu, for example, notes that the regime regarded hippies not as an ideological problem, but as an esthetic or moral problem.[59] Socialist regimes, one might argue, were the heritage of a form of struggle, to quote Foucault again, "against forms of exploitation which separate individuals from what they produce," a struggle that had, of course, characterized the working-class movement.[60] What hippies, punks, and yogis did was not part of these struggles. They fought against a regime of subjectification that wanted to create a "new man" as an untiring, always working, and constantly functioning human machine, as Jochen Hellbeck noted. Perhaps the regime was unable to grasp the political challenge hippies and others posed because the regime thought about politics in terms of class conflict and imperialism, but not as a struggle against a regime of subjectification; and perhaps this was one reason why these drop-outs were ultimately dangerous for the regimes.

To conclude, then, this is a rich volume that gives much food for further thought and inquiry. We may look forward to more exhaustive and empirically rich studies about the spiritual, bodily, and spatial practices that hippies, punks, yogis, and many others engaged in. As a historian of Western Europe, I long for more detailed examinations of what music did to feelings and bodies, how activists decorated rooms and how this affected them, what they did with their bodies when meditating or practicing yoga, and not least, how this could become politically meaningful. Beyond the specific case studies, the volume also challenges us to think about European history of the late twentieth century across the Iron Curtain. If we can observe, as I have suggested in this conclusion, similar critiques of the state and society on both sides of the Iron Curtain, and similar practices that questioned and challenged social norms, then what does this mean for our conceptualization of the era? Is it still useful to frame this period as the age of the Cold War, which implies a rather strict opposition between East and West? Or might it be more productive to think about developments that sometimes took place at the fringes of society, but that nevertheless indicate a certain convergence? And if so, what might a different narrative look like? In this conclusion I have suggested interpreting what the various drop-outs did in terms of "technologies of the self" and changing cultures of subjectivity—a very Western perspective as far as I can tell. Of course, all this conclusion can offer are some very preliminary thoughts. Much more empirical research and conceptual thinking will be necessary to arrive at a genuinely European history of the late twentieth century.

## NOTES

1. For my work on the alternative left in West Germany, see Joachim C. Häberlen, "Ingrid's Boredom," in *Learning How to Feel: Children's Literature and Emotional Socialization, 1870–1970*, ed. Ute Frevert, Pascal Eitler, and Stephanie Olsen (Oxford: Oxford University Press, 2014), ———, "Sekunden der Freiheit: Zum Verhältnis von Gefühlen, Macht und Zeit in Ausnahmesituationen am Beispiel der Revolte 1980/81 in Berlin," in *Ausnahmezustände: Entgrenzungen und Regulierungen in Europa während des Kalten Krieges*, ed. Dirk Schumann and Cornelia Rau (Göttingen: Wallstein, 2015), ———, "Feeling Like a Child: Visions and Practices of Sexuality in the West German Alternative Left during the Long 1970s," *Journal for the History of Sexuality* 25, no. 2 (2016), Joachim C. Häberlen and Jake Smith, "Struggling for Feelings: The Politics of Emotions in the Radical New Left in West Germany, c. 1968–84," *Contemporary European History* 23, no. 4 (2014).

2. See Philipp Gassert, "Narratives of Democratization: 1968 in Postwar Europe," in *1968 in Europe. A History of Protest and Activism, 1956–1977*, ed. Martin Klimke and Joachim Scharloth (New York: Palgrave Macmillan, 2008), Belinda Davis, "What's Left? Popular and Democratic Political Participation in Postwar Europe," *American Historical Review* 113, no. 2 (2008). See also, with regards to West Germany, Ulrich Herbert, ed., *Wandlungsprozesse in Westdeutschland: Belastung, Integration, Liberalisierung 1945–1980* (Göttingen: Wallstein, 2002).

3. Sven Reichardt, *Authentizität und Gemeinschaft: Linksalternatives Leben in den siebziger und frühen achtziger Jahren* (Berlin: Suhrkamp, 2014), 68, Sven Reichardt and Detlef Siegfried, eds., *Das Alternative Milieu: Antibürgerlicher Lebensstil und linke Politik in der Bundesrepublik Deutschland und Europa 1968–1983* (Göttingen: Wallstein, 2010).

4. See for example, Pascal Eitler and Jens Elberfeld, eds., *Zeitgeschichte des Selbst: Therapeutisierung—Politisierung—Emotionalisierung* (Bielefeld: Transcript, 2015), Sabine Maasen et al., eds., *Das beratene Selbst: Zur Genealogie der Therapeutisierung in den "langen" Siebzigern* (Bielefeld: Transcript, 2011), Maik Tändler, "Therapeutische Vergemeinschaftung: Demokratie, Emanzipation und Emotionalisierung in der 'Gruppe,' 1963–1976," in *Das Selbst zwischen Anpassung und Befreiung: Psychowissen und Politik im 20. Jahrhundert*, ed. Maik Tändler and Uffa Jensen (Göttingen: Wallstein, 2012).

5. Ulrich Bröckling, *Das unternehmerische Selbst: Soziologie einer Subjektivierungsform* (Frankfurt am Main: Suhrkamp, 2007). The emphasis on creativity

and self-determination distinguishes the neoliberal self Bröckling and others are describing from the ideal of a "new man" common among Bolsheviks after 1917. The "new man" they envisioned was, as Jochen Hellbeck has noted, a "human machine, an untiring worker, or an unfettered, integrated 'personality.'" See Jochen Hellbeck, *Revolution on My Mind: Writing a Diary under Stalin* (Cambridge, MA: Harvard University Press, 2006), 5.

6. Thomas Lemke, Susanne Krasmann, and Ulrich Bröckling, "Gouvernementalität, Neoliberalismus und Selbsttechnologien: Eine Einleitung," in *Gouvernementalität der Gegenwart: Studien zur Ökonomisierung des Sozialen*, ed. Thomas Lemke, Susanne Krasmann, and Ulrich Bröckling (Frankfurt am Main: Suhrkamp, 2000), 30.

7. Luc Boltanski and Eve Chiapello, *The New Spirit of Capitalism* (London: Verso, 2005).

8. On New Ageism, see Pascal Eitler, "'Alternative' Religion: Subjektivierungspraktiken und Politisierungsstrategien im 'New Age' (Westdeutschland 1970–1990)," in *Das alternative Milieu: Antibürgerlicher Lebensstil und linke Politik in der Bundesrepublik Deutschland und Europa, 1968–1983*, ed. Sven Reichardt and Detlef Siegfried (Göttingen: Wallstein, 2010), ———, "'Selbstheilung': Zur Somatisierung und Sakralisierung von Selbstverhältnissen im New Age (Westdeutschland 1970–1990)," in *Das beratene Selbst: Zur Genealogie der Therapeutisierung in den "langen" Siebzigern*, ed. Sabine Maasen et al. (Bielefeld: Transcript, 2011).

9. Toomistu in this volume.

10. Toomistu in this volume.

11. See Theodor W. Adorno, "Dissonanzen: Musik in der verwalteten Welt," in *Dissonanzen: Einleitung in die Musiksoziologie,* vol. 14 in *Gesammelte Schriften* (Frankfurt am Main: Suhrkamp, 1973).

12. Costache in this volume.

13. Hayton in this volume. For an example from West Germany, see Anon., "Torschlusspanik um 10 (Discotheken)," in *ABBLDIBABBLDIBIBBLDIBABBLDIBU: Schülerzeitung der HCO*, December 2, 1973, 8–10.

14. See for example, Büro für anti-utopische Forschungen, *Betonzeit: Ein Pamphlet gegen die Stadtlandschaft und ihre Verbesserungen* (Cologne: Eigenverlag, 1980). On West German youth movements demanding "autonomy," see also David Templin, *Freizeit ohne Kontrollen: Die Jugendzentrumsbewegung in der Bundesrepublik der 1970er Jahre* (Göttingen: Wallstein, 2015).

15. Gordeeva in this volume.

16. Hayton and Mitchell in this volume.

17. Michel Foucault, "Technologies of the Self," in *Technologies of the Self: A Seminar with Michel Foucault*, ed. Luther H. Martin, Huck Gutman, and Patrick H. Hutton (London: University of Massachusetts Press, 1988).

18. See Monique Scheer, "Are Emotions a Kind of Practice (and Is That What Makes Them Have a History)? A Bourdieuan Approach to Understanding Emotion," *History and Theory* 51, no. 2 (2012).

19. See Tändler, "Therapeutische Vergemeinschaftung." ———, *Das therapeutische Jahrzehnt: Der Psychoboom in den siebziger Jahren* (Göttingen: Wallstein, 2016).

20. Fürst in this volume.

21. It would be interesting to know whether there was a psychoboom similar to what can be observed in West Germany. See Tändler, *Therapeutische Jahrzehnt.*

22. Asavei in this volume.

23. To give only two examples from West Germany, see Wolfgang Seiler, *Grenzüberschreitungen: Zur Sprache des Wahnsinns* (Giessen: Focus, 1980), Herbert Röttgen and Florian Rabe, *Vulkantänze: Linke und alternative Ausgänge* (Munich: Trikont-Verlag, 1978).

24. Toomistu in this volume.

25. See Gilles Deleuze and Félix Guattari, *A Thousand Plateaus*, trans. Brian Massumi (Minneapolis: University of Minnesota Press, 1987).

26. Herbert Röttgen, "Sumpf," *Das Blatt*, November 4–17, 1977, 14–15.

27. Gordeeva in this volume. On Tunix, see Michael März, *Linker Protest nach dem Deutschen Herbst: Eine Geschichte des linken Spektrums im Schatten des "starken Staates", 1977–1979* (Bielefeld: transcript, 2012).

28. Asavei in this volume.

29. Fürst in this volume.

30. See Häberlen, "Feeling Like A Child."

31. Fichter in this volume.

32. Toomistu in this volume.

33. Hayton, Mitchell, and Fürst in this volume.

34. Toomistu in this volume.

35. Hayton, Kan, and Kazakov in this volume.

36. Anon., "Bericht von einer Frauenfete," in *Info BUG* 87 (1977): 4–5.

37. Toomistu in this volume.

38. Costache in this volume.

39. See for example, *Wandmalereien & Texte: Nehmt der Langeweile ihren Sinn* (Berlin: Kramer, 1979). For a discussion of the Italian Indiani Metropolitani, see also Pablo Echaurren, *La casa del desiderio: '77: indiani metropolitani e altri strani* (Lecce: Manni Editore, 2005).

40. Fürst in this volume.

41. Mitchell in this volume.

42. Asavei in this volume.

43. Costache in this volume.

44. Studies on nude gymnastics in the context of the German life reform movement might be instructive in this regard. See Maren Möhring, *Marmorleiber: Körperbildung in der deutschen Nacktkultur (1890–1930)* (Cologne: Böhlau, 2004).

45. Toomistu in this volume.

46. Wasiak in this volume.

47. Gordeeva in this volume.

48. See Richard Ivan Jobs, "Youth Movements: Travel, Protest, and Europe in 1968," *American Historical Review* 114, no. 2 (2009).

49. Gordeeva in this volume. See also the comments on the "revolution against loneliness" in Angelo Ventrone, *"Vogliamo tutto": Perché due generazioni hanno creduto nella rivoluzione 1960–1988* (Rome: Editori Laterza, 2012), 348–351.

50. Mitchell in this volume.

51. Hayton in this volume. Note that this is a common phrase in German.

52. Boltanski and Chiapello, *Spirit*.

53. See Philipp Ther, *Die neue Ordnung auf dem alten Kontinent: Eine Geschichte des neoliberalen Europa* (Berlin: Suhrkamp, 2014).

54. Kazakov in this volume.

55. On DAF, see Rüdiger Esch, *Electri_City: Elektronische Musik aus Düsseldorf 1970–1986* (Berlin: Suhrkamp, 2014). On parody and mockery, see also Alexei Yurchak, *Everything Was Forever, Until It Was No More: The Last Soviet Generation* (Princeton: Princeton University Press, 2006).

56. Asavei in this volume.

57. Toomistu in this volume.

58. Michel Foucault, "The Subject and Power," *Critical Inquiry* 8, no. 4 (1982): 781.

59. Toomistu in this volume.

60. Foucault, "Subject," 781.

# Bibliography

Andjelic, Neven. *Bosnia-Herzegovina: The End of a Legacy*. Portland: Frank Cass Publishers, 2003.

Andreescu, Gabriel. *Reprimarea Miscarii Yoga in Anii 80*. Iasi: Polirom, 2008.

———. *MISA: Radiografia Unei Represiun*. Iasi: Polirom, 2013.

Assmann, Jan. "Communicative and Cultural Memory." In *Cultural Memory Studies: An International and Interdisciplinary Handbook*. Edited by Astrid Erll, Ansgar Nünning, and Sara B. Young, 109–18. Berlin: Walter de Gruyter, 2008.

Aune, Margrethe. "The Computer in Everyday Life: Patterns of Domestication of a New Technology." In *Making Technology Our Own?* Edited by Merete Lie and Knut H. Sørensen, 91–120. Oslo: Scandinavian University Press, 1996.

Babeți, Coriolan. "The Bertalan Case: The Artistic Experiment as an Exercise of Neurotic Sublimination." In *Primary Documents: A Sourcebook for Eastern and Central European Art since the 1950s*. Edited by Laura J. Hoptman and Tomáš Pospiszyl. New York: MOMA, 1999.

Babuna, Aydın. "Bosnian Muslims during the Cold War: Their Identity between Domestic and Foreign Policies." In *Religion and the Cold War: A Global Perspective*. Edited by Philip Muehlenbeck. Nashville: Vanderbilt University Press, 2012.

Banac, Ivo. "Bosnian Muslims: From Religious Community to Socialist Nationhood and Postcommunist Statehood, 1918–1992." In *The Muslims of Bosnia-Herzegovina: Their Historic Development from the Middle Ages to the Dissolution of Yugoslavia*. Edited by Mark Pinson, 129–53. Cambridge, MA: Harvard University Press, 1994.

Beck, Ulrich. *The Cosmopolitan Vision*. Translated by Ciaran Cronin. Cambridge: Polity Press, 2006.

Bek, Ul'rikh [Beck, Ulrich]. *Chto takoe globalizatsiia? Oshibki globalizma—otvety na globalizatsiiu*. Translated by A. Grigor'ev and V. Sedel'nik. Moscow: Progress-Traditsiia, 2001.

Boehlke, Michael and Henryk Gericke, eds. *too much future—Punk in der DDR*. Berlin: Verbrecher Verlag, 2007.

Bougarel, Xavier. "Bosnian Muslims and the Yugoslav Idea." In *Yugoslavism: Histories of a Failed Idea, 1918–1992.* Edited by Dejan Djokić. London: Hurst and Company, 2003.

Boym, Svetlana. *The Future of Nostalgia.* New York: Basic Books, 2002.

Bringa, Tone. *Being Muslim the Bosnian Way: Identity and Community in a Central Bosnian Village.* Princeton: Princeton University Press, 1995.

Brintlinger, Angela and Ilya Vinitsky, eds. *Madness and the Mad in Russian Culture.* Toronto: University of Toronto Press, 2007.

Brown, Timothy and Lorena Anton, eds. *Between the Avant-Garde and the Everyday: Subversive Politics in Europe from 1957 to the Present.* New York: Berghahn Books, 2011.

Buck, Hannsjörg F. *Mit hohem Anspruch gescheitert: Die Wohnungspolitik der DDR.* Münster: Lit Verlag, 2004.

Bursten, Ben. *Psychiatry on Trial: Fact and Fantasy in the Courtroom.* Jefferson, NC: McFarland, 2001.

Bushnell, John. *Moscow Graffiti: Language and Subculture.* Boston: Unwin Hyman, 1990.

Butler, Judith. *Bodies That Matter: On the Discursive Limits of Sex.* New York: Routledge, 1993.

Buxbaum, Roman, Clément Chéroux, Marc Lenot, and Quentin Bajac, eds. *Miroslav Tichý Catalogue.* Paris: Éditions du Centre Pompidou, 2008.

Clough, T. Patricia. "The Affective Turn: Political Economy, Biomedia, and Bodies." In *The Affect Theory Reader.* Edited by Gregory J. Seigworth and Melissa Gregg. Durham: Duke University Press, 2010.

Crowley, David and Susan E. Reid. "Socialist Spaces: Sites of Everyday Life in the Eastern Bloc." In *Socialist Spaces: Sites of Everyday Life in the Eastern Bloc.* Edited by David Crowley and Susan E. Reid. Oxford: Berg, 2002.

Cucu, Ioan and Toma Cucu. *Psihiatria sub Dictatura/Psychiatry under Dictatorship.* Piatra Neamt: f.e, 2005.

Cushman, Thomas. *Notes From Underground: Rock Music Counterculture in Russia.* Albany: State University of New York Press, 1995.

Devic, Ana. "The Forging of Socialist Nationalism and Its Alternatives: Social and Political Context and Intellectual Criticism in Yugoslavia between the Mid-1960s and 1992." PhD diss., University of California, San Diego, 2000.

Dolinin, Viacheslav. *Istoriia leningradskoi nepodtsensurnoi literatury.* Edited by B. Ivanov and B. Roginskii. St. Petersburg: DEAN, 2000.

———. *Ne stol' otdalennaia kochegarka: Rasskazy, vospominaniia.* St. Petersburg: Izdatel'stvo Novikovoi, 2005.

——— and Boris Ivanov, eds. *Samizdat: Po materialam konferentsii '30 let nezavisimoi pechati. 1950–80 gody.'* St. Petersburg: NITs "Memorial," 1993.

Dubin, Boris. *Slovo—pis'mo—literatura: Ocherki po sotsiologii sovremennoi kul'tury.* Moscow: Novoe Literaturnoe Obozrenie, 2001.

Easton, Paul. "The Rock Music Community." In *Soviet Youth Culture.* Edited by Jim Riordan. Bloomington: Indiana University Press, 1989.

Evans, Jennifer V. *Life among the Ruins: Cityscape and Sexuality in Cold War Berlin.* New York: Palgrave Macmillan, 2011.

Felsmann, Barbara and Annett Gröschner, eds. *Durchgangszimmer Prenzlauer Berg: Eine Berliner Künstlersozialgeschichte der 70er und 80er Jahre in Selbstauskünften.* Berlin: Lukas Verlag, 1999.

Fenemore, Mark. *Sex, Thugs and Rock 'n' Roll: Teenage Rebels in Cold War East Germany.* Oxford: Oxford University Press, 2007.

Foucault, Michel. *Discipline and Punish: The Birth of the Prison.* Translated by Alan Sheridan. London: Allen Lane, 1977.

Fürst, Juliane. "Where Did All the Normal People Go?: Another Look at the Soviet 1970s." *Kritika: Explorations in Russian and Eurasian History* 14, no. 3 (2013): 621–40.

———. "Love, Peace and Rock 'n' Roll on Gorky Street: The 'Emotional Style' of the Soviet Hippie Community." *Contemporary European History* 23, no. 4 (2014): 565–87.

Fulbrook, Mary. "The Limits of Totalitarianism: God, State and Society in the GDR." *Transactions of the Royal Historical Society Sixth Series* 7 (1997): 5–52.

Gakkel, Vsevolod. *Akvarium kak sposob ukhoda za tennisnym kortom.* St. Petersburg: Amfora, 2007.

Gal, Susan and Gail Kligman. *The Politics of Gender after Socialism.* Princeton: Princeton University Press, 2000.

Galenza, Ronald and Heinz Havemeister, eds. *Wir wollen immer artig sein . . .: Punk, New Wave, HipHop und Independent-Szene in der DDR 1980–1990.* Berlin: Schwarzkopf & Schwarzkopf, 2005.

Gildea, Robert, James Mark, and Anette Warring. *Europe's 1968: Voices of Revolt.* Oxford: Oxford University Press, 2013.

Giustino, Cathleen M., Catherine J. Plum, and Alexander Vari, eds. *Socialist Escapes: Breaking Away from Ideology and Everyday Routine in Eastern Europe, 1945–1989.* New York: Berghahn Books, 2015.

Gölz, Christine and Alfrun Kliems, eds. *Spielplätze der Verweigerung: Gegenkulturen im östlichen Europa.* Cologne: Böhlau, 2014.

Gorsuch, Anne and Diane Koenker, eds. *The Socialist Sixties: Crossing Borders in the Second World.* Bloomington: Indiana University Press, 2013.

Grashoff, Udo. *Leben im Abriss: Schwarzwohnen in Halle an der Saale.* Halle: Hasenverlag, 2011.

———. *Schwarzwohnen: Die Unterwanderung der staatlichen Wohnraumlenkung in der DDR.* Göttingen: V&R Unipress, 2011.

Håpnes, T. "'Not in Their Machines': How Hackers Transform Computers into Subcultural Artefacts." In *Making Technology Our Own? Domesticating Technology into Everyday Life.* Edited by Merete Lie and Knut H. Sørensen, 121–50. Oslo: Scandinavian University Press, 1996.

Hahn, Anne and Frank Willmann. *Satan, kannst du mir noch mal verzeihen: Otze Ehrlich, Schleimkeim und der ganze Rest.* Mainz: Ventil Verlag, 2008.

Hall, Stuart and Tony Jefferson, eds. *Resistance through Ritual: Youth Subcultures in Post-War Britain.* London: Hutchinson, 1976.

Hayton, Jeff. "'Härte Gegen Punk': Popular Music, Western Media, and State Response in the German Democratic Republic." *German History* 21, no. 4 (2013): 523–49.

Hebdige, Dick. *Subculture: The Meaning of Style*. London: Routledge, 1979.

Herzog, Dagmar. *Sexuality in Europe: A Twentieth-Century History*. Cambridge: Cambridge University Press, 2011.

Hodkinson, Paul and Wolfgang Deicke, eds. *Youth Cultures: Scenes, Subcultures and Tribes*. London: Routledge, 2007.

Irwin, Zachary T. "The Islamic Revival and the Muslims of Bosnia-Hercegovina." *East European Quarterly* 17, no. 4 (1984): 437–58.

Ivanov, Sergey A. *Holy Fools in Byzantium and Beyond*. Oxford: Oxford University Press, 2006.

Jarausch, Konrad H., ed. *Dictatorship as Experience: Towards a Socio-Cultural History of the GDR*. Translated by Eve Duffy. New York: Berghahn Books, 2006.

Josephson, Paul. *Would Trotsky Wear a Bluetooth? Technological Utopianism under Socialism, 1917–1989*. Baltimore: Johns Hopkins University Press, 2009.

Kan, Aleksandr. *Poka ne nachalsia Jazz*. St. Petersburg: Amfora, 2008.

———. *Kurekhin: Shkiper o Kapitane*. St. Petersburg: Amfora, 2012.

Karčić, Fikret. "Islamic Revival in the Balkans 1970–1992." *Islamic Studies* 36, nos. 2/3 (1997): 565–81.

Kasakow, Ewgeniy. "Models of 'Taboo Breaking' in Russian Rock Music: The Ambivalence of the 'Politically Incorrect.'" *Kultura: Russian Cultural Review* no. 4 (2009): 22–26.

———. "Subkultur? Verbieten! Zur Geschichte einer russischen Sommerlochdebatte." In *Emo—Porträt einer Szene*. Edited by Martin Büsser, Jonas Engelmann, and Ingo Rüdiger, 122–31. Mainz: Ventil Verlag, 2009.

———. "Die Fantasie von der Macht fernhalten: Michail Lifschitz–Westmarxist im Osten." In *Ästhetik ohne Widerstand: Texte zu reaktionären Tendenzen in der Kunst*. Edited by Annette Emde and Radek Krolczyk, 37–52. Mainz: Ventil Verlag, 2013.

———. "NOM—Charms Enkel, Laibachs Söhne." *Zonic: Magazin für Kulturelle Randstandsblicke und Involvierungsmomente* no. 20 (2013): 30–34.

———. "Dissens und Untergrund: Das Wiederaufkommen der linken oppositionellen Gruppen in der späten Brežnev-Zeit." In *Goldenes Zeitalter der Stagnation? Perspektiven auf die sowjetische Ordnung der Brežnev-Zeit*. Edited by Boris Belge and Martin Deuerlein, 75–95. Tübingen: Mohr Siebeck, 2014.

———. "Von der Staats- zur Herrschaftskritik? Notizen zur Entwicklung der anarchistischen und marxistischen Staatstheorie." In *Begegnungen feindlicher Brüder: Zum Verhältnis von Anarchismus und Marxismus in der Geschichte der sozialistischen Bewegung*. Vol. 3. Edited by Philippe Kellerman, 185–205. Münster: Unrast Verlag, 2014.

Kazakov, Evgenyi [Kasakow, Ewgeniy]. "Ubiitsy 'belykh khalatov.' Sotsialisticheskii kollektiv patsientov: Maloizvestnye stranitsy istorii 'novykh levykh.'" *Neprikosnovennyi zapas* no. 5 (67) (2009): 122–32. http://magazines.russ.ru/nz/2009/5/ka10.html.

———. "Maoistskie i khodzhistskie organizatsii v FRG." *Neprikosnovennyi zapas* no. 1 (69) (2010): 160–70. http://magazines.russ.ru/nz/2010/69/ka18.html.

————. "'Ty tozhe ubil Kennedi!': Situatsionistskaia teoriia i 'novye levye' v FRG." *Neprikosnovennyi zapas* no. 5 (85) (2012): 272–85. http://magazines.russ. ru/nz/2012/5/k20.html.

————. "Organy samoupravleniia shkol'nikov FRG: Ot vnutriinstitutsionnogo protesta k uchastiyu v politicheskoi zhizni." In *Ostrova utopii: Pedagogicheskoe i sotsial'noe proektirovanie poslevoennoi shkoly (1940–1980e)*. *Kollektivnaia monografiia*. Compiled and edited by I'lia Kukulin, Mariia Maiofis, and Petr Safronov, 519–46. Moscow: Novoe Literaturnoe Obozrenie, 2015.

————. "The Razlatsky-Isaev Case: Pro-Marxist Opposition in the Soviet Provinces, Part I." *The Stanford Post-Soviet Post*, March 14, 2013. https://postsovietpost. stanford.edu/node/173.

————. "The Razlatsky-Isaev Case: Pro-Marxist Opposition in the Soviet Provinces, Part II." *The Stanford Post-Soviet Post*, April 17, 2013. https://postsovietpost.stanford.edu/history/razlatsky-isaev-case-pro-marxist-opposition-soviet-provinces-0.

Kessler, Erwin. *The Self-punishing One: Ştefan Bertalan, Florin Mitroi, Ion Grigorescu: The Art and Romania in the 80s and 90s*. Bucharest: Romanian Cultural Institute, 2010.

Kligman, Gail. *The Politics of Duplicity: Controlling Reproduction in Ceausescu's Romania*. Berkeley: University of California Press, 1998.

Konrád, György. *Antipolitics: An Essay*. Translated by Richard E. Allen. New York: Harcourt Brace Jovanovich, 1984.

Kowalczuk, Ilko-Sascha. "Von der Freiheit, Ich zu sagen: Widerständiges Verhalten in der DDR." In *Zwischen Selbstbehauptung und Anpassung: Formen des Widerstandes und der Opposition in der DDR*. Edited by Ulrike Poppe, Ilko-Sascha Kowalczuk, and Rainer Eckert. Berlin: Ch. Links, 1995.

Kowalczyk, Angela. *Punk in Pankow. Stasi-"Sieg": 16jährige Pazifistin verhaftet!* Berlin: Anita Tykve Verlag, 1996.

Kushnir, Aleksandr, ed. *100 magnitoal'bomov sovetskogo roka*. Moscow: Agraf, 2003.

Levada, Iurii. *Ishchem cheloveka: Sotsiologicheskie ocherki, 2000–2005*. Moscow: Novoe Izdatel'stvo, 2006.

Lindenberger, Thomas. "Die Diktatur der Grenzen." In *Herrschaft und Eigen-Sinn in der Diktatur: Studien zur Gesellschaftsgeschichte der DDR*. Edited by Thomas Lindenberger. Cologne: Böhlau, 1999.

Lindner, Bernd. *DDR: Rock & Pop*. Cologne: Komet Verlag, 2008.

Lovell, Stephen. *The Russian Reading Revolution: Print Culture in the Soviet and Post-Soviet Eras*. Basingstoke: Macmillan, 2000.

Lygo, Emily. *Leningrad Poetry 1853–1975: The Thaw Generation*. New York: Peter Lang, 2010.

Marquardt, Sven with Judka Strittmatter. *Die Nacht ist Leben: Autobiographie*. Berlin: Ullstein, 2014.

Medvedev, Zhores A. and Roy A. Medvedev. *A Question of Madness: Repression by Psychiatry in the Soviet Union*. New York: Macmillan, 1971.

Morozova, Marina A. *Anatomiia otkaza*. Moscow: RGGU, 2011.

Muggleton, David. *Inside Subculture: The Postmodern Meaning of Style.* Oxford: Oxford University Press, 2000.

Muniz, Albert and Thomas O'Guinn. "Brand Community." *Journal of Consumer Research* 27, no. 4 (2001): 412–32.

Oushakine, Sergei. "The Terrifying Mimicry of Samizdat." *Public Culture* 13, no. 2 (2001): 191–214.

Pehlemann, Alexander and Ronald Galenza, eds. *Spannung. Leistung. Widerstand: Magnetband-Kultur in der DDR, 1979–1990.* Berlin: Verbrecher Verlag, 1999.

Pudovkina, Elena. "Klub 'Derzanie.'" *Pchela* nos. 26/27 (2000). http://www.pchela.ru/podshiv/26_27/club.htm.

Ramet, Sabrina Petra. "Islam in Yugoslavia Today." *Religion in Communist Lands* 18, no. 3 (1990): 226–35.

———, ed. *Rocking the State: Rock Music and Politics in Eastern Europe and Russia.* Boulder, CO: Westview, 1994.

Reichardt, Sven. *Authenzität und Gemeinschaft: Linksaternatives Leben in den siebziger und frühen achtziger Jahren.* Berlin: Suhrkamp, 2014.

Rink, Dieter. "Der Traum ist aus? Hausbesetzer in Leipzig-Connewitz in der 90er Jahren." In *Jugendkulturen, Politik und Protest: Vom Widerstand zum Kommerz?* Edited by Roland Roth and Dieter Rucht. Opladen: Leske + Budrich, 2000.

Risch, William Jay. "Soviet 'Flower Children': Hippies and the Youth Counter-Culture in 1970s L'viv." *Journal of Contemporary History* 40, no. 3 (2005): 565–84.

Rogov, Kirill, ed. *Semidesiatye kak predmet istorii russkoi kul'tury.* Moscow: OGI, 1998.

Romanov, Diusha. *Istoriia Akvariuma: Kniga fleitista.* Moscow: Olma-Press, 2001.

Satter, David. *Vek bezumiia: Raspad i padenie Sovetskogo Soiuza.* Moscow: OGI, 2005.

Saunders, Anna. *Honecker's Children: Youth and Patriotism in East(ern) Germany, 1979–2002.* Manchester: Manchester University Press, 2007.

Savitskii, Stanislav. *Andergraund: Istorii i mify leningradskoi neofitsial'noi literatury.* Moscow: Novoe Literaturnoe Obozrenie, 2002.

Schroeder, Klaus. *Der SED-Staat: Partei, Staat und Gesellschaft, 1949–1990.* Munich: Carl Hanser Verlag, 1998.

Schwell, Alexandra. *Anarchie ist die Mutter der Ordnung: Alternativkultur und Tradition in Polen.* Münster: Lit, 2005.

Seigworth, Gregory J. and Melissa Gregg. "An Inventory of Shimmers." In *The Affect Theory Reader.* Edited by Gregory J. Seigworth and Melissa Gregg. Durham: Duke University Press, 2010.

Severiukhin, D., V. Dolinin, B. Ivanov, and B. Ostanin, eds. *Samizdat Leningrada. 1950e—1980e gody: Literaturnaia entsiklopediia.* Moscow: Novoe Literaturnoe Obozrenie, 2003.

Shepanskaia, Tat'iana. *Sistema: Teksty i traditsii subkul'tury.* Moscow: OGI, 2004.

Siegelbaum, Lewis. *Borders of Socialism: Private Spheres of Soviet Russia.* Basingstoke: Palgrave, 2006.

Simpson, Patricia Anne. "Born in the 'Bakschischrepublik': Anthems of the Late GDR." In *Transformations of the New Germany.* Edited by Ruth A. Starkman, 89–111. New York: Palgrave Macmillan, 2006.

Smirnov, Il'ia. *Vremia kolokolchikov.* Moscow: INTO, 1994.

Sørensen, Knut H. "Domestication: The Enactment of Technology." In *Domestication of Media and Technology*. Edited by Thomas Berker, Maren Hartmann, Yves Punie, and Katie Ward, 40–61. Maidenhead: Open University Press, 2006.

Strauss, Sarah. *Positioning Yoga: Balancing Acts across Cultures*. Oxford: Bloomsbury Academic, 2005.

Streeter, Thomas. *The Net Effect: Romanticism, Capitalism and the Internet*. New York: New York University Press, 2011.

Swede, Mark. "All You Need is Lovebeads: Latvia's Hippies Undress for Success." In *Style and Socialism: Modernity and Material Culture in Post-War Eastern Europe*. Edited by Susan Reid and David Crowley, 189–208. Oxford: Berg, 2000.

Szulecki, Kacper. "'Freedom and Peace are Indivisible': On the Czechoslovak and Polish Dissident Input to the European Peace Movement, 1985–1989." In *Transnational Perspectives on Dissent and Opposition in Central and Eastern Europe*. Edited by Robert Brier. Osnabrück: Fibre, 2012.

Thomas, Douglas. *Hacker Culture*. Minneapolis: University of Minnesota Press, 2003.

Troitsky, Artemy. *Back in the USSR: The History of Rock in Russia*. London: Omnibus Press, 1987.

Vail', Petr and Aleksandr Genis. *Mir sovetskogo cheloveka 60-e*. Moscow: Novoe Literaturnoe Obozrenie, 2001.

Valieva, Iuliia, ed. *Sumerki 'Saigona.'* St. Petersburg: Samizdat, 2009.

Vassileva-Karagyozova, Svetlana. "Voluntary Social Marginalization as a Survival Strategy in Polish Postcommunist Accounts of Childhood." *The Sarmatian Review* 29, no. 1 (2009). http://www.ruf.rice.edu/~sarmatia/109/291vassil.htm.

Vatulescu, Cristina. *Police Aesthetics: Literature, Film, and the Secret Police in Soviet Times*. Stanford: Stanford University Press, 2012.

Velikonja, Mitja. *Religious Separation and Political Intolerance in Bosnia-Herzegovina*. College Station: Texas A & M University Press, 2003.

Vesse, Sesil' [Vaissié, Cécile]. *Za vashu i nashu svobodu: Dissidentskoe dvizhenie v Rossii*. Moscow: Novoe Literaturnoe Obozrenie, 2015.

Wasiak, Patryk, "Playing and Copying: Social Practices of Home Computer Users in Poland during the 1980s." In *Hacking Europe: From Computer Cultures to Demoscenes*. Edited by Gerard Alberts and Ruth Oldenziel. London: Springer, 2014.

Yurchak, Alexei. *Everything Was Forever, Until It Was No More: The Last Soviet Generation*. Princeton: Princeton University Press, 2005.

Zdravomyslova, Elena. "Kul'turnyi andergraund 1970-kh: Leningradskoe kafe 'Saigon' glazami zavsegdataia i issledovatelia." In *Raznomyslie v SSSR i Rossii (1945–2009)*. Edited by B. M. Firsov. Saint Petersburg: Izd. Evropeiskogo universiteta v Sankt-Peterburge, 2010.

Zhuravlev, Oleg. "Studenty, nauchnaia innovatsiia i politicheskaia funktsiia komsomola: Fizfak MGU v 1950–1960-e gody." In *Raznomyslie v SSSR i Rossii (1945–2009)*. Edited by B. M. Firsov. Saint Petersburg: Izd. Evropeiskogo universiteta v Sankt-Peterburg, 2010.

# Index

absurdity: of life, mastered through irony, parody, withdrawal, 17; of Necrorealists, 76–77; as Yellow Submarine's response to absurdity of outside world, 185
Agamben, Giorgio, 77
Akhmatova, Anna, 65
Akvarium (band), 262
Alekseeva, Liudmila, 108–9
AlösA group (punks), 217
*Anarkhiia* (fanzine), 239
Anderson, Sascha, 223
Appadurai, Arjun, 43–44
"Appeal to the Governments and People of the USSR and the USA, An": and formation of the Trust Group, 130–31, uniqueness of, 132
"Appeal to Young America," 134
Arbeitsgruppe Wohnungspolitik, 282, 290
Augustine, Saint, 32
Atari: as meaningful object, 161
Aune, Margarethe, 158
authenticity, 8, 12, 16, 306, 308
autonomy, 305, 312

Babeţi, Coriolan, 74–76
*Bajtek* (magazine): divided into sections dedicated to brands, 167;

Grzybowska computer fair sponsored by, 165; sponsored by ZSMP, 162
Bălaşa, Sabin, 66–67
Banac, Ivo, 86
bards (songwriters), shaped Soviet rock music, 241; *magnitizdat* and, 267
Batovrin, Sergei, 130, 143, 146–47
Beal, Becky, 18
The Beatles, 44, 180, 182, 185, 193, 198; "Let It Be," 190; Maksim Kapitanovskii, *The Beatles are to Blame*, 144; songs of, as shorthand, 179; "Strawberry Fields Forever," 187; *The Yellow Submarine* (film), and "Yellow Submarine" (song), 184
Beauvoir, Simone de, 34
Beck, Ulrich, 142–43, 150
Bertalan, Ştefan, 74–76
Besson, Tatjana, 223
Between East and West. *See Trust Group*
Bivolaru, Gregorian, 23; accused of immoral sexual practices, 31; context for interest in yoga, 25; correspondence held in Securitate archives, 28; correspondence with Western individuals and institutions, 30; granted political asylum in Sweden, 24; as "Guru Grig," 34–35;

327

*kanal*, 108; responses to Blok Questionnaire, 116, 121; as scholar and critic, 110
Strauss, Sarah, 28, 38n20
student activism: part of a larger movement, 93; and repression, late 1970s and 1980s, 99–100; across Yugoslavia, 96; Yugoslav nationalist and religiously inflected, 89–90
student movements: Sarajevo madrassa students as part of, 85; in Yugoslavia, 89
students: conflicts with madrassa administration, 95–98; madrassa, 15; madrassa, strike of (January 1972), 85, 90, 96–97; secular and Muslim, common concerns of, 93
style, 310; as a crucial element of punk subculture, 210–11; jeans, 194–95; punk DIY aesthetic and a society of shortages, 213; in studying "dropping out" and "creating one's own," 10–11; style clusters, 161; styles of self-fashioning, 51–52
subculture: Hebdige's definition of, 6
subjectivity, 304, 305, 308, 311, 312, 314; of the late socialist subject, 181; Soviet hippie and imaginary elsewhere, 47, 57
Sudakov, Oleg "Manager," 235, 239

Tallinn, 9, 41; early center of Hare Krishna movement in the USSR, 54; GrOb farewell concert in, 243; hippie tradition to gather in on May 1, 43; Tallinn Polytechnic Institute, 48;
*tamizdat*, 234
Tamm, Mihkel Ram, 54, 55–56, *56*, 61n64
Tantrism: Bivolaru's interest in, 31–32; Tantric yoga, 32, 36; Tantric sex, 33
tape recorders, 267, 271
Tartu, Buddhist studies at University of, 54; Lotman's study circle, 184
Thaw (1956–1964), 42, 67; Thaw generation, 190

"37" (journal), 107, 111
"The Twelve" 115, 116, 117, 118
therapy, 333, 35, 308; art therapy and psychodrama at Gătaia Psychiatric Hospital, 70; Tichý's photographs as self-therapy, 74
Tichý, Miroslav, 71–74
Tiumen', 236, 238
Tolstoyans, 129
tradition: little memory of Russia's pacifist tradition, 129; new punk generation rejected tradition of the Siberian school, 246; references of punks, 241; unofficial poets as heirs to Russian poetic, 111; of writers resisting appropriation of poets, 114
Transcendental Meditation Affair (Romania), 25–27; Bivolaru caught up in, 34
*Transponans* (journal), 114
Tröger, Frank, 223
Troianskii, Sergei: arrest, 135–36, 152n27; death of (2004), 136; leader of Free Initiative, 134
Troitsky, Artemy, 239, 240, 256, 257, 258, 262, 264–65, 272
Tropillo, Andrei, and rock *magnitizdat*, 267–68, access to a recording studio, 267
Trust Group: announcement "Concerning the Trust Group," 141; attempts to expose, 136–37; formation, 130; and counterculture, 134; criticism and misperceptions of members, 150; offshoots of, 142; persecution of by police and KGB, 133; and public diplomacy, 132; scientists' involvement in, 139–40, 143; social makeup of, 136
Tsaritsyno: annual gathering of hippies on June 1, 135

Umweltbibliothek, 288
unofficial literature: goals differ from human rights *samizdat* texts, 109; relationship with official literature,

.

# About the Contributors

**Maria-Alina Asavei** is a lecturer and postdoctoral researcher in the Department of Russian and East European Studies at Charles University in Prague and an independent curator of contemporary art. Dr. Asavei is a former honorary research fellow at the City University of New York (CUNY) and at the American Research Center in Sofia (ARCS). Her research interests revolve around critical theory, cultural studies, aesthetics, ethnography, memory studies, and forms of artistic engagement during and after totalitarian regimes. Her most recent publications include "Beauty and Critical Art: Is Beauty at Odds with Critical-Political Engagement?" (*Journal of Aesthetics and Culture*, 2015) and "Visual Chronicles from the Balkans and Central Europe: Samplers Remembered" (*Journal of Ethnology and Folkloristics*, 2015).

**Irina Costache** received her PhD in Comparative Gender Studies from the Central European University in 2014 with a thesis on sexualities in Ceaușescu's Romania. Dr. Costache's essay on nudism and the bohemian lifestyle in Romania after World War II appeared in Cathleen M. Giustino, Catherine J. Plum, and Alexander Vari, eds., *Breaking Away from Ideology and Everyday Routine in Eastern Europe, 1945–1989* (Berghahn Books, 2013). In 2016, Irina Costache authored a study on LGBT youth in Romanian high schools.

**Madigan Andrea Fichter** is assistant professor of History at Holy Family University in Philadelphia. She has published an article, "Yugoslav Protest: Student Rebellion in Belgrade, Zagreb, and Sarajevo in 1968," in the journal *Slavic Review*, and is working on a book about counterculture and student opposition movements in the socialist Balkans in the 1960s and 1970s.

**Juliane Fürst** is senior lecturer in Twentieth-Century History at the University of Bristol. She is the author of *Stalin's Last Generation: Post-War Soviet Youth and the Emergence of Mature Socialism* (OUP, 2010) and the editor of *Late Stalinist Russia: Society between Reconstruction and Reinvention* (London, 2006). She is currently working on a history of the Soviet Hippie movement and preparing a monograph titled *Flowers through Concrete: The World of the Soviet Hippies* (forthcoming with OUP). Together with Josie McLellan she ran the Arts and Humanities Research Council-sponsored project "Dropping out of Socialism" (2009–2014).

**Irina Gordeeva** is lecturer in Russian History at the Russian State University for the Humanities (Moscow). She is the author of the monograph *Zabytye liudi: Istoriia rossiiskogo kommunitarnogo dvizheniia (Forgotten People: A History of the Russian Communitarian Movement)* (AIRO-XX, 2000). Her current project examines the history of the pacifist movement in Russia from the Tolstoyans at the beginning of the twentieth century to the independent peace activism of the late Soviet period.

**Jeff Hayton** is assistant professor of Modern European History at Wichita State University. He received his PhD from the University of Illinois at Urbana-Champaign in 2013. Currently, he is revising his manuscript, *Culture from the Slums: Punk Rock, Authenticity and Alternative Culture in East and West Germany*, for publication, and has published on popular culture, rock'n'roll, and German history.

**Anna Kan** is a postgraduate student at the University of Bristol. She graduated from St. Petersburg State University and St. Petersburg State Theater Arts Academy. Her research interests are the social and cultural history of the late Soviet Union, especially the underground rock scene, its musicians, and their relations and/or interactions with the Soviet authorities. She is currently working on a PhD thesis on underground rock musicians and the authorities in Leningrad, 1972–1992.

**Evgenyi Kazakov** [Ewgeniy Kasakow] is a PhD candidate in History at the University of Bremen (Germany).

**Josie McLellan** is reader in Modern European History at the University of Bristol. She is the author of *Antifascism and Memory in East Germany* (OUP, 2004) and *Love in the Time of Communism: Intimacy and Sexuality in the GDR* (CUP, 2011). Her research on gays and lesbians in East Berlin, undertaken as part of the Dropping Out project, has been published in *History Workshop Journal, Central European History,* and *Cultural and Social History.*

**Peter Mitchell** gained his PhD in History from the University of Edinburgh in 2015. His thesis, "Contested Space: The History of Squatting in Divided Berlin c. 1970–c. 1990," explores the relationship between urban space, opposition and conformity, mainstream, and alternative cultures, as well as questions of identity and belonging in postwar Germany. His postgraduate research was funded by an Arts and Humanities Research Council doctoral studentship. He now lives in Berlin where he works as a part-time lecturer at the Humboldt University.

**Terje Toomistu** is an anthropologist and documentary filmmaker whose works often draw on various cross-cultural processes, queer realities and subjectivities, and cultural memory. She holds MA degrees (*cum laude*) in Ethnology and in Communication Studies from the University of Tartu, Estonia, where she is pursuing a PhD degree in Ethnology. In 2013–2014, she was a Fulbright fellow at the University of California, Berkeley. She is currently directing a documentary film focusing on the hippie movement in the Soviet Union (forthcoming in 2017).

**Patryk Wasiak** has a PhD in Cultural Studies from the University of Social Sciences and Humanities in Warsaw. He is currently a lecturer at the Institute for Cultural Studies at the University of Wrocław, Poland. He is working on a book on consumer culture, home technologies, and the "imaginary West" in post-socialist Poland. He has published articles in *Cahiers du Monde Russe*, *Zeitschrift für Ostmitteleuropa-Forschung*, *International Journal of Communication*, and *Zeithistorische Forschungen*.

**Josephine von Zitzewitz** is a Leverhulme Early Career Fellow in Russian Literature at the University of Cambridge. Her monograph, *Poetry and the Religious-Philosophical Seminar in Leningrad 1974–1980: Music for a Deaf Age*, was published by Legenda in May 2016. She has written numerous articles on the poetry of the "second culture" in the late Soviet Union. Having held a lectureship at Oxford University, she is now working on a project that examines the role of *samizdat* journals as social networks.

Lightning Source UK Ltd.
Milton Keynes UK
UKHW02n0518020918
328099UK00011B/345/P